CO-DETERMINATION

ENDORSEMENTS

Conflict to Co-determination

The economic crises and political situations in South Africa and Africa are not conducive to the survival and sustainability of companies. Co-determination is a model that encourages unions and companies to view and consider their positional approach when dealing with operational and strategic issues. This does not necessarily mean unions should abandon their fundamental principles when dealing with the mandates and interests of their constituencies, however.

It is common cause that some unions view co-determination in a negative light, in the sense that a union that participates in co-determination is seen as sleeping in the same bed as the employer. I think this perception emanates from the South African historical perception that companies are not trustworthy, and that their interests lie with the profit margin without taking their staff complement into consideration.

My experience with this model is that it is a platform or vehicle that union leaders can utilise to enhance the interests of their constituencies. Simultaneously, they can have a clear vision of the challenges that the company is facing and the kind of assistance and role they can play to assist in the situation. At the same time, they are also saving their constituencies' work and retain sustainable membership. Union leaders sometimes make a serious mistake if they don't interact with companies or have insufficient information prior to taking a decision.

Co-determination promotes collective decision-making between a company and a union. The company decision alone is no longer applicable in terms of this model; it is gone and buried. Marikana is a classic example of company and union decisions that were far apart from each other, and at the end of the day, both parties suffered the negative consequences.

Motebang Botsane, National Office Bearer of the Transport and Services Worker Union (TASWU); full time Shop Steward from IBL.
Mr Botsane played a significant role in the transformation of Interstate Bus Lines.

Central to the reasonable and justifiable management of the ever-present conditions for creating conflict in the workplace, is acceptance by the representatives of capital, who are positioned in various highly-placed company structures, that of equal importance for the successful running of the enterprise is acknowledgement of the positive role that the people who possess labour (intellectually or physically) can play in ensuring the sustained growth of the enterprise.

In democratic South Africa, there remains a need for the conscious recognition of the diverse nature of the productive forces found in the workplace, as well as a desirability for the interaction of these forces as equal partners through democratic practices, with the aim of harnessing the collective brain power of all the recognised stakeholders populating and surrounding the enterprise, for the purpose of working towards the benefit of the enterprise and all who make a living out of its proceeds.

The object and purpose of the LRA, as seen in Chapter 1 [section 1(a) and section 1(d)(iii)] of the Act, together with the provisions for the establishment of Workplace Forums (Chapter 5 of the LRA), which *inter alia* are envisaged to promote employee participation in decisions that affect their working lives, is to provide employees with greater participation in matters affecting the quality of their lives. In so doing they give effect to the fundamental rights guaranteed in the Constitution of the Republic of South Africa Act 108 of 1996, which collectively aim to achieve this mutually beneficial arrangement of harnessing the collective brain power of all stakeholders populating and surrounding the enterprise.

Co-determination gives structure towards the realisation of this objective.

Rapesha Meshack John Ramela, CEO: Commuter Bus Employers Organisation

Prior to 1994, bargaining had many different dimensions, with the focus being on who could gain and who could retain. Shared economic empowerment, other than shareholder advancement and investor interest, was not considered. With the dawn of democracy, the creation of a new model based on collective bargaining was introduced, with a lot of emphasis being placed on creating controlled bargaining environments. This did not take into account a model of shared capital gains for all who worked in industries. It seemed like a safe haven as it reduced industrial action, or better-controlled strikes, with the introduction of laws regulating such strikes. The introduction of this book and the research and studies that have gone into it bring a new dimension of shared ownership, where those concerned take equal control of their future and destiny, and where all share in the growth and welfare of the entity. The introduction of co-determination opens a new debate, and, more importantly, endeavours to bring about shared economic empowerment.

Gary Wilson, General Secretary: SARPBAC (South African Road Passenger Bargaining Council)

The Labour Relations Act (66 of 1995) places a high premium on collective bargaining, with a focus on employers and employees engaging each other for some mutually beneficial relationships. Sections 78 to 94 of the aforementioned Act enable the establishment of workplace forums, which are intended to promote employees' interest in the workplace while enhancing efficiency. When employees and employers work towards common goals, new heights will be achieved in organisations, entities and businesses. Due to many factors, this seems to be only a pipe dream to most role players, however. Factors such as different goals, varying cultural diversities and an imbalance of economic power are often cited as reasons why a process of co-determination cannot work in South Africa as it does in the Scandinavian and European countries, but the reasons are not limited to the above. This book, however, puts different perspectives and working models on display that will hopefully create a new wave for industries to ride.

Douglas Roye Els, CCMA Dispute Management Commissioner (Free State)

Public road transport operations in South Africa fall under the ambit of the South African Road Passenger Bargaining Council (SARPBAC).

Prior to the establishment of SARPBAC in 1997, conditions of employment within the Road Passenger Transport sector were regulated by Wage Determination 452, or alternatively by agreements concluded within other industrial councils. The terms of employment and working conditions were far from uniform amongst the different operators within the industry. Labour's demand for the establishment of a single National Bargaining Council was resisted by employers, who thought that there would be a propensity for Labour to cherry pick and endeavour to settle collective agreements at the highest prevailing levels. This in fact proved to be the case, together with a number of other contributing factors. The move to transport contracts and the manner in which government passenger subsidies were determined bedeviled wage negotiations within the National Bargaining Council.

During the 20 years since the establishment of SARPBAC, there have been pitifully few occasions when wage negotiations have been concluded within the SARPBAC National Bargaining Forum without third party interventions and/or strike action. Wage negotiations tend to be adversarial, with very little attempt made to find win-win solutions that take cognisance of prevailing conditions and try to meet the needs of all stakeholders. This situation is not peculiar to the road passenger transport industry, but is, sadly, prevalent in many other sectors within South Africa. The stark reality is that national wage negotiations are simply not working in the long-term interests of the industry or its stakeholders.

It has often been said that one cannot expect a different outcome when one continues to tackle an issue in the same way. Something has to change and this is true for labour relations in South Africa.

The well-being of company stakeholders requires the well-being of the company. Employers and employees have a shared and joint responsibility to ensure the success and well-being of the company. One party cannot expect to "win" at the expense of the other. Employers need labour and labour needs employers – the parties are inextricably linked by an umbilical cord that determines success or failure.

Co-determination, as has been introduced at Interstate Bus Lines, is new to the South African context and is still in an early trial stage. Only time will tell whether it can prove to be a success here as it is in other arguably more developed countries like Germany.

What is inescapable, however, is that the path we have been walking has not successfully addressed growing employer/employee issues or contributed to improving labour relations. A new approach is long overdue and co-determination might warrant a closer look and consideration. This book will hopefully contribute to an understanding and evaluation of co-determination as a possible way forward.

Barry W. Gie, Previous Bus Line Executive

First published in 2019

ISBN: 978-1-86922-755-5 (Printed)
ISBN: 978-1-86922-756-2 (ePDF)

Published by KR Publishing
P O Box 3954
Randburg
2125
Republic of South Africa

Tel: (011) 706-6009
Fax: (011) 706-1127
E-mail: orders@knowres.co.za
Website: www.kr.co.za

Printed and bound: Tandym Print, 1 Park Road, Western Province Park, Epping, 7475
Typesetting, layout and design: Cia Joubert, cia@knowres.co.za
Cover design: Marlene de Villiers, marlene@knowres.co.za
Editing and proofreading: Jennifer Renton, jenniferrenton@live.co.za
Project management: Cia Joubert, cia@knowres.co.za

CO-DETERMINATION

The answer to South Africa's industrial relations crisis

Edited by:

Dr Rica Viljoen
Henk van Zyl
Dr Joyce Toendepi
Stefan Viljoen

kr publishing

2019

DEDICATION

For Dr George Lindeque

This publication is also dedicated to all those human resources practitioners who have developed processes and new knowledge to enhance the management and development of those in the world of work.

ACKNOWLEDGEMENTS

This book serves as an acknowledgement to the workers of our rainbow country who keep our economy ticking.

From the blog *The Reading Point*, the following dedication is spoken over our workers in South Africa and the world:

Stand for something without falling for something.

From each according to his ability, to each according to his needs.

God sells us all things at the price of workers.

Labor disgraces no man; unfortunately, you occasionally find men who disgrace labor.

Let us celebrate the Labour, Those built up this Great Land, Happy May Day.

It was thus important for us to launch this book on Workers Day.

TABLE OF CONTENTS

ABOUT THE EDITORS

Dr Rica Viljoen's model on inclusivity, introduced in her doctorate thesis, was acknowledged as one of the 10 most promising contributions to the field of Management, Spirituality and Religion by the Academy of Management in 2008. Since then, this approach to hearing the voices of the whole social system has been applied in 42 different countries with over 100,000 participants. Rica has been presented with the CEO award for her contribution to the field of study nationally and internationally by the Institute of People Management (IPM), for which she also acts as ambassador, and has received two additional awards from the Academy of Management for her contribution. She is an adjunct faculty member of the Henley Business School in South Africa, associated with Reading University, and a senior research associate at the University of Johannesburg. Rica is also the founder and managing director of Mandala Consulting, an organisational development and research house. She works closely with Dr Don Beck and Dr Loraine Laubscher, who are international experts on Spiral Dynamics. As the founder of the African Centre of Human Emergence, she engages with the the various Centres for Human Emergence to study geo-political trends and how they impact people and the organisations they form. Rica has published numerous academic chapters and books to ensure that untold stories find their way into mainstream publications.

Henk van Zyl worked as a HR professional in the transport industry for 36 years, of which 20 were at the Executive level. For more than 19 years he gained extensive knowledge and experience in Employee Relations at Interstate Bus Lines at the Bargaining Council level. His interest in, and passion for, employee relations resulted in him developing and implementing an advanced ER Co-determination Model, the first in South Africa, whereby unions are engaged at the strategic and executive levels to take responsibility for creating wealth for employees and all stakeholders. Henk is currently a Specialised Facilitator: Co-determination at Metamor Consulting. During his corporate career, his passion for HR management resulted in IBL becoming the first company to implement the South African Board of People Practices' (SABPP) Human Resource Management Standards in the Free State and the passenger industry. Henk was subsequently nominated to be the SABPP's Ambassador of the Year in 2017. His ability to understand the thinking patterns of different human niches enables him to relate to people across all levels.

Dr Joyce Toendepi is an effective and efficient strategic planner who has the capability and expertise to devise and promote innovative solutions that challenge mainstream thinking. She has a particular interest in professional leadership and leadership development issues, and believes that raised levels of consciousness within social systems will eventually result in cohesion and total transformation. Joyce also has an extensive understanding of the leadership requirements and challenges facing the African continent, which is why she wants to dedicate most of her research space to authentic leadership and how it can benefit Africa. Joyce is an articulate communicator who is adept at negotiation, can influence important decisions, and is able to manage professional relationships with tact and common sense.

Joyce is also an innovative planner who applies forward-thinking methodologies to add value to various business models, and is a confident leader with expertise in market and industry analysis to position various businesses for market leadership. As a keen multi-cultural researcher, she is well published and grounds her work deeply in academic thought. Joyce's areas of interest include Leadership and Organisational Development, Strategic Management, Systems Thinking and Change Management. She is associated with the University of Johannesburg.

Stefan Viljoen has a vast knowledge of organisational development, business management and management practices, gained from his various qualifications, including a Bachelor of Commerce Degree in Business Management, a Bachelor of Commerce Honours Degree in Strategic Management, a Post Graduate Diploma in Management Practice, and his current Masters of Commerce Degree in Business Management. In addition, Stefan has seven years' experience working within a business consulting environment. With this solid pedigree, Stefan is an expert in managing complex client interactions while proactively engaging with all internal and external stakeholders in order to influence the outcome of a project. Throughout Stefan's career, he has successfully achieved and exceeded company objectives and targets.

As an ambitious and energetic industry specialist, he is inspired and motivated by success through the achievement of organisational goals. Offering the innate ability to align challenges with opportunities, he has acquired the broad knowledge required to guide organisations to achieve their short- and long-term business goals. He is strategically involved in business management, where his unique combination of financial knowledge, people management abilities and understanding of business see him stand out amongst his peers. As a dynamic self-starter, Stefan provides excellent communication capabilities and offers experience in multi-cultural and multi-disciplinary team settings. He further provides admirable relationship management skills across all levels, and is able to apply his knowledge and experience to different circumstances and environments through an intelligent and hardworking approach.

ABOUT THE CONTRIBUTORS[i]

Marius Meyer lectures in HR Management at Stellenbosch University and is the former CEO of the SA Board for People Practices (SABPP), the professional body for HR practitioners and the Education and Training Quality Assurance Body for HR in South Africa. Previously Marius lectured in HRD at the University of South Africa and the University of Johannesburg, and he is still involved in academic work for North-West University and the University of Cape Town. Marius has been a HRD practitioner, consultant, academic and manager for the last 23 years, and is registered as a Master HR Professional and Mentor with the SABPP. He was an advisory board member for the African Society for Talent Development, as well as South Africa's first talent management magazine, *Talent Talks*. Marius is a regular speaker at local and international conferences and the author of 22 books and over 300 articles. He has a passion for leadership, strategy, governance, change management and people development. The latest output of his team is the National HR Competency Model, as well as a full set of national HR standards, the first set of national HR standards in the world. A comprehensive HR audit framework has now been developed to audit the application of these HR standards within companies. In addition, under his leadership, the Minister of Justice approved SABPP HR professionals in South Africa as Commissioners of Oaths.

Penny Abbott has had a long and successful career at executive level in Human Resource Management across a spread of South African companies, in industries ranging from food and pharmaceuticals to mining and cement. In 2002 she took up a position as Senior Vice President, Human Resources, with Holcim Limited, based in Switzerland, covering global human resource management across the company's operations in 70 countries with over 70 000 employees. Returning home to South Africa in 2007, she combined consulting work in her South African franchise of Clutterbuck Associates (the leading mentoring and coaching consultancy from the UK) with studying for her M Phil in Human Resource Development, which she completed at the University of Johannesburg. She also completed her doctoral research at UJ on the socio-economic impact of HR. Penny has been a Chartered HR Practitioner since 1985, was elected a Mentor of the SABPP in 2006 and a Master HR Practitioner in 2009. She has co-authored a book published in 2010 entitled "A Guide for Coachees", and is a regular contributor of conference presentations and journal articles on a variety of subjects. Penny is also Research and Policy Advisor for SABPP.

Vusi M. Vilakati is an African consciousness and leadership development scholar and practitioner. He is passionate about the intersections between identity, locatedness or positionality and context in the facilitation and embodiment of African

---

i   The sequence of the contributors is according to how their chapters appear in the book.

spiritual consciousness, values and practices within organisations. He believes that in the emerging VUCA business and public leadership context, Africa urgently needs to develop future referenced, contextually attuned and globally responsive leaders to translate business goals and leadership toward the continent's social and economic advancement. As a insightful civic organisation leader, speaker, facilitator and researcher, Vusi's experience spreads across a number of key organisational roles in strategic planning, policy formulation, seminary lecturing, leadership training, facilitating diversity management initiatives, organisational transformation and change, and coordinating in-service training, recruitment, selection and team-building. His interests are African consciousness in leadership development and coaching, the role of business in society, corporate citizenship, cross-cultural management, the contribution of emerging economies to global geo-economics, outcomes-based and ethical leadership, leadership effectiveness, systems thinking, holistic leadership development, and the economic and human advancement of Africa. Vusi holds a Diploma in Construction Studies, a MA in Theological Studies (UP) and a MPhil HRM in Personal and Professional Leadership. He is currently a PhD candidate :Leadership in Performance and Change at the University of Johannesburg.

As a project leader involved in large scale IT projects, **Dr Tonja Blom** developed an interest in the effects of change. Working in the Slovak Republic, she witnessed the severe impact of change at the national, organisational and local levels, as individuals, organisations and the economy were forced into major changes related to ideologies, systems, procedures and habits, which were somewhat similar to those experienced in South Africa post-1994. After returning to South Africa, she became involved in HR system implementations and strategic HR in a global manufacturing organisation. Tonja completed her Doctorate in Business Leadership in 2015, focusing on organisational change and leadership. Her unique contribution presents a practical roadmap for companies looking to navigate change. A further significant contribution relates to her application of diversity in an African context and alternative modalities to alleviate stress, fear and anxiety to ensure optimal cognitive functioning.

Dr Nceba Ndzwayiba (PhD: Wits) is the General Manager: Enterprise and Supplier Development at Netcare Limited: SA, the Director of the Netcare Foundation, a former Board member of the Health and Welfare SETA, and the Chairperson of the ETQA Sub-Committee of the HWSETA Board. He has over 15 years' experience in several sectors of the South African economy including Aviation, Private Healthcare and Pharmaceuticals, Hospitality and Tourism, National Legislature and the Vocational Education and Training Sector.

Professionally, Nceba has made a significant contribution to the strategic areas of Human Capital Development, Organisational Change and Development, Organisational Diversity and Equity, Broad-Based Black Economic Empowerment and Socio-Economic Transformation. Nceba infuses his passion for social justice into his professional and academic work, as is evident in his publications in international peer reviewed journals, and the annual guest lectures he offers at the University of Stellenbosch, Henley Business School and the University of the Witwatersrand. He locates his work at the intersections of business, society and the politics of being and doing human.

Nceba's work is grounded in postmodern, postcolonial and decolonial critical philosophy, with a sharp focus on the interplay between the economy, race, gender, dis/ability, sexuality, class and real transformation.

FOREWORD

Igniting new hope for employers and labour – a collaborative approach to labour stability and building great companies

This book by Henk van Zyl, Rica Viljoen and others takes you on an interesting journey of how Interstate Bus Lines (IBL), which started as a family-owned passenger bus company based in the Free State, emerged from being a disengaged, conflict ridden affair to the Great Company it has become. The journey to the co-determination environment that was successfully implemented two years ago started when the company reacted to recommendations included in the report of the BEQ study undertaken by Mandala Consulting. The seed of hope was planted when the then HR Manager, Henk van Zyl, convinced the Board to invest in people development interventions, thereby prioritising its employees as the greatest and most valuable asset of the company.

Over the years, the HR department invested in building genuine trust between union leadership and the management of the company. Trust can be referred to as the bedrock of embarking on a successful Co-determination Model in any company, as demonstrated in the IBL case. As you will learn from this book, the model focuses on creating adequate communication forums for social partners. On those platforms, emphasis is placed on a shared vision as well as joint responsibility for decision-making for the sustainability of the company. In order to support the core, which is sustained trust, the following equally valuable interventions had to be undertaken: engaging in team-building and RBOs (relationship-building initiatives); appropriate and targeted training, which, amongst others, exposed parties to understanding the thinking patterns of diverse people; emotional intelligence workshops; and strategic planning sessions. Furthermore, the Co-determination Agreement was developed based on benchmarking models from other countries, but most importantly, it was workshopped in sessions wherein senior leaders of the company and the relevant unions actively participated in robust discussions that eventually led to an agreement.

Another key factor of the successful implementation was the agreement between parties to ensure the election of high-level shop stewards who could engage at different levels, including strategic issues. The Co-determination Model is supported by three other important agreements - the Collective Recognition and Procedural Agreement, the Close Shop Agreement and the Dispute Prevention and Resolution Policy. For the co-determination to be successfully implemented, the aforementioned agreements and policy had to be in place. Furthermore, we are cognisant of the fact that co-determination remains a work in progress, and requires continuous investment in the form of best human resources practices and interventions.

This model is well in line with what the South African government refers to in its slogan, "Together we can do more". It is a practical approach wherein employers and labour can proactively do more together to eliminate causes of conflict, save jobs that are usually at risk due to protracted strikes, reduce poverty that is further exacerbated by a loss of income during protracted strikes, and contribute towards the joint management of the factors of production by employers and labour unions. The model further presents an opportunity for the real empowerment of union leaders and employees of companies, who will gain an understanding of business principles. This is essential for union representatives, who need to jointly plan and make strategic decisions through a co-determination model. I recommend that you take time to read and internalise the principles contained in this wonderful and progressive work of Dr Rica Viljoen et al.

George Mokgoto
CEO Interstate Bus Lines
Leader of Co-determination

PREFACE

Firstly, this was a lovely book to author and edit, as we authors believe that co-determination is really the only way to go in South Africa and other emerging economies. Our traditional corporate ways of managing employee relations can lead to a few negative scenarios. Sometimes leadership is scared of the unions, thus too much power is given to them and the organisation becomes unmanageable. Alternatively, leadership may assume that workers only want to make claims and thus do not speak to them, leading the workers to lean towards unions, which disturbs the power dynamic in the organisation. In another scenario, unions do not really represent the workforce and intimidation is the order of the day. A way thus needs to be found where the rights of all stakeholders are not only protected, but are able to flourish into real relatedness and functional interaction, seeing that the ultimate, superordinate goal for all is the same.

Second, co-determination works successfully in Germany, yet although a few companies have tried it in South Africa, there are not many success stories. Why is this? Is it that in the German model, co-determination is institutionalised? Or could it be that we in African and other emerging economies organise differently and have an alternative way of thinking?

Third, it was lovely to author a book that integrates Organisational Development (OD) as a field of study with Employee Relationships (ER). Human Resources (HR) in companies are often so fragmented that the full function is managed in a disjointed way. This book crosses the boundaries between the functionalities and argues theoretically, and attempts to show practically, that the integration of different fields of HR can have huge benefits for organisations. If OD is done correctly, ER will be a much more fulfilling field; and if ER embraces co-determination, OD can add real strategic business value.

Fourth, we never anticipated such a rich book - full of African philosophy, stories, narratives, cases and theory – all in a kaleidoscope of different angles studying the same topic. To all the authors who contributed… you are amazing. You are the thought leaders of the future. Your wisdom will linger long after this book is published.

Fifth, different role-players worked together in various disciplines over decades to reach the point where insights on a progressive book on co-determination can be shared. The book was conceptualised academically and practically implemented – often during times when the odds were seriously against us from a union, employee and employer perspective. Even the professional bodies did not always assist functionally. With the workers experiencing all the dynamics, the book became personal to us. If eople create magic together, it is hard not to acknowledge it. There are more dedications here than usual, for his purpose. The acknowledgements of the book were written in the spirit of lived history that made this publication possible. For us, this is sacred work. We walked this journey.

Years before the concept of co-determination became known to me, and before Henk van Zyl and I implemented it successfully in Interstate Bus Lines, Dr George Lindeque, the Executive Director of Human Resources at Eskom, implemented such a concept in the company. The intent of this book is not to share the case of Eskom, but rather to acknowledge the deep, authentic and courageous footprints that were left on the industry by those of the calibre of Dr Lindique and other HR practitioners like him.

During the 1980s, as most Human Resource practitioners reported manually on the number of strikes, Dr Lindeque conceptualized "inspraak"[ii] - an African version of co-determination. Inspraak means so much more than co-determination, however; it means that workers have a say in the organisation – which was very progressive for his time and even for the future. This book attempts to remember what worked before us, acknowledge what is currently working, and challenge leaders and Human Resource practitioners to do what is right for their companies, their employees, their societies and their shareholders.

In 2014, labour strikes in the platinum industry in South Africa resulted in more than R11 billion in wages being lost. In 2015, this figure decreased but still almost R7 billion was lost due to industrial action, the Department of Labour reported. Investor confidence declined rapidly as companies like Barclays disinvested due to economic instability, and the almost junk status of our economy impacts negatively on all stakeholders in the economy.

It is becoming increasingly clear that new ways of thinking about leadership and ensuring labour stability are critical, not only for organisational sustainability, but for South Africa as a whole, as well as for other emerging economies.

In this book, a concerted effort is made to critically analyse the changes in the external environment, study the social fibre of our society, and find alternative ways of addressing not only diversity of thought but also labour relationships. Co-determination is positioned as a way that may facilitate co-operation between various stakeholders and assist role-players to address tough labour issues without compromising principles. The case of Interstate Bus Lines is presented as an example of a successful implementation of such a strategy and approach. Practical guidelines are provided that the practitioner may find helpful. Ultimately, the importance of ethical conduct and a principle-based scope of practice are stressed in introducing a SABPP stance towards labour relations and the management thereof in South Africa. The book proposes a shift from the current destructive conflict model and positions co-determination as the solution for sustainable employee relations.

In **Chapter 1**, Marius Meyer, CEO of the South African Board of People Practices (SABPP), deals with the changing world of work. A convincing argument is made for a new way of engaging with unions and employees in organisations. The

---

ii   Inspraak is an Afrikaans word; we struggled to find an English word to translate it into. It basically
     implies that people have a voice in a shared concern.

outcome of a scenario planning session facilitated by Clem Sunter indicates clearly that co-determination is the way to go for South African organisations and other emerging economies. Current models of 'industrial' or 'labour' relations have evolved from the industrial revolution and the establishment and growth of the manufacturing sector all over the world. Now, with the Fourth Industrial Revolution that is fueled by significant technological advancement and innovation, traditional models of labour relations are challenged, so much so that the future world of work requires new ways of positioning and managing employment relations. This chapter explores options of understanding how employment relations could be transformed against the backdrop of the rapid changes required in the future world of work. These future trends are unpacked to assist readers to explore new approaches of leveraging employment relations in a totally different workplace. Moreover, by adapting a futuristic approach to employment relations in the new world of work, four labour market scenarios developed by the SABPP for 2030 are discussed with a view of linking them to the achievement of the goals of the National Development Plan (NDP).

Chapter 2 considers the epistemic and ideological embedding of African spiritual consciousness and its implications for employment relations in the emerging South African labour context. It begins with an overview of the historical and political legacies; structural and economic factors, including the impact of emerging economic players; and sociocultural influences that have shaped and are shaping Africa's labour practices. The central piece discusses African spiritual consciousness, in particular the wisdom, practices and values that need to be translated and integrated into evolving forms of employment engagement, leadership development and practice at the individual, team and organisational levels. The last section explores how the African spiritual and human values and practices of identity facilitation and creativity, solidarity and cooperation, belonging and connective engagement, and consultative decision-making contribute towards the emerging model of co-determination. This chapter is authored by Vusi Vilikati.

Different people think differently. They ask different questions of existence and organise differently, thus it is critical to understand the thinking systems of different organisations. In the second part of **Chapter 3**, the organisational being is described. Spiral dynamics is used to describe the kaleidoscope of differences that play out in daily organisational life. Human niches and the manifestation thereof as Purple in organisations impact relations in the following ways:
- Want to speak to their leader rather than the union
- Collective
- Want to be consulted and included
- Access to top management
- Management must listen
- Integrated
- Want to be respected

- Want to be consulted
- Need a sense of belonging

Further, the following spiral dynamics thinking systems are described: dealing with Purple; the forgotten system – Beige; the colour Red; the colour Blue; and the colour Orange - the universal leadership dilemma. Blue and Orange leaders leading Purple and Red people are discussed, before Rica Viljoen concludes with a section on meshwork and the importance of valuing all thinking structures.

The new world of work described in **Chapter 4** is demanding new orientations and approaches to social change for organisations to be sustainable in the midst of complexity and uncertainty. Transdisciplinary measures that can bring together collaborative efforts are being called for. Inclusive measures like co-determination, which can influence and move stakeholders towards a collectively desired state, have been seen as sustainable options. However, for co-determination to be an effective concept in South Africa, it needs to be supported by relevant legislation and suitable structures of involvement that recognise peoples' values, norms and customs. This chapter was written by Joyce Toendepi.

Chapter 5 deals with the concept of 'inclusivity' as a radical transformational process and describes Viljoen-Terblanche's (2008) inclusivity model. Through optimising the Doing and the Being in an organisation, human energy can be released that can be wired around organisational strategy and result in measurable business indicators. This model was used in the Interstate Bus Lines (IBL) case study described in Chapters 9 and 10. Inclusivity, conceptualised here, can be measured by the Benchmark of Engagement (BEQ). Viljoen argues that co-determination is a radical transformational process undertaken through the adaptation of inclusivity as strategy. Four phases of the implementation of a change process are outlined.

Chapter 6 deals with human reactions to change. It is critical for leadership to realise that during the implementation of co-determination, these reactions will impact business as usual. This chapter deals with our inherent need for predictability and order, before discussing stress and anxiety and the impact thereof on individuals and organisations. During the initial implementation of a strategy of co-determination, leadership is scared of losing power to the unions; unions are scared that they will be seen to be on the side of management; and workers are concerned about their shop stewards' loyalty. Change management processes are critical during this phase of a change process, Rica Viljoen and Tonja Blom maintain.

In **Chapter 7**, the importance of leadership during a radical transformational process is underlined. In this chapter, it is argued that systemic leadership is needed to comprehend, influence and lead multi-cultural systems. The new world of work is demanding leadership that can catalyse the process of systems shift from the narrow short-termism approach to a more long-term collaborative multi-stakeholder perspective. Rica Viljoen and Joyce Toendepi describe the challenges of the new world of work as including interactive technology; the effects of globalisation, diversity, trust and multi-culturalism; and the complexities thereof. These issues demand new leadership perspectives to effectively tackle workplace challenges for the benefit of the collective. The world will be unable to achieve an effective eradication of the identified Millennium challenges with its current business models and approaches to public and private governance. Leaders who are able to recognise these challenges and harness them for sustainable systems change will be able to build the necessary positive pathways for a sustainable future. The new world of work requires fearless trans-disciplinary approaches to social change that emphasise re-thinking inclusive growth and development. As a result, new approaches that partner across sectors seem favourable for devising sustainable solutions. Co-determination is positioned in this book as an approach that leadership can adopt and use in the facilitation of collaboration amongst various stakeholders, in an effort to support the radical change efforts at hand.

During the research phase of this book, some progressive attempts towards co-determination were found in the South African domain. **Chapter 8** tells some of these stories in the form of mini-cases on Eskom, Cashbuild, Interstate Bus Lines, Solms-Delta, a chicken farm, and Mangwanani, the African Spa. This chapter by Rica Viljoen and Tonja Blom concludes with insights gained on co-determination in practice.

The next chapter, **Chapter 9**, showcases the case study of Interstate Bus Lines. Emphasis is placed on the preparation of the system to build trust and inclusivity for the implementation of co-determination. This forms the core case for the book, and spills over into other chapters. Henk van Zyl shares his oral history and lived experiences in Interstate Bus Lines over three decades. Rica Viljoen was involved as strategy consultant for more than 20 years and also contributed to the chapter.

What actually happened with regards to co-determination in IBL is illustrated in **Chapter 10**. The philosophy followed to create trust in Interstate, an institutional framework for co-determination and practical advice to implement co-determination are shared. The chapter was written by Henk van Zyl for the practitioner who wants to adopt a strategy of co-determination in their organisation.

Chapter 11 is presented for the human resource practitioner, thus practical advice from lessons learned during the implementation of co-determination at IBL are shared. These issues, including how to strike, how to engage, how to develop shop stewards, how to solicit the buy-in of leadership, how to deal with leadership and how to align the needs of all the role-players, are discussed in a practical manner from his lived experience by Henk van Zyl.

Chapter 12 draws from post-modernist and post-structuralist critical theories to argue the importance of challenging and changing normalised European enlightenment Cartesian ideas of who is, and what it means to be, human. Drawing on Franz Fanon's idea of socio-genesis and Melissa Steyn's critical diversity literacy, the chapter explains the origins and the processes that systematised racism, sexism, homophobia, ableism, patriarchy, and Christionormativity across all spheres of life, and the ways in which these 'isms' are consciously and unconsciously reproduced in organisational discourses. The chapter advances that these 'isms' need to be named and called out, with the intention of producing new forms of thinking about our collective humanity in which we can be "different but equal" humankind. The author argues that this uncomfortable yet critical work is essential for the success and sustainability of co-determination and deepening democracy for all. Nceba Ndzwayiba concludes by arguing that new ways of organising are critical, and that co-determination is such a strategy.

Actual solicited documents can be found in the appendices, which share examples such as contracts and agreements necessary for the co-determination process.

The reader is invited to suspend their traditional views on how employee relations must be dealt with, and in doing so will hopefully be tempted to tread into an alternative way of doing things here – a true African way. You may just be surprised by the magic of Africa and inclusivity.

Chapter

1

THE CHANGING WORLD OF WORK

Penny Abbott and Marius Meyer

INTRODUCTION AND BACKGROUND

This new book on employment relations is published at a time when labour markets around the world are challenged, and employers, employees and labour unions are presented with opportunities to become part of a new workplace revolution, creating a workplace that is totally different from the one we have experienced since early in the 20th century. The time for innovation in thinking and planning in a different and more dynamic way in response to the demands of the new world of work has arrived. Co-determination is one such innovation.

Projections concerning the South African labour market into the future are almost invariably gloomy. It seems that unemployment will not reduce significantly, and the shortage of skills which hampers strategy execution for many South African organisations will not improve any time soon, as the education system from early childhood to university fails to meet the needs of both young people and employers. One of the major factors influencing the way in which the labour market develops is the economy. At present, any debate over the South African economy is marked by entrenched ideological differences between politicians, business leaders, union leaders and other key stakeholders, and an apparent inability to dialogue constructively to find an accepted way forward. Some progress was made in this regard with the framework agreements reached in the National Economic and Labour Council (Nedlac) in early 2017, but these framework agreements are still solidly founded within the "old" world of work. Protests, also in early 2017, by metered taxi drivers against Uber as their competition, accompanied separately by protests by Uber drivers against employment relations management practices by the company, is a good example of tension within the labour market in response to development in the "new world of work". These events ask the question: To what extent has the labour market and its key stakeholders adapted to the new world of work?

Organisational effectiveness experts (CEOs) and Human Resource (HR) practitioners working at higher levels in organisations are required to participate in the strategy formulation processes of the organisation, not only to implement agreed upon strategies. In order to play this role, they need good frameworks and a proper analysis of the environment to be able to advise the executive team on probable developments affecting the labour market in general, as well as the employees of today and of the future.

Recognising this need for HR executives, in March 2016, the SA Board of People Practices (SABPP) convened a group of 50 senior HR practitioners, academics and consultants under the facilitation of Clem Sunter, who is recognised within South Africa and globally as a top scenario planner, to think about how the labour market could evolve under different scenarios. The purpose of this session was to develop a set of labour market scenarios in South Africa.

Strategy teams of organisations can use scenarios as the basis for their strategy formulation – either to act now, or to have a contingency plan for the probability of one of the scenarios increasing or decreasing significantly. We probably won't get the story of the future exactly right, but we will get the idea of the future and be able to plan accordingly. Clearly, co-determination, or decisions on how to take an organisation forward made jointly by management and employees, will be better founded if the strategy-making processes of the organisation result in strategies that take account of likely futures.

THE SCENARIO FORMULATION PROCESS

In this chapter, different scenario planning model outputs are discussed. All speak to the same realisation; if we do not find inclusive ways to do things differently in South Africa, the future will be rendered bleak. Let us first explore general and business approaches to scenario planning, and then share the SABPP's approach to labour market scenarios with you.

In his book, *A Time Traveller's Guide to Our Next Ten Years*, Frans Cronje explains that due to their complexity, political, social and economic systems can only be understood in the framework of complex systems theory (which was developed in the natural science disciplines). Extremely complex systems are characterised by the following:

- A very large number of participants (stakeholders).
- These participants interacting regularly with each other.
- Through that interaction, directing feedback into the system based on how satisfied they are with their circumstances in that system.

In any given situation, it is likely that some of these stakeholders will be satisfied and therefore prefer to maintain the status quo, but others will not have their expectations met and will want to change the system to improve their own circumstances. Obviously, this leads to conflict and the resolution of this conflict depends on relative power within the system. The disruption of a complex system can be sudden and dramatic, and most often is not predicted, therefore a wide view of the components of the complex system must be developed.

As outlined in the various books of Clem Sunter and Chantel Illbury[1], the creation of scenarios is an outside-in process that starts with looking at the *Rules of the Game* – these are patterns which can be seen now and are fairly certain to apply over a period of 20 to 30 years. One example would be the aging of the population in Europe and Japan.

Having thought about these as constants or assumptions, the process continues with identifying *Key Uncertainties* – patterns which can be seen now, but we have no idea which way they will develop. An example of this would be the enormous wave of migrants moving across the world, and in particular from Africa and the Middle East moving to Western Europe. At this point it is very far from clear for how long the wave will continue and how Europe will handle the matter, but the issue has huge consequences in many ways. In some parts of the world, the increase in immigrant populations has created serious conflict, fuelled xenophobia and resulted in a major backlash against immigrants. In countries with strong immigrant populations, immigrants responded by highlighting the role they play as a significant labour and talent pool in many countries. The strong anti-immigrant stance of President Donald Trump in the USA has not only helped him to ascend to power, but has influenced anti-immigration policy, not only in America, but also in other parts of the world. In South Africa, there are large immigrant populations from different parts of the world, such as China, Zimbabwe, Malawi, Somalia and Mozambique. During 2017, the Department of Home Affairs began preparing a revision to South African policies for the treatment of economic migrants and asylum-seekers.

Based on this discussion about the dynamics in the labour and broader environment, the SABPP labour market's working group synthesised two polarities to describe the two key trends, which framed four possible stories of the future. These stories were fleshed out; "flags" were identified to indicate the direction in which the future is developing; and finally the group agreed on probabilities for each of the four scenarios. These key trends, stories, flags and eventual scenarios will be described throughout this chapter.

RECENT SOUTH AFRICAN SCENARIOS

Any exposition of future labour market scenarios in South Africa would be incomplete without recognising the strong history of scenario planning in South Africa over the last 30 years. In the early 1990s, an unprecedentedly representative group of South Africans from all political persuasions, business and civil society leaders put together the first set of South African socio-political scenarios – the now famous Ostrich and Flamingo scenarios, which supported leaders to enter constitutional negotiations in good faith, resulting in the transition to democracy in 1994. In Figure 1.1 below the scenarios of Sunter[2] are presented.

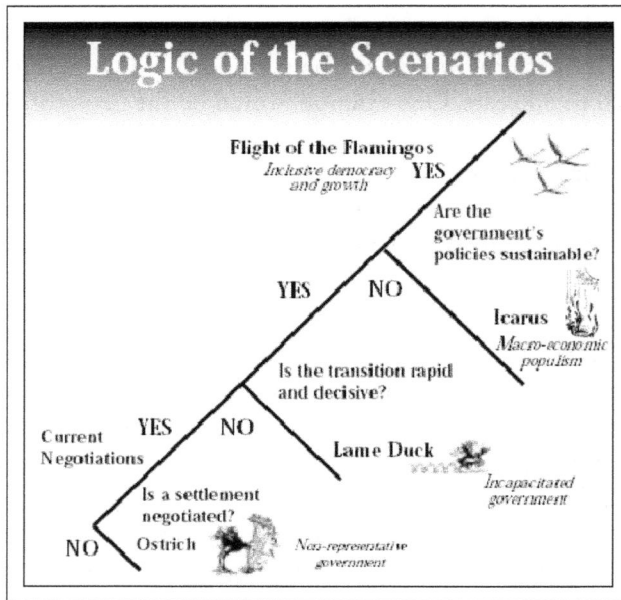

Figure 1.1: Logic of scenarios[3]

Sunter[4] indicated that various scenarios could apply to South Africa. Interestingly, the transition to a stable democracy in 1994 was highly successful, and hailed a "miracle" against all the odds of civil war and a bloodbath, as suggested by some commentators at the time. The negotiated settlement resulted in a democratic dispensation and the adoption of a Constitution praised as one of the most progressive in the world. Likewise, a more inclusive multi-party democracy was created, and the economy performed relatively well at the turn of the millennium.

Building on this initial effort of scenario planning, the question was whether South Africa would continue to grow and prosper once the euphoria of the period from 1994 to 1999 evaporated. Subsequently Chantel Illbury and Clem Sunter wrote a set of general South African scenarios during the 2000s.[5] In Figure 1.2 below, four scenarios for South Africa are described by Sunter.[6]

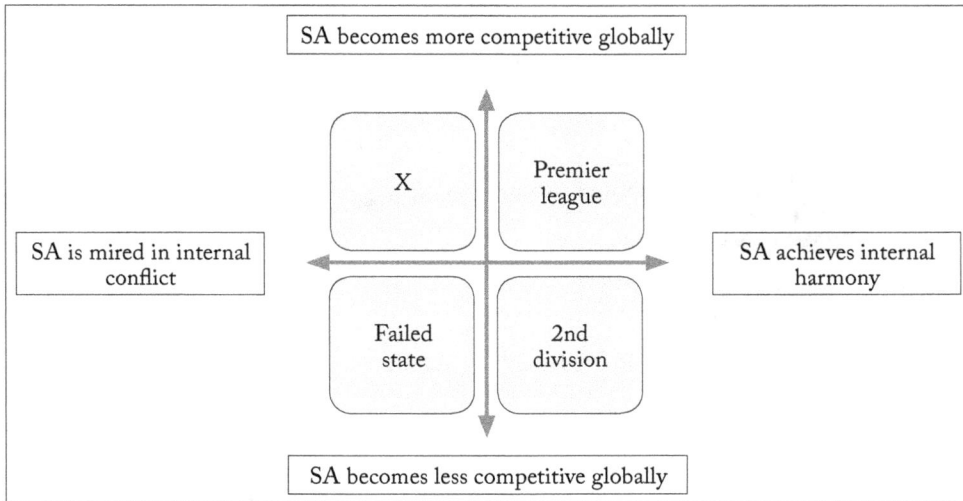

Figure 1.2: South African scenarios[7]

It is clear that the possibility of becoming a failed state was high during the early 2000s. South Africa achieved its best period of economic growth since 1994 and managed to escape the failed state scenario, yet did not manage to elevate itself to the premier league, despite pockets of excellence in certain areas such as banking, finance, auditing and corporate governance. The successful hosting of the FIFA World Cup in 2010 was one of the highlights of this period, but unfortunately the country failed to capitalise on this opportunity of growth and excellence, which turned out not to be sustainable. At best, the country ended up in the 2nd division scenario, thus regressing to less competitiveness as a result of poor education, skills gaps, increased corruption and low levels of productivity.

In 2014, Frans Cronje from the South African Institute of Race Relations identified four politico/economic scenarios for South Africa, which can be seen in Figure 1.3 below.

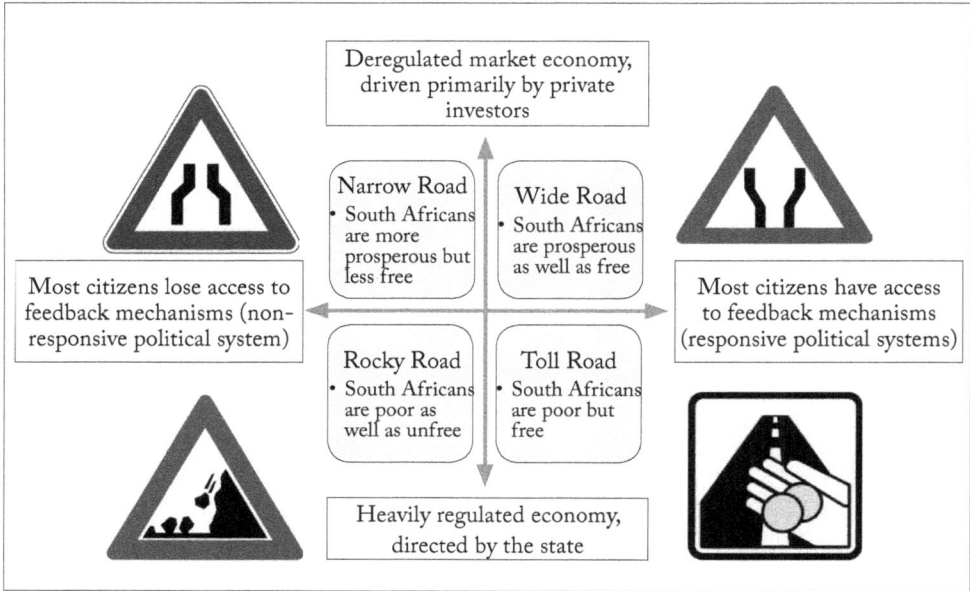

Figure 1.3: Political and social scenarios[8]

The four scenarios were described as the rocky road, the toll road, the narrow road and the wide road. The tensions between the various extremes of the two axes in these scenarios can be seen in developments since 2014. State actions have demonstrated an inconsistency between promoting private sector investment, for example in the vehicle manufacturing industry, and a state-directed economy, as frequently alluded to by many politicians. Similarly, sometimes we see indications that the political system is not responsive to feedback from citizens, as when service delivery protests do not result in any tangible improvements, but at the same time we observe an increase in demands for the political system to become more responsive, notably in advances by opposition parties in the 2016 local government elections.

In 2016, the SA Institute of Risk Management (IRMSA) published the second edition of its *SA Risk Report*[i], which contained the results of a scenario-planning workshop with Clem Sunter, combined with the results of its second risks survey. Their scenarios are shown in Figure 1.4 below.

---

i   Available as a free download from www.irmsa.co.za.

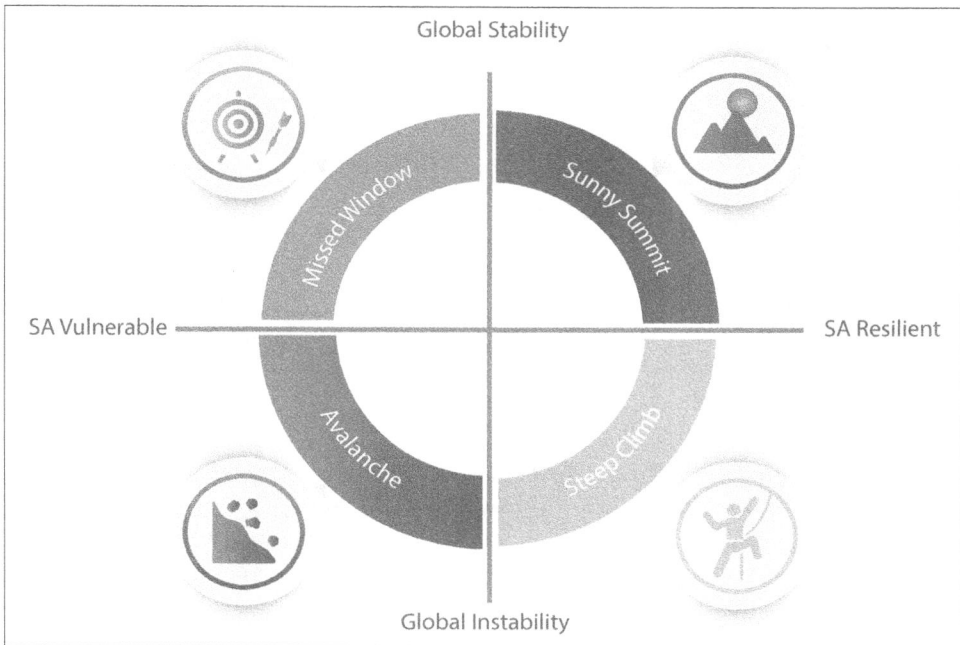

Figure 1.4: The South African Institute of Risk Management scenario planning (2016)[9]

In Figure 1.4 above, four scenarios are presented, namely avalanche, steep climb, missed window, and finally a sunny summit. The axis of SA Vulnerable and SA Resilient was defined on the basis of whether the National Development Plan (NDP) was implemented or not. While the NDP has been accepted by business leaders and other stakeholders as an excellent blueprint for socio-economic and political transformation, the inability of the key stakeholders to implement the NDP has resulted in the country being extremely vulnerable, so much so that the missed window, avalanche and steep climb scenarios appear to be the current options for South Africa. Later in this chapter we will elaborate more clearly on how the labour market should be developed to contribute in a more meaningful way to achieving the objectives of the NDP.

Also in 2016, an NGO in the land-reform sector produced a set of land-reform scenarios[ii] as shown in Figure 1.5 below.

---

ii   Available as a free download from www.landreformfutures.org.

Figure 1.5: Land return scenarios

The current slow progress in land reform is leading to increased conflict, marginalisation and political radicalism, as can be seen in Figure 1.5 above. This situation may become unbearable if solutions are not found for the land crisis. The scenarios identified in the figure above help to frame the discussion towards deriving sustainable solutions for the land situation.

FLAGS – AS UNFOLDING EVENTS

"Flags", as described earlier, are key trends (or unfolding events), which, if watched closely, will indicate the possible scenarios that are becoming more or less likely. During a SABPP debate over labour market scenarios for 2030, Clem Sunter[10] noted that, "Over the past 12 years, I have realised that our clients get quite frustrated if you offer them only a suite of different scenarios for whatever economy, market or industry they are contemplating the future of. It is like offering different pathways without any signposts to suggest which one you are on, and where it is heading. Thus, I now put as much effort into identifying flags that would indicate you are moving from one scenario into another one as we do into developing the themes of the scenarios themselves. Flags can range from tipping points that might precipitate a different chain of events (like a jump in interest rates) to ones which are a sign that you have already switched scenarios (like a rise or drop in the unemployment rate). I tend to consult experts in the field under consideration (whether it is the global economy, a country's political future or the stock market) about the flags they are watching out for. The purpose of flags is to remove the tint from the glasses we all wear when we look at the future. The tint may be caused by emotional make-up of being a natural optimist or pessimist, or by simple bias. The fact is that as the flags rise, they cannot be ignored".[iii]

---

iii Sunter, C. 2017. *Scenarios, Flags, Probabilities*. Retrieved from: http://www.clemsunter.co.za/scenariosflagsprobabilities.html

Flags from other scenarios

It is important to consider issues identified by other scenario development groups when considering the South African labour market, as the labour market does not evolve in isolation.

In their flag-watching book referenced earlier, Illbury and Sunter describe some major global flags which are laid out in Table 1.1 below.

Table 1.1: Major global flags

Rules of the Game	**Key Uncertainties**
The Religious Flag – competition between the major religions of the world	The Red Flag – Russia's intentions and actions
The Grey Flag – population aging	The Anti-Establishment Flag – fury of the middle class against the super-rich, who get richer by the day as real economies fail to grow while financial markets explode
The Green Flag – climate change	The Porous Border Flag – Middle East migrants to Europe
	The New Technology Revolution – a new major wave of technology is due - will this come from smart energy, smart medicine or something else?

In Table 1.1 above, the rules of the game and key consistencies of some major global flags are listed. It is interesting to note that some countries, regions or continents may be more affected by certain flags than others. For instance, the religious flag may be more prevalent in the Middle East and Europe than other regions, while it is also possible for this flag to spill over to other areas (more recently the religious flag has become prominent in the USA). Likewise, the grey flag is prevalent in countries like Germany and the UK, while it is not an issue in African countries with its large youth populations. It is also interesting to note that in some countries certain flags may be downplayed, ignored or discarded. Examples include President Donald Trump's challenging of the green flag, or countries that are slow to adapt to the technology revolution. The vastly different and diverse approaches for dealing with immigrants are good examples of how much confusion can be created when countries respond differently to immigration in a world that had been expected to become more global.

The above approaches to scenarios for South Africa provide some interesting lessons and opportunities for leveraging scenario planning in navigating planning, policy-making and decision-making in the business and political environments. In particular, the IRMSA scenarios present some useful options for consideration when starting to explore labour market scenarios. Major South African flags as identified by IRMSA are described in Figure 1.6 below.

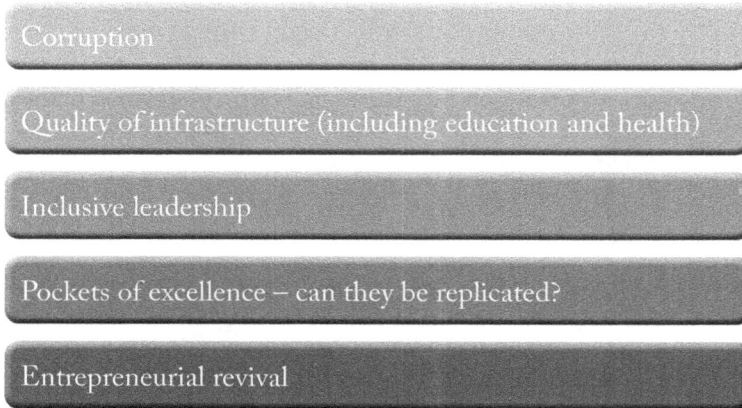

Corruption

Quality of infrastructure (including education and health)

Inclusive leadership

Pockets of excellence – can they be replicated?

Entrepreneurial revival

Figure 1.6: Major South African flags[11]

The IRMSA flags represent some interesting questions for stakeholders in the labour market:
- How is corruption distorting the labour market, and what can we do about it?
- How good is our labour market infrastructure and education specifically?
- How inclusive is our leadership in the labour market (government, labour, business)?
- Do we have pockets of excellence in the labour market that can be replicated?
- To what extent does the labour market contribute to (or stifle) entrepreneurial revival?

The above questions are a useful point of departure when analysing the South African labour market and exploring different approaches and options for labour market development. Sometimes one tends to jump to conclusions and solutions too quickly in the absence of a proper understanding of the dynamics, realities and factors that contribute to the labour market, hence the need for a sound labour market analysis. Ensuring that the labour market is responsive to changing conditions and a totally different world of work is indeed a challenge to first realise, and then to address in a proactive and dynamic manner. Building on an understanding of the broader labour market dynamics within the context of a changing business environment enables decision-makers to consider the impact, opportunities and risks of different labour market scenarios.

THE SABPP's LABOUR MARKET SCENARIOS

The SABPP HR Leaders Working Group on labour market scenarios brainstormed the rules of the game and key uncertainties we will face, as facilitated by Clem Sunter. In essence, the HR leaders unpacked two key issues, i.e. the rules of the game (the forces that are present and will continue in the labour market) and the key uncertainties (the forces that could change the way the labour market functions). Figure 1.7 below shows the results of the working group from March 2016.

Rules of the Game	Key Uncertainties
World of work is changing - technology driven	Education and skills development systems - will they adapt to meet employers' needs?
Employee characteristics - young people will be the majority in organisations	Balance of power - will de-unionisation in the private sector continue and how will shifting power relationships play out?
Transformation - ownership of economy and exercise of managerial power remains an imperative	Economic growth - will the NDP be implemented and economic growth achieve targeted levels?
Protection of worker gains - legislation will continue to be more protective than laissez-faire	Tolerance of inequality - will the status quo of inequality provoke major social unrest externally to organisations and internally?
Structural unemployment and huge differences between formal and informal employment will continue	

Figure 1.7: Rules of the Game and Key Uncertainties for the SA labour market

A large part of the issues above requires a "changing world of work" perspective, also often referred to as "the new world of work" or the "future world of work".

What do we mean by "The new world of work"?

There are many publications on the nature of the new world of work and the drivers that will shape that new world. Three of these are highlighted here to illustrate the general agreement on key features of that world of work.

In their book, *The 2020 Work place*, Meister and Willyerd identified three major forces of work as seen in Figure 1.8 below.[12]

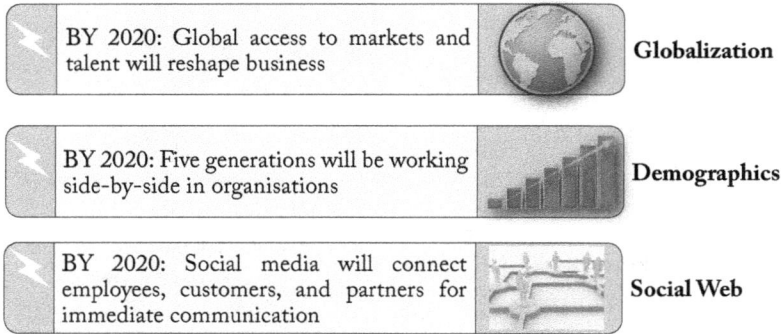

BY 2020: Global access to markets and talent will reshape business	**Globalization**
BY 2020: Five generations will be working side-by-side in organisations	**Demographics**
BY 2020: Social media will connect employees, customers, and partners for immediate communication	**Social Web**

Figure 1.8: Three major forces of work[13]

In Figure 1.8 above, Meister and Willyerd outlined three major forces shaping the UK's Chartered Institute for Personnel and Development (CIPD) in their 2013 publication, *Megatrends – the trends shaping work and working lives*.[14] They identified important trends affecting the work itself, the workforce and the workplace. This can be seen in Figure 1.9 below.

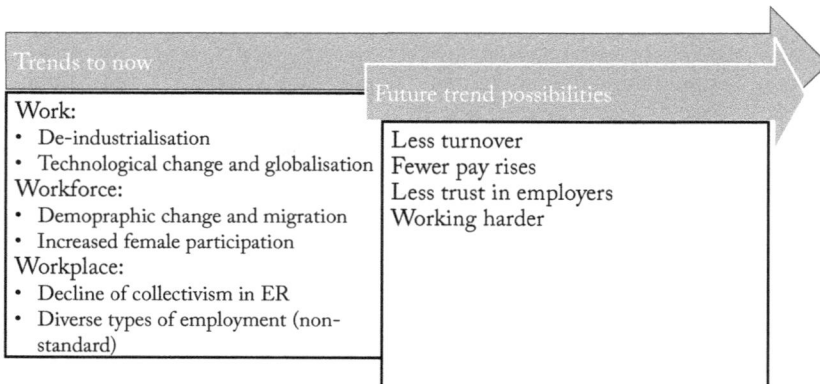

Trends to now

Future trend possibilities

Work:
• De-industrialisation
• Technological change and globalisation
Workforce:
• Demopraphic change and migration
• Increased female participation
Workplace:
• Decline of collectivism in ER
• Diverse types of employment (non-standard)

Less turnover
Fewer pay rises
Less trust in employers
Working harder

Figure 1.9: Current and future trends[15]

The major shifts in the demand for well-educated people are illustrated in the 1997 book, *Workforce 2020: Work and Workers in the 21st Century,*[16] which uses data from the US. In Figure 1.10 below, the workforce gap in 2020 is clearly visible.

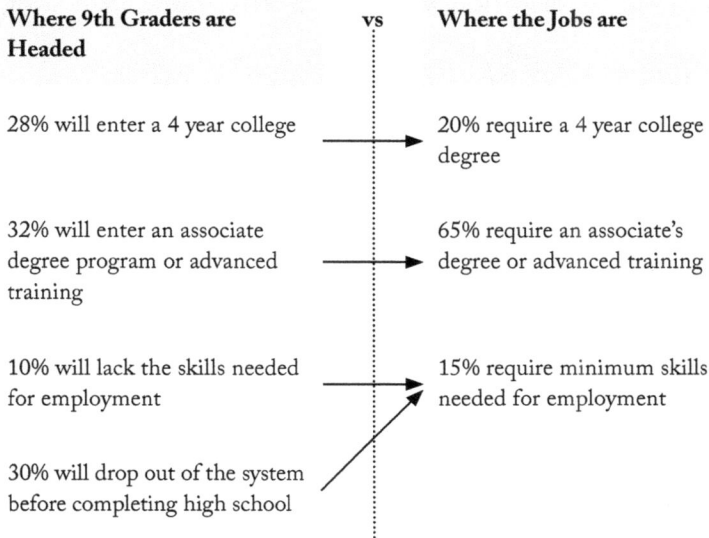

Where 9th Graders are Headed   vs   **Where the Jobs are**

28% will enter a 4 year college   20% require a 4 year college degree

32% will enter an associate degree program or advanced training   65% require an associate's degree or advanced training

10% will lack the skills needed for employment   15% require minimum skills needed for employment

30% will drop out of the system before completing high school

Figure 1.10: The workforce gap in 2020[17]

Figure 1.10 above displays the workforce trends and concurrent gaps. Changes in the workplace since this book was published in 1997 would most probably change the demand percentages (the right-hand column in the above figure) so that the four-year college degree requirement would be higher.

Clearly, the supply situation in South Africa (the left-hand column in the above figure) would be different. The White Paper of the Department of Higher Education and Training[18] has set a target of 1.6 million students at university (from 937 000 in 2011) and 2.5 million students in TVET colleges (from 345 000 in 2010 and an estimated 650 000 in 2013) by 2030. These figures represent a 25% and 39% increase respectively. Assuming a demand situation, which is less knowledge intensive than the US, it can still be seen that the gap will be extremely high.

Research by the Oxford Martin Programme on Technology and Employment[19] has identified the following key trends:

- New technologies are not creating many jobs.
- Technology has increased the range of tasks skilled workers can perform.
- New "high-touch" (as opposed to "high-tech") jobs are being created.
- Many new personal service jobs are being created.

The trends identified by the CIPD imply that employees in the future will be (even) more pressurised and the workplace climate will be less supportive.

Meister and Willyerd identified more positive qualitative aspects of the future world of work in 2010, which are laid out in Table 1.2 below. Some of these factors are already evident in South African workplaces, whilst others are possibly less likely to emerge.

Table 1.2: Qualitative aspects of the future world of work

1.	You will be hired and promoted based upon your reputational capital.
2.	Your mobile device will be your office.
3.	Recruiting will be done on social networking sites.
4.	Web commuters will force corporate offices to reinvent themselves.
5.	Companies will hire entire teams.
6.	Job requirements for CEOs will include blogging.
7.	Your corporate curriculum will use video games, simulations and other reality games as key modes of delivery.
8.	The world will be networked and you will need a networked mind set.
9.	Outsourcing will be replaced by crowd-sourcing.
10.	Corporate social networks will flourish and grow inside companies.
11.	You will elect your leader.
12.	Work-life flexibility will replace work-life balance.
13.	Corporate social responsibility will be a key business driver that is used to attract employees.
14.	Diversity will be a business imperative.
15.	The lines between marketing, communication and learning will blur.
16.	Social media literacy will be required for all employees.
17.	Building a portfolio of contract jobs will be the path to obtaining full-time employment.
18.	Corporate app stores will offer ways to manage work and personal life better.

These aspects described in Table 1.2 above apply more specifically to knowledge workers than other workers, for whom the new world of work could be less attractive if it is further characterised by a lack of job security and fluctuating incomes.

According to the CIPD, whilst the actual work and workplace will change, as outlined above, the nature of the workforce itself will also change. Popular descriptions of the attributes of the so-called "millennials" concentrate on their values (civic-minded, family-focused, favour lifestyle and experience over money and prestige) and wants (being able to express themselves, constant challenge), as well as their education level. However, one aspect not often covered is their financial situation. As a result of their higher education levels, millennials often start their careers carrying debt from their student days. They also face a shortage of jobs, and as a result, their ability to save and buy their first homes is very constrained. They are used to cheap credit but they understand that their financial long-term future is uncertain, especially as governments will be unable to fund their retirements. There is thus often a preference to spend today rather than save for tomorrow. The absence of a national savings culture exacerbates the problem. Ultimately, the middle class find it difficult to cope with their financial, career and family demands. However, the new free public higher education system is expected to alleviate this burden.

The National Development Plan (NDP)

The National Development Plan (NDP) is the blueprint for making South Africa a successful country. The following are policy goals of the NDP:
- Maintaining fiscal discipline and macro-economic stability.
- Achieving a sustained GDP growth of 5.4%.
- Reducing unemployment to 14% by 2020 and 6% by 2030.
- Overhauling the civil service to improve efficiency and implementation.
- Promoting market competitiveness.
- Reducing the cost of living.
- Reducing impediments to investment.
- Creating jobs via entrepreneurship and reduced regulation, as well as a public works programme.

The new world of work trends outlined above will challenge the achievement of these goals considerably, demonstrating that some creative solutions will need to be found by all stakeholders. In fact, it may be argued that an inability to adapt to and leverage the new world of work will make it almost impossible to achieve the goals of the NDP. The sad reality is that we are lagging behind in our progress towards achieving most of the goals of the NDP, including GDP growth and reducing unemployment. With unemployment rising to almost 27% in recent times, we are highly unlikely to achieve the NDP target of 14% by 2020 and 6% by 2030, unless radical changes are implemented over a short period of time.

FOUR POSSIBLE SCENARIOS FOR THE SA LABOUR MARKET THROUGH TO 2030

Applying the Rules of the Game and Key Uncertainties to the South African labour market, the two key axes of possible change were identified by the SABPP working group facilitated by Clem Sunter in 2016 as follows:

- The extent of adoption or denial of the new world of work by the South African government, employers and unions.
- The extent to which labour market stakeholders can collaborate to find new ways of jointly influencing the future. One of the immediate key uncertainties discussed here was the adversarial nature of relationships between employers and organised labour created by the legislative framework for collective bargaining, and the need to amend labour legislation to curb the right to strike in light of the high level of intimidation and violence that was taking place, as well as the need for remedying the financial devastation occasioned by protracted strikes which were no longer in the best interests of the parties.

Combined, these two axes produce the following four possible scenarios portrayed in Figure 1.11 below.

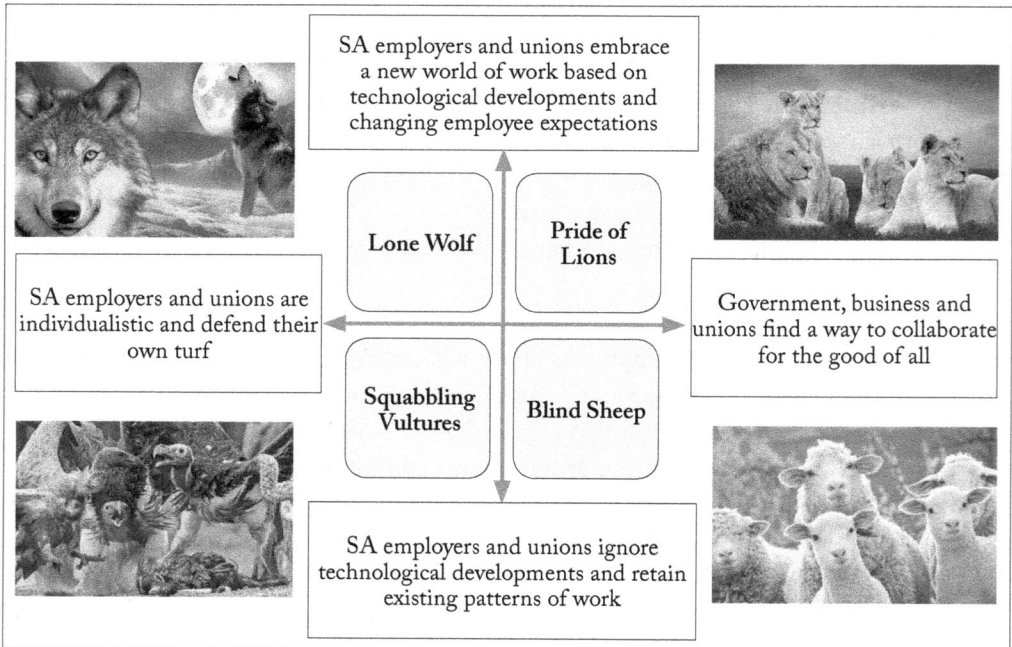

Figure 1.11: Four possible scenarios in the South African market in 2030[20]

The possible situation under each of these four scenarios is described in the next four sections.

1. Lone Wolf

In this scenario, many employers are innovating and making fundamental changes to the ways in which work is done. More outsourcing and the use of freelance employees lead to decreases in permanent employment among large employers. The number of start-up businesses is increasing, but the transition of these to medium-sized enterprises is reducing and failures are increasing. Game-changer business models such as Uber and Airbnb are emerging rapidly and traditional businesses fail to find a suitable response, and may exit the market altogether. The structure of the labour market is changing, skewing even more to the ICT and service industries. Unskilled people are trapped in low-wage, unprotected employment.

Economic growth is accelerating, but unemployment and the income inequality of employees are also accelerating, leading to high levels of social and industrial unrest. No suitable model of pay and benefits has been found to protect people who are forced to move out of the formal sector into informal employment.

Unions have found themselves occupied almost exclusively in trying in vain to protect the job security of their members, and traditional industries in the mining and metals sectors disappear. As unions lose membership and credibility, new "one man band" unions spring up and cause continued unprotected strike action due to a lack of expertise and infrastructure.

Employer organisations fragment and lose bargaining power. The collapse of central bargaining councils results in many employee benefit schemes being transferred to large insurance companies, and as a result many workers lose track of their benefits.

The government tries to keep control through tightened labour legislation, which is increasingly avoided by new enterprises. In addition, corruption and anti-competitive behaviour flourish, further exacerbating the situation.

The education system improves to some extent, but mismatches with the labour market continue to result in a lack of employment for young people leaving the system.

2. Squabbling Vultures

In this scenario, a resistance by all parties to recognise the fundamental, technology driven changes to the world of work results in continued low economic growth as South African products and services become less attractive and less competitive to the rest of the world. A lack of consumer-led economic growth leads to higher inflation, less employment and more poverty as people's incomes fail to keep up with the high cost of living. Corruption and anti-competitive practices flourish.

The NDP continues to exist only on paper. Business insists on a free market approach, resists government intervention and pulls out of centralised bargaining structures. Broad-Based Black Economic Empowerment (B-BBEE) fails to be broad-based and continues to benefit the connected few. As a result, high levels of corruption continue. Unions, losing members and political influence, become more confrontational, and their approach brings some businesses to their knees, causing more unemployment. Government continues to try to use legislation and control to protect workers, but is unable to counteract the consequences of poor economic growth. The collapse of bargaining councils, as with the Lone Wolf scenario, results in many employee benefit schemes being transferred to large insurance companies, and as a result many workers lose track of their benefits.

The education system fails to improve, and each year hundreds of thousands of young people leave school with no prospects of employment. Employers find ways around immigration restrictions to bring in skilled and professional workers, and illegal immigrants continue to flood into South Africa.

3. Blind Sheep

In this scenario, economic growth also continues to be low due to the inability of the private sector and State Owned Enterprises to adapt to the new world of work. Clinging to the status quo, the parties (government, business and unions) recognise their mutual interdependence and reach social compacts, which move towards co-determination in an effort to reduce industrial and social unrest. Labour market institutions remain largely unchanged in structure and purpose, but dialogue within them is characterised by cooperation and willingness to abandon fixed negotiating positions, recognising the severity of the economic situation.

Jointly governed labour market institutions bring some changes to the education system to match the needs of employers, but this is done within the old concept of the world of work, resulting in the skills produced missing the requirements of the new world of work.

Due to the increased levels of trust between social players, corruption decreases and the private sector accepts that anti-competitive behaviour is detrimental to the economy.

This scenario could also be described as moving the deck chairs on the Titanic; the collaborative, trusting nature of relationships is unsustainable due to the continued low economic growth – the new partnerships see no results and therefore fragment.

4. Pride of Lions

In this scenario, economic growth accelerates on the back of an innovative and adaptive private sector, supported through social compacts between government, business and labour which have found new ways of dealing with the protection of vulnerable employees, new ways of encouraging employers to employ and train young people, and new ways to match the education system to the needs of the new world of work.

The new structures and collaborative approach enable flexibility as the structure of the economy and completely new business models emerge, flourish and are in turn transcended and disappear. To reach these social compacts, the parties have abandoned fixed, ideologically-based approaches, and have found new ways to accommodate the genuine and fundamental interests of different segments of the population.

Government has implemented the NDP and South Africa has an efficient and politically independent civil service, and as a result, service delivery has improved and the lives of poor South Africans continue to improve, albeit slowly. Once again, the South African people have found a way to navigate a seemingly impossible transition. Under the Pride of Lions scenario, the pockets of excellence that emerged during the Lone Wolf scenario are replicated and multiplied to such an extent that they have become the norm in driving national innovation, productivity, competitiveness and growth. Significant job creation and entrepreneurial activity lead to a drastic reduction in unemployment on the back of a strong integrated education and skills development system, which caters for all segments of the labour market.

FLAGS TO WATCH

In considering the labour market scenarios outlined in the previous section, it is evident that the two most important factors to take into account are the new world of work and collaboration. Understanding the impact of these two flags is the key to strategic planning around these scenarios, as per Figure 1.12 below.

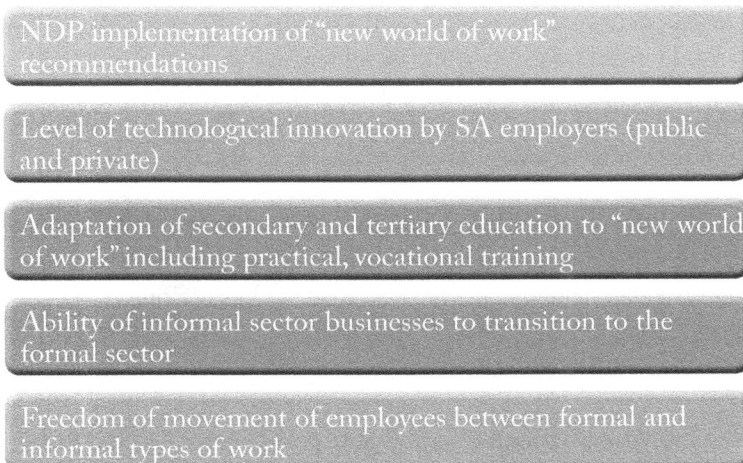

NDP implementation of "new world of work" recommendations

Level of technological innovation by SA employers (public and private)

Adaptation of secondary and tertiary education to "new world of work" including practical, vocational training

Ability of informal sector businesses to transition to the formal sector

Freedom of movement of employees between formal and informal types of work

Figure 1.12: Embracing the new world of work[21]

In Figure 1.12 above, the new world of South African work realities is presented. The question is whether the three key stakeholders (government, business and labour) are able to embrace the new world. Some radical changes to current thinking, planning and practice are required to create and leverage the new world of work, including:

- parties working actively together to implement the NDP's recommendations for the new world of work;
- putting technological innovation at the centre of economic, business and government development;
- creating the best possible education system relevant to the new world of work;
- converting the informal sector to the formal sector and setting these businesses up for success; and
- eliminating barriers to the movement of people between formal and informal types of work.

In Figure 1.13 below, a more all-encompassing approach to reaching an inclusive, collaborative approach to labour market development is set out.

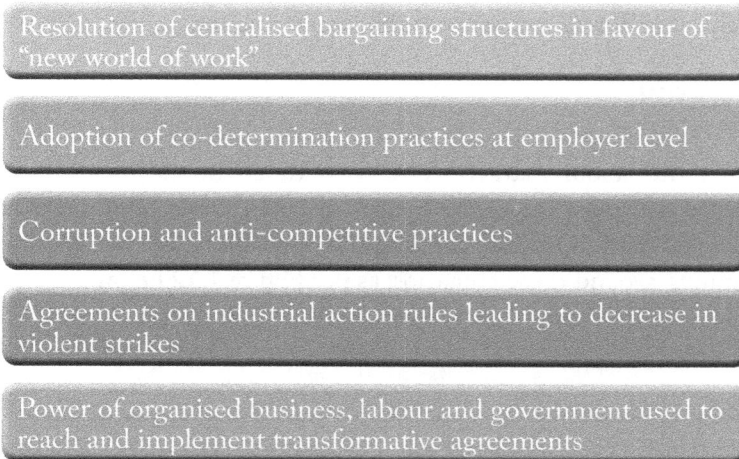

Resolution of centralised bargaining structures in favour of "new world of work"

Adoption of co-determination practices at employer level

Corruption and anti-competitive practices

Agreements on industrial action rules leading to decrease in violent strikes

Power of organised business, labour and government used to reach and implement transformative agreements

Figure 1.13: Reaching an inclusive, collaborative approach to labour market development

The above areas in Figure 1.13 present many opportunities for creating and implementing significant strategies towards collaboration between the three main stakeholders in the labour market. The following are key actions:

- Leveraging "new world of work" thinking and practices when reconsidering centralised bargaining structures.
- Co-determination practices at the employer level.
- Clear plans to address corruption and anti-competitive practices.
- Agreement on new industrial action rules aimed at a decrease and eventual elimination of violence during strikes.

- Utilising and balancing the power of organised business, labour and government to reach and implement transformative agreements.

WHAT THE FUTURE HOLDS ACCORDING TO SCENARIO PLANNING

HR practitioners working at higher levels of organisations are required to participate in the strategy formulation processes of their organisations to implement agreed upon strategies. In order to play this role, they need good frameworks and a good analysis of the environment to be able to advise the executive team on probable developments affecting the labour market in general, as well as individual employees of today and of the future.

Recognising this need for HR executives, in March 2016, the SABPP convened a group of 50 senior HR practitioners, academics and consultants under the facilitation of Clem Sunter, who is recognised within South Africa and globally as a top scenario planner, to think about the way in which the labour market could evolve under different scenarios. The purpose of this session was to develop a set of labour market scenarios for South Africa.

THE SOUTH AFRICAN BOARD OF PEOPLE PRACTICES' STANDARDS (SABPP)

The scenarios developed in Clem Sunter's session in March 2016 were formulated in the context of a set of national HRM standards. The SABPP is a quality assurance and professional body for HR practitioners in South Africa, which developed the first set of national HRM standards for South Africa in 2013. These standards also turned out to be the first set of national HRM standards in the world. The purpose of the national HRM standards initiative was to create a common framework of sound HR practice, to reduce inconsistency in practice, and to improve the overall standard and quality of HR work aligned to business objectives. The following set of 13 national HR standards was developed:

1. Strategic HR Management
2. Talent Management
3. HR Risk Management
4. Workforce Planning
5. Learning and Development
6. Performance Management
7. Reward and Recognition
8. Employee Wellness
9. Employment Relations Management
10. Organisation Development

11. HR Service Delivery
12. HR Technology
13. HR Measurement

These standards challenged organisations to improve their HR practices, thereby contributing to a more mature internal and external labour market. The SABPP standards can help an organisation to create the processes needed to implement co-determination. The greater the extent to which employers adopt these standards, the better the possibility of developing a mature labour market, especially if a critical mass of employers across economic sectors make the standards work. For instance, if all employers apply the talent management standard (Standard Element 2), better talent will be developed within organisations. This will then enlarge talent pools within organisations, and consequently externally. Ultimately, all organisations and the country at large will benefit from such an inclusive and standardised approach to people and human capital development. Likewise, if all organisations actively champion sound employment relations in accordance with the employment relations management standard (Standard Element 9), a more stable and productive labour relations climate will be created and maintained to the benefit of society as a whole.

The 2013 SABPP strategic HR management standard (Standard Element 1) requires organisations to "…analyse the internal and external socio-economic, political and technological environment and provide proactive people-related business solutions". At present, many HR executives acknowledge a lack of depth in their environmental scanning. The Vital Science Monitor discussed in Chapter 3, together with the social environmental analysis in Chapters 2, 3 and 4, can assist strategic HR practitioners to adhere to this standard.

The HRM standards challenge organisations to get their HR functions right. From the perspective of this book on co-determination, the HR standards should be integrated to achieve sustainable business and HR success. In essence, the book proposes an integration of the application of the employment relations standard (Standard Element 9) and the organisation development standard (Standard Element 10), while simultaneously leveraging and implementing the other 11 HR standards. A successful implementation of co-determination requires such an integrated approach to HR standards implementation. For instance, if employee wellness (Standard Element 8) is not implemented, co-determination is unlikely to work, because successful co-determination is dependent on employee wellness, good skills levels (Standard Element 5), as well as appropriate rewards and recognition (Standard Element 7).

The national HRM standards form a strong foundation for sound employment relations in the workplace. Not only do they define excellent practice within specialised HR areas such as employment relations, employee wellness and organisation development (OD), but they also encourage cross-functional implementation across these areas of specialisation. In essence, to make co-determination work, we propose an OD approach to HR management and employment relations in particular. Currently, Viljoen and van Zyl are co-creating co-determination standards with the SABPP, as co-determination presents an innovative approach to dynamic collaboration on employment relations in the workplace (this standard will be discussed in more detail in Chapter 8).

However, it is important to understand the purpose of scenarios when doing labour market planning. According to Brian Whittaker, the convenor of the Land Reform Futures scenario team, *"These scenarios are not forecasts of what will happen or proposals for what should happen. They are stories about what could happen under different circumstances. They are designed to trigger thinking about a future that is coming at us faster than we will be able to respond if we don't make time for the courageous conversation".* [iv]

Whilst the purpose of depicting labour market scenarios is to assist organisations to think about the future and how it could affect each organisation so that they can prepare contingency plans, the outcome of the scenarios make it clear that organisations should play an active role in shaping the future.

These "courageous conversations" will ask that the various parties respond effectively by committing to real engagement and being prepared to accept outcomes other than those that each party prefers. A deep grasp of the socio-political environment is thus required. This real engagement will require time and the necessary skills to build durable long-term relationships. Through these relationships, a new way forward could be found. Professor Clayton Christensen of Harvard Business School, an important business theorist, has advocated for organisations to innovate and grow, not relying solely on profits and returns on assets but on market-creating innovation, with job creation and job sustainability coming from market innovation. [v] Michael Porter supports this, articulating a Shared Value model in which business "sees societal problems as opportunities for business innovation and competitive advantage". [22]

The SABPP work group concluded that, at present, South Africa finds itself somewhere in the Squabbling Vultures scenario, although there are increasing calls for moves towards collaboration. The SABPP calls on stakeholders to reflect on the scenarios and commit to collaboration to influence the future. The unique South African adaptation of the German Co-determination Model at the transport company Interstate Bus Lines, as discussed later in this book, shows what is possible when companies explore new and innovative approaches and paradigms to employment relations in the workplace. Thus, in this chapter and throughout the book, we are challenging readers and stakeholders in the broader employment relations landscape to transform the labour market to the benefit of all stakeholders and society at large.

---

iv   Brian Whittaker, Executive Director of Vumelana Advisory Fund and convenor of the Land Reform Futures scenario team.

v   For an interesting South African example of the application of his thinking, see: Skae, O. 2nd March 2016. Creating win-win solutions for businesses. *Business Day.*

CONCLUSION

This chapter attempted to set the scene for positioning employment relations in the context of understanding the labour market and considering different labour market scenarios, as we move closer to the 2030 workplace and the eventual goal of ensuring the successful implementation of the NDP.

This book on employment relations in the new world of work presents a radical departure from the current approaches to HR, employment relations and organisation development. It offers new approaches to thinking about and planning around employment relations in the workplace. While employment relations in the past were seen as the responsibility of the employment relations manager, this book essentially approaches employment relations from an organisational culture and leadership perspective based on the reality of the new world of work.

We would like to acknowledge Clem Sunter for facilitating the labour market scenarios session for the SABPP, and we want to thank all HR managers and academics for their contribution to this project.

REFERENCES

Chartered Institute for Personnel and Development. (2013). *Megatrends – the trends shaping work and working lives.* Retrieved from: www.cipd.co.uk.

Cronje, F. (2014). *A Time Traveller's Guide to Our Next Ten Years.* Cape Town: NB Publishers.

Department of Higher Education and Training. (2014). *White Paper for Post-school Education and Training: Building an Expanded, Effective and Integrated Post-School System.* Retrieved from: http://www.dhet. gov.za/SiteAssets/Latest%20News/White%20paper%20for%20post-school%20education%20 and%20training.pdf.

Illbury, C & Sunter, C. (2011). *Mind of a Fox Trilogy.* Tafelberg: Human and Rousseau; Sunter, C. 2015. *Flagwatching.* Tafelberg: Human and Rousseau.

Judy, R.W. & d'Amico, C. (1997). *Workforce 2020: Work and Workers in the 21st Century.* Indianapolis, IN: Hudson Institute.

Meister, J.C. & Willyerd, K. (2010). *The 2020 Workplace: How Innovative Companies Attract, Develop, and Keep Tomorrow's Employees Today.* New York: HarperCollins.

Oxford Martin Programme on Technology and Employment. (2013). *Future Tech.* Retrieved from: http:// www.oxfordmartin.ox.ac.uk/downloads/academic/The_Future_of_Employment.pdf.

Porter, M. & Kramer, M. (2011). Creating Shared Value. *Harvard Business Review,* Jan-Feb.

The South African Institute of Risk Management (IRMSA). (2016). *SA Risk Report.* Retrieved from: https://c.ymcdn.com/sites/www.irmsa.org.za/resource/resmgr/2016_Risk_Report/IRMSA_2016_ Risk_Report.pdf.

SABPP. (2016). *SABPP Labour Market Scenarios 2030: People and Work – How will the South African Labour Market Change over the next 14 years?* Retrieved from: http://sabpp.co.za/wp-content/ uploads/2017/01/Labour-Market-2030-Scenarios.pdf.

Sunter, C. (2017). *Scenarios, Flags, Probabilities.* Retrieved from: http://www.clemsunter.co.za/ scenariosflagsprobabilities.html.

Vumelana Advisory Fund. (2016). *Land Reform Futures: Four scenarios for land reform in South Africa.* Retrieved from: www.landreformfutures.org.

ENDNOTES

1   Illbury & Sunter, 2011.
2   Sunter 2011.
3   Ibid.
4   Ibid.
5   Illbury & Sunter, 2011.
6   Sunter 2011.
7   Ibid.
8   Cronje, 2014.
9   The South African Institute of Risk Management (IRMSA), 2016.
10 Sunter, 2017.
11 IRMSA, 2016.
12 Meister & Willyerd, 2010.
13 Ibid.
14 Chartered Institute for Personnel and Development, 2013.
15 Ibid.
16 Judy & d'Amico, 1997.
17 Ibid.
18 Department of Higher Education and Training, 2014.
19 Oxford Martin Programme on Technology and Employment, 2013.
20 SABPP, 2016.
21 Ibid.
22 Porter & Kramer, 2011.

Chapter

2

THINGS ARE DONE DIFFERENTLY HERE
An African spiritual consciousness perspective on co-determination

Vusi M. Vilakati

INTRODUCTION

Despite the expansion of the South African economy over the last two decades, the engagement between business, labour and society has been complex and challenging.[1] The recurrent tensions that characterise the employment relations landscape are increasingly bringing to the public's attention countless ethical and socio-economic issues. Questions have been raised about a host of issues, including corporate governance, executive compensation, corruption, the inequality of labour and capital, and discrimination in the workplace.[2] There is a growing public awareness and call for a healthier relationship between business and labour, that could accelerate socio-economic sustainability and advancement.

As business struggles with these labour and developmental issues, one cannot help but notice that the simmering tensions in the South African labour market are a contradiction to the economic growth reported by a number of countries in sub-Saharan Africa. From the beginning of this century, adages such as Africa's turn, Africa rising, African renaissance, emerging Africa, the new scramble for Africa and the assertion of the 21st century as the African century have been prevalent across the globe. Regrettably, Africa's celebrated growth has not effectively translated to the continent's holistic advancement.[3]

Noting Africa's economic growth over the last decade, Chimhanzi[4] dispassionately posits that Africa's economic growth is jobless, not inclusive and not widely shared. Whether it is this perceived 'rise of Africa' or the purported 'new scramble for Africa', beneath the surface of this growth veneer are perpetual processes of production, distribution, employment relations, and capital patterns that lack the practical intent toward Africa's holistic advancement.[5] Complicit in these processes are factors of globalisation and massive capital outflows, which adversely impact domestic resource mobilisation and hamper the continent's economic growth.[6]

The recent Marikana tragedy in the South Africa mining context, along with its political ramifications, highlighted the importance of finding dynamic solutions to the tension between business outputs, labour and socio-economic advancement. It seems that even corporate social responsibility initiatives do not adequately bridge the gulf between business and society,[7] thus there has to be an urgent, well thought out response. After this tragic event, Webber Wentzel's Africa mining head, Peter Leon, boldly called on South Africa to consider adopting the two-tier German board system of co-determination, which allows for up to 50% worker representation in the company structure.[8]

At a broader level, the prolonged tensions that characterise the South African labour market are a convergence of the typical historical legacies, current political and socio-economic factors and the future requirements shared by many African countries. These factors necessitate dynamic, contextually attuned and globally responsive processes of consultation, engagement and decision-making between business, labour and society.[9] With the expansion of global markets, the growing fluidity of the labour market, as well as the growing interdependence of resources and suppliers, the need to evolve employment relations and human resources management practices in Africa has become urgent.[10]

Besides the economic, legal and ethical responsibilities of making a profit, the idea of corporate citizenship in African countries has wider ramifications than in developed countries. South African labour and business thus need to rewire the employment relationship and evolve their organisational development strategies. Broadening the understanding of the fundamental role of a business organisation in society lies at the heart of this reconfiguration. Such a process will ask questions about how business organisations are creating shared value[11] and incorporating social and economic sustainability into their human resource management strategies.[12]

Adapting relevant co-determination models may assist in emolliating the tension between the failing promises of neoliberal capitalist markets[13] and the cause for the advancement of sociality and business substantiality. In part, this requires an adaptive intelligence and contextual intelligence. If business is going to make a substantial impact toward the holistic advancement of society, the art of adapting and adopting contextual developmental needs is critical for business sustainability. With regards to employment relations, this will include adopting contextual values and practices and incorporating them into human resource development strategies. Contextually attuned businesses will realise relevance through creating responsible and responsive frameworks for the co-determination of work and the movement of capital.[14]

To fundamentally reconfigure the 'goal' of business in society is one of the ways through which organisations can respond to the United Nations Sustainable Development Goals (SDGs). The SDGs are a 'new global social contract' for promoting human dignity and realising a just and inclusive society at national and global levels. These SDGs are often summed up in 5Ps – People, Planet, Prosperity, Peace and

Partnership. Taking them into consideration, I believe achieving holistic advancement in Africa, and in South Africa in particular, requires an ecosystemic approach that promotes a harmonious co-existence between business, labour and society.

To realise such a dream will require innovative strategies for adapting employment relations strategies to meet the emerging world of work and business. The employment relationship within the context of internalisation, globalisation and the fourth industrial revolution will be a tight balancing of paradoxes and tensions between economic, social and ecological objectives.[15] Business leaders will require dynamic skills for making their businesses locally relevant and globally responsive.[16] Key to this chapter is the need to integrate the wisdom of African spiritual consciousness (ASC) into processes of corporate governance, and the structuring of collective agreements in order to create trust, belonging, inclusivity and a dynamic organisational culture.

More specifically, this chapter focuses on how the values, attitudes and behaviours of ASC can restore the practice of humanity to the heart of business by creating an inclusive employee relations culture.[17] I consider the contextual epistemic and ideological embedding of co-determination to be a consultative and partnering process in South African business and labour practices. The storyline of the chapter unfolds thematically as follows:

- **Theme 1: 'Securing the base' for Africa's advancement** - reflecting on the historical, current and future requirements for South Africa's new world of work.
- **Theme 2: Co-determination in the South African context of employment relations** - a brief overview of co-determination in South Africa.
- **Theme 3: The rediscovery of the wisdom of ASC** – a discussion of the philosophy and essential practices of ASC.
- **Theme 4: Approaching co-determination from an African perspective** through bottom-up, Africa-centred and adaptive practices of humanity by harnessing the connectedness of human life, creating an engaged employment environment, and nurturing socially and economically responsive business organisations.

'SECURING THE BASE' FOR AFRICA'S ADVANCEMENT

At a recent lecture at the University of the Witwatersrand, a world-renowned African literary author, Ngũgĩ wa Thiong'o, gave a lecture entitled, 'Secure the Base, Decolonise the Mind'. During the lecture, Ngũgĩ posed the question, Why is Africa, the home of 30% of the world's remaining minerals, still the poorest of all the continents? This question echoes with stark familiarity across disciplinary boundaries as an unquenchable thirst for understanding the incongruence between Africa's material resourcefulness and the slow pace of its social and economic development.

Africa's resourcefulness and its ramifications for business and labour are to an extent shaped by the ongoing distrust between unions, business and government. The complexity of the employment relationship between employees, employers, states, markets and contracts should be seen in the light of each particular country's historical timeline, along with its current and future requirements. While discussing these factors is beyond the scope of this chapter, it is worth pointing out that the advent of democracy in South Africa has not sufficiently translated into a dynamic economic and political consensus. There are still tensions between the different ideological vantage points of stakeholders (state, employees, unions, business) with regards to the nature of engagement processes and the competing social and economic outcomes that each stakeholder anticipates.[18]

In addressing the challenge of development in South Africa, there is a need to demystify and disentangle the neo-liberal claim that the freedom to pursue rationality and self-interest leads to social and economic growth.[19] Instead of finding ways of holding the social and economic agendas in creative tension, capitalist illusions and communist ideals continue to strain the country's labour market. The challenge for South Africa and many other African countries is the lip service they pay to the wisdom of ASC.

For Africa to advance, business and labour should disinvest themselves of the tendency to shy away from African human values that promote peace, social cohesion, solidarity and cooperation, simply because they do not fit the inherited neo-colonial market policies. Ntibagirirwa[20] made a very important point when he suggested that the full participation of Africans in the emerging economy will effectively happen if the cultural wisdom, beliefs and values of its people are elevated and integrated into business and labour policy frameworks.

Allowing African ways of thinking, doing and being to shape the interactions between labour and capital promises to deconstruct the dominant global economic frameworks that continue to leave Africa in a perpetual state of underdevelopment. The worst manifestation of the dominance of western consciousness is the labelling of African cultures as obstacles to development and presenting African consciousness as paternalistic or an impediment to the spirit of creativity, initiative and innovation.[21] Instead, the integrative nature of African wisdom is an essential component of economic cooperation and can be a creative catalyst for business, labour and socio-economic advancement.[22] Seen against the background of African cultural wisdom, employment relations and economic growth and development are product of the synergy of multiple actors: the state, the market, shareholders, stakeholders, unions and individual employees.[23] This view eliminates any possibility of distinctions between producers and consumers, employees as recipients and shareholders as accumulators. It proposes a view of the human being as a producer and a consumer, or a buyer and a seller, and an agent of personal and societal transformation.

Noting all these variables, the task of securing a strong African consciousness for leveraging the relationship between labour and business in South Africa will entail:
- converting the moral impetus that gained them political independence into

strong regional networks and policy frameworks, along with national strategies for reorganising and expanding the economy, including radically transforming the large oligopolistic firms that dominate and determine Africa's market trends;[24]

- an imaginative, innovative and contextually attuned process of identifying, integrating and translating the wisdom of African human and spiritual consciousness into evolving forms and practices of employment relations, leadership development, business goal setting and organisational strategies;[25] and

- linking co-determination to the theory of the firm and making employee participation a major factor in framing the country's corporate governance system.[26]

Ultimately, the hope is to discover how ASC, with its supportive ontologies and epistemologies, promises to broaden the scope of employee participation in the workplace, strengthen the cause of human dignity, restore the practice of humanity, foster an appreciation for the dignity of work, and engender the conceptualisation of the organisation as a community of solidarity.

CO-DETERMINATION WITHIN THE SOUTH AFRICAN CONTEXT

Employment relations in South Africa over last three decades initially focused on securing basic workers' rights, before increasingly shifting toward an interaction between the labour market and the economy, and instituting programmes to address labour market inequalities such as union structures and collective bargaining processes. According to Barker[27], any labour relations framework should be based on the principles of fairness, equity and humanness, and recognise the employee not as a product or set of skills but as a human being.

The emerging South African world of work is increasingly demanding a more structured way of employee participation and consensus building, including the strengthening of the processes of co-determination across all levels of the company.[28] In South Africa, the associational adaptations of the German model of co-determination go as far as providing a framework for consensus building, establishing agreements pertaining to social and economic policy, and improving employment conditions.[29] Suggestions for implanting the German two-tier board system of co-determination have not gained traction in the South African labour market.

Co-determination, or *Mitbestimmung* in German, is an attempt to increase purposeful cooperation, engagement, participation and involvement between employers and employees based on partly uniform interests and the common good. It is a consultative institutional framework for the participation of employees and their representatives in the regulation of working conditions, as well as planning and decision-making, to leverage the conflict relationship between capital and labour.[30]

Co-determination is also based on notions that are central to human flourishing, namely working for a living with the goal of creating a productive workplace and resolving conflicts through dialogue rather than force.[31] The foundational ingredients are equality of capital and labour, the consideration of equality and human dignity, the need for stability through social cohesion and development, and enabling creative partnerships between shareholders, stakeholders and employees.[32]

Co-determination, which is deeply rooted in the tradition of German corporate governance, gradually arose through consensual collective agreements, which paved the way for social consensus and was subsequently codified into the Co-determination Act of 1976.[33] German co-determination also grew out of a move towards developing a trustful collaboration between all members in a cooperative enterprise, and the solidarity that guilds and unions attain in the process of collective bargaining. It also came as a consequence of the anthropocentric orientation of Catholic social teaching, which was sympathetic to labour as a remedy for the deprivation and dispossession of workers in the industrial revolution.[34]

Importing, translating and integrating the principles of co-determination into the South African organisational context broadens our conceptual understanding of employment relations. It not only includes internal HR standards such as reward and recognition, employee wellness, and talent and performance management, but also takes into account external labour market factors and stakeholders such as shareholders, the state and international policy frameworks. Of critical importance in implementing co-determination is recognising work as an important aspect of the development of human personality and the priority of human dignity over economic efficiency.[35]

In order to make co-determination work, a dynamic, inclusive and integrated approach to organisational development and employment relations is needed, which keeps all stakeholders in a constant dialogue about the welfare and future of employees, the growth and sustainability of organisations, and the socio-economic dynamics of context. It is also important to integrate the processes of co-determination with organisations' insights, as well as the values and attitudes from the ASC perspective.

AN AFRICAN SPIRITUAL CONSCIOUSNESS APPROACH

> African communities are increasingly being dismembered by the everyday practices of Euro-colonial and Eurocentric institutions that require we move away from indigenous African culture, tradition, social values and customs.
>
> George J. Sefa Dei

In Africa, the growth and sustainability of organisations depend on their innovative strategies for creating shared value and assuming a systems approach in shaping their ideologies, processes, and outcomes. Using the systems approach to creating shared value is deeply resonant with the integrative, cooperative and connective perspectives of ASC. Futuristic organisations have to embrace strategic and contextually attuned ideologies and processes to respond effectively to the internal and external factors of business and labour. As suggested by Dei[36] , there is an important case for translating and integrating the wisdom of ASC into employment relations, organisational development and strategic HR frameworks.

The African ways of being, thinking, doing and seeing the world

Integrating ASC into organisational development and employment relations requires authentic voices that will favour African human experiences by deconstructing the often reductionist narratives of the Western thinkers that frequently thrive on universalisms that evade the uniqueness of the African context and identity facilitation processes.[37] Such a process requires a local and relational, creative and receptive, and narrative and metaphor-generating consciousness that will embody the relational and generous ontology and epistemology of the African people.[38]

The African conceptions of personhood, identity facilitation and reality are an attempt to capture the attitudes of mind, logic and perception behind the manner in which African culture influences the way its people think, act and speak in different situations of life.[39] ASC is a narrative, subjective and experiential paradigm that is mainly characterised by a relational and contextual intuition and consciousness. It dynamically integrates emerging insights, values and attitudes with current existential (political, economic, social and technological) realities in order to facilitate African people's identities and agency in the emerging business and labour context.[40]

Making a case for African spiritual consciousness is not nostalgic myopia or being an uncritical guardian of tradition, but is rather a critical, conceptual and reconstructive appreciation of the fact that African people embody their beliefs about existence and reality. Those interested in discovering and integrating it into organisational developments and employment relations processes should critically engage traditional views, domesticate intellectual resources from other cultures, and participate in daily experiences with a curious awareness.[41] The goal is to reveal the beliefs and values that make us less productive and less prosperous and glean positive insights that will enhance our human existence and benefit the changing African context.

Language is also an important part of conceptualising African personhood. At many levels, using colonial elements (synthetic and analytic elements) of language have led to the misconception of the African person.[42] Although there are biological and psychological structures that are universal for all human beings, the cultural and linguistic coding of these structures alter the ontological and phenomenological appreciation of selfhood.[43] The cultural and linguistic relativity also render the perception of ontological issues of existence relative.

An immersion into the African existence reveals a particular cosmology and ontology that shapes their lived experiences and values. Foundational to this worldview is a holistic, indivisible and anthropocentric ontology that includes a dynamic relationship with God, ancestors, each other and the natural environment, creating an eco-systemic field of energy and existence. From this indivisible cosmic whole, three realities can be theoretically distinguished, i.e. the macro-, meso-, and micro-cosmos.[44]

The macro-cosmos refers to the universe (and all its contents) in which God is encountered as the source and purpose of creation; the meso-cosmos refers to the spiritual realm (situated in the world of the individual and transcendent) where energies interchange; and the micro-cosmos refers to the physical domain (the cognitive, affective, behavioural and motivational daily existence) of the individual, which is influenced by the meso-cosmos and macro-cosmos.[45]

Table 2.1 lists the key characteristics of each domain within the African cosmology. Notable in these features is the interrelated nature of these domains. The African system of thought and personhood shares the following characteristics:

- The unity of the person with their environment.
- The vital life force that connects people intrinsically with others and nature.
- The unique space-time consciousness, intelligence and moral capacity.
- The desire to collectively develop without high levels of competition.

Table 2.1: Domains of an African cosmology

The macro-cosmos	The meso-cosmos	The micro-cosmos
• The universal reality domain in which God is encountered. • The spiritual and religious realm of existence that enfolds all human existence. • The place where God exists transcendentally with ancestors (the living dead) and can be eminently/inherently experienced in daily routines of life. • Anchored in this domain all life is spiritual.	• The domain of the spirits – a no man's land. • The spiritual world where all forces coincide – ancestors, malignant spirits and sorcerers' operational realm. • Situated in the world of the individual and collective imagination – involves ancestors, human and animal life and the natural physical reality. • The spirits in this realm influence human behaviour – almost to the point of regulation and control.	• The domain of the individual and their daily collective existence. • Wholly influenced by the macro-cosmos and meso-cosmos based on the following principles: survival of the community (tribe); union with nature; co-operation; interdependence; collective responsibility. • In this domain, Western psychological values of 'individuality', 'uniqueness' and 'differences' are often replaced by 'communality', 'group orientation' and 'agreement'.

The macro-cosmos	The meso-cosmos	The micro-cosmos
• There is an open door between sensible (perceptible and physical) and non-sensible (non-perceptible and spiritual). • Philosophically, in this domain, there is no distinction between the sacred and worldly, religion and non-religion, and spiritual and physical. • Everything belongs together in this realm like one big ecosystem – no dissection of the world and people – the collective functioning of people and natural reality. • People and nature live in partnership.	• The space that gives form to good and bad fortune, desires, fears and hope for success. • Behaviour cannot always be explained in empirical and rational terms; it is always attributed to powers beyond. • This is the domain of human dreams and motivation. • Forces in this domain are channelled through some rituals in order to translate them into goodwill and protective care for the individual – in bad instances, they can come as punishment.	• Self-concept is 'we'/ 'us' rather than 'I'. • The logical choice is an outcome of the objective personal and subjective collective sense of being. • The individual is an active force that is expected to contribute positively towards the community. • Characterised by co-operation rather than competition. • Values and ethics are normative rather than individualistic. • Personal development is community achievement.

The nature of reality that underpins this system of being and doing stresses a complete or holistic ontological viewpoint, and the need for connective, harmonious belonging and co-existence between nature, culture and society. The African worldview is an integral bridge between the subjective, objective, inter-subjective, and inter-objective worlds of research and existence.[46] Forster[47] called the emerging consciousness and approach to individuals and systems a relational and generous ontology.

This worldview is rooted in an African indigenous knowledge system that works with an African epistemology that centres on the inner spiritual dimensions of knowing and making connections with the aspects of existence. African epistemology also hinges on:

- the acceptance of different ways of knowing and conceptualising reality;
- viewing knowledge as situational, positional, contextual, cumulative and emergent;
- taking responsibility for the individual and collective actions; and
- integrating personal (body, mind and soul) experience with the social and metaphysical worlds.

Understanding the grounding of this epistemology enables a process of recovery from the spirit injury, the depersonalisation of selves and the negation of the wisdom of

African humanness.[48] It is also an affirmation of the motivational and intuitive power of spirituality that enables the constitutive imagination required for integrating context-informed knowledge - insights, perceptions, emotions, memory and actions – into processes of self-expression and communication in personal, team and organisational settings.[49]

A further consideration for African thought is the axiological position linked to the inherent reality and ways of knowing and understanding the world. The values espoused in African human consciousness emphasise caring, sharing, belonging, creativity, connectedness, reciprocity, cooperation, compassion and empathy.[50] There is also a recognition that for human beings to develop, flourish and reach their full potential, they need to conduct their relationships in a manner that promotes the well-being of others, i.e. humanness (*botho, Ubuntu, buntfu, edubantu*). These are often captured in the common Nguni idiom, *umuntu ngumuntu ngabantu* – I am a person through other people[51], or as per Shutte[52], I participate, therefore I am.

Being human in the African sense is to be part of a living organism or network of relations that includes all of society - the living, the living-dead and future generations – held together with an intersubjective understanding of the mutuality, sharing and reciprocal nature of existence. Inter-subjectivity from an African perspective suggests that a person grows more fully human, more truly in their identity, through engagement with other persons.[53]

Many traditional African communities evaluate their systems of thought, values, beliefs and practices within the history and context of their communities, often privileging responsibilities over rights, community over individual, and peaceful coexistence over dominance or control.[54] It is important for understanding human agency in the workplace to reclaim these understandings of reality, knowledge, values and ethical orientations.

At the heart of African spiritual consciousness is a collective analogy of being that transcends the idea of the individual self, which often is at the centre of dominant Western thought.[55] Africa's past, the present and its future requirements dynamically buttress this consciousness.

Being African and spiritual and conscious

At the most basic level, ASC recognises Africa as an ideological and geographical location, which captures the heart and spirit (priorities, motivations, meaning, giving features, and essence) of the African peoples, and the desire to discover how they live out this consciousness in their personal, interpersonal and professional dimensions of life.

Being spiritual is beyond a religious orientation. It is a matter of discovering the essence of 'being'; what it means to exist and to belong and to be connected with the whole spectrum of reality.[56] Walach defined spirituality as an experiential realisation of connectedness with reality beyond the immediate goals of the individual. It gives rise to a holistic knowing that manifests cognitively, emotionally and motivationally. The concept of 'spirit' is intangible in its essence and true depth.[57] Tolle contends that the essence of spirit is 'being' – the innermost, ever-present, invisible, indestructible true nature.

The spirit is the part of being that gives conscious awareness of self, connects us to the universe, and exists with no time, space and age limitations.[58] Being spiritual is about making connections between the personal, communal, environmental and transcendental aspects of one's existence.[59] Spirituality has a number of functions:[60]

- **Transcendental** - intrapersonal and transpersonal transcendence or connectedness that provides mental attitudes that enable calmness and balance in different life situations.
- **Structural** - certain values or belief systems (e.g. theological and metaphysical principles) lead to appropriate behaviour in life and work situations. For example, in an organisation, the organisational structure and ethics code should lead to certain behaviours.
- **Value-guidance** - acquiring knowledge, clarifying personal values (or universal principles) and growing one's sense of identity and beliefs leads to awareness and competent and ethical behaviour.

The importance of understanding the spiritual life dimension helps us hold the psychological, sociological and spiritual aspects that shape organisational culture in creative tension. People have three forms of intelligence: linear (logical) mental intelligence (IQ), associative emotional intelligence (EQ), and uniting spiritual intelligence (SQ).[61] Spiritual intelligence provides the integrative bridge from the right and left brain thinking models, leading to a transcendent form of thinking that elevates leaders to an increased level of self-awareness, other awareness and reality awareness.[62]

I have laboured on this concept because the spiritual life dimension is central to the shaping of identity within ASC. Often in common discourse, people try to commodify and relegate spirituality to private feelings, but this is not the case within most African cultures. In reality, Africa is replete with spirit and connectedness. African life refutes any amputations of the self and emphasises connectedness, belongingness, identifications, wellbeing, love, compassion, and peaceful co-existence with self, others and nature. The connecting values in African human experience include humility, healing, wholeness, compassion, sacredness and collective empowerment.

The third aspect of ASC is the idea of lived consciousness. To contextualise and understand African consciousness we need to see it within the broader framework of human consciousness. In consciousness, we can realise our connectedness; even universal connectedness. Consciousness in contemporary research has a trans-disciplinary nature; contemporary studies on consciousness can be classified into spiritual/mystical, neurophysiological, cognitive, neuropsychological and depth-psychological.[63]

Consciousness research can either take an objective empirical approach (biological and sociological – studying the functions of the brain), or a subjective phenomenological approach, such as in religion, philosophy and psychology.[64] The African philosophical presuppositions above suggest an integral approach to African reality and personality. The best way to work towards a dynamic and holistic appreciation of human beings is to take into account the 'four quadrants' of human existence, i.e. the intentional, behavioural, cultural and social.[65] This broad spectrum of research embraces the exterior individual (behavioural), interior individual (intentional), exterior collective (social), and interior-collective (cultural) realities of existence.

African consciousness rejects all forms of reductionism and founds itself on the integral approach to life. From an African perspective, consciousness is located within a material and communicative world of relatedness and relationships. As a collaborative social phenomenon, it presupposes a multiplicity of worldviews.[66] Consciousness is also bound to time, locality, relationships, narratives, memory and present experiences. Context, relationships and language are vehicles through which consciousness is mediated to the external world as logical and intelligible.[67]

While consciousness may be situational, contextual and language oriented, it has an intrinsic capacity to shape the world. Consciousness is local and relational, receptive and creative, cooperative and narrative about the generation of symbols. From an ethical perspective, African consciousness is an intellectual, affective and relational strategy that refuses to reduce the human being to a set of mechanical functions. Any consciousness and forms of existence that fail to create human relationships are morally bankrupt and incoherent.

In essence, ASC is an all-inclusive embrace and recognition of all possible sources of identity and meaning for African people, as shaped or being shaped by historical and political legacies; geographic, national and socio-cultural influences; past and current structural economic factors; and diverse ideological and religious knowledge and experiences.[68] Recognising African identities and personhood involves reclaiming and liberating African knowledge production by interrogating dominant discourses, setting the agenda, designing the Africa we want, and rediscovering African indigeneity as a space, concept and embodiment of African humaneness, aspiration and dreams.[69]

CONSIDERATIONS FOR THE EMERGING WORLD OF WORK

Thus far, I have detailed the developmental challenges facing Africa, as well as the need for an inclusive and consultative approach to organisational development and employment relations. I have also given a basic overview of the need for implementing co-determination in the South African organisational context. However, in large part I have explored African spiritual consciousness as a dynamic, integrative and inclusive way of seeing, thinking, being and doing in the world. I now want to explore how to translate and integrate the wisdom and values of ASC into the workplace at the individual, group and organisational levels.[70]

From an organisational development and employment relations perspective, African spiritual consciousness is concerned with optimising individual creativity and functioning; liberating and harnessing collective connectivity and synergistic co-creation; and recognising and strengthening our common existence, belonging and cooperation through proactive participation in decision-making processes. This consciousness promises to be an antidote to the South African business and labour context that has a strong market orientation, which is often disconnected from the country's developmental priorities, leaving a substratum of weak individuals, families and communities.[71]

The foundational ideology within this African perspective takes a relational, receptive, creative, and inclusive ontology that is prevalent in most traditional African cultures.[72] This ontology offers an integrative cosmology and shares deep resonances with the integral theory and research perspective, the inclusivity theory and the human niches theory. The ideological grounding of ASC and the theoretical basis of co-determination all share the aspiration of inclusivity, connectedness and a peaceful, cohesive and flourishing humanity.

In South Africa, the SABPP's HR Standard on Employment Relations Management and a growing number of organisations are supportive of the core aims of co-determination.[73] Envisaged through this model of co-determination is a dynamic, responsible, ethical, sustainable and mutually beneficial partnership between business, labour and society.

The employment relationship

The common variables of an employment relationship include employees, employers, states, markets, and contractual agreements. Due to contextual and ideological diversity across occupations, industries, countries, time, and organisational levels of functioning, there is no singular conceptual basis for understanding these stakeholders.[74] Yet this is not to say that we cannot make some claims regarding the need for dignity and respect for individuals, as well as for creating good labour practices that promote respect, inclusivity and the improvement of socio-economic conditions by creating opportunities for employees.[75]

There is a common case for structuring mutually beneficial partnerships between employees and employers, as well as leveraging the competing economic interests of all stakeholders in the context of unequal power relations embedded in complex socio-political inequalities. Central to this conversation is the systemic process of ideologically understanding each of these stakeholders, i.e. understanding the processes through which each of them arrives at their common or competing interests in the tension between labour and capital.

The 'employee' and the organisation

Integrating ASC into our understanding should firstly relate it to existing ideas of who exactly is an 'employee', as well as the process of their motivation, agency, and engagement within an organisation and the anticipated outcomes of the relationship. To avoid the legal maze of conceptions, for the purposes of this chapter, it is sufficient to define an employee as anyone who sells their labour. Employees are frequently conceptualised as an economic or a behavioural being, yet seeing employees as purely rational economic and self-interested (*homo ecomomicus*) agents with the goal of maximising income and leisure often leads to the 'instrumentalisation' of people as factors of production and maximising capital.[76]

The 'employee' in the proposed Co-determination Model reflects a wider variety of intrinsic goals that go beyond a selfish desire for income and leisure. In particular, from an ASC perspective, these intrinsic goals include a desire for voice, equity, justice, power and control, social identity and exchange, individual fulfilment and self-determination that is rooted in a strong sense of 'calling', membership, belonging and connectedness to an authentic community. From an HR and employment relations perspective, understanding and investing in people's growth and enabling an inclusive organisational culture that optimally engages employees intellectually, affectively and socially, is critical.

Seeing employees as mechanistic rationally bound economic entities reduces human dignity to a particular set of capabilities, rendering them vulnerable to all sorts of distortions. The relational ontologies that underpin ASC, inclusivity theory and integral theory use a systems approach to understanding the relatedness of reality, making labour more than a transactional commodity and rather a means of transformation within a web of relations that promotes cohesion and reciprocal value.[77] The corresponding challenge that ASC presents to the employee is the need to engage constantly in an eco-systemic manner. ASC hosts a wide terrain of motivational factors that liberate others, and collective creativity, synergistically contribute to the welfare of others and foster a contextually attuned organisational culture.

ASC and organisational development principles of co-determination

Business organisations are conceptually constituted in three forms: as being owned and constituted by shareholders, implying the dominance of shareholder interests; as a combination of capital and labour, i.e. nothing more a legal fiction concealing a nexus of contracts; or as institutions, i.e. a creation of partnership with an appeal to social and economic reality.[78] Understanding the nature of the organisation empowers practitioners to understand the particular pathways to take in implementing processes of co-determination. The reality is that if an organisation prioritises shareholder interests or binds itself to the notion of contractual arrangements, the power relations and processes of co-determination become relative.[79]

From an organisational development and sustainability perspective, the partnership between the stakeholders of the employment relationship are committed to co-creating the future, maintaining a high level of engagement, adequately sharing power and responsibilities, proactively preventing, managing and rapidly resolving disputes, as well as jointly formulating business strategies.[80]

From an ASC perspective, an organisation is an integrative system that incorporates the micro, meso, and macro aspects of reality that the African concept of consultative dialogue, planning, decision-making and consensus building. In a number of African countries, this is what happens within constructs such as *Indaba, Lekgotla, Dare, Inkhundla* and *Imbizo*. These forms of organisational dialogue work from the premise of a community of practice,[81] which in this regard is a circular, experiential learning and an inclusive dialogical process of facilitating meetings, decision-making, conflict resolution, and building teams and organisational culture.[82]

In the Swazi language, there is an idiom that says *injobo lenhle itfungwelwa ebandla*, which translates to beautiful traditional attire is a product of collective effort. Creating a culture of engagement invokes the African values of community sharing and compassion, cooperation and solidarity, and a custodianship of the past, present and future resources.[83] Whether the engagement is about internal or external factors, the art of huddling together in a circuit-like conversation to analyse ideas, processes and outcomes; tease out each other's assumptions; address possible faults; discuss issues of efficiency; and propose alternatives, are the same in the processes of strategy formulation, collective bargaining, organisational development or managing the employment relationship.[84]

At best, organisational dialogue and employee engagement are a constant dance.

In a circle holding hands, to the music and rhythm of drums and marimba, I danced with all, I danced in the centre for all to see, and then I danced with all. As the night went on, we all became alive in a way we had never known, and our dance moved the mountains around to become one with us.[85]

Employee participation in the boardroom

Conversations about employees' participation and representation in organisations' administrative and management bodies are still contested; organisations' strategies and governance frameworks are traditionally characterised by the interplay between managers and shareholders.[86] While the latter wish to maximise the long-term value of the business, executives maximise their own utility, for which compensation, prestige and power often take precedence. It is also important to explore whether business goals are structured in a way that is responsive to the socio-cultural context of the country and translate into broader social and economic advances.

This particular consideration of an integrative and inclusive approach to individual growth, organisational effectiveness and socio-economic advancement has the support of the SABPP, as manifest in its definition of Employment Relations Management:[87]

> *Employment relations is the management of individual and collective relationships in an organisation through the implementation of good practices that enable the achievement of organisational objectives compliant with the legislative framework and appropriate to socioeconomic conditions.*

Co-determination at the executive level of the organisation introduces a third interest group, employees, to the supervisory board and thus to the firm's decision-making process.[88] The participation of employees at this level of the organisation invokes the inherent values of solidarity, sharing, responsibility, custodianship and the holistic worldview emanating from African spiritual consciousness.[89] For South Africa, the conversation should focus on whether the labour framework as it stands provides sufficient avenues for this consciousness to prevail, and not on the semantics about whether to legislate on the two-tier board system. It is clear that an inclusive framework for employment relations promises a culture of respectful engagement, a more trusting environment, and greater accountability regarding the movement of capital within organisations and broader society.

For South Africa to advance and benefit from economic growth, it is vital that all stakeholders consider broadening their understanding of the implications of co-determination for business and labour. For the implementation of co-determination to be contextually attuned and relevant to the socio-economic challenges facing the country, it will require reflective, relational, inclusive and integrative employment relations and organisational development strategies. In contemplating approaches to employment engagement, the values and practices, insights and values inherent within the African spiritual consciousness perspective are supportive of constructive frameworks of engagement and need no adaptation to be integrated into individual, group and organisational levels.

CONCLUSION

In this chapter, the concept of African spiritual consciousness was discussed in relation to the process of implementing co-determination in South Africa. The broader socio-economic challenges and the seeming neglect of African priorities and consciousness are backdrop issues to the surface tensions experienced by organisations in dealing with employment issues. Practical suggestions for translating and integrating ASC within the South African labour market were also provided. The current employment relations conversation relating to the implementation of a local Co-determination Model holds good prospects for advancing the country's labour market and advancing South Africa.

REFERENCE LIST

Addison, J. (2009). *The Economics of Codetermination: Lessons from the German Experience*. New York: Springer Verlag.

Afolayan, S. (2011). African Literature: A Showcase for Africa's Leadership Problems. *Matatu: Journal for African Culture & Society*, 39 (June), 27–39.

Ajulu, R. (2001). Thabo Mbeki's African Renaissance in a Globalising World Economy: The Struggle for the Soul of the Continent. *Review of African Political Economy*, 28(87), 27-42. https://doi.org/10.1080/03056240108704501.

Backhaus, J. (1989). *Codetermination: A Discussion of Different Approaches*. Edited by Hans G. Nutzinger. Berlin; New York: Springer-Verlag.

Barker, F. S. (2007). *The South African Labour Market* (5th ed.). Pretoria: Van Schaik.

Bendeman, H., Venter, R., Levy, A. & Dworzanowski-Venter, B. (2015). *Labour Relations in South Africa*. Cape Town: Oxford University Press.

Bertsch, A. (2012). Updating American Leadership Practices by Exploring the African Philosophy of Ubuntu. *Journal of Leadership, Accountability & Ethics*, 9(1), 81–97.

Bolden, R., & Kirk, P. (2009). African Leadership: Surfacing New Understandings through Leadership Development. *International Journal of Cross Cultural Management* 9(1), 69–86. https://doi.org/10.1177/1470595808101156.

Booysen, L. (2014). The Development of Inclusive Leadership Practice and Processes. In *Diversity at Work: The Practice of Inclusion*, edited by B.M. Ferdman & B.R. Deane, 296–329. San Francisco: John Wiley & Sons, Inc.

Bramucci, A., & Zanfei, A. (2015). The Governance of Offshoring and Its Effects at Home. The Role of Codetermination in the International Organization of German Firms. *Economia e Politica Industriale* 42(2), 217-244.

Branham, C. (2016). Stuck in the Middle: Curbing Income Inequality with the Better Bargain Plan. *Kansas Journal of Law & Public Policy*, 25(2), 187-224.

Bridger, E. (2014). *Employee Engagement*. London: Kogan Page.

Brooke, R. (2008). Ubuntu and the Individuation Process: Toward a Multicultural Analytical Psychology. *Psychological Perspectives*, 51(1), 36-53.

Budd, J.W. (2012). *Labor Relations: Striking a Balance*. New York: McGraw-Hill/Irwin.

Budd, J.W., & Scoville, J.G. (2005). *The Ethics of Human Resources and Industrial Relations*. Ithaca, NY: Cornell University Press.

Carmody, P. (2011). *The New Scramble for Africa* (1st ed). Cambridge, UK; Malden, MA: Polity Press.

Carroll, A.B., Brown, J., & Buchholtz, A.K. (2017). *Business & Society: Ethics, Sustainability & Stakeholder Management*. Boston, MA: Cengage Learning.

Chimhanzi, J. (2012). Whither Africa? *Development*, 55(4), 503-508. https://doi.org/10.1057/dev.2012.71.

Corner, P.D. (2008). Workplace Spirituality and Business Ethics: Insights from an Eastern Spiritual Tradition. *Journal of Business Ethics*, 85(3), 377–389. https://doi.org/10.1007/s10551-008-9776-2.

Coyle, S.M. (2017). Integrating Spirituality in Marriage and Family Therapy Training. *Australian and New Zealand Journal of Family Therapy*, 38,(1), 142–55. https://doi.org/10.1002/anzf.1195.

Creamer, M. (2012). Leon Proposes Employee Codetermination at Board Level. Retrieved from: http://www.miningweekly.com/print-version/leon-proposes-employee-codetermination-at-board-level-2012-11-14.

Dalitso, Sulamoyo. (2010). I Am Because We Are': Ubuntu as a Cultural Strategy for OD and Change in Sub-Saharan Africa. *Organization Development Journal*, 28(4), 41–51.

du Toit, C. (2008). Black Consciousness as an Expression of Radical Responsibility: Biko an African Bonhoeffer. *Religion and Theology*, 15(1), 28–52. https://doi.org/10.1163/157430108X308145.

Eidenmüller, H. (2016). Corporate Co-Determination German-Style as a Model for the UK? Retrieved from: https://www.law.ox.ac.uk/business-law-blog/blog/2016/07/corporate-co-determination-german-style-model-uk.

Fein, E. (2015). Reviewing the Practice Turn in Social, Organizational and Leadership Studies from an Integral Perspective. *Integral Review: A Transdisciplinary & Transcultural Journal for New Thought, Research, & Praxis*, 11(3), 93–116.

Forster, D.A. (2010). A Generous Ontology: Identity as a Process of Intersubjective Discovery – an African Theological Contribution. *HTS Teologiese Studies / Theological Studies*, 66(1), 1–12. https://doi.org/10.4102/hts.v66i1.731.

Gade, C.B.N. (2012). Different Interpretations among South Africans of African Descent. *South African Journal of Philosophy*, 31(3), 484–502.

Giacalone, R.A., & Jurkiewicz, C.L. (2003). Handbook of workplace spirituality and organizational performance. Armonk, N.Y: M.E. Sharpe.

Grant, R. (2014). *Africa: Geographies of Change*. 1 edition. New York: Oxford University Press.

Gutto, S. (2013). In Search of Real Justice for Africa and Africans, and Her/Their Descendants in a World of Justice, Injustices and Impunity. *International Journal of African Renaissance Studies - Multi-, Inter- and Transdisciplinarity*, 8(1), 30–45. https://doi.org/10.1080/18186874.2013.834553.

Hountondji, P.J. (1996). *African Philosophy: Myth and Reality*. Bloomington, IN: Indiana University Press.

Jackson, T. (2013). Reconstructing the Indigenous in African Management Research. *Management International Review*, 53(1), 13–38. https://doi.org/10.1007/s11575-012-0161-0.

Kankonde, P. (2015). A Reflection on the Necessity for an 'Ontological Turn' in African Studies with Reference to the Ecologies of Knowledge Production. In *ResearchGate*, 2015. Retrieved from: https://www.researchgate.net/publication/281631558_A_Reflection_on_the_Necessity_for_an_'Ontological_Turn'_in_African_Studies_with_Reference_to_the_Ecologies_of_Knowledge_Production.

Karsten, L., & Illa, H. (2005). Ubuntu as a Key African Management Concept: Contextual Background and Practical Insights for Knowledge Application. *Journal of Managerial Psychology* 20(7) 607–620. https://doi.org/10.1108/02683940510623416.

Kaufman, B.E. (2005). The Social Welfare Objectives and Ethical Principles of Industrial Relations, 23–59. In JW. Budd & JG. Scoville, eds. *The Ethics of Human Resources and Industrial Relations*. Champaign, IL: Labor and Employment Relations Association,

Khoza, R.J. (2012). *Attuned Leadership: African Humanism as Compass*. Rosebank, Johannesburg: Penguin Group.

Lakoff, G., & Johnson, M. (1999). *Philosophy in the Flesh: The Embodied Mind & Its Challenge to Western Thought*. New York: Basic Books.

Lancaster, B.L. (2004). *Approaches to Consciousness: The Marriage of Science and Mysticism*. Basingstoke, UK: Palgrave Macmillan.

Lawrence, A.G. (2003). *Transitions to Economic Democracy: Corporations, Collective Action*, Councils and Codetermination in Twentieth Century Germany and South Africa. Ph.D., City University of New York, 2003. Retrieved from: http://0-search.proquest.com.ujlink.uj.ac.za/businesspremium/docview/288407311/abstract/80A6C040674741PQ/21.

Lawrence, A.G. (2014). *Employer and Worker Collective Action*. Cambridge, UK: Cambridge University Press.

Letseka, M. (2011). In Defence of Ubuntu. *Studies in Philosophy and Education An International Journal*, 31(1 (October 2011): 47–60. https://doi.org/10.1007/s11217-011-9267-2.

Luce, S. (2014). *Labor Movements: Global Perspectives* (1st ed.). Cambridge: Polity.

Lutz, D.W. (2009). African Ubuntu Philosophy and Global Management. *Journal of Business Ethics* 84(S3 (October 2009): 313–328. https://doi.org/10.1007/s10551-009-0204-z.

Manda, D.L. (2007). The Importance of the African Ethics of Ubuntu and Traditional African Healing Systems for Black South African Women's Health in the Context of HIV and AIDS.,. http://researchspace.ukzn.ac.za/handle/10413/152.

Maree, J. (1991). Worker Participation: A Case for Co-Determination. *Indicator South Africa* 8(4 (January 1, 1991): 85–88.

Martins, L., & José Manuel Rodríguez Álvarez. (2007). Towards Glocal Leadership: Taking up the Challenge of New Local Governance in Europe? *Environment and Planning C: Government and Policy* 25(3 (June 1, 2007): 391–409. https://doi.org/10.1068/c0641.

Mbigi, L. (2005). *The Spirit of African Leadership*. Randburg: Knowres Publishing.

Mbiti, J.S. (2015). *Introduction to African Religion: Second Edition*. Long Grove, Illinois: Waveland Press.

McGaughey, E. (2015). The Codetermination Bargains: The History of German Corporate and Labour Law,. Retrieved from: https://papers.ssrn.com/sol3/papers.cfm?abstract_id=2579932.

McMahon, G., Barkhuizen, N., & Schutte, N. (2014). The Impact of Globalisation on South African Businesses: Some Leadership Thoughts. *Mediterranean Journal of Social Sciences* 5(9: 215–220. https://doi.org/10.5901/mjss.2014.v5n9p215.

Meyer, W.F. (2008). *Personology: From Individual to Ecosystem*. Johannesburg: Heinemann.

Milliken, F.J., Schipani, CA., Bishara, ND. & Prado, AM. (2015). Linking Workplace Practices to Community Engagement: The Case for Encouraging Employee Voice. *Academy of Management Perspectives*, 29(4), 405–21. https://doi.org/10.5465/amp.2013.0121.

Mogale, R.S. (2012). The Epiphany of Ubuntu in Knowledge Development: An African Way By. *The Journal of Pan African Studies* 4(10) 240–248.

Moloi, T.M. (2016). Afrikan Contribution to International Relations Theory: An Afrocentric Philosophical Enquiry. *Journal of Pan African Studies* 9(1). Retrieved from: http://www.jpanafrican.org/docs/vol9no1/9.1-15-T-new-Moloi.pdf.

Muswaka, L. (2014). The Corporate Responsibility for Human Rights: A Conceptual Framework. *Mediterranean Journal of Social Sciences*, March 1, 2014. https://doi.org/10.5901/mjss.2014.v5n3p219. The Two-Tier Board Structure and Co-Determination: Should South Africa Follow the Germany Example? *Mediterranean Journal of Social Sciences*, 5(9), 142–47. https://doi.org/10.5901/mjss.2014.v5n9p142.

Nafukho, F.M. (2006). Ubuntu Worldview: A Traditional African View of Adult Learning in the Workplace. *Advances in Developing Human Resources*, 8(3), 408–415. https://doi.org/10.1177/1523422306288434.

Nkomo, S.M., & Ngambi, H. (2009). African Women in Leadership: Current Knowledge and a Framework for Future Studies. *International Journal of African Renaissance Studies - Multi-, Inter- and Transdisciplinarity*, 4(1), 49–68. https://doi.org/10.1080/18186870903102014.

Nsamenang, A.B. (1995). Factors Influencing the Development of Psychology in Sub-Saharan Africa. *International Journal of Psychology*, 30(6), 729–39. https://doi.org/10.1080/00207599508246598.

Nsamenang, B.A. (2006). Human Ontogenesis: An Indigenous African View on Development and Intelligence. *International Journal of Psychology*, 41(4), 293–97.

Ntibagirirwa, S. (2009). Cultural Values, Economic Growth and Development. *Journal of Business Ethics*, 84(S3), 297–311. https://doi.org/10.1007/s10551-009-0203-0.

Himes, KR., OFM. (2005). *Modern Catholic Social Teaching: Commentaries and Interpretations*. Washington, D.C.: Georgetown University Press.

Oladipo, O. (2006). *Core Issues in African Philosophy*. Ibadan: Hope Publications.

Porter, M.E., & Kramer, M.R. (2011). Creating Shared Value. *Harvard Business Review*, 89(1/2), 62–77.

Prescott, R.C. (2008). *Mortal Grounding: Cosmology and Consciousness*. Bloomington: AuthorHouse.

Roth, M. (2010). Employee Participation, Corporate Governance and the Firm: A Transatlantic View Focused on Occupational Pensions and Co-Determination. *European Business Organization Law Review*, 11(01), 51. https://doi.org/10.1017/S1566752910100044.

Rukuni, M. (2007). *Being Afrikan*. Johannesburg: Penguin Global.

Sefa Dei, G.J. (2012). Reclaiming Our Africanness in the Disaporized Context: The Challenge of Asserting a Critical African Personality. *Journal of Pan African Studies*, (9), 42.

Sefa Dei, G.J. (2013). Critical Perspectives on Indigenous Research. *Socialist Studies*, 9(1), 27–38.

Sefa Dei, G.J. (2014). Personal Reflections on Anti-Racism Education for a Global Context. *Encounters on Education*, Vol. 15, 239-249. https://doi.org/10.15572/ENCO2014.13.

Severino, J.M., & Ray, O. (2013). *Africa's Moment*. 1 edition. Cambridge: Polity.

Shutte, A. (2001). *Ubuntu: An Ethic for a New South Africa*. Pietermaritzburg: Cluster Publications.

Subban, L. (2017). Fact Sheet – Towards a Co-Determination Model for South Africa. *HR Today: SA Board For People Practices Daily News*.

Taylor, D.F.P. (2014). Defining Ubuntu for Business Ethics – a Deontological Approach. *South African Journal of Philosophy*, 33(3), 331–45. https://doi.org/10.1080/02580136.2014.948328.

Tesar, G., & Kuada, J, eds. (2013). *Marketing Management and Strategy: An African Casebook*. London; New York: Routledge.

Thimm, A.L. (1987). Codetermination and Industrial Policy: The Special Case of the German Steel Industry. *California Management Review*, 29(3), 115–33.

Thomas, M, & Thompson, A. (2013). Empire and Globalisation: From 'High Imperialism' to Decolonisation. *The International History Review*, 36(1), 142–170. https://doi.org/10.1080/07075 332.2013.828643.

Tolle, E. (2009). *A New Earth: Create a Better Life*. London: Penguin.

Van Stapele, N. (2014). Intersubjectivity, Self-Reflexivity and Agency: Narrating about 'Self' and 'Other' in Feminist Research. *Women's Studies International Forum*, 43), 13–21. https://doi.org/10.1016/j. wsif.2013.06.010.

Van den Berg, A., Grift, Y. & van Witteloostuijn, A. (2011). Works Councils and Organizational Performance. *Journal of Labor Research*, 32(2), 136–56. https://doi.org/10.1007/s12122-011-9105-x.

Veldsman, T.H. (2013). People Professionals Fit for Emerging Economies. In *Talent Management in Emerging Markets (Ed.)*, 179–202. Randburg: Knowres.

Vilakati, V.M., Schurink, W, & Viljoen, R. (2013). Exploring the Concept of African Spiritual Consciousness. *Academy of Management Proceedings*, 2013(1), 12714. https://doi.org/10.5465/ AMBPP.2013.12714abstract.

Vilakati, V.M. (2016). African Leadership. In T.H. Veldsman & A.J. Johnson. *Leadership: Perspectives From the Front Line*. Randburg: KR Publishing.

Viljoen, R. (2015). *Organisational Change & Development: An African Perspective*. Knowres Publishing.

Walach, H. (2011). Neuroscience, Consciousness and Spirituality - Questions, Problems and Potential Solutions: An Introductory Essay. In *Neuroscience, Consciousness and Spirituality*, edited by Harald Walach, Stefan Schmidt, and Wayne B. Jonas, 1–22. Netherlands: Springer Science & Business Media.

Wilber, K. (2006). *Integral Spirituality: A Startling New Role for Religion in the Modern and Postmodern World*. 1 edition. Boston: Shambhala.

Wilkinson, A., & Townsend, K. (2016). *The Future of Employment Relations: New Paradigms, New Developments*. London: Palgrave Macmillan.

Zelazo, P.D., Moscovitch, M., & Thompson, E. (2007). *The Cambridge Handbook of Consciousness*. Cambridge: Cambridge University Press.

Zohar, D. (2012). *Spiritual Intelligence: The Ultimate Intelligence*. New York: Bloomsbury Publishing.

Zohar, D., & Marshall, I. (2007). *SQ - Kecerdasan Spiritual*. Bandung: Mizan Pustaka.

ENDNOTES

1   Bendeman et al., 2015.

2   Ajulu, 2001.

3   Carmody, 2011.

4   Chimhanzi, 2012.

5   Ibid.

6   Thomas & Thompson, 2013.

7   Carroll, Brown, & Buchholtz, 2017.

8   Creamer, 2012.

9   Carmody, 2011.

10   McMahon, Barkhuizen, & Schutte, 2011.

11   Porter & Kramer, 2011.

12   Wilkinson & Townsend, 2016.

13   Luce, 2014.

14   Lawrence, 2014.

15   Wilkinson & Townsend, 2016.

16   Martins & Álvarez, 2007.

17   Vilakati, 2016.

18   Barker, 2007.

19   Ntibagirirwa, 2009.

20   Ibid.

21   Ibid.

22   Ibid.; Lutz, 2009.

23   Ntibagirirwa, 2009.

24   Lawrence, 2014.

25   Vilakati, Schurink, & Viljoen, 2013.

26   McGaughey, 2015.

27   Barker, 2015, p.2.

28   Creamer, 2012.

29   Lawrence, 2014.

30   McGaughey, 2015; Lawrence, 2003; Backhaus, 1989.

31   McGaughey, 2015.

32   Lawrence, 2003.

33   McGaughey, 2015.

35   Himes, 2005.

36   Dei (2012)

37   Sefa Dei, 2012.

38   Nafukho, 2006; Karsten & Illa, 2005; Taylor, 2014.

39   Mbiti, 2015.

40   Vilakati, Schurink, & Viljoen, 2013.

41   Sefa Dei, 2013.

42   Oladipo, 2006; Afolayan, 2011; Gutto, 2013.

43   Afolayan, 2011.

44   Mbiti, 2015; Mogale, 2012; Khoza, 2012; Nafukho, 2006; Taylor, 2014; Brooke, 2008; Nsamenang, 1995; Oladipo, 2006; Mbigi, 2005.

45   Meyer, 2008.

46   Forster, 2010; Wilber, 2006; Vilakati, Schurink, & Viljoen, 2013.

47   Forster, 2010.

48   Sefa Dei, 2014.

49   Lakoff & Johnson, 1999; Sefa Dei, 2012.

50   Lutz, 2009; Bertsch, 2012; Khoza, 2012; Taylor, 2014.

51   Manda, 2007.

52   Shutte, 2001.

53   van Stapele, 2014; Shutte, 2001.

54   Sefa Dei, 2012.

55   Moloi, 2016; Gade, 2012; Lutz, 2009; Nkomo & Ngambi, 2009; Oladipo, 2006.

56   Walach, 2011.

57   Tolle, 2009.

58   Prescott, 2008.

59   Giacalone, & Jurkiewicz, 2003.

60   Coyle, 2017.

61   Zohar & Marshall, 2007.

62   Wilber, 2006; Zohar & Marshall, 2007; Walach, 2011.

63   Zelazo, Moscovitch, & Thompson, 2007.

64   Walach, 2011; Lancaster, 2004.

65   Wilber, 2006.

66   Viljoen, 2015.

67   du Toit, 2008; Walach, 2011; Vilakati, Schurink, & Viljoen, 2013.

68   Vilakati, Schurink, & Viljoen, 2013; Vilakati, 2016; Viljoen, 2015.

69   Jackson, 2013; Sefa Dei, 2013.

70   Wilber, 2006; Viljoen, 2015.

71   Vilakati, 2016.

72   Bolden & Kirk, 2009; Taylor, 2014; Kankonde, 2015.

73   Subban, 2017; Viljoen, 2015.

74   Budd, 2012; Bramucci & Zanfei, 2015.

75   Booysen, 2014; Viljoen, 2015; Subban, 2017.

76   Kaufman, 2005; Tesar & Kuada, 2013.

77   Budd & Scoville, 2005; Budd, 2012.

78   McGaughey, 2015.

79   Backhaus, 1989.

80   Bridger, 2014; Subban, 201; Viljoen, 2015.

81   Mbigi, 2005; Rukuni, 2007; Veldsman, 2013; Milliken et al., 2015.

82   Vilakati, 2016.

83   Nafukho, 2006; Brooke, 2008; Letseka, 2011.

84   Vilakati, Schurink, & Viljoen, 2013; Vilakati, 2016.

85   Vilakati, 2016.

86   Eidenmüller, 2016; Van den Berg, Grift, & Witteloostuijn, 2011.

87   Subban, 2017.

88   Addison, 2009.

89   Lutz, 2009; Nsamenang, 2006.

Chapter

3

ORGANISATIONAL BEING:
Human Niches Inclusivity

Rica Viljoen

INTRODUCTION

In his 2006 book, *The Crucible – Forging South Africa's Future*, Don Beck[1] described that thinking systems are deep-core intelligences that form as a coping response to changing life conditions. He promised Clare Graves[2] that he would always work theoretically purely, and over the years highlighted the following assumptions:

- Human nature is not static; it changes as it adapts to new systems. Yet, the old systems must be integrated and transcended, or the benefits of this thinking system will not serve us.
- When a new system is activated, our rules for living change to adapt to the new conditions.
- We live in an open system of values where an infinite number of ways of living are available – there is no final state to which we all must aspire.
- An individual, organisation and/or society can respond positively only to the memes with which they relate.

GRAVESIAN PRINCIPLES THAT UNDERPIN HUMAN NICHES

Spiral dynamics is thus a coiled spring of value systems, worldviews and mind-sets, each the product of its times and conditions.[3] In Table 3.1 below, the 12 Gravesian principles are described.

Table 3.1: Applications of the 12 Gravesian principles

Principle	Application
1	The interaction of two sets of forces determine thinking systems: • Existential problems in a specific milieu. • Neuropsychological coping mechanisms in the brain.
2	Human development is an emergent, oscillating process of thinking systems to newer, more expansive complex systems.
3	Thinking systems oscillate between a focus on how to change and control it and how to adapt to it.
4	As conditions of existence change, people adapt their bio-psycho-social beings.
5	People anchors in a human niche are psychosocially congruent with parts of the system.
6	People may not always be equipped to move to different complex systems.
7	An individual can stabilise at one or a combination of thinking systems.
8	With each value system, there are gifts and side effects.
9	A person or a collective may regress to previous thinking systems.
10	Thinking systems can be described as low, stuck or high. When low manifestations occur, side-effects of the thinking system appear. When a system is stuck, an individual is so deeply rooted in his or her thinking system that alternative systems cannot emerge. A high manifestation reflects the gift that a thinking system or a human niche holds.
11	Personality, intelligence, race and gender do not correlate with human niches.
12	One thinking system is not better or worse than another – congruence or appropriateness to the external environment and the conditions of existence are critical.

Questions of existence of human niches

A human niche, Laubscher[4] explained, is something at which humans excel. In answer to the question of existence that people and groups of people unconsciously ask, a specific human niche or way of being crystallises. The human niches are described and integrated with spiral dynamics as follows:

Turquoise:	How can the galaxy be sustained?
Yellow:	How can you and I survive?
Green:	How can we sacrifice for the benefit of the world and peace?
Orange:	How can I conquer the material world and take calculated risks?
Blue:	How can we sacrifice to prepare for the future?
Red:	How can I get power?
Purple:	How can we sacrifice for the benefit of the community, family or elders?
Beige:	How do I survive?

Various systems all bring unique gifts according to their different niches. Theoretically, each shift from system to system allows individuals and society to transcend and include the gift offered by the previous system. However, owing to the tension that must be built up to let go of a specific thinking structure and embody a new niche, the previous system is often rejected. While we as social systems continue to reject previous niches, we will never be integral as a collective whole.

Organising archetypes of human niches

In Figure 3.1 below the archetypes of different thinking systems are presented.

BEIGE	PURPLE	RED	BLUE	ORANGE	GREEN	YELLOW	TUR-QUOISE
Expressive	Sacrificial	Expressive	Sacrificial	Expressive	Sacrificial	Integral	Holistic
Survival (Band)	Tribal (Order)	Exploitive (Empire)	Authority (Structure)	Strategic (Enterprise)	Social/ (Network)	Systemic (Flow)	Holistic (Organism)
Instinct (Driven)	Safety (Driven)	Power (Driven)	Order (Driven)	Success (Driven)	People (Driven)	Process (Oriented)	Synthesis (Oriented)

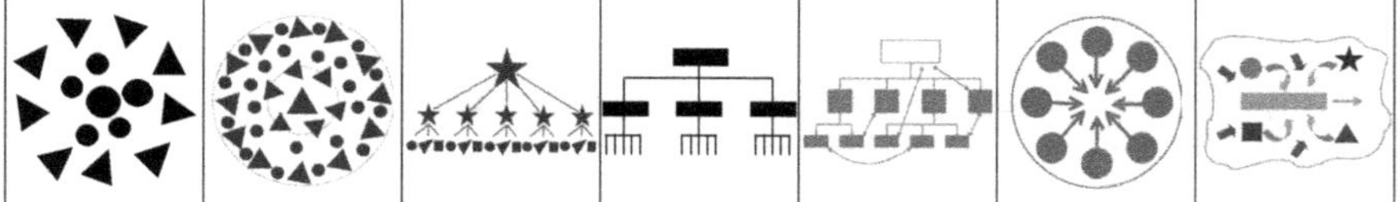

Figure 3.1: Archetypes of different thinking systems (adapted from Laubscher)[5]

The different colours that are used to distinguish the various thinking systems are indicated in the first line of Figure 3.1 above. In the second line, the oscillating nature of the spiral is indicated with a rhythm of expressive (idealistic) to sacrificial (collective) and back again to a different organising capability as individualistic. This nature occurs for all the thinking systems. The first six systems function on fear; BEIGE fears not being able to survive, PURPLE is fearful of being excluded from the community, RED is fearful of losing power, BLUE is concerned about moral decay and that rules are broken, ORANGE is driven by not achieving, and GREEN is preoccupied with the survival of the planet. A huge chasm occurs after GREEN, when YELLOW emerges from the egoless GREEN pattern. YELLOW is driven by hope – hope for self and hope for the collective. This continues in emerging systems. If we design strategy or models we must design them from a place of hope.

In order to weave together a collective tapestry of being and inclusivity in an organisation, all the different human niches should be respected and valued, but must be kept responsible for collective goals. BEIGE must be sustained; PURPLE must be able to bring its soulful nature, insight of humanity and self-organising humane rhythm to the table; RED has to bring energy and daily rejuvenation of willingness to make things happen; BLUE's structure and compliance are needed; ORANGE's calculated risk and enterprising ability have to be utilised; and GREEN has to bring inclusivity and participation. YELLOW leadership has the capacity to wire together the various gifts in an integral approach towards systemic healing, enabling a sustained transformation.

A description of each human niche that explains the nature of the system follows, after which the archetype is presented. The archetype is a symbol of the organising pattern that describes the underlying thinking in a system. In the bottom line of Figure 3.1 above, the various motives or drivers of the systems are described. Laubscher[6], in her 50-year immersion in spiral dynamics theory and even longer study of African and

Eastern philosophies, determined the percentages of occurrence of a specific human niche in South African societies in her PhD thesis. Listed in the blocks below are descriptions of the respective niches.

More emphasis is placed on the systems that typically play out in business. Further knowledge of spiral dynamics can be accessed by reading *Inclusive Organisational Transformation through Inclusivity, Organisational Change and Development.*[7] It is not the purpose of this chapter to provide a complete account of the various systems – rather, an overview is presented. The parts that are presented here are the parts that we carefully selected to prove context for the drama that is playing out.

The various human niches are summarised below.

Beige

Beck and Cowan[8] described BEIGE as automatic, autistic and reflective. They say that this thinking system centres on the satisfaction of the very basic human biological needs, and that it is driven by deep brain programmes, instincts and genetics. According to them, BEIGE shows little awareness of self as an undifferentiated being. As people with Beige codes survive at the most basic level, the key focus of this question of existence is to satisfy physiological needs; to sometimes form protective, supportive bands; to exist as biological units; and to simply to make it through the night or day.

BEIGE is based on the primal desire to survive; its key traits are therefore involved with self-preservation. Laubscher[9] noted that BEIGE's outlook is survival at every level of being, while Beecroft[10] explained that with BEIGE thinking, the mind, spirit and body are fully focused on survival. BEIGE is highly instinctive and those tribal people who remain untouched by the complexities of higher levels are often able to see, hear and smell better, and can, for example, sense changes in the weather.[11] Laubscher reported that BEIGE people have 26 senses; they can even smell water. She passionately asked who can still today smell water, or know which leaves to suck on to survive alone in the desert.

BEIGE people act immediately in the interests of their survival[12] which is a pressing daily issue, hence BEIGE people must be totally in touch with what it takes to survive otherwise they will not. Laubscher[13] warned that if our society fails to heed the warnings of climate change and there is catastrophic collapse, it is possible that the survivors will be those who are best able to remember and access their BEIGE instincts. Current statistics indicate that 1 out of 127 people are dislocated or refugees, with merely a backpack, children that cannot be fed, and nowhere to go. These external conditions ask for BEIGE thinking to deal with the contextual dynamics. Loraine Laubscher and Rica Viljoen are currently busy with a study to ensure that the description of BEIGE is rich and populated in theory.

Low BEIGE people function like drug addicts, with only the next fix in mind; they will use the last money that is intended for food for their mothers to buy alcohol.

Recently one of the four largest mining houses in the world launched a project to take beggars off the street. It failed because within weeks the beggars indicated that they would much rather take control into their own hands as to where they slept and found food and drink. High-functioning BEIGE people cope relatively well in society under strict conditions that may seem peculiar to others. One business leader was doing quite well in her IT job when one day management decided to change the kettle to an urn, which caused her to have a break-down. A kettle had to be bought for her so that the water would be the correct heat, otherwise things would fall apart.

The observant reader may become aware that more references are used for the description of BEIGE in this text - more so than for other thinking systems. A large scale effort is being made to populate BEIGE with deeper, richer and more recent evidence – just as was the case with PURPLE five years ago. Most of the text available on BEIGE describes it from another thinking system. Effort is now made internationally to immerge into BEIGE and describe the phenomenon in an ethnographic way. The research process is almost complete and will be published in a book called *Spiral Dynamics in Action: Humanity's Master Code.*[14]

Companies cannot deny that some members of their workforce are BEIGE. In a more idealistic interpretation of the theory, claims are made that if we heal poverty, we will transcend BEIGE. All current research shows that to a degree some people will move, but a great percentage of BEIGE will remain BEIGE. We must also remember that one thinking system is not better than another – it just has different gifts to offer the world. The question to be asked is whether you would still have the intelligence to survive if you were dropped in a desert today, whether it is the Sahara or a concrete desert?

In Figure 3.2, the dynamics of BEIGE are visually displayed.

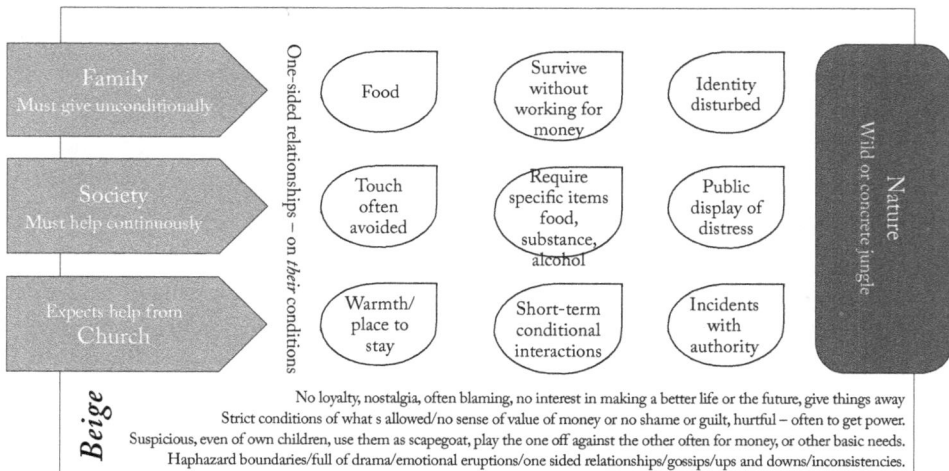

Figure 3.2: The dynamics of BEIGE

As per Figure 3.2 above, it is clear that life conditions are viewed as a wild, almost physical or concrete jungle, where everyone is for their own. It is a world full of drama, emotional eruptions, one-sided relationships, up and downs, and inconsistencies. Boundaries are haphazard – much is expected, but on the other hand, much is given away. From a psychological point of view, loyalty is eroded and a lot of blaming takes place. There is no interest in making things better, for example a sick person has an operation but is told that nothing will ever be better again. Money, presents, clothes and physical goods are given away without any money motive, only to look for the same objects the next day.

BEIGE are suspicious, even of their own children or parents; they often use their children as scapegoats. One child may support their father daily, while another sees their father once a year, however the first child must hear the whole time how good the other child is. They play people off each other for money or to meet other basic needs; their ability to manipulate people is impressive.

Strict conditions around them are allowed, which have to do with what they eat, what can be in their house, and who they allow close to them. As there is no sense of money, shame or guilt, they often lash out with hurtful behaviour that becomes impossible for those who love them.

As building blocks, people with an active BEIGE code acknowledge the church, society and family, but all these entities only have to fulfil basic roles, which is to fulfil basic needs and deal with the essential question of existence, namely survival.

Often their identity is disturbed; there are public display of distress, which often lead to incidents with authority. They can survive without working for money – a real superpower in a capitalist system. I like to call them the invisible ones.

They require specific items to feel a sense of worth; this may the next meal, the next sleeping tablet that makes them feel in control for a few hours, other substances or alcohol. Where they stay is important – if in the Southern continent they must have a place that is north. They are suspicious of food – this may be because it may be old, poisoned or have garlic in it. Physical touch is also an issue here. They avoid it, are scared of it, feel claustrophobic, and have a sense of shame for smelling and being dirty. Eye contact is thus elusive; they do not want to see judgement in the eyes of others. It is important to remember that we are not dealing with intelligence but with thinking systems.

Lastly, as per Figure 3.2 above, society's boundaries do not apply to them – they are fluid and move to where they can be left alone and construct a lifestyle that serves them – invisibly.

9% of South African's population is BEIGE

Purple

Although most descriptions of PURPLE portray it as animalistic, traditional and tribal, the contribution of Loraine Laubscher, and later Rica Viljoen and Loraine Laubscher, to position PURPLE as a rich, narrative, story-telling and wise system illustrates the deep relatedness that PURPLE brings to the kaleidoscope of differences.

In Figure 3.3 below, the inter-subjective interrelatedness of African PURPLE is presented.

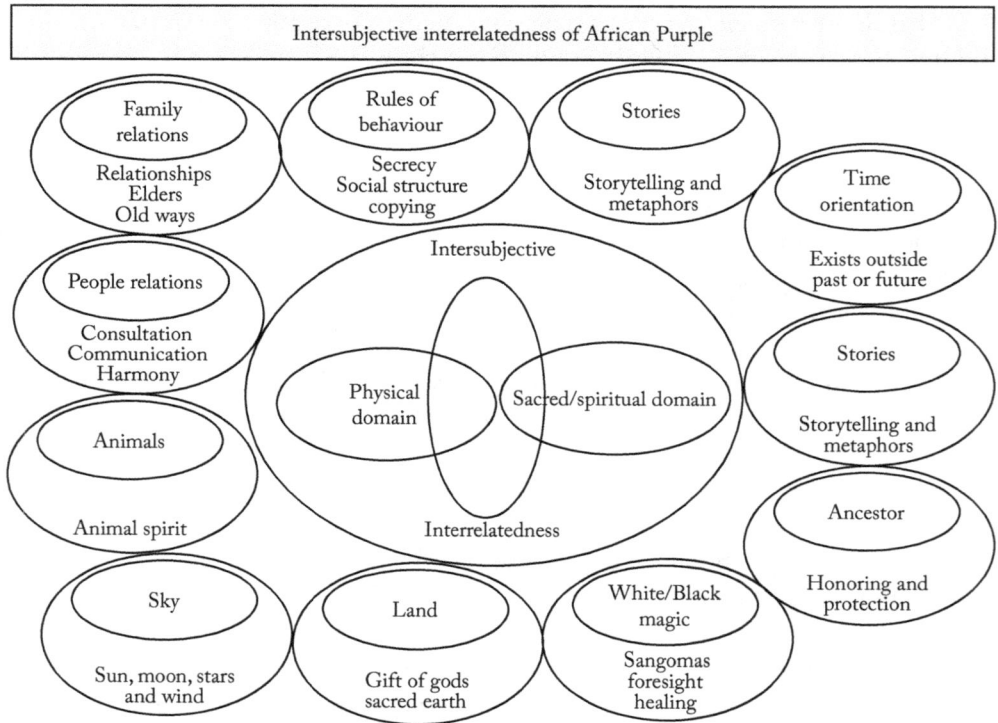

Figure 3.3: The dynamics of PURPLE[15]

Figure 3.3 above illustrates that PURPLE are the keepers of family relations and traditional ceremonies; they are the protectors of the old ways who honour individual and collective rituals. Consultation and harmony are important, and they express a sense of enchantment and magic in life's mysteries. Animals are interwoven in the ecology of day-to-day human life; a tribe or clan often has a totem animal with characteristics that describe people who belong to the collective. This is sometimes helpful for the individual as collective traits are ascribed to them.

Children are also incorporated, and elders play an important role in family relations and society. PURPLE people are deeply bound to the positionality of their place in history, land and ancestry. They are aligned with the forces of nature, the sky and other natural occurrences; their souls belong to the land where they were born. PURPLE celebrates rituals, traditions and the community. Identity resides in being part of the collective, while music, like drumming and dancing, forms an integral part of celebrating and interacting with each other.

PURPLE people speak in stories, metaphors and examples. They do not like to expose the impact of leadership publicly, i.e. they save face and leaders are supported and respected publicly. In the same way, other team members must not be publicly disciplined or ridiculed – or even rewarded. A collective regulating mechanism is inherently present, which can be seen when PURPLE groups collectively engage without rules and regulations. A toyi-toyi[i] march is an example of this; intuitively PURPLE people attract each other like mercury – there are collective struggle songs that were orally passed on by previous generations, and a very clear organising pattern is perceived. This self-organising can also be seen when the traffic in Dar es Salaam, Cairo, Mumbai and Rio de Janeiro is studied – the whole system acts with relatively few incidents and accidents, and without any traffic police or compliance processes.

Traditions, especially human traditions such as funerals, are celebrated. Often the ancestors or forefathers are consulted and acknowledged. Specific rituals celebrate the passing of a soul to a different plane, and there is a particular way of facilitating this movement to the spiritual realm. These traditions are also oral. Often, first-born children must go and find an uncle or relative to explain the ways of the collective if their father has passed on.

Children are very important in PURPLE, partly because they must later provide for the elders. Further, it is critical for PURPLE that children have better lives than they did, thus a good education is key. Good shoes are also a prerequisite, as PURPLE people must often walk long distances. The way in which PURPLE children are disciplined is humane, yet definite. The whole is always kept in mind.

For people with PUPRLE codes as their centre of gravity, doing business entails a focus on relatedness, respect and a sense of dignity and belonging. They consult often with all relevant parties. PURPLE people greet others every time they see them as an acknowledgement of the awareness of membership of the whole. It is important to them to interact with their chiefs, elders, nanas, fathers or top managers. One should not make the mistake of thinking that PURPLE people are backwards or lazy, or that human niches correlate with intelligence. In fact, highly intelligent PURPLE leaders are often very successful in organisations due to their relational ability and their ability to resonate with others. What should be considered is that the ontology (how the world is perceived), the epistemology (how the individual relates to the world), and the organising capability (the archetypes in Figure 3.1 above) differ significantly between human niches. PURPLE people just want to organise in a PURPLE way, and find the

---

i   Another word for a protest march

BLUE way of governance, structure, policy and standard operating procedures quite mechanistic, lifeless, and, in fact, boring and reductionist.

Low PURPLE presents a thinking system that is darker in terms of magic and superstition. PURPLE people here are submissive, act collectively, and withdraw into an alternative conceptualisation of reality that is based on ecological constructs. The old ways are respected and lived by. Arrested PURPLE people exhibit good relations. There is a social structure that is kept, and over time the roles of the society often overwrite rules of organisations. Sometimes social pandemics such as xenophobia or tribalism can manifest in a protection to secure the future of the collective. High PURPLE is royal, wise, deep and has a story-telling ability. They are relational and represent all the gifts that PURPLE can offer.

Vusi Vilikati[16] warned that we should consider the way in which PURPLE identity is constructed, so that we do not attempt to use BLUE and ORANGE ways to try and develop PURPLE thinking – it will just slide off. One must intervene with organisational effectiveness or strategic HR interventions from within a system should we try to influence it, and not patronisingly from another system.

Companies with populations that can be described by PURPLE dynamics should strategise, translate and manoeuvre ways of taking the workforce with them in an effort to optimise the human energy in the system to perform.

65% of the South African population is PURPLE

Most organisational development initiatives in South Africa fail because strategists and business leaders do not consider that their workers are predominantly PURPLE. Ignoring this very important fact is an indicator that a good shareholder analysis was not done, that the socio-economic factors were not considered, or that there is an assumption that others are like us. Companies may just be surprised at the rich insights and soul that are unleashed when PURPLE ways are adopted. The fear that things will not happen, or that leadership will not make money or will lose control, is a stereotypical view, as within the very nature of PURPLE these aspects are evident; the way to release it in a system is just a different way.

By superimposing BLUE thinking, governance, organising and rules on PURPLE people, there will be a huge loss, as digital rules and regulations reduce the complexity and gifts of PURPLE wisdom and organising capability. The picture below portrays the impossibility of enforcing BLUE standard operating procedures, issues of discipline and rank, as well as activating in relation to the PURPLE self-organising structure. Relationships come first in PURPLE. Through solid relationships we can all play our own part in the human ecology. In Figure 3.4, the organising archetypes of PURPLE and BLUE are compared.

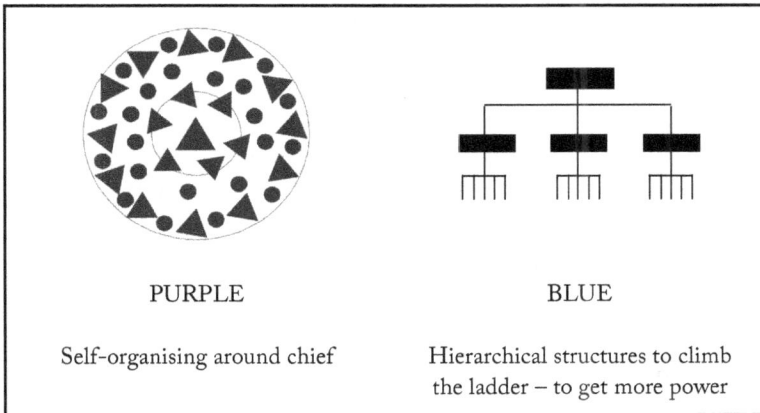

PURPLE

Self-organising around chief

BLUE

Hierarchical structures to climb
the ladder – to get more power

Figure 3.4: Organising archetypes of PURPLE and BLUE

It can be seen in Figure 3.4 above that the way in which PURPLE and BLUE organise are radically different. In the words of Laubscher[17], "BLUE rules glide off PURPLE beingness".

SPIRAL DYNAMICS IN INTERSTATE BUS LINES

Henk van Zyl insisted that a scientific cultural-sensitive culture study be done. The Benchmark of Engagement (BeQ) was used as a diagnostic tool, which indicated that most workers (90%) were PURPLE, yet 94% of management were BLUE. The climate study also showed high levels of risk-taking and low levels of rule following. These are aspects that are very important for quality behaviour.

The clash in thinking systems was clear; PURPLE people do not ask commercial questions. Laubscher[18] explained that PURPLE people are concerned with their elders, relationships and the old ways. They are close to nature, often worship their ancestors, and define 'self' differently than most academic books do. PURPLE has an analogue thinking system; PURPLE people think in metaphors and stories, not in bullet points and slide shows. Management at IBL (both ORANGE and BLUE), however, have digital thinking systems; they think linearly and point by point. Rules are important, and they conserve today for the future. Unlike PURPLE, they are on time; PURPLE could potentially pose a big problem for a bus company, since being on time is one of the drivers of success in this world. Another issue in terms of time was discipline. Due to the collective nature of PURPLE, strict and direct enforcement of rules and discipline is frowned upon by them. A way had to be found where PURPLE felt that they belonged, and that they were consulted on issues regarding production and discipline. Over the years a lot had been done in this organisation to build trust, thus co-determination became the logical next step.

As indicated before, more than 90% of the workers were PURPLE, while 3% RED was visible in the system. In effect, IBL is a PURPLE company. The leaders had to move through their own thinking structures to a place where they were unseen in order to see the social system of IBL as a whole. BLUE management and BLUE compliant systems did not value the PURPLE thinking system. A BLUE CEO was appointed with strong PURPLE residue, and an ORANGE CEO supported the CEO. BLUE compliance structures were implemented. The HR person assisted with the translation of different thinking structures to perform a BLUE system function. In effect, a way to align PURPLE's energy around BLUE practices was required. As can be seen in the organising archetypes in Figure 3.4, BLUE thinking is autocratic, digital and linear, while PURPLE thinking is inclusive and circular. A PURPLE way of doing was needed.

This book is a tribute to the lived history of Henk van Zyl, who through his visionary leadership, ability to speak PURPLE (amongst other colours), unwavering belief and ethical considerations created the catalytic transformation at IBL. This is a change that will be sustainable for years to come. If companies that function in collective societies adopt this progressive approach of van Zyl, it will enthuse the human dynamics and performance of all social systems that are willing to do what they must do more inclusively. This, in turn, could lead to doing humanity differently.[ii]

Red

A huge amount of energy is needed to break away from the collective of PURPLE to become RED – a thinking structure that is not concerned with what has been, or with whom people are in relation to their families. Rather, the question emerges of WHO AM I? RED energy is needed to let go of the seduction of returning to the traditional ways, to be pulled back into the ways society wants things to be done, and for the individual voice to become. As Laubscher[19] explained, RED people want to understand who they are – they want to be acknowledged for their unique contribution, and really have a need to be powerful. As can be seen in Figure 3.5, to let go of the South PURPLE sense of nature and community and to become more integral,

RED is needed. This thinking system allows individuals to individualise – to know who they are if they are not the tribe.

In low RED, behaviour easily becomes bullying, gas-lighting, persistence and even entitlement. This may even manifest in violence. Arrested RED is a place where people found the worth of RED, and how to use or misuse its power. They will probably

---

ii   Dr Nceba Ndzwayiba wrote a masterful PhD thesis on 'Doing Human Differently'. The words
     above were inspired by his meaningful thesis.

not adopt another thinking system as the RED power-driven system gives them the power that they thrive on. They forever embody the worth of asking questions about self and obtaining power and acknowledgement instantly. High RED becomes hero- or warrior-like. They can jump in to save others, but do it to feel more powerful.

In Figure 3.5 below, it can be seen that different thinking systems should come together around a superordinate goal. This means that people who are BEIGE, YELLOW, PURPLE, RED, BLUE or GREEN all have a gift to offer to the whole.

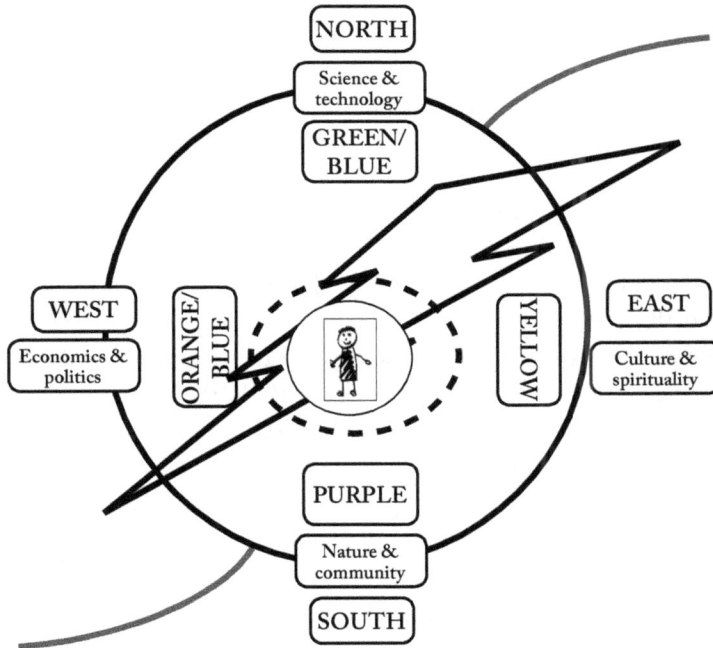

Figure 3.5: The role of RED in individualisation[20]

RED acts as a spark plug to the rest of the system. Here consciousness begins to reside at an individual level and the enmeshment with the culture is broken in Jungian terms; RED is needed to start the effort of self-individuation. Without moving through RED, BLUE, ORANGE and GREEN will never be embodied.

Sometimes in organisations, RED people appear to be troublemakers and agitators; they seem to be against authority and concerned with self-interest, yet leadership can utilise RED thinking to enable others to progress and move forward. By learning how to deal with the 15% of RED in South Africa as a country, one can ensure that leaders have the power and that they can control the powerful passion energy of RED. Without RED energy, PURPLE may seem very down and slow. RED employees love being the employee of the month and getting individual attention. RED often rejects things that PURPLE built as they are viewed as being backwards and old school.

RED union members may be very scared that co-determination may erode their influence on PURPLE people, or that the other members will trust management to such a degree that they will lose power. RED has the capacity, the energy and the followership to create strikes, uprisings and uncontrollable managerial realities. RED is able to keep a system hostage, and instead of managing the minority group, a small percentage of RED can keep a whole system captive owing to the power dynamic. In the true fashion of Loraine Laubscher, this is the part that facilitates her. If RED can be rewired into a positive system, it may lead the system to a more functional place. Laubscher, in the case studies shared in *Organisational Change and Development*[21], explained that if RED is given formal power positions and trained properly, their energy may sometimes be utilised positively. Jung[22] warned, however, "Do not give a man a sword that cannot dance". Basic planning, organising, leading and control skills can assist.

> In IBL, over a period of 30 years, Henk van Zyl went so far as to train each worker to understand not only their own personality types, but also those of their loved ones. It must be added here that the rest of the industry frowned on this, as if the theory was too advanced for bus drivers. Further, all the workers participated in various forms of soft skills development, and even supported a large-scale emotional intelligence drive. PURPLE workers were also taught how to function in a BLUE system. Special attention was given to assisting individuals to act in teams. IBL has an interesting team-based operating model that will be published in a book on new organisational design principles for the new world of work. Business acumen skills also assisted RED people to understand BLUE and even ORANGE systems. Understanding the importance of bringing energy to the PURPLE grouping, and being acknowledged for this, would help greatly. Henk's own ability to effortlessly translate between thinking systems, and to ensure understanding of the larger reality, helped greatly in facilitating trust and inclusivity, which prepared the system for progressive models and strategies to follow. RED workers were deliberately involved and trained. The involvement was seen as meaningful, and the workers became supportive towards management.

Low RED may be impulsive, entitled and even aggressive. Arrested RED people are cemented in the power that a position of authority gives them, and feel that they are deserving of that power. It is their time now. High RED people are often the energetic battery of a team.

---

15 % of South African population is RED

Blue

BLUE is a system that is firstly collective, and asks how the individual can sacrifice for the benefit of the future for all. They want to save today to use later, and they want to sacrifice for the whole. They follow the rules and are reliable; they want to help PURPLE people be more structured, early-starting and rule following. They are pre-occupied with the idea of ensuring that moving forward, if we follow rules and structures today, there will be a future for all. They are very happy to start at a lower level in the organisation, but believe that through rules and regulations, personal development programmes and performance appraisals, they can climb the corporate ladder. Rules and the application thereof should apply to all and fairness is valued in the system. BLUE are loyal, but expect loyalty in return. They often rely on the job descriptions provided by the organisation to fulfil their duties; things that fall outside the official job description are ignored. BLUE is typically hyper polite in meetings, and they are very proper. Direct conflict does not surface, and family secrets are swept under the rug. Sometimes gossip happens outside official forums, but in these forums they are polite and politically correct. Here the individual voice is replaced by a collective forum. If you do not fit in, you fit out.

Some of the PURPLE residue remains in the BLUE code. People with BLUE as the centre of gravity also acknowledge their forefathers . They stoically hang pictures in oval frames on dining room walls, and often the things from one generation are saved for the next. For BLUE, it is important what the neighbours will say, and keeping up with the Jones applies; everyone wants to be better than his or her neighbours. They ask: "What will happen if you have an accident and your kitchen is dirty?"

BLUE brings roles and regulations to organisations. They believe in a proven structure, i.e. while you do what you are supposed to do, everything will go well! They ask organisational questions and attempt to bring the whole together. They dress the part and speak the part. The tribe in PURPLE and the gang in RED become the BLUE corporate. Standard operating procedures, good governance and rule-following are the order of the day. They are truly "Corporate Johnnies"[iii]. Males often hunt or camp together; one must walk, talk and act the part. Suits are important, and a clean-cut professional look is critical while they uphold a corporate manoeuvre. A woman, for example, may either wear a necklace or earrings, but not both.

It must be stated that BLUE is good for companies that must comply with corporate governance. In the case of IBL, standard operating procedures are critical. Rules and regulations are more than guidelines; it is important to keep to the norms of the industry, and to ensure that there is a licence to operate. In effect, it is a BLUE world.

A radical new way of operating and dealing with decisions and ownership may be challenging to all the different thinking systems. In fact, BLUE may feel that they are losing control and that their efforts to comply are failing miserably. BLUE thinks digitally, while PURPLE thinks in analogue or pictures. Translation between the niches is needed for the different sides to understand each other.

---

iii A popular term to refer to employees who belong in corporates and act in a BLUE way.

BLUE thinking creates behaviour that can be described as decent, reliable well-structured and consistent. As it is constructed around the task at hand or functional activities, personal relationship are typically not viewed as important. If we work hard together we may have a relationship, which may end abruptly if someone changes companies. For PURPLE, relationships come first.

A large percentage of well-functioning organisations are BLUE.[23] Rules are followed, compliance is optimal, and everyone knows what is expected of the whole. In these organisations there are rules and responsibilities, i.e. one needs to follow standard operating procedures and comply with them. Risks are isolated, and the rules ultimately apply. The organisation is there to provide a return on investment for its stakeholders, and a hierarchical operating structure exists. There are various levels of supervision and management, and a bus company must act according to BLUE, e.g. employees must be on time and there cannot be breakdowns. Rule following is critical. To manage routes, ticket machines and cash, BLUE digital logic is needed, yet the question may be asked whether there is no other way of organising that will fit the thinking system and questions regarding the existence of the employees more closely.

10% of the South African population is BLUE

Most leadership in South Africa is BLUE. In a study of 195,004 management members across industry boundaries, 94.3% indicated that they were BLUE. It seems that BLUE workers follow BLUE rules, which is viewed as compliant with BLUE processes, and these people are therefore promoted. In this way, the cycle of BLUE leadership is enforced.

Orange

ORANGE is a thinking structure that is invoked when the risk-adverse nature of BLUE turns into a risk-taking space. ORANGE is commercial, deal making and entrepreneurial. Although they deeply value the risk-adverse nature of BLUE, they cannot help but see how to grow a business, make more money or succeed. If the rest of the system understands them and allows them to be enterprising on the organisation's behalf, they can be of great benefit to a system as they are not stuck with what has happened in the past, but are risk-taking enough to diversify income streams. ORANGE leaders often breathe new life into systems that have become stagnant. Hopefully, they find themselves high enough in the organisation to enable new ways of doing. They are often willing to implement spiral dynamics as they can see the economic value-add thereof. ORANGE people are not too rigid in clinging to organisational hierarchy – they are willing to use other structures in their endeavours to succeed. ORANGE is needed to diversify income streams to pro-actively identify other streams of revenue, as well as to change strategies continuously so as to not be caught in what cannot be.

The risk of BLUE, as with PURPLE, is the unwillingness to consider new ways of thinking, as only ways that have worked for generations before seem to be valued. Moving from organisational patterns that have worked for one's forefathers to something unknown is indeed difficult, and the same applies to a business that is working and making money. Why do things differently when they work, and why give power away? The visible risk-taking of RED and the calculated risk-taking of ORANGE are also contradictory to the risk-adverse natures of PURPLE and BLUE. It is not that easy to overcome resistance, however if the internal rule-following structure can be overcome, a more entrepreneurial, innovative and free thinking system may lead to alternative ways of doing things differently, while being sustainably and materialistically successful.

The complexity of diversity of thought occurs when different systems reside in the same system. In 2012 at IBL, more than 90% of workers belonged to a PURPLE system, while only two people in top management belonged to an ORANGE system. That means that only 002% of the population was ORANGE. ORANGE is needed, however, as it is the way to innovation, building enterprises and ensuring success for all. As explained earlier, every system has a gift. The gift of PURPLE is being relational and loyal; the gift of ORANGE is to make money and be enterprising; and the gift of BLUE is to comply. We need all the different thinking structures to build a sustainable organisation, however, we must also make sure that the systems, structures and practices we build are congruent with the thinking of the people who must implement them. In the case of IBL, this thinking was largely PURPLE. The COO of IBL is a healthy ORANGE.

> # 1% of the South African population is ORANGE

Green

GREEN is a collective thinking system that is pre-occupied with nature, the earth and humanity at large. If you would like to determine whether you are mostly GREEN, ask yourself the following:
The earth feels:
- so proud about the innovation over the last 100 years;
- so sad, as one out of 127 of my children is a refugee; and
- so scared, as humanity is killing me and stripping me of my resources.

If you have a GREEN thinking system, 80% to 90% of your day is pre-occupied with thoughts like the above, i.e. GREEN is deeply concerned with the survival of the earth and humanity at large.

Green avoids conflict, and wants all to be equal and to consult all. However, in business, GREEN is often seen as slow in terms of decision-making. Often GREEN hears all sides of the arguments and then gets a bit stuck as they understand the different perspectives. This again strengthens the perception that GREEN may change direction as they hear different voices. The gift of GREEN is best explained by the African saying: "If you want to go fast, go alone; if you want to go far, go together".

Viljoen[24] argued that a GREEN expatriate who wants to give back to society often works best in PURPLE systems. The circular structure of PURPLE and GREEN in Figure 3.5 above can be compared to see the similarity. In PURPLE there is a chief in the middle, while in GREEN there is no leader in the middle as leadership is shared. Beck[25] once said in an interview that when assisting South Africa to form the new democracy, the only mistake made by him and the design team of the constitution was that different role players attempted to solve the South African conditions through a GREEN philosophy. However, GREEN does not have enough teeth to manage aggression, especially that of RED. His insight was that leaders should design business solutions from YELLOW, disregarding their own human niche. The YELLOW niche is described next.

0.1% of the South African population is GREEN

When Henk van Zyl measured his psychological map[iv, 26] the first time in 2002, he indicated a GREEN thinking system. The instrument also showed an emerging YELLOW thinking structure. This transition happened in 2006; where Henk had been inclusive and participative, he became functional, systemic, organic and integral.

Yellow

A new thinking structure emerges from the old GREEN. Where all the previous systems function on fear, YELLOW people are hopeful. The codes in the first tear all are fear-driven. BEIGE is fearful that it will not survive, PURPLE that it loses connectivity to the tribe, RED that it may lose power, BLUE that there is decline in the fabric of society, ORANGE that it may not succeed and GREEN that it will not be included, or that there will not be peace.

YELLOW is hopeful as it sees the beauty in all the different codes. BEIGE can survive, PURPLE automatically cares, RED provides energy, BLUE is rule-following and compliant, ORANGE is enterprising, and GREEN wants everyone to

---

iv   An instrument from Clare Graves that measures thinking systems

be included. To weave this tapestry of differences together, YELLOW leadership or YELLOW thinking becomes important. YELLOW also asks the question of what to do to put life into part of the system that is not breathing, so that the whole can become functional and integral.

An organisation has no choice but to strategise from second tier YELLOW, because doing it from BLUE and/or ORANGE fails from a sustainability perspective. Without YELLOW thinking, companies will continue to create the same level of problems with the same level of thinking. YELLOW is prepared to let go of preconceived ways of organising to obtain worth. YELLOW leadership is characterised by trust, integrity, friendliness and fairness; they are value driven and one of their values is people. They also want to assist people to reach their full potential.

From the YELLOW thinking of Henk van Zyl, a model of sharing ownership, decisions, discipline and control materialised in a way that served each stakeholder's best interests.

> ## 0.001% of the South African population is YELLOW

Turquoise

Loraine Laubscher echoed Don Beck by saying that life conditions in the outer world stimulate the adaptive intelligence to deal with changing conditions. Both believe that we should work with what the world needs, rather than focus too much on systems that are not yet manifesting in the outer world. Beck explained that morphing occurs on an ongoing basis for TURQUOISE; this thinking system is adapting all the time. They can find the systems that they need, and the whole is seen as interconnected and even interplanetary.

> ## 0.0000001% of the South African population is TURQUOISE

MESHWORK, INCLUSIVITY IN PRACTICE

Beck[27] and Viljoen described the process of integrating different thinking systems around a systemic problem as a meshwork. A meshwork is a process through which the thinking and behaviour of different codes are wired together into an inclusive, aligned force of energy in a system. The BEIGE, PURPLE, RED, BLUE, ORANGE, GREEN and YELLOW people all find themselves in a space where they can contribute not only insight, but can leverage the system in a collective whole through leadership. The question to be asked is how to weave the various strings of gifts together into an inclusive, integrated and conducive whole. Co-determination is such a process of a meshwork.

CONCLUSION

It is crucial for employers to take the bio-psycho-social make-up of their workers into account in the design and translation of strategy, design and delivery of organisational development initiatives, and design and implement other organisational interventions accordingly. By understanding the social fabric created by the different human niches inside the organisation, the way to connect, to engage, and ultimately to ensure that everyone is on the same page, is enabled. The psychological map is available to determine different human niches on an individual level, while the BeQ is available to determine the organisational levels of spiral dynamics. Graves[28] said that at each stage of human existence, the adult man is off on his quest for this Holy Grail, i.e. the way of life by which he believes men should live. The Human Niche Theory may offer insight into the organisational BEING, and by following an inclusivity process such as co-determination, the organisational DOING can also be optimised.

REFERENCES

Beck, D., & Linscott, G. (2006). *The crucible: Forging South Africas future: In search of a template for the world*. Columbia, MD: Published and distributed by Dherie Beck, representing Coera.us and the Center for Human Emergence.

Beck, D.E., Larsen, T.H., Solonin, S., Viljoen, R., & Johns, T.Q. (2018). *Spiral dynamics in action: Humanity's Master Code*. Chichester, West Sussex: John Wiley & Sons.

Graves, C. (1974). Human nature prepares for a momentous leap. *The Futurist*, April. p.72-87.

Jung, C.G. (1954). On the Nature of the Psyche. In H. Read, et al. (eds.). *The Collected Works of C.G. Jung* (vol. 8). Princeton: Princeton University Press.

Laubscher, L.I. (2013). *Human Niches: Spiral Dynamics for Africa*. Ph.D dissertation. Modderfontein: Da Vinci Institute. Retrived from: https://www.mandalaconsulting.co.za/Documents/Thesis%20-%20Loraine%20Laubscher.pdf.

Vilikati, M.V., Schurink, W., & Viljoen, R. (2013). Exploring the concept of African Spiritual Consciousness. *Academy of Management Proceedings, 2013, Orlando*. Retrieved from: https://www.mandalaconsulting.co.za/Documents/Articles/28%20Vusi%20Vilakati%20AOM%20Article.pdf

Viljoen R.C. (2014). *Inclusive Organisational Transformation: An African Perspective on Human Niches and Diversity of Thought*. Gower. Farnham, UK. ISBN: 978-1-86922-540-7

Viljoen, R. (2015). *Organisational Change and Development: – an African perspective*. Bryanston: KR Publishing.

ENDNOTES

1   Beck & Linscott, 2006.
2   Graves, 1974.
3   Graves, 1974.
4   Laubscher, 2013.
5   Laubscher, 2013.
6   Laubscher, 2013.

7   Viljoen, R. 2015.
8   Beck & Cowan, 1996.
9   Laubscher, 2013.
10   Beecroft, 2014.
11   Laubscher, 2013.
12   Beecraft, 2014.
13   Laubscher, 2013.
14   Beck, Larsen, Solonin, Viljoen, & Johns, 2018.
15   Laubscher, 2013.
16   Vilikati, 2013.
17   Laubscher, 2013.
18   Laubscher, 2013.
19   Laubscher, 2013.
20   Viljoen, 2014.
21   Viljoen, 2015.
22   Jung, 1953.
23   Viljoen, 2008.
24   Viljoen, 2015.
25   Beck, 2016.
26   Graves, 1974.
27   Beck & Linscott, 2006.
28   Graves, 1971.

Chapter

4

CO-DETERMINATION CONCEPTUALISED

Joyce Toendepi and Rica Viljoen

INTRODUCTION

The new world of work requires fearless trans-disciplinary approaches to social change that emphasise re-thinking inclusive growth and development. As a result, new approaches that partner across sectors seem favourable for devising sustainable solutions, and co-determination is one of the initiatives at hand for South Africa and the African continent at large.

Co-determination is a concept of employee consultation and participation in company decisions, which originated in Germany in 1848.[1] Based on the *Labour and Employee Handbook*[2] , co-determination rights effectively apply where the consent of the works councils is mandatory. In Germany, enforceable co-determination is now a highly developed system of board level worker consultations and engagement.[3] Similarly, the concept is now widely used throughout the European Union countries with variations. Co-determination was introduced in South Africa through workplace forums in Chapter 5 of the Labour Relations Act (LRA)[4], as the old system of industrial relations of 1920 were not adding value to the production of goods and services.

The purpose of this chapter is to provide basic explanations regarding co-determination, how it is being used worldwide as a consultation and participatory process in company decision-making at both the lower and board levels, its advantages and disadvantages, and how South Africa adopted it.

THE CONCEPT OF CO-DETERMINATION

According to Bramucci and Zanfie[5], co-determination is a concept that legally recognises the rights of employees to be consulted and to take part in company decisions. When co-determination was introduced in Germany as far back as 1848, it was seriously affected by employers' fear of their decision-making power being undermined.[6] It was the 1920 Works Council Act that gave workers participation rights and paved the way for worker representation on supervisory boards.[7]

The meaning of the term 'co-determination' was expanded by Page[8] to embrace worker participation with regards to their working conditions, as well as the economic planning of the company. In Germany, co-determination was legalised through acts of parliament, i.e. the Works Constitution Act and the Co-determination Law. It is this institutionalisation of co-determination that differentiates its operationalisation in Germany from other countries worldwide.

Co-determination is a dual level system that gives the works council the right to decide on the hiring and firing of employees at a lower level in the organisation, as well as workforce representation on supervisory boards that the employees themselves elect at the corporate level.[9] The supervisory board is elected for a period of four years and the elected worker representatives automatically become full board members with voting powers.[10] This places the internal stakeholders on an equal footing with the employers, as both sides have vested interests in the sustainability of the organisation. Page[11] explained that such a relationship creates a balance of interest that spills out across the country to stabilise the whole economy and create social order. The World Economic Forum[12] emphasised the need for bold steps to improve working conditions and to take a broader stakeholder perspective. Unfortunately, the current business models cannot enhance good governance that can foster the sustainability of organisations if employees' concerns are relegated.

Page[13] listed the objectives of co-determination as:

- equality of capital and work;
- democracy in the economy; and
- social development and control of economic power.

The main goal of co-determination is to settle conflicts and disputes between employers and employees through the use of dialogue and co-decision-making.[14] For this reason, collaborative strategies are the basis for co-determination in its endeavour to protect workers' rights. Heiner[15] elaborated that co-determination is not a democratisation of the workplace process, but it seeks to empower workers through the works council representation that will act in the best interests of the organisation and safeguard employment. In other words, it is an inclusive participatory approach where the works council influences management decisions.

The majority of workers in the new world of work will be millennials, which calls for fundamental changes to the current HR policies and procedures. Millennials were described by Brack and Kelly[16] as continuous learners who prefer an unstructured flow of information, hence they depend on networks and communities. Co-determination by construction fosters information exchange. Kraft, Stank and Dewenter[17] observed that co-determination advocates argue that the system facilitates the harnessing of information from all employees, which could have otherwise been lost. Viljoen[18] concurred, stating that in the new world of work, the voices and gifts of all individuals and groups will assist in building progressive organisations. Due to the transparency built into the co-determination process, conflict between employers and employees is reduced, if not eliminated, due to the good flow and processing of information. Timeliness of information delivery also keeps organisations agile and hence competitive. In co-determination, negotiation and the sharing of organisational goals promote the development of alternative strategies that move the organisation ahead of its competitors. According to Page[19], all decisions reached under the practice of co-determination are unanimous, implying consensus. This process promotes harmony and peace within the organisation.

Kraft et al.[20] noted that due to good information flow, productivity can increase and the organisation will be competitive, yet, it is frequently supposed that co-determination increases turnaround time, affects flexibility and limits innovation; three factors that have an impact on competitiveness. However, Kraft et al.[21] found that co-determination has a marginal impact on such factors. Due to the high levels of transparency induced by co-determination, the authors found that worker motivation was enhanced, which may accelerate innovation in projects.

EMPLOYEE INVOLVEMENT IN SA

Co-determination is a construct that seeks to create an informed organisation, where decisions are based on the collective wisdom of both the employers and employees. Leadership is positioned as the change agent in co-determination. Upon democratisation, South Africa re-entered the international market, yet the imperatives of a more open economy demanded that value-added products be created and productivity levels improved. Success in restructuring the industries and the economy at large lay in management and labour finding mutual ground to operate on.[22]

WHY FORUMS WERE ESTABLISHED

Co-determination in South Africa has more to do with capital realising that despotic control is not sustainable, and that these struggles are a direct outcome of struggles by organised workers who are strong and able to push back the frontier of control and gain greater direction of their lives in production.[23] In Germany, however, corporate governance is shaped by a legal tradition that dates back as far as 1920.[24]

Buhlungu[25] thus asserted that co-determination and worker participation in South Africa cannot be separated from the struggle for democracy. The strategies used are about the demands and struggles of South African workers and unions, particularly black unions. It seems that works forums were established and favoured by workers because there was a void in the regular in-plant negotiations, and as a result an in-house committee was deemed appropriate. The forums had a striking feature of strong emphasis on consensual interaction.

According to Webster and Macun[26], the unions tended to be reactive and lacked initiatives and the capacity to frame creative and imaginative proposals. Because of where the South African unions were coming from, Webster and Macun described them as "masters in resistance politics". Due to the structure of trade unions in South Africa, white collar and middle management are excluded from forums.[27] Page[28] and Heiner[29] pointed out that due to the increase in global competition and flexibility required by the rapidly changing markets in Europe, works councils were forced to take on managerial tasks and even present more favourable alternatives in order to preserve production at home. Thus, the danger of co-determination in Europe around 1994 seemed to be degenerating into co-management, which stimulated a different set of challenges as there was no clarification on the delimitation of the duties of the supervisory board. In South Africa the relationship between unions, works councils and boards is sticky, whereas in Germany, 80% of the works council representatives are affiliated to a labour union.[30] Heiner[31], however, insisted that employers tend to want to block external representatives of the unions from attaining board level representation, which is one of the South African challenges.

The ILO[32] observed that worker participation in decision-making demands special training to equip workers and their representatives with special skills, because for worker representatives to be able to exert influence, whether through representation on management boards or in the process of consultation, negotiation or joint decision-making, they must be capable of understanding the questions under discussion and appreciate the effects of the decision to be taken.

The flow of information within the works forums is relatively high and has tended to increase over time, however in some companies there still is hesitation by management to fully disclose financial information.[33] Summers[34] had argued that the provision of more complete and reliable information concerning the profitability and prospects of the enterprise can make the representatives more ready to accept terms at the bargaining table however, which will promote the common long-term goal of company success. Union representatives who are fully informed and understand the problems of the enterprise might well be less aggressive in their bargaining demands, and employer representation might well be less adamant in resisting union demands.

CHARACTERISTICS AND LIMITATIONS OF WORKS FORUMS IN SOUTH AFRICA

South African works forums can be distinguished from internal workplace representation in that there is no statutory support. The German works councils, on the other hand, have legislation to articulate and regulate them.

Companies are spending considerable amounts of time and money on the running and servicing of works forums. Many companies have establishments throughout the country and they have to fly delegates to these regular meetings. In countries like Germany, it is suggested that this amounts to 1% of the annual wage bill. A second characteristic of forums that were established during the 1980s and 1990s is their vulnerability, as they depend on charismatic managers and when they leave the company, maintaining continued commitment becomes a problem. In the absence of formal statutes or agreements, these experiments of participation will always be subject to the cycle of changing support by management and labour.[35]

Webster and Macun identified the inadequate training of workplace representatives as a drawback of forums. Trade unions in Germany play a pivotal role in supporting and resourcing works councils, thus members of the councils are well qualified to engage with management. The length of service of many works councillors also provides necessary experience in the functioning of the councils.[36]

The presence of employee representatives on the board does, however, raise difficulties when it comes to providing them with special roles and responsibilities. Summers[37] suggested that the decision-making process must be structured in such a way that guarantees employee directors the chance to effectively participate in corporate decisions.

Webster and Macun[38] noted other limitations of works forums in South Africa as including a reluctance by employees and their representatives to identify with the goals of the enterprise. This is deeply rooted in the low trust dynamic that arose from the apartheid workplace regime, which has resulted in suspicion of any involvement in decision-making. High levels of mistrust exist between the employees, employers and the unions in South Africa, however the IBL case study presents a lot of hope for co-determination in the country. According to McLaverty[39], where participation is done properly, it does contribute to the efficiency of decision-making and also reduces workplace alienation. Viljoen[40] advocates for the unleashing of the voices of the minority for a better co-creation of the future of the organisation.

Webster and Macun[41] explained that both management and shop stewards are well schooled in adversarial bargaining and find it difficult to adjust to co-determination. Further, the forums are not based on legal rights but on the sheer power of the union representatives in the workplace. Indeed, both unions and management remain cautious about existing forums and the provision in the Act for workplace forums. Unions are concerned that new forms of workplace representation will undermine established union structures, while management uncertainties with regard to the statutory forums arise from a fear that the proposed forums will substantially curtail their prerogative to make unilateral decisions, by giving workers statutory rights to consultation and co-decision-making. Therefore, it remains to be seen whether Chapter 5 of the LRA has the potential to take South African corporate governance in the direction of the German style of co-determination.

CO-DETERMINATION, CULTURE AND STRUCTURES OF INVOLVEMENT

The process of co-determination can also be used to harness an inclusive culture. Viljoen[42] noted that inclusivity offers great potential for organisations, as it enables them to use the gifts of their diverse employees effectively. Toendepi[43], meanwhile, pointed out that it is the duty of the leaders to conscientise employees on the benefits of inclusivity and how individual and group differences are valued in the organisation. The primary aim of works councils in co-determination is to resolve conflicts by following collaborative strategies.[44]

There is a structural challenge in the South African context, in that co-determination was imported and imposed as a way to mitigate the failures of the old system of industrial relations created in 1920. As South Africa emerged from the apartheid workplace system, co-determination was viewed as disarming the workers by promoting a view that capitalism and the workers had shared interests. Toendepi[45] argued that it is the structures of involvement that created the challenges and not the co-determination process. Trust levels were very low in the system, yet the magnitude of change required from both management and employees was very high, i.e. the leadership of organisations needed to be role models for the new value system being introduced. Mistrust emanated from the socio-political environment that was prevailing in the country.

At IBL, workers trusted their leaders fully, to the extent that when co-determination was facilitated, three different unions participated in the co-creation of different organisational structures and forums to facilitate shared decision-making in the organisation.[46] Van der Ohe[47] asserted that there will be a positive impact on productivity when workers feel trusted by management to work towards a common goal.

Toendepi[48] proposed that the hierarchical structures of involvement be revisited for their lack of fit with the indigenous context and suggested that a circular structure of involvement where everybody is invited to participate be introduced. At the time of the introduction of works forums, South Africa was still using more of a formal societal structure, which was defined by discriminatory tendencies, formalisation, centralisation and a hierarchical control that suited the minority. Structural hierarchy emphasises spatial aspects, according to Dawson.[49] It is top-down; rigid; concentrates on size, position and power; and pays no particular attention to interrelationships and how the system's networks rely on new levels of openness, trust, integrity and effective feedback.[50]

Toendepi[51] suggested that the circular structure is more suited to the South African context, because it collapses the hierarchical structure and permits engagement across the same level. It further incorporates all stakeholders' interests and acknowledges the role and relevance of societal values and norms. The circular structure is systemic because its major concern is about the interrelationships between the key variables.

Every participant in a circular structure has to be committed and take responsibility for decisions made, thus it enhances effective collaboration as knowledge is shared freely through clear and flexible communication channels.

Toendepi[52] observed that in the African tradition, at *imbizos* or *padares* (small group discussions), the participants sit in a circular formation either around a fire or under a big tree. This sitting formation diffuses the hierarchy and implies that everyone's contribution is valid and that all people are equal. The leadership in that setting is seen as being open and courageous by lowering themselves to the level of the people. At these discussion groups, participants expose their thinking and desire to influence others. Structural changes are a functional adaptive reaction to the internal environment and are not necessarily designed to change the physical positions that constitute organisations, hence co-determination may provide an evolution in how organised labour interacts with business.

From a spiral dynamics point of view, Professor Clare Graves explored the essence of human nature as pertaining to distinct ways of thinking or structure of thought. Butters[53] defined 'spiral dynamics' as a system that describes the conceptual models that humans use to explain the world around them. Similarly, Viljoen[54] said that spiral dynamics refers to the "oscillating, ever-emerging essence of the thinking systems". In human systems, structures include how people make decisions; in this regard, Viljoen and Laubscher[55] noted that 65% of South Africans can be classified as PURPLE.

Viljoen[56] explained that people who operate in the PURPLE thinking system are extremely concerned about safety and security, adding that PURPLE is a collective system that takes the circular shape where self is defined in terms of others. She continued that PURPLE can smell intent, which is why in 1994 there was a general acceptance of co-determination, but the low trust levels that existed in the system created challenges. In the proceedings of the *imbizos/padares*, a great deal of consultation takes place before a collective stance is taken. For co-determination to be effective in the South African context, therefore, circular structures of involvement need to be introduced. Such structures treat organisational people or citizens in general as active participants in shaping their reality, and also respects the customs, values and norms of participants. According to Dawson[57], however, people are capable of adapting to their work circumstances and the environment created for their benefit.

CONCLUSION

Co-determination as a form of inclusive participation and a co-responsibility process, if done well, improves trust levels, unleashes minority voices, sorts out relationships, and above all improves the process of decision-making within an organisation. An organisation's success is of great importance to both the workers and the employers. Germany's example has been used in this write-up because it has well laid out elements of worker representation. For co-determination in South Africa to succeed as it has in Germany, it should be backed by legislation and be flexible enough to embrace inclusivity by engaging all thinking systems through appropriate involvement structures. The structures should take great care of peoples' values, customs and norms.

REFERENCES

Addison, J. T. (2009). *The economics of co-determination: lessons from German experiences*. New York: Palgrave MacMillan.

Brack, J., & Kelley, K. (2012). *Maximising Millennials in the workplace*. Retrieved from: www.execdev. unc.edu.

Bramucci, A., & Zanfei, A. (2015). The Governance of offshoring and its effects at home. The Role of Codetermination in the International organisation of German firms. *Journal of Industrial and Business Economics*, 42(2), 1-30.

Buhlungu, S. (1999). A Question of Power: Co-determination and Trade Union Capacity. *African Sociology Review*, 3(1), 111-129.

Butters, A. M. (2015). A Brief History of Spiral Dynamics. *Approaching Religion*, 5(2), 67-78.

Dawson, B. (2007). *Bertalanffy Revisited: Operationalising General Systems Theory based on Business Model. The General Systems Thinking, Modelling and Practice*. Retrieved from: http://citeseerx.ist.psu.edu/viewdoc/download?doi=10.1.1.463.2671&rep=rep1&type=pdf.

Heiner, M. (2007). *Co-determination in Germany. The Recent Debate*. Retrieved from: http://ns2.sise.ucl.ac.be/cps/ucl/doc/etes/documents/WDW004.pdf.

Kluge, N. (2011). *Worker participation in the boardrooms throughout Europe*. Düsseldorf: Hans Bockler Foundation.

Kraft, K., Stank, J., & Dewenter, R. (2011). Co-determination and Innovation. *Cambridge Journal of Economics*, 35, 145-172.

McLaverty, P. (2017). *Public Participation and Innovation in community governance*. London: Routledge.

Muswaka, L. (2014). The Two-Tier Structure and Co-determination: Should South Africa follow the German Example? *Mediterranean Journal of Social Science*, 5(9), 142-147.

Page, R. (2011). *Co-determination in Germany - a Beginners guide*. Retrieved from: https://www.boeckler.de/pdf/p_arbp_033.pdf.

Summers, C. W. (1982). Co-determination in the United States of America: A projection of problems and potentials. *Journal of Comparative Corporate Law and Securities Regulation*, 4, 155-191.

Toendepi, J. (2013). *A Systemic Perspective to Wealth Creation through Learning and Adaptation: An analysis of South Africa's competitiveness*. Riga, Latvia: Lambert Academic Publishing.

Toendepi, J. (2017). *Transformation Leadership as a Catalyst to higher levels of Consciousness in Social Systems. Johannesburg*. Retrieved from: https://www.mandalaconsulting.co.za/Documents/Thesis/Joyce%20Toendepi%20Thesis%202016.pdf

Viljoen, R., & Laubscher, L. (2015). Spiral dynamics integral. In R. Lessem & A. Schieffer (eds.). *Integral Polity*. Farnham: Gower Ashgate.

Viljoen. R. (2015). *Organisational Change and Development: an African Perspective*. Randburg: Knowledge Resources.

Von der Ohe, H. (2015). Trust and engagement. In H. Nienaber & N. Martins (eds.). *Employee Engagement in a South African context*. Bryanston: KR Publishing.

Webster, E., & Macun, I. (2009). *A trend towards co-determination? Case study of South African enterprises*. Retrieved from: https://www.ajol.info/index.php/ldd/article/viewFile/138018/127588

World Economic Forum. (2016). *Davos Conference*. Geneva: World Economic Forum.

ENDNOTES

1   Muswaka, 2014.
2   Labour and Employee Handbook, 2010.
3   Kludge, 2011.
4   Webster & Macun, 2009.
5   Bramucci & Zanfie 2015.
6   Page, 2011.
7   Kraft, Stank & Dewenter, 2011.
8   Page, 2011.
9   Bramucci & Zanfei, 2015; Kraft, Stank & Deventer, 2011.
10 Page, 2011.
11 Ibid.
12 World Economic Forum, 2016.
13 Page, 2011.
14 Bramucci & Zanfei, 2015.
15 Heiner, 2007.
16 Brack & Kelly, 2012.
17 Kraft, Stank & Dewenter, 2011.
18 Viljoen, 2015.
19 Page, 2011.
20 Kraft et al., 2011.
21 Kraft et al., 2011.
22 Ministry of Labour, 1994.
23 Buhlungu, 1999.
24 Mintz, 2006, cited in Muswaka, 2014.
25 Buhlungu, 1999.
26 Webster & Macun, 2009.
27 Ibid.
28 Page, 2011.
29 Heiner, 2007.
30 Addison, 2009.
31 Heiner, 2007.
32 The ILO, 1989.
33 Webster & Macun, 2009.
34 Summers, 1982.
35 Webster & Macun, 2009.
36 Ibid.
37 Summers, 1982.
38 Webster & Macun ,2009
39 McLaverty, 2017.
40 Viljoen, 2015.
41 Webster & Macun, 2009.
42 Viljoen, 2015.
43 Toendepi, 2017.
44 Page, 2011.
45 Toendepi, 2013.
46 Viljoen, 2015.

47   Von der Ohe, 2016.
48   Toendepi, 2013.
49   Dawson 2007, cited in Toendepi, 2013.
50   Toendepi, 2013.
51   Ibid.
52   Ibid.
53   Butters 2015.
54   Viljoen 2015.
55   Viljoen & Laubscher, 2015.
56   Viljoen, 2015.
57   Dawson, 2007.

5

THEORETICAL UNDERPINNINGS OF CO-DETERMINATION AS RADICAL TRANSFORMATION PROCESSES

Rica Viljoen

INTRODUCTION

Sustainability and social innovation are increasingly important to organisations, societies, geo-political regions, and ultimately, humanity. The unintended implications of the interplay and claims of ecological, cultural, socio-economic and rising levels of consciousness internationally require radical new ways of organising. In the face of these external changes, organisations and societies must adapt. A transition towards sustainability and social innovation requires co-creation, co-evolution and the redesign of current relatedness.

As early as 1974, Clare Graves wrote an article entitled, *Human Nature Prepares for a Momentous Leap*, and a bio-psycho-socio system of human development was shared. Don Beck and Christopher Cowan built further on the deep-rooted academic work of Graves. They quoted Graves as saying that humanity was at the beginning of, not merely a transition to, a new level of existence, "but (was at) the start of a new movement in the symphony of human history".[1] Beck colour-coded the Gravesian map of worldviews to ensure accessibility and explain the transferability of the same organising patterns to a single person, an organisation or an entire situation. A universal language is presented in this chapter for dealing with changing life conditions and the corresponding thinking that can respond to these changing realities.

Csikszentmihalyi[2] applied the term "memes" in the following context: "A meme is any permanent pattern of matter or information produced as an act of human intentionality." Laubscher[3] appreciated the worth of all the different thinking systems, and offered the term "human niches" to describe the result of the self-organising capability of the thinking structures. These human niches are in fact archetypes; they are patterns of meta-design that encapsulate the what, why and how social systems are designed or co-designed. In the first section of this chapter, the Gravesian psychological map as developed by Graves[4] and explained by Beck, Laubscher and Viljoen[5] is described.

To weave together a sustainable organisation or society, different worldviews must be respected, integrated and aligned around a commonly shared goal. The manner in which different worldviews are combined impacts the culture of a social system. Ultimately, social systems adapt to external life conditions through the emergence of human systems with different levels of complexity, organisation and consciousness. Graves warned that individuals, organisations and societies "respond positively only to those managerial principles, motivational appeals, educational formulas and legal or ethical codes".[6] Trans-disciplinary integration and collaboration must happen through courageous dialogue; inclusivity is required. The second part of this chapter positions inclusivity as a radical transformational process, as significant behavioural changes are required from all stakeholders to co-create a future that everyone wants.

The process of inclusivity suggests the incorporation of a 'doing' component (strategy) and a 'being' component (behaviour). If an integral process emerges where individual gifts come to the organisational or collective domain, in an environment that is conducive to trust and respect, human capacity to perform is unleashed. This human energy must be wired in terms of a shared purpose by leadership at all levels of the organisation. Although this chapter does not address the impact and importance of leadership on social systems (Chapter 7 deals with this), the importance of leadership in radical behavioural transformation cannot be denied. The focus here is on the optimisation of organisational or systemic beingness and capacity, where healthy, cooperative interactions are spontaneous across the whole system.

A holistic, integral process of thinking is needed, where responsible and conscious meta-design thinking creates sustainable and highly functioning social systems. The last part of this chapter deals with a strategic framework and architecture that can enable an aggressive participation process of co-determination. The importance of creating strategic architecture is underlined, as a natural design that fits the social dynamics of the system is required. Shifts towards more appropriate and sustainable ways of interacting around organisational tasks, structures and relationships are proposed. Although only discussed later in the book, the case of Interstate Bus Lines (IBL), where a model of inclusivity, strategy and co-determination was engineered, forms the practical application of the theoretical approach that is shared here. Realistic and auto-ethnographical tales á la Sparkes[7] are used to integrate the narratives of the organisation as a reference point. In this organisation, an integrated, interconnected and interdependent model emerged, which allowed for engagement, pride and growth at the individual and collective levels. The transformational journey of IBL is used as context for this part of the book. The chapter concludes with some insights into inclusivity and organisational doing and being that are focused on a shared purpose such as co-determination.

During one of my first interventions with IBL I met a humble elderly bus driver. I remember clearly that there were holes in a thin-washed shirt that showed a religious emblem. His official work clothes almost hid the old shirt. Peter[i] did not finish school,

---

i   Pseudonym

but he was arguably one of the wisest people I ever met. His insight into the group process that was facilitated was enhancing. On asking him to share the basis for his intelligent interpretation of dynamics, he nonchalantly said that if I had studied humans on buses for 30 years like him, I would be wise too.

At the end of our intervention, Peter asked me whether he could pray for the group. He opened his jacket to display his most precious possession - the shirt that was given to him by his congregation when he became a religious elder. Peter explained that the work we did in the group process was aligned with the spirit of his company, Interstate Bus Lines. Since the process would make things better, and since IBL provided a livelihood to at least five times the number of actual employees, he prayed that it would be sustained.

BACKGROUND AND CONTEXT

The auto-ethnographical note above reflects the start of a deep, theoretical radical transformation process in IBL. Little did I know that this would be the start of a 25-year journey with the company. Over the years, the results of numerous culture studies showed no manifestations of racism or diversity issues as they pertained to multi-nationalism. These results were different to those of other organisations that were studied in South Africa over the same period of time. Rich multi-cultural lessons were learned from leadership and the bus drivers. Over time, the deep roots of trust and inclusivity grew into a progressive co-determination engagement model, where unions and management crafted organisational strategy and collectively took responsibility for the management of performance and discipline of the organisation. The key role player in this system was the HR Manager, Henk van Zyl. He was wise beyond his time in constructing a puzzle of human relatedness that would benefit all.

Peter's blessing was prophetic, as IBL has become one of the few companies in the history of South Africa where, even today, co-determination has been implemented with great results.

This chapter is viewed as critical, since the understandings and applications of this theory can greatly assist the successful implementation of co-determination. There is no ultimate way of successfully implementing co-determination, but there are certainly deep-rooted prerequisites. This chapter on multi-culturalism is one of them.

INCLUSIVITY AS RADICAL TRANSFORMATIONAL PROCESS

A mind, once stretched, never regains its original dimensions.

Holmes (n.d.)

The eclectic, systemic Inclusivity Model displayed in Figure 5.1 below is viewed as a roadmap to organisational transformation. The concepts in the model are metathemes that are positioned as variable concepts that are open to interpretation by the organisation or the social system. The author believes that on reflection, the reader can become aware of his or her own basic assumptions and beliefs regarding these concepts. This awareness can lead to greater insight into one's own behaviour and that of others, and ultimately to enhanced consciousness. The way in which the individual, group or organisation views the concept is more important than studying its theoretical definition. In this sense, the framework is phenomenological in nature.

The bottom part of the model describes the waves of change in the global external world. These are changes that no organisation can escape. Due to the forces of the new world of work, leadership must adapt since the strategies and styles that worked effectively in the past are no longer recent or applicable, and the different outcomes cannot be expected while clinging to old behaviours. The way in which leadership manages the ever-changing organisations must change. The first triangle in the framework predicts this reality.

Systems thinking principles, as described by Senge[8], always influence the way in which living systems such as organisations are viewed. The essence of change is determined by these principles. Change is paradoxical and complex, and causes self-organising in systems (systems will always move to equilibrium and therefore resist change). The second triangle in the framework refers to these principles.

The third triangle represents the rising levels of consciousness at the individual level, the impact of the self on others, and insight into one's own unconscious patterns. Consciousness at the group level refers to the limitation of destructive unconscious patterns and group dynamics, and to the acknowledgement of own patterns. On the organisational level, consciousness refers to the application of moral and ethical behaviour and social consciousness both within and outside the organisation. In this way, transformation becomes the most pressing intent of the individual, the group and the organisational psyche.

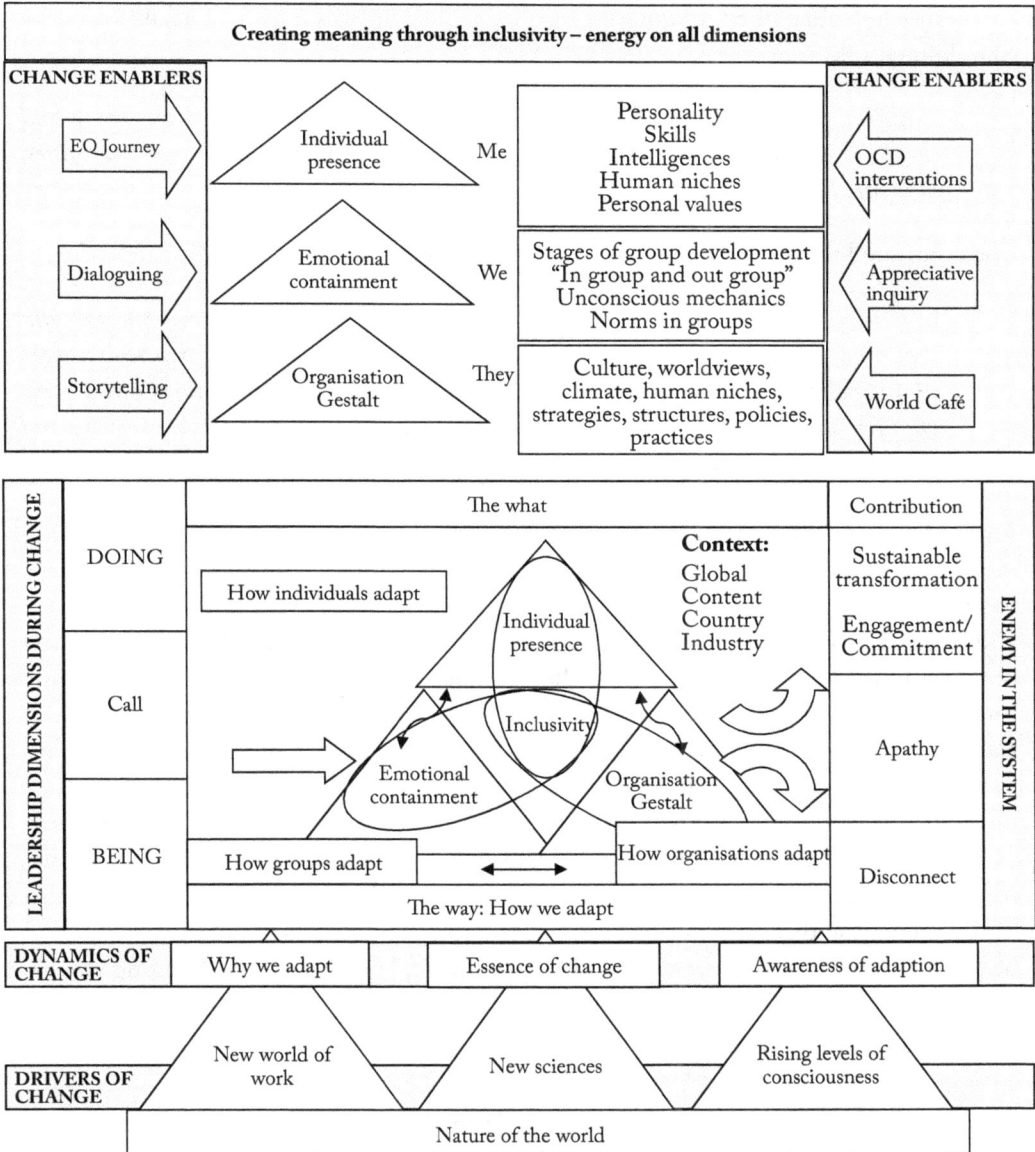

Figure 5.1: Viljoen's Inclusivity Model (adapted from Viljoen-Terblanche)[9]

The radical organisational methodology of inclusivity is visually described in this framework as the optimisation of the interplay of the diversity dynamics in the individual, group, organisational and contextual domains. The interplay manifests itself as energy in a system to perform. It is the task of leadership, through the aligning of the 'doing' and the 'being', to enable the system to engage in strategic conversation in a conducive way. The energy in the system can be described as virtuous (engaged), neutral (apathetic) or vicious (disconnected).

Viljoen-Terblanche[10] uniquely positioned inclusivity as a transformational process. She defined it as follows:

> *A radical organisational transformational methodology which aligns the doing and the being aspects of the organisation around commonly defined principles and values, co-created by all.*

She continued with a further explanation of inclusivity as an organisational process:

> *It is a systemic approach that focuses on underlying beliefs and assumptions and challenges patterns within the individual, group and organisational psyche to engage in an inclusive manner with the aim of achieving a shared consciousness that will manifest in sustainable business results within the context of the specific industry and national culture in which the company operates.*[ii; 11]

Jung[12] described the journey of integrating opposites, of becoming aware and of taking ownership of own behaviour, as the process of individuation – the metamorphosis to crystallise individual essence. Through a process of inclusivity, individuals, groups and organisations also engage in a process of metamorphosis, during which the organisational doing (strategy) and the organisational being (relatedness) become integrated and conscious. Leaders at all levels of the organisation become aware of themselves and others, as well as of themselves in relation to others. This also applies to societies in which different groupings should become integrated. Paradoxically, they must become more of who they are in relation to others, rather than faking sameness or merely assimilating, and, thereby, collectively co-creating societal doing and being. Metamorphosis, as a process of vicissitude, implies hardship and effort, but also exponential growth. A radical transformational process in terms of inclusivity seems to be a difficult, but satisfying, process with sustainable, life-giving and changing results.

Prerequisites for Inclusivity

The following aspects are critical prerequisites for an inclusivity journey:
- Strong, committed leadership from the top.
- Co-creation of strategies and action plans.
- Translation of both the doing and the being.
- Individual accountability through clearly contracted performance measures linked to strategy and rigorous performance management.
- Building the Emotional Intelligence of leadership (leadership development).

ii   As inclusivity is a systemic phenomenon, the supportive definition was added. Due to the reciprocal nature of diversity factors on individual, group and organisational domains, a simplistic definition will not capture the complex essence thereof. By presenting the detailed, integrated and comprehensive definition, the systemic nature of the phenomenon is acknowledged.

- Allowing and encouraging diversity of thought.
- An in-depth understanding of the different thinking systems (as describe in Chapter 3 of this book).
- The realisation that inclusivity is a radical organisational transformational process.
- Ethical behaviour on the part of leaders.

It is also critical to build the following aspects in an organisation, as described in the Benchmark of Engagement (BeQ):

Individual domain aspects:	Respect, Regard, Resilience, Personal Responsibility
Group domain aspects:	Support, Leadership, Diversity, Accountability
Organisational domain aspects:	Trust, Alignment, Adaptability, Inclusivity, Ethics

Benchmark of Engagement – a multi-cultural philosophy to build inclusivity

The chapter is not dedicated to the BeQ model and philosophy to build trusting organisations. It is, however, a prerequisite for successful radical organisational transformation. Figure 5.2 below visually describes the approach. In their book, *Employee Engagement in South Africa*, Martins and Nienaber[13] dedicate three chapters to this approach, should the reader require more detail. A sample report is included with the practical documents in the appendices of the book. In Figure 5.2 below, a snapshot of the BeQ theory is presented.

Constructs for the BeQ

Within the context of the country:

I-Engage	Assumptions About Me	Respect Self-regard Resilience Personal responsibility Corporate citizenship
We-Engage	Assumptions About We	Support Leadership Alignment Valuing diversity Accountability
They-Engage	Assumptions About Them	Trust Business orientation Adaptability to change Inclusivity Ethics

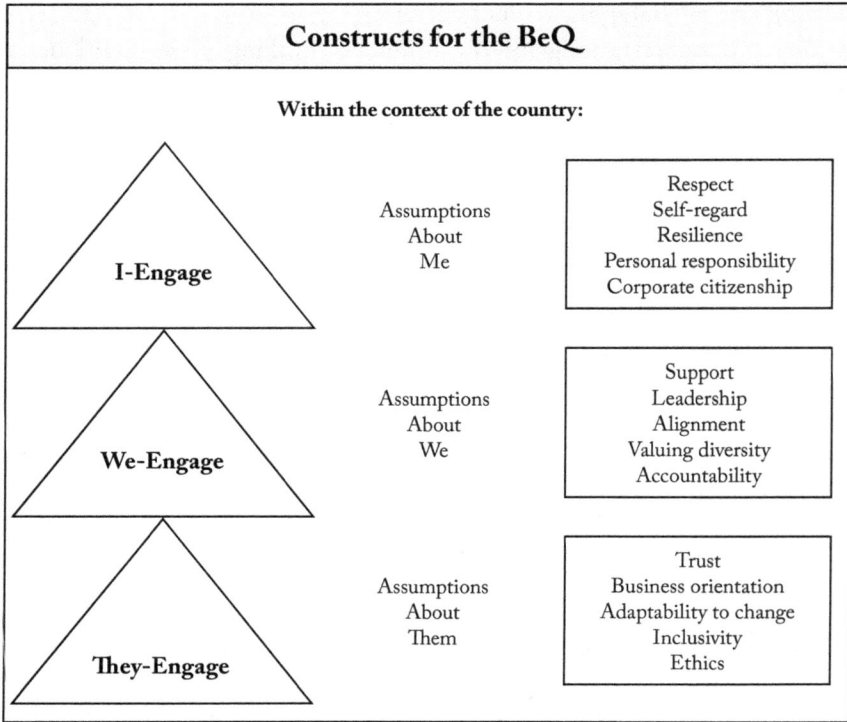

Figure 5.2: BeQ Constructs[14]

A systemic interplay of the individual, group and organisational dynamics, as represented in the figure above by the assumptions about the me, the we and the them, release human energy in the system to perform (see Figure 5.2). These constructs are described by the BeQ. By wiring the energy around organisational doing, the benefits, as shown in Figure 5.3 below, can be observed.

Re-wiring the organisation to have innate momentum to perform sustainably

Vicious Cycle:
Disengagement
Absenteeism
Staff turnover
Apathy
Low morale
Negative behaviour
Poor service delivery
Incidents and accidents

Leads to

High Expectations

Enabling Work Environment

Virtuous Circle

Reinforces

Contribution and Commitment

Results in

Leads to

Low Expectations

Tight Control by 'Us'

Vicious Circle

Alienated Reaction by 'Them'

Reinforces

Results in

Virtuous Cycle:
Unleashing voice
Productivity
Staff retention
Employee satisfaction
Creativity/Innovation
Value based behaviour
Customer experience
Safe behaviour
Stakeholder experience

Disconnected 30%-44%	Apathetic 45-59%	Involved 60-74%	Engaged >75%

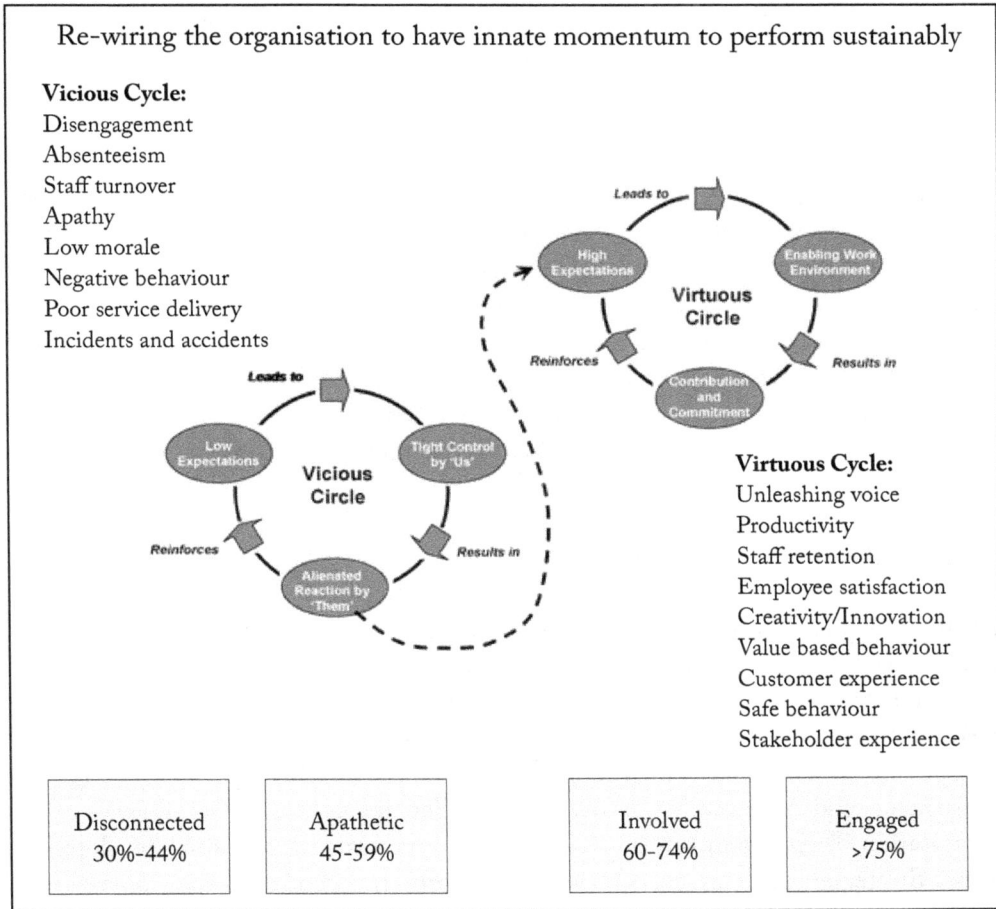

Figure 5.3: Human energy in the system to perform[15]

The three phases of a radical inclusivity transformational process

In Figure 5.3 above the different categories of human energy in the system to perform are clear. These categories are: engaged, involved, apathetic and disconnected. If the human energy is engaged, a virtuous cycle can be created in the organisation. This positive energy results in positive business indicators such as the unleashing of voice, high productivity, staff retention, high levels of employee satisfaction, creativity and innovation, value-based behaviour, high levels of customer experience, safe behaviour and high stakeholder experience. However, if the energy is low, a vicious cycle is created where disengagement, absenteeism, high staff turnover, high levels of apathy, low morale, negative behaviour, poor service delivery and high levels of incidents and accidents manifest.

Three distinct phases must be followed in an inclusivity journey, each of which has specific characteristic dynamics and dilemmas.

Phase 1: New foundation

This phase is characterised by vulnerability in terms of individual leadership, as well as in terms of the fragile group relationships. Resistance to change is experienced throughout the system. The value of psychometrical testing in identifying development areas for leadership development and the optimisation of group dynamics are identified as a critical part of this phase. Further, the use of a multi-cultural sensitive diagnostic tool like the Benchmark of Engagement (BeQ) is critical – both as a diagnostic tool for what, where and how to intervene, but also to describe different thinking systems in the organisation, to start the organisational dialogue, and to serve as a pre-measure for the journey.

Phase 2: The filtering through process

During this phase, everybody participates in training and development. This includes all the stakeholders in different ways, on different topics and with different complexity. There are typically a DOING and a BEING part. In the DOING part, strategy is co-created. In the BEING part, the focus is on relatedness and diversity of thought to generate human energy in the system to do the DOING. Strategy maps are constructed, and Balanced Scorecards are compiled and contracted at all levels of the organisation. These are linked to performance appraisals and individual development plans. Strategies, such as co-determination, form the centre of the conversation. Organisational development initiatives are implemented according to the inclusivity strategy, focused on identified development areas. This process is circular in nature in the form of co-operative inquiry as described by Viljoen.[16] It is not a linear process but organic, inclusive, multi-faceted and integral.

Phase 3: Cementing the future

During this phase, employees take personal responsibility for the process of creating the culture of inclusivity, shared ownership, delivering on plans and discipline. The collective commitment becomes so strong and respected that it is difficult to reverse the strategy after it has been filtered through to all levels. This implies that companies really should ensure that leadership is strong, committed and enabled to deal with a workforce that has voice and accepts personal authority. Leadership capacity is built in the system, thus innovation starts to happen and performance indicators reflect positively.

Co-determination is such a transformational process; it unleashes human energy at the individual, group and organisational levels. Both organisational doing and being is needed in such an inclusivity process.

The below-mentioned model in Figure 5.4 explains that there are different parts to strategy, namely:
- a diagnostic phase (the bubbles on the top left);
- the construction of strategic architecture (the group of bubbles on the top and to the right); and
- the strategic planning process and translation thereof (the bubbles in the right bottom corner).

If a process of inclusivity is followed, the benefits in the bubbles in the left bottom corner are unleashed.

Companies seldom do scenario planning often enough; they do not spend enough time on strategic architecture and do not translate strategy in an inclusive manner. IBL makes sure that everyone participates in the strategy session, including external union members, board members and shop stewards. Human Resources ensures the translation of strategy through the organisation, and line managers are held responsible for the execution of strategy through performance appraisals.

Organisational doing: Constructing a sustainable organisation

Doing strategy right

In Figure 5.4 below, the strategic planning process that is followed by IBL is shared.

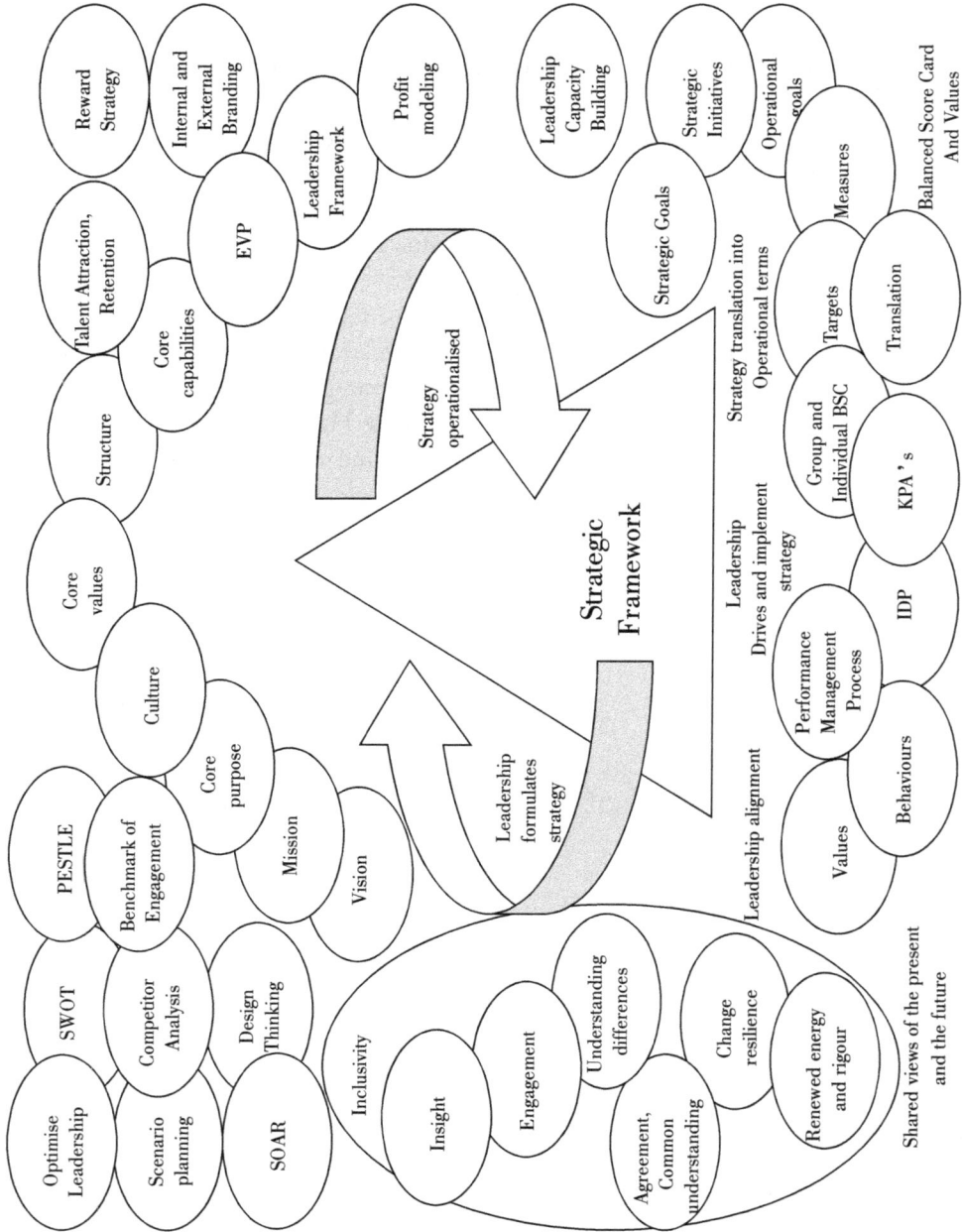

Reward Strategy

Internal and External Branding

Profit modeling

Leadership Capacity Building

Strategic Initiatives

Operational goals

Balanced Score Card And Values

Talent Attraction, Retention

EVP

Leadership Framework

Strategic Goals

Measures

Core capabilities

Strategy translation into Operational terms

Targets

Translation

Structure

Strategy operationalised

Group and Individual BSC

KPA's

Core values

Strategic Framework

Leadership Drives and implement strategy

Culture

Performance Management Process

IDP

Core purpose

Leadership formulates strategy

Behaviours

PESTLE

Benchmark of Engagement

Mission

Vision

Leadership alignment

Values

Shared views of the present and the future

SWOT

Competitor Analysis

Design Thinking

Inclusivity

Insight

Engagement

Understanding differences

Change resilience

Renewed energy and rigour

Optimise Leadership

Scenario planning

SOAR

Agreement, Common understanding

Figure 5.4: Inclusive strategy process[17]

Strategising for radical organisational transformation: co-determination

Strategy is so integrated in the way in which things are done at IBL, that Henk van Zyl, as HR Manager, utilised the integral, inclusive strategic framework towards co-determination. This framework can be seen in Figure 5.5 below.

IBL Institutional Framework

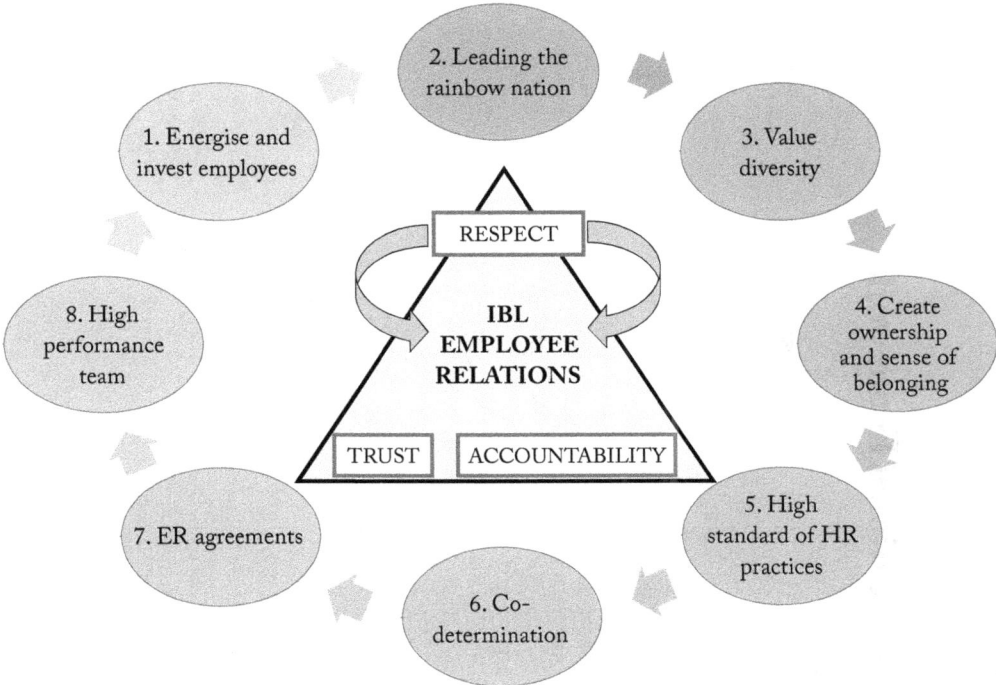

Figure 5.5: Institutional framework of IBL[18]

Figure 5.5 illustrates the eight different steps that should form part of an inclusive co-determination journey. All the following steps should be implemented:
- Energise and engage employees.
- Lead the Rainbow Nation.[iii]
- Value diversity.
- Ownership and a sense of belonging.
- High standard of HR practices.
- Co-determination.
- Employee relations agreements.
- High performance team.

---

iii A story is told in the spiral dynamics circle that after Desmond Tutu worked with spiral dynamics, he called our country the Rainbow Nation.

All of these building blocks centre around the values, in this case, respect, responsibility and trust, in an effort to optimise employee relations in the organisation. In Figure 5.6 below, more detail of these eight steps in the co-determination journey is provided.

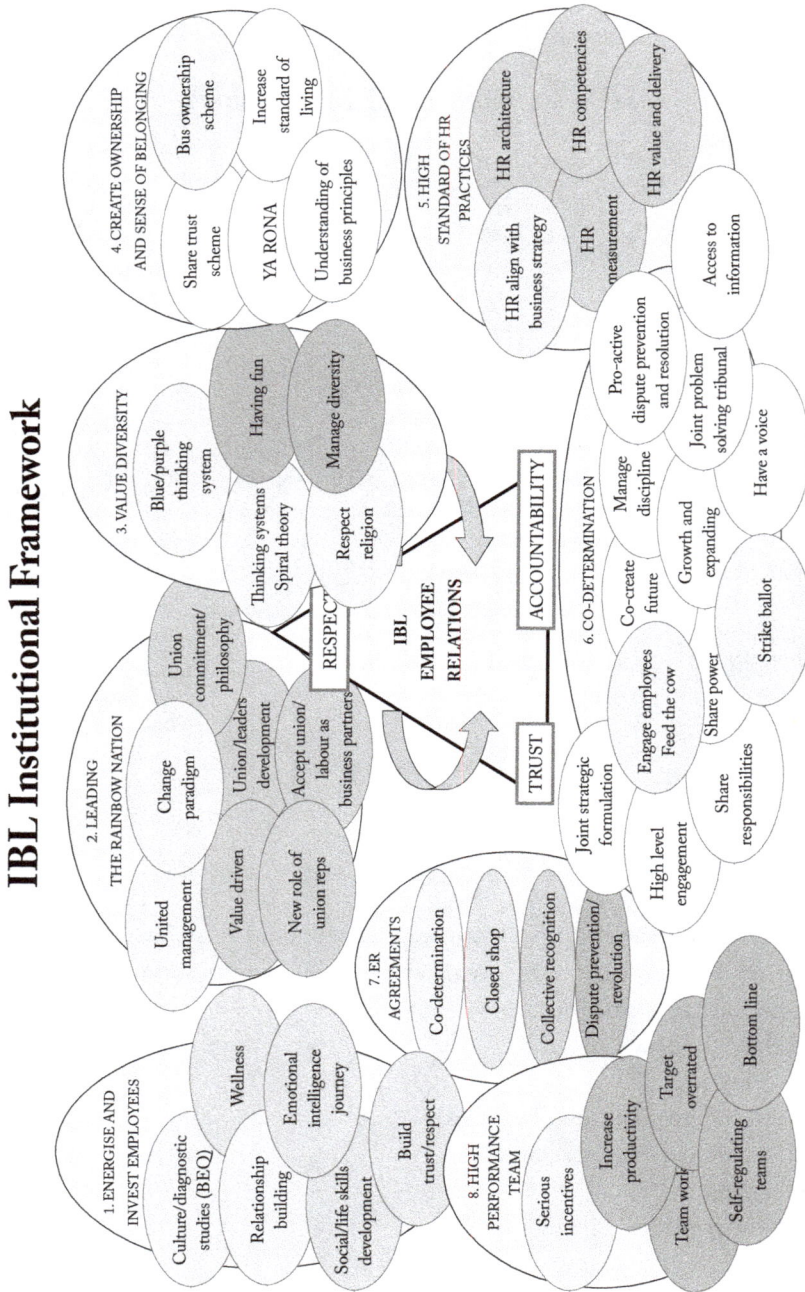

Figure 5.6: Comprehensive IBL institutional framework[19]

In Figure 5.6 above, the strategic doing process of co-determination, as implemented by IBL, is indicated. It should be highlighted that the process starts with an initial BeQ study to ensure that the dynamics on the individual, group, organisational and contextual levels are described in detail. Further, the philosophy and theory of spiral dynamics are deeply integrated into all the steps that directly impact behaviour. Next, excellent HR practices segment changes into practices. Lastly, without courageous leadership, an approach like this is almost impossible.

It is truly remarkable that, in an ER model, which is typically law-driven and BLUE[iv], the first four steps focus only on the relationship and resonant side of behaviour at the individual, group and organisational levels. Even the 5th step above is relational, where HR practices come in to ensure the cementing of the behavioural approach, before the actual contracting on co-determination starts. The fact that the model comes full circle by focusing on achievements and the high-performance part of the task execution is significant; the human energy is transformed into collective action to do business together.

The values of respect, trust and accountability are central to the approach and the framework.

Application of the co-determination framework

In this chapter, the theory of inclusivity, as a radical change method, was explained. Without inclusivity co-determination cannot be implemented – in fact, inclusivity is a critical pre-requisite for co-determination. Further, the Benchmark of Engagement, which is the first step of such an approach and can be seen in Figure 5.5 in the first bubble on the top left, has been introduced and discussed. In Chapter 3, with the discussion on spiral dynamics, the focus was placed on diversity of thought and the wonderful energy that our Rainbow Nation can unleash. In the words of Madiba:

"The time to build is upon us. We have at last achieved our emancipation. We pledge ourselves to liberate all our people from the continuing bondage of poverty, deprivation, suffering and discrimination. Let freedom reign. The sun shall never set on so glorious a human achievement. God bless Africa."

Nelson Mandela (10 May 1994)

If one integrates the findings of Clem Sunter and the dynamics and changes of the new world of work, and considers the social landscape in which businesses in South Africa operate, it becomes clear that strategic approaches that enable inclusivity, facilitate the co-creation of strategy, and lead to co-determination, are the way to go.

---

iv Spiral dynamics are discussed in Chapter 3. BLUE refers to a thinking structure that is risk adverse, long-term orientated, structured, and compliant.

CONCLUSION

The inclusivity framework uniquely positions the phenomenon of inclusivity as a radical transformational process. Co-determination is such a process. This integral process strongly suggests that by aligning the workforce around 'doing' and 'being', sustainable organisational transformation can be achieved.

Alvin Toffler in Power Shift[20] said:

> *"We actually have an immense repertoire of organisational forms to draw on – from jazz compos to espionage networks, from tribes and clans and councils of elders to monasteries and soccer teams. Each is good at some things and bad at other things. Each has its own unique ways of collecting and distributing information and ways of allocating power."*

Inclusivity is a **multi-dimensional** concept that is determined by sub-constructs at the individual, group and organisational levels. The national culture also impacts on the willingness of employees to engage. It is **not a quick fix.** It is hard work and some individuals will be lost during the process. It must not be perceived as merely a few mechanistic interventions, but as **a journey** – a new way of behaving. In designing a transformational strategy, careful consideration should be given to all sub-categories in terms of all domains, because a simplistic, mechanistic and disintegrated approach will not lead to sustainable transformation. It is **only a skilful and systemic design that acknowledges the causal interrelations that determine willingness to engage that will have a significant impact.** Almost no reference is made to the detail of the inclusivity process in this chapter, and nor were there explicit references to specific doing or being interventions. The process is experienced as an interrelated growth process which describes the **way** in which the processes happened. Inclusivity is experienced at **all levels of the organisation**. The organisational being should be optimised. That is the focus of the next chapter.

The doing side of an organisation, namely strategy and the translation and how it manifests in co-determination were described in this chapter. The theory of how to involve people through inclusivity on both the doing and the being side should further be explained. Chapter 3 focuses on this.

The different parts of the co-determination framework is described in different sections of this book. Different chapters of the book deal with critical pre-requisites for successful co-determination that should not be underestimated. These are that:
- co-determination is a radical transformational process, as new behaviours are required of everyone in the organisation (this chapter);
- the concept of inclusivity is a non-negotiable (this chapter);
- humans react in different ways to change – often not in a functional manner (Chapter 6); and

- without leadership, first from the top and later throughout the system, such a process cannot be implemented successfully (Chapter 7).

Inclusivity does not mean that there is similarity in terms of the group dynamics of the sub-groups within the system. If a climate is inclusive then the leader's natural style will emerge and his or her typology preferences will have a direct impact on the sub-climate that is created. Inclusivity relies heavily on the **leadership depth** within the organisation. The maturity level of the leaders within an organisation is of critical importance in the success of this approach. If the ego strength of the leader is not highly developed, then the leadership will not be shared within the group as willingly. Official conversations are dictated by the co-created objectives, goals and initiatives. Uniqueness and differences in terms of reasoning processes are allowed. On the other hand, non-conformity with values and principles will not be allowed, and non-performance will not be valued. The **maturity level** of the top leadership and union leadership is of critical importance in the success of this approach. Chapter 7 focuses on the important role that leadership must play for ensuring the success of such a radical transformational process.

In this chapter, it was argued that the best organising system is the one that is most congruent with the external life conditions and the corresponding thinking systems inside the organisation, and that through a radical transformational process such as co-determination through inclusivity, sustainable transformation, not only for the organisation but for the society, can be enabled. The human reaction to change should not be underestimated during a radical transformational process. This is described in the chapter to follow.

REFERENCES

Beck, D.E & Cowan, C.C. (1996): *Spiral dynamics: mastering values, leadership, and change*. Cambridge: Blackwell. p. 319.

Csikszentmihalyi, M. (1993), *The Evolving Self: A Psychology for the Third Millennium*, New York: HarperCollins, p. 120.

Graves, C. (1974): Human nature prepares for a momentous leap. *The Futurist*, April. p.72-87.

Interstate Bus Lines. (2015). IBL Strategy. Available at Interstate Bus Lines: Bloemfontein.

Jung, C.G. (1954). On the Nature of the Psyche. In H. Read, et al. (eds.). *The Collected Works of C. G. Jung* (vol. 8). Princeton: Princeton University Press.

Laubscher, L.I. (2013). *Human Niches: Spiral Dynamics for Africa*. Ph.D dissertation. Modderfontein: Da Vinci Institute. Retrieved from: https://www.mandalaconsulting.co.za/Documents/Thesis%20-%20Loraine%20Laubscher.pdf.

Martins, N. & Nienaber, H. (2016). *Employee engagement in a South African context*. Bryanston: KR Publishing.

Martins, E., Martins, N., & Viljoen RC. (2017). *Organisational Diagnostics*. Bryanston: KR Publishing.

Sparkes, A. C. (2007). Embodiment, academics, and the audit culture: a story seeking consideration. *Qualitative Research*, 7(24), 521-550.

Senge, P.M. (1993). *The fifth discipline*. London: Random House.

Toffler, A. (1986). *Powershift*. NY: Bantam Books.

Viljoen, R. (2016). Engagement in multi-cultural environments: Reflections and theoretical development. In N. Martins & H. Nienaber. (2016). *Employee engagement in a South African context*. Bryanston: KR Publishing.

Viljoen R.C. (2014). *Inclusive Organisational Transformation: An African Perspective on Human Niches and Diversity of Thought*. Farnham, UK: Gower. ISBN: 978-1-86922-540-7

Viljoen, R. (2015). *Organisational change and development – an African perspective*. Bryanston: KR Publishing.

Viljoen-Terblanche, R.C. (2009). *Sustainable organisational transformation through Inclusivity*. Unpublished PhD thesis. Unisa: Midrand. Retrieved from: http://uir.unisa.ac.za/bitstream/handle/10500/726/00thesis.pdf;sequence=2

Wilber, K. (1996). *A brief history of everything*. Boston. Shambhala Publishing.

ENDNOTES

1   Beck & Cowan, 1996, p. 319.
2   Csikszentmihalyi, 1993, p. 120.
3   Laubscher, 2013.
4   Graves, 1974.
5   Beck, 1996, Laubscher, 2013 & Viljoen, 2014; 2015; 2016.
6   Wilber, 1996, p. 7.
7   Sparkes, 2007.
8   Senge, 1993.
9   Viljoen-Terblanche, 2009, p. 347.
10 Viljoen-Terblanche, 2009, p. 360.
11 Ibid.
12 Jung, 1954.
13 Martins & Nienaber, 2016.
14 Viljoen in Nienaber & Martins, 2016.
15 Viljoen, 2014.
16 Viljoen, 2014.
17 Viljoen-Terblanche, 2009, p. 349.
18 IBL, 2015.
19 IBL, 2015.
20 Toffler, 1986.

6

HUMAN REACTIONS TO CHANGE

Tonja Blom and Rica Viljoen

INTRODUCTION

"Change means alteration, whether in the position, the state or the nature of a thing. Progress implies change, but not vice versa; not all changes are progressive."

Francisco J. Ayala (in Rosen & Rosen[1])

We live in an age of unprecedented change; change has become all pervasive, permeating every aspect of modern life.[2] Modernism is characterised by change, and the future has become unstable, unpredictable and non-recurring, which can cause a sense of loss and/or anxiety for individuals, organisations and society. Taleb[3] listed feelings of membership in the extended disorder family, namely uncertainty, variability, imperfect and incomplete knowledge, change, chaos, volatility, disorder, entropy, time, the unknown, randomness, turmoil, stressor, error, dispersion of outcomes and un-knowledge. In this modern day and age, such extended disorder has become the norm for society, organisations and individuals.

South Africa has been experiencing extraordinary change and transformation across all sectors of business, society and community, yet in all probability, when we look back at this period in history, the turbulence and amount of change will be nothing compared to that which is yet to come. However, because of the large amount of change in today's organisations, employees increasingly encounter new problems. This means that employees encounter problems with no procedures to follow and no obvious answers or solutions for new and unfamiliar situations. Co-determination, as a radical organisational transformation, asks employees, union representatives, unions and leadership to change, however human realities to change should not be underestimated and must managed deliberately.

Dahl[4] postulated that organisational change increases frustration and destabilises the organisation, which, in turn, increases employee stress and turnover. Broader and more extensive degrees of change further increase employee stress and turnover. Dahl's research indicated that service departments are more negatively affected by change, probably because services are characterised by more rapidly changing, dynamic conditions. Furthermore, if organisations change multiple core dimensions at the same time, employees are more likely to receive stress-related medication for insomnia and depression.

Through their research related to organisational change, Blom and Viljoen[5] found the work environment to be perceived as chronically stressful. At an individual level, the stressful work environment, coupled with the resultant unpredictability in the modern organisation, causes fear, stress and anxiety, which can easily result in a vicious cycle. In addition to the above, they found a lack of trusted outlets within the organisational setting where stress could be minimised. Viljoen-Terblanche[6] thus stressed the importance of leaders taking employees along with them during the transformational process.

This chapter attempts to elucidate change, human reactions to change, and the stress and anxiety that results.

CHANGE

Unintended social, environmental and economic consequences of rapid population growth, resource consumption, economic growth and commercial activity, alongside global trends in an increasingly interconnected and interdependent world, drive organisational change.[7] Managing change is difficult and amplified by the fact that there is little agreement on which factors most influence change initiatives, as both soft and hard measurable factors have a role to play.[8]

Viljoen-Terblanche[9] suggested that diversity is a driving force for change; organisations may be impacted by a combination of individual, group, organisational, South African and/or global diversity. The author extended the concept of diversity to "diversity of thought" – a much broader concept which includes aspects such as personality type, diverse intelligences, complexity handling and world views.

Change is generally implemented for positive reasons, but the low success rate of change programmes is often attributed to employee resistance.[10] Rosenberg and Mosca[11] attributed resistance to the poor execution of change strategies, inadequate communication and a lack of employee involvement schemes. According to Werkman, large, bureaucratic organisations with mechanistic structures can hinder change through too much managerial power and too many procedures and rules. Since communication in large, bureaucratic organisations is less personal and more formal, management's ability to effectively communicate organisational change is essential to mitigate the personal reasons for resistance to change, such as fear of the unknown, lack of understanding, disruption of routine, or perceived loss of security.[12]

Resistance to change

Lewin[13] first used the term "resistance to change" in the context of individual resistance to change, however use of the term evolved to refer to the resistance of organisations to make transitions and their inability to quickly and effectively react to change.[14] In the change literature, resistance to change is a recurring theme.[15]

The conventional change management literature[16] argues that resistance has different appearances, varying from foot-dragging and withdrawal, to material sabotage, whistleblowing[17], strikes, working to rule and symbolic sabotage.[18] Organisational change is desirable and inevitable, however, and people resisting change are framed as irrational.[19]

Because organisational change requires employees to adapt to new conditions, environments, contexts and positions, a certain level of change readiness[20] and resilience[21] is required. This highlights the role of individual competency, the potential individual contribution to make positive change, individual learning[22] and individual adaptation in order to participate in and not resist organisational change.[23] During organisational change, fear and uncertainty about the future could "lead some employees to leave and others to have mental problems".[24]

Negative emotions relating to organisational change

Organisational change is a primary cause of stress for individuals[25] due to feelings of uncertainty, insecurity and threat.[26] When organisational change occurs, individuals are often stressed by role overload, role ambiguity and role boundaries, which can affect human resource potential.[27]

Change compels employees to adapt to new circumstances, but retaining some stability enables them to maintain a sense of identity and understanding.[28] Because one of the main aspects of human nature is people's inherent need for predictability and order[29], one should bear in mind that major organisational change may be experienced in ways that contradict this basic need and deplete employees' adaptive resources.[30] Although scant attention has been paid to investigating such possibilities, research has shown that an overemphasis on organisational change may come at the expense of other important organisational factors, such as commitment or satisfaction.[31] Other studies have indicated that the potential for negative outcomes is particularly heightened when the rate of change is perceived as being too frequent.[32]

When change is perceived as a discrete event with a beginning and an end, employees are better able to predict and adjust their behaviour accordingly.[33] Alternatively, when an organisation is in a state of continuous flux, employees are unable to align their thoughts and actions with the expectations of organisational leaders. Marks[34] proposed a saturation effect, i.e. employees can handle only so much disruption. Bernerth et al.[35] implicitly suggested that there may be a moment where change becomes too much; exhaustion is the central mechanism through which change fatigue drives employees' affective reactions (such as less commitment) and behavioural intentions (such as turnover intention).

Conceptually, exhaustion emerged from Maslach and Jackson's[36] early work on employee burnout. Originally deemed to be only one of the three components of burnout (emotional exhaustion, depersonalisation and diminished personal accomplishment), exhaustion has more recently emerged as the central variable in understanding the burnout process.[37] Exhaustion is a feeling of being depleted or overextended beyond one's capacity to handle workplace demands. The energy to perform basic job tasks disappears and employees are left feeling drained.[38] Burnout is a serious, multi-factorial syndrome which may be caused by organisational factors (as opposed to employee-related factors) such as the presence of severe, improper, unsupported working conditions and improper leadership style practices.[39]

Dahl's[40] research examined the effect of organisational change on the likelihood that individual employees leave the organisation or receive stress-related medication. The author found that employees of organisations with large degrees of change have a significantly higher risk of experiencing stress (receiving prescriptions for stress-related conditions) and/or leaving the organisation. Dahl further argued that organisational change can lead to employee frustration and uncertainty, because organisational change threatens the identity and implicit contract of the organisation with its employees. Furthermore, increased frustration, uncertainty, fear and the instability induced by organisational change will increase the stress on employees while increasing the risk of employees leaving the organisation.

Research by Loh et al.[41] found the relationship with one's superior to be a key source of pressure. Distinguishing acceptable stress from excessive stress has a significant impact on the success of organisational change.[42] The overwhelming effect of stress on employees can be devastating and the cost to the organisation enormous[43], with detrimental consequences including higher absenteeism, lower productivity, lower job satisfaction and low morale.[44]

HUMAN REACTIONS TO CHANGE

There are currently huge changes in virtually all dimensions of the socio-economic environment.[45] Concerns focusing on issues such as business, government, politics, education, health and social care, religion, management, leading, investing, borrowing, buying, owning, working and innovating are permeating societies as never before.[46] Unfortunately, the reality is that humans do not take kindly to change. Wild ideas scare people; they fill them with anxiety and doubt. Straying grotesquely from the beaten path makes humans fearful and even self-destructive.[47]

Blom and Viljoen[48] found that organisational change results in fear, stress and anxiety. Furthermore, human reactions to change could stem from the individual, groups, community, the organisation, leadership, management or a combination of these. Fear of the unknown, habit, self-interest and economic insecurity, as well as a failure to recognise the need for change, distrust, perceptions and scepticism, were all identified as factors that contribute to stress and an individual's resistance to change.

South African organisations are constantly changing. Not only are organisations busy with radical changes, which result in the upheaval of a lot of known elements, but the frequency rate of change is also extremely high. Through their interviews with people who had recently undergone major organisational change, Blom and Viljoen[49] found that organisations are typically busy with more than three major changes at any point in time. In addition, the authors found that there was no mourning (shock, disbelief, discard and eventual realisation). The individuals who were interviewed still seemed to be in a state of shock and/or disbelief. The required processes of discarding and realisation, or "clarify, crystallise and change", had apparently not started. In Figure 6.1 below, Viljoen-Terblanche[50] portrays superimposed different change models to present a comprehensive gestalt of how humans react to change during radical transformation efforts such as co-determination.

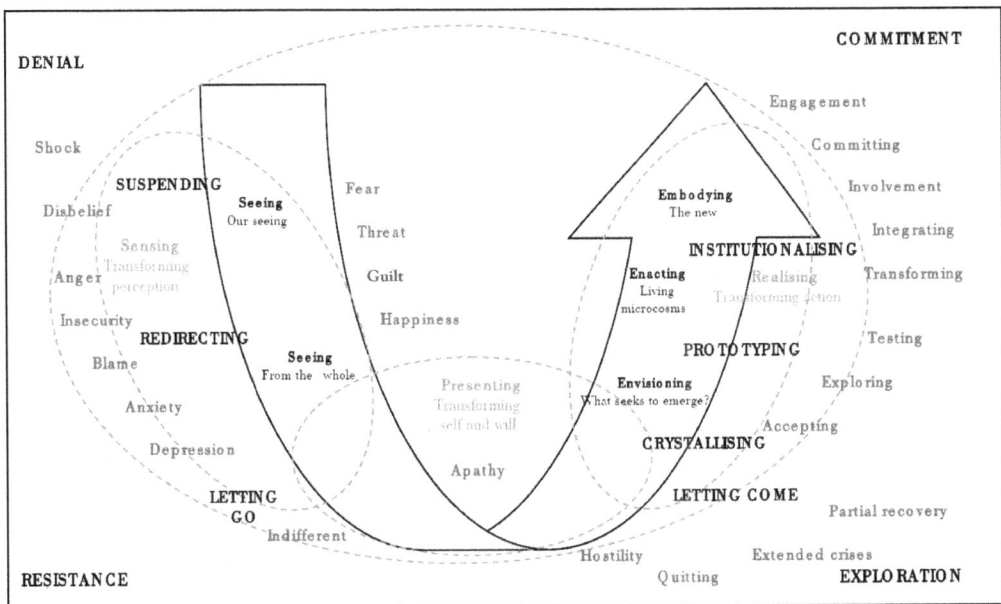

Figure 6.1: Models of comprehensive gestalt[51]

Blom and Viljoen[52] found that all of the above factors are influenced by increased stress levels, which in turn result in stress-related behaviours, coupled with decreased cognitive capacity. While certain change models acknowledge emotions and their role, the impact of stress appears to be ignored, despite the fact that elevated stress levels could hamper individual movement towards change acceptance.

THE IMPACT OF STRESS IN THE SOUTH AFRICAN ORGANISATIONAL CONTEXT

Life in general has become more stressful. Time pressures within time-compressed lifestyles[53] are stressors faced by many working individuals. Unrelieved stress becomes perpetual, and will undeniably influence organisational change efforts negatively. Dahl[54] confirmed this, indicating that despite the long-standing focus on change management, the average organisation is unable to control the process of change without significant negative consequences. Numerous research reports have revealed that employees who experience large-scale change report higher levels of stress, more anxiety and increased feelings of uncertainty.[55]

Within an organisational change context, Blom and Viljoen[56] found stress, anxiety, reduced autonomy, reduced ability and even total shutdown. One would assume that it is unlikely that an individual would be unable to function optimally, given such feelings. However, in the South African context, poverty, migrant labour, energy supply challenges, public anger, alcohol abuse and domestic violence are added stressors. Statistics on rape, crime, violent crime, uncontrolled shootings, domestic violence, racial and political violence, and road accidents are commonly available.[57]

It is unlikely that many individuals would remain unaffected by the above. Given these added stressors, coupled with organisational change, there could well be a moment when change becomes overwhelming. The additional stress caused by organisational changes therefore creates huge challenges for leadership and organisations.

Our inherent need for predictability and order

Our brains have an inherent need for predictability and order[58], yet in response to a diverse range of challenges, organisations are increasingly engaging in change initiatives.[59] Such organisational change necessitates that employees adapt to new circumstances, which may contradict this basic need while depleting employees' adaptive resources.[60]

Ambiguity activates the threat circuitry in the brain[61], as does reduced autonomy. Stress also reduces working memory and results in significant cognitive impairment, affecting basic perception as well as decision-making.[62] To a large extent, organisational change implies turmoil, ambiguity, uncertainty and a loss of control. This, in turn, may heighten employees' feelings of anxiousness.[63] However, when we feel in control, this results in an up-tweak of the brain, hormones and immune system, controlling upshifts in our physiology.[64]

Typically, the brain and spinal cord work together, but when in a stressful situation, the spinal cord will act before the information enters the brain for processing.[65] The human brain is wired to make general assumptions from experience, i.e. humans think much less than we believe we do and most of our actions are instinctive. Humans get lost in the details; they only react.[66] With stress, the brain disconnects more often from the task at hand.[67] Individuals are particularly stressed by organisational change, to such an extent that many participants are not able to function optimally; they disconnect from the task at hand or are unable to think of ways to improve their situation.[68]

The concept of optimal stress arose from the Yerkes Dodson Law. This law is depicted in Figure 6.2, indicating the familiar inverted U diagram.[69] The inverted U is often drawn with stress or arousal on the horizontal axis and performance on the vertical axis. Common management practice assumes through the application of the Yerkes Dodson Law that a reasonable amount of pressure, anxiety or fear in the environment leads to higher performance than if stress is not present.[70]

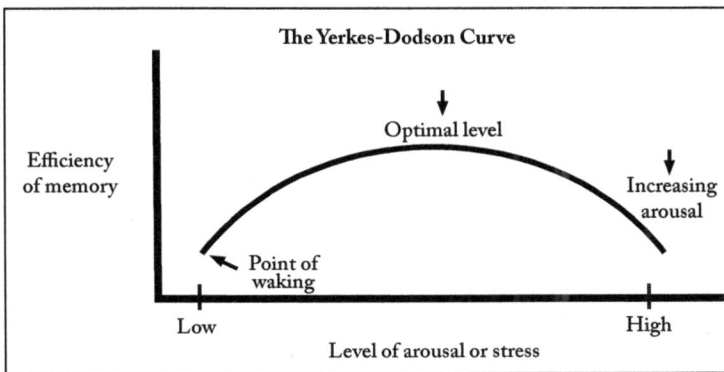

Figure 6.2: Yerkes Dodson Law[71]

Figure 6.2 indicates that increasing stress is beneficial to performance until an optimum level is reached, after which performance declines.[72] However, "stress", "arousal" and "performance" do not appear at any time in the original paper.[73] Their work explored the relationship between the strength of stimuli (threat of electrical shock – demand) and task acquisition (choosing the right box – performance) in mice. Selye[74] observed that the individual determines whether the stressor is to be eustress or distress. Whether a particular demand represents eustress or distress is determined not only by the amount of demand perceived by the individual, but also by an individual's perceptions of the demand's other characteristics.[75]

It is not at all clear that Yerkes and Dodson's[76] findings should be applied to human work environments and considered the truth regarding the beneficial effects of optimal workplace stress.[77] It is also unfortunate that the inverted U form, as well as the principles derived from it, continue to be included in contemporary management texts[78], completely disregarding the potential for negative outcomes which are heightened by a too frequent rate of change.[79]

Stress and anxiety defined

Given the prominence of stress and anxiety, ensuring a uniform definition and understanding of these concepts are important. Stress and anxiety are close companions, which often trigger each other. Stress comes from a feeling that certain circumstances should not be happening, while anxiety stems from the feeling that something should be happening but is not. In both stress and anxiety, our inner experience is that we want to be somewhere other than where we are.[80]

Various definitions of stress exist and differ depending on whether stress is being defined by psychologists, medical practitioners or management staff. Stress, as used in the literature, may refer to external influences acting on individuals[81]; physiological reactions to such influences (Selye's original stress concept)[82]; the psychological interpretation of both the external influences and the physiological reactions[83]; and adverse behavioural reactions exhibited in work or social situations, or both.[84]

However, the most apt definition comes from the founding father of stress research, Selye, who introduced the concept of stress as a medical and scientific entity.[85] He coined the term "stress" to describe a set of physical and psychological responses to adverse conditions or influences, applying the engineering term "stress" (a force which causes deformation in bodies) to describe the stereotypical response of an organism to a wide range of chemical, biological or physical stimuli. He also recognised that stress included both a neurological and a physiological reaction. This concept of neurophysiology distinguished psychology (content of thoughts in the brain) from neurology (the way the brain processes that content).[86] He further defined stress as "…the non-specific response of the body to any demand placed upon it" and differentiated between eustress and distress, i.e. eustress is good stress, while distress occurs when demands placed on the body exceed its capacity to expend energy in maintaining homeostasis[87].

Anxiety

"Anxiety is the most powerful and pervasive of all emotions"[88], which can easily dominate all brain processes, distort experience and sharply interfere with the mind/brain. The singularly intolerable to the brain is anxiety. Anxiety is also the great enemy of intelligence and development, and is peculiarly contagious.[89] According to Lazarus[90], anxiety is a feeling of uneasiness and apprehension about a situation, typically one with an uncertain outcome.

Fear and anxiety both reflect the high end of the arousal continuum, however fear is a response to a specific threat, while anxiety is vague and relatively unfocused.[91] Various authors have explained that anxiety is a product of the human biological response to stressful experiences in society[92], whereas fear is a form of arousal that prepares us to fight back rather than give up, driving us toward group unity.[93]

The Merriam-Webster Dictionary[94] defined anxiety as "fear or nervousness about what might happen; apprehensive uneasiness of mind over an impending or anticipated ill; an overwhelming sense of apprehension and fear marked by physiological signs (such as sweating, tension and increased pulse), by doubt concerning the reality and nature of the threat and by self-doubt about one's capacity to cope with it". Speilberger[95], meanwhile, defined anxiety as an "…unpleasant emotional state or condition, which is characterised by subjective feelings of tension, apprehension, and worry, and by activation or arousal of the autonomic nervous system". More specifically, anxiety can be defined as "a cognitive-affective response characterised by physiological arousal (indicative of the sympathetic nervous system activation) and apprehension regarding a potentially negative outcome that the individual perceives as impending".[96]

LeDoux[97] defined anxiety as unresolved fear, while Sapolsky[98] suggested that anxiety is a sense of disquiet or disease created by dread and foreboding. The sensations of anxiety are so closely related in the neural structures of the brain that Ohman and Mineka[99] argued that panic, phobic fear and post-traumatic stress disorder all reflect the single underlying response of anxiety. Berceli[100] added to this, arguing that, "Anxiety is unresolved fear". Interestingly, anxiety and depression are predicted to be the single major burden of disease within the next two decades.[101]

Anxiety has a worry and emotionality component; worry is the cognitive aspect that results in troubling thoughts and beliefs about one's own ability to deal with a situation, while emotionality is the affective aspect resulting in physiological responses such as muscular tension, stomach butterflies, increased heart rate, perspiration, restlessness and pacing.[102] Ormrod[103] identified state and trait anxiety. The former is a temporary condition elicited by a particular stimulus; an individual might experience state anxiety while working on a challenging problem or project. The latter is a relatively stable situation of affairs, such that an individual is chronically anxious in certain situations.

The problem with merely passing through a stressful or anxious time is that nothing has really changed; we may have left a difficult situation behind, but we have not yet changed. We have, in fact, reinforced our weakness in the face of stress or anxiety. This leaves us even more vulnerable to the next source of distress.[104] Furthermore, Selye[105] demonstrated that the same neuro-physiological effects of stress were experienced, irrespective of whether the stress situation was positive or negative.

Penn[106] indicated that anxiety becomes pathological when it persists and disrupts an individual's social and/or occupational functioning. The participants in Blom's[107] research reported increased anxiety, stress and fear levels, uneasiness and feelings of worthlessness. They also mentioned a loss of autonomy and relatedness during periods of organisational change. It seems clear that all the individuals interviewed experienced anxiety during organisational change. The organisational challenge therefore seems to be how to find workable methods to reduce stress and anxiety before it becomes persistent, intense, chronic or recurring, not justified by real-life stresses, problematic and hampering individual functioning.

STRESS AND THE SOUTH AFRICAN ORGANISATION

Unfortunately, if we seek security in today's organisations, counter to our instinctive foundations, it may only heighten our anxieties and further our suspicions. The security that we seek and that we inherently know was provided by early groups does not exist in the culture of the groups that support our survival today. This causes confusion and sows further seeds of mistrust, while planting questions about trustworthiness.[108]

Stress in South African society is very real. Given the large percentage of PURPLE in this country and their interconnectedness, the likelihood of societal stress impacting on individuals is high. In addition, increased stressors will probably result in a downshift of human niches. Knowing that organisational change increases stress, it seems unreasonable to expect optimal performance or even enthusiasm during times of organisational change, because organisational change adds further stressors to an already stressed individual. Again, this underscores the importance of finding workable interventions to alleviate individual stress, more so during times of organisational change.

Organisational ecologists[109] have long argued that organisational change and transformation are rarely completely positive experiences, especially when the core features and core identities of the organisation are subject to change. The authors added that there are substantial obstacles to fundamental structural changes in organisations, because changes can fuel undesirable effects on employees such as increased uncertainty, fear, frustration and occupational stress.

Organisations are built on high levels of internal trust and reliability, where employees are loyal and committed to the organisation and the implicit contract they have with it. Fundamental changes - shifts in core strategies or goals - threaten these values.[110] Organisational changes have often been viewed as a threat to organisational identity[111], and this is especially true where the identity is well established in the organisation. Changes that deeply influence the identity erode its reliability and accountability, leading to frustration and confusion. A destabilisation process follows, which involves significant costs to reshape operations and realign the organisation.[112] Corbitt[113] confirmed this, stating that the overwhelming effect of stress on employees can be devastating to them, and the cost to the organisation enormous. Furthermore, a disruption in the social environment affects individuals' higher-order thinking.[114] Organisational stressors are concerned with aspects of employees' jobs or organisation that can lead to adverse physical and psychological reactions, or strain that can be chronic or acute.[115]

Stressors are also associated with absenteeism[116], which seems a likely outcome when the other effects of traumatic events are considered. People exposed to traumatic events exhibit a range of negative psychological reactions, including emotional numbing, social withdrawal, irritability, fearfulness, depression, sleep disturbances, substance abuse and marital problems.[117] These people are also more likely to experience protracted medical problems.[118]

Examples of internal pressures are ineffective leadership, morale problems, a high turnover of capable people, absenteeism, labour problems, increased political behaviour in the organisation and turf fights.[119] Instead of minimising workplace stress levels, organisations are encouraged to manage stress to optimal levels.[120]

The theoretical framework of Lazarus and Folkman's[121] psychosocial model of stress and coping provides an effective basis for explaining the role of perceived available support. Blom's[122] PhD data confirmed this, indicating that organisations are unable to handle or support increased stress levels. In addition, all participants indicated that they had sought support outside of the organisation.

CHANGE AND/OR CHAOS IN THE CHANGING WORLD OF WORK

The impact of stress on individuals

The impact of stress on individuals has been reiterated throughout this study. In relating the information in this chapter to the case study and the collected data, it becomes clear that many individuals operate in fight/flight/freeze mode on a daily basis. Slumped body postures, reduced ability and skewed perceptions all indicate increased stress, while aggression, defensiveness, resistance, emotional behaviours, hostility and anger are all indicative of a stressed organism.

Laubscher[123] highlighted the fact that when under stress, our human niches close down as the question of existence changes to cope with new life conditions. ORANGE and BLUE human niches can become RED in times of stress, while PURPLE human niches can regress to BEIGE.

Organisational change is a complex adaptive system

Organisational change is complex, with disequilibrium and instability morphing and evolving in unpredictable ways. Such complexity and unpredictability tax the ability of individuals, leaders and their organisations. Thoughts on complexity theory and chaos theory naturally developed alongside Blom's[124] data findings. Complexity is generally used to characterise something with many parts that interact in multiple ways. Complex systems investigate how the relationships between parts give rise to the collective behaviours of a system, and how the system interacts and forms relationships with its environment.[125]

Complexity theory is rooted in chaos theory, which views chaos as extremely complicated information as opposed to the absence of order. Chaos theory concerns deterministic systems whose behaviour can, in principle, be predicted. Chaotic systems are predictable for a while and then appear to become random.[126] Chaos theory recognises that the future is unknowable, yet allows for the possibility of an awareness of a variety of future states. Moreover, chaos theory suggests that complete and accurate information, which is necessary for rational decision-making, is unobtainable.[127]

Unpredictability and chaos manifest during times of organisational change. Individual behaviour becomes unpredictable owing to increased stress, while accurate information sharing is challenging because of a constantly changing future state. Both chaos and complexity theory reiterate the necessity to boldly re-evaluate traditional organisational problem-solving methods.

Organisations are complex systems; Grant[128] described the common features of complex systems as unpredictability, self-organisation, inertia and chaos. A by-product of organisational struggles for survival and adaptation is organisational change, as current processes and methods struggle to keep abreast of competitors while exhausting those individuals involved. Cost reductions and chasing of profit margins can no longer sustain organisations, thus without effective adaptation methods, organisations may perish. With effective adaptation methods, new behaviours can emerge.

The science of complexity yielded three principles to be applied to organisational change. Firstly, complex adaptive systems are at risk when in equilibrium, which is the precursor to death.[129] In organisational terms, equilibrium equals stagnation. Organisational change is a direct result of the struggle to adapt and evolve in the continuous struggle for survival. The data clearly indicated that change is the new stability - organisations are in a constant state of disequilibrium.

Secondly, complex adaptive systems exhibit the capacity of self-organisation and emergent complexity.[130] The accelerating complexity in organisations demonstrates this principle.

Thirdly, complex adaptive systems tend to move towards the edge of chaos when provoked by complexity. An important corollary to this principle is that a complex adaptive system, once it has reached a peak or a golden era in the case of an organisation, must go down to go up, i.e. the system must be pulled far enough out of its usual arrangements before it can create substantially different forms and arrive at a more evolved basin of attraction.[131]

This principle holds true for individuals who need to regress before upshift becomes possible, and relates to the regression of human niches when under stress in order to upshift. This is displayed in Figure 6.3.

Figure 6.3 confirms that different people excel differently. PURPLE, as the predominant human niche in Africa, brings with it innate wisdom and goodwill, thus organisational thinking systems must embrace this. This requires organisations, which predominantly fall within the BLUE human niche, to alter their thinking system which believes that the organisation is always right. The BLUE organisation needs to alter and/or adjust its dogmatic and mechanistic thinking to embrace more humanistic methods in order to be understood by PURPLE.

Stress results in a downshift of the human niche (see Figure 6.3 below). Stress in South Africa is very real, as is stress in organisations, and repeated stress responses in organisations are a reality. Individual stress in organisations undergoing any form of change can no longer be ignored.

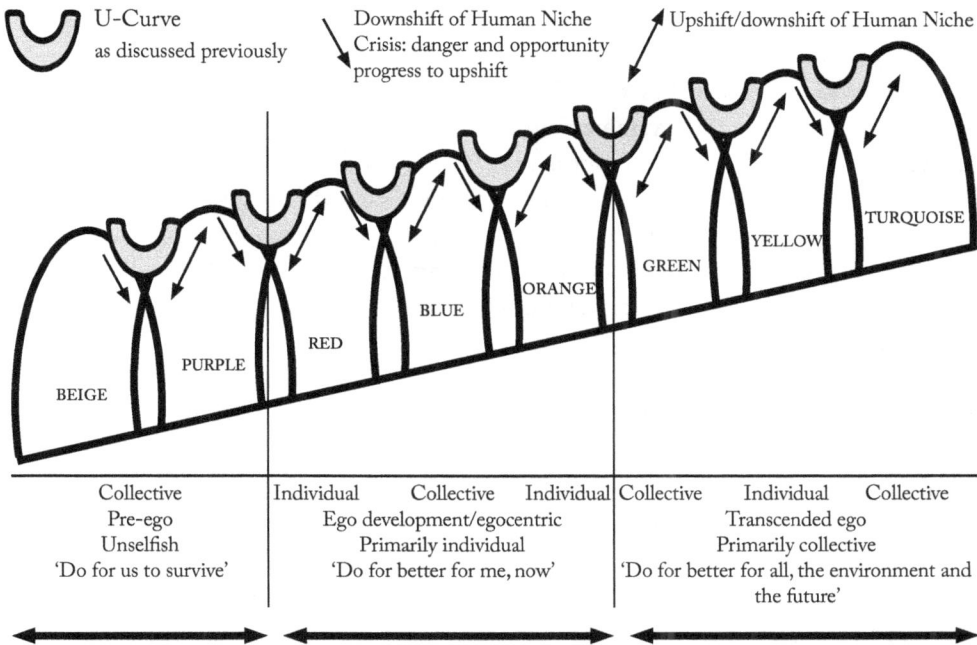

Figure 6.3: Downshift of the human niche when under stress

Organisational change creates ambiguity and uncertainty, yet PURPLE[i] seeks group safety; the organisation remains one of the fundamental groups in which PURPLE operates. When safety and security are removed, PURPLE can no longer function optimally. Organisational change initiators need a deep awareness of PURPLE as well as relevant strategies that can address the uncertainties created by organisational change.

However, Figure 6.3 also indicates that once downshifted, an upshift becomes possible. In the researcher's opinion, today's organisations need alternative interventions that could assist the individual to firstly reduce stress and anxiety, and secondly to allow the individual to regress to the BEIGE human niche from where upshift becomes possible. This thought should serve as a further building block element in the emerging conceptual change framework.

A living system cannot be directed, only disturbed[132], and living systems are easily disturbed. Complex adaptive systems are characterised by weak cause and effect links; large changes may have little effect, while small changes may result in a huge effect. Many organisations have attempted large scale change, which had hardly any impact.

All of the above hold true for organisational change. We thus have to reframe our reference of organisational change as organisations need to be in a constant state of adaptive ability. Because change is complex, it is constantly moving towards the edge

---

i   Refer to the theory in Chapter 3 on human niches

of chaos. Organisational change is a complex adaptive system whose very survival depends on adaptive equilibrium. Two laws play a role here – Einstein's[133] second law of thermo dynamics says that the energy in a system will wind down without external interaction, while systems thinking[134] teaches that a system will move back into a state of equilibrium. To adapt is not that easy. Viljoen[135] described the stages of change, as conceptualised by Beck[136], by explaining that if a system is in gamma, it is really stuck. To move through this gamma stage, solid leadership is important. For as long as employees distrust leadership, unions can step into this relationship. To now start trusting that both leadership and unions have their best interests at heart can be tremendously challenging.

CONCLUSION

An analogy can be drawn between organisational change and working the land. When working the land, a team of oxen is yoked with the plough-boy in front. The plough-boy makes few, if any, decisions - his only function is to follow, albeit from the front. The driver of the team of oxen is at the back or on the side of the team, sometimes sitting in the wagon from where he directs and drives the team and the plough-boy. Occasionally, the plough-boy knows where to go and leads the entire team, with the driver merely determining the tempo or pace of work.

Furthermore, each ox has its special place in the team. Generally, the two tamest oxen are at the back to stabilise the entire operation. The driver knows each ox intimately, knowing what can be expected of each and every one. Each ox is placed according to its ability, strength and skill. When an ox becomes ill or "stressed", it has to be replaced by a fresh ox, and the unfit ox has to be treated or rested.

Similarly, during organisational change, the leader should be guiding from behind, allowing the leaders of teams to take up their roles. The leader should be intimately familiar with the strengths, abilities and condition of each and every employee, while ensuring role clarity for all involved in organisational change. The strengths of every employee should be aligned to job requirements where these strengths can best be utilised to achieve organisational objectives. Leaders have to consider the replacement of unfit role players, for whatever reason.

The need for a new frame of reference when embarking upon organisational change like co-determination is clear, as the reality of fear, stress and anxiety, as well as the impact thereof on individual functioning, is evident. The first and often lasting emotion when discussing organisational change is fear; productivity is impossible when individuals are caught up in the vicious cycle that is fear, stress and anxiety. The strengths of every individual can only be fully utilised when their stress levels are in a state of homeostasis or at least reduced. In the next chapter, the importance of leadership during a radical change process is described.

REFERENCES

Ackoff, R.L. (2010). *Systems Thinking for Curious Managers*. New York: Triarchy Press.

Einstein, A. (1967). In M.J. Klein, *Thermodynamics in Einstein's Universe*, in Science, 157 p. 509.

Armenakis, A., & Bedeian, A. (1999). Organisational change: a review of theory and research. *Journal of Management, 25*(3), 293-315.

Atkinson, P. (2005). Managing resistance to change. *Management Services, 49*(1), 14–19.

Avey, J.B., Wernsing, T. S., & Luthans, F. (2008). Can positive employees help positive organisational change? *Journal of Applied Behavioural Science, 44*(1), 48-70.

Bar-Yam, T. (2002). *General features of complex systems. Encyclopaedia of life support systems*. Oxford: EOLSS UNESCO Publishers.

Bateh, J., Castaneda, M.E., & Farah, J.E. (2013). Employee resistance to organisational change. *International Journal of Management and Information Systems, 17*(2), 113-116.

Baumeister, R.F., Twenge, J.M., & Nuss, C.K. (2002). Effects of social exclusion on cognitive processes: anticipated aloneness reduces intelligent thought. *Journal of Personality and Social Psychology, 83*(4), 817-827.

Beck, D., Larsen,T., Solonin, T., Viljoen, R.C., & Thomas, T.Q. (2018). *Spiral dynamics in Action: Humanity's Master Code*. London: Wiley.

Beer, M., & Nohria, N. (2000). Cracking the code of change. *Harvard Business Review*, May/June, 133–141.

Beehr, T.A., Jex, S.M., Stacy, B.A., & Murray, M.A. (2000). Work stressors and coworkers support as predictors of individual strain and job performance. *Journal of Organizational Behavior*, 21, 391–405.

Berceli, D. (2012). *The revolutionary trauma release process: transcend your toughest times* (5th ed.). Vancouver: Namaste Publishing.

Bercovitz, J., & Feldman, M. (2008). Academic entrepreneurs: organisational change at the individual level. *Organisation Science, 19*(1), 69-89.

Bernerth, J.B., Walker, H.J., & Harris, S.G. (2011). Change fatigue: development and initial validation of a new measure. *Work and Stress, 25*(4), 321-337. Doi:10.1080/02678373.2011.634280.

Blom, T. (2015). *Fusing Organisational Change and Leadership into a Practical Roadmap for South African Organisations*. Master's Thesis. Pretoria :University of South Africa.

Bloom, H. (2010). *The genius of the beast. a radical re-vision of capitalism*. New York: Prometheus Books.

Carr, J.B., & Brower, R. S. (2000). Principled opportunism. *Public Affairs Quarterly*, Spring, 109-138.

Carter, R., Williams, S., & Silverman, W.K. (2008). Cognitive and emotional facets of test anxiety in African American school children. *Cognition and Emotion*, 22, 539–551.

Certo, S.C. (2003). *Supervision: concepts and skill building* (4th ed.). New York: McGraw Hill.

Chen, I.S. (2011). Choosing the right channels of communication and moderating stress levels during organizational change. *International Journal of Management and Innovation, 3*(1), 43-44.

Code, S., & Langan-Fox, J. (2001). Motivation, cognitions and traits: predicting occupational health, well-being and performance. *Stress and Health*, 17, 159-74.

Cohen, S. (2004). Social relationships and health. *American Psychologist*, 59, 676-684.

Corbitt, C.M. (2005). The cost of job stress. *Meditation Media*, July. Retrieved from: <https://www.mediate.com/articles/clarkM1.cfm>.

Coy, P. (3 November 2008). Surviving the storm. *Business Week*, pp. 48 – 50.

Cropanzano, R., Rupp, D.E., & Byrne, Z.S. (2003). The relationship of emotional exhaustion to work attitudes, job performance, and organisational citizenship behaviors. *Journal of Applied Psychology*, 88, 160-169.

Cummings, T.G. & Worley, C.G. (2005). *Organisation development and change*, Mason, OH: Thomson.

Dahl, M.S. (*28* February 2009). *The cancer of organizational change*. Preliminary Draft.

Darling, J.R., & Heller, V.L. (2011). The key for effective stress management: importance of responsive leadership in organisational development. *Organisational Development Journal, 29*(1), 1-26.

Di Virgilio, M.E. & Ludema, J.D. (2009). Let's talk: creative energy for action through strategic conversations. *Journal of Change Management, 9*(1), 76-85.

Eisenbach, R., Watson, K., & Pillai, R. (1999). Transformational leadership in the context of organisational change. *Journal of Organisational Change Management, 12*(2), 80–88.

Fleming, P., & Spicer, A. (2003). Working at a cynical distance: implications for power, subjectivity and resistance. *Organisation, 10*(1), 157-179.

Ford, J.D., Ford, L.W., & D'Amelio, A. (2008). Resistance to change: the rest of the story. *Academy of Management Review, 33*(2), 362–377.

Fram, E.H. (1992). Stressed out consumers need timesaving innovations. *Marketing News, 26*(5), 10-11.

Grady, J., & Grady, V. (2011). Organisational mistrust: exploring the issues, pondering its fate. *Organisational and Social Dynamics, 11*(1), 41-58.

Halbesleben, J.R.B., & Buckley, M.R. (2004). Burnout in organisational life. *Journal of Management*, 30, 859-879.

Hannan, M.T., & Freeman, J. (1989). *Organizational ecology*. Cambridge: Harvard University Press.

Hannan, M.T., Baron, J.N., Hsu, G. & Koğcak, Ő. (2006). Organizational identities and the hazard of change. *Industrial and Corporate Change*, 15, 755-784.

Hansson, A., Vingard, E., Arnetz, B.B., & Anderzen, I. (2008). Organisational change, health, and sick leave among health care employees: a longitudinal study measuring stress markers, individual, and work site factors. *Work and Stress*, 22, 69-80.

Hayles, N.K. (1991). *Chaos bound: orderly disorder in contemporary literature and science*. Ithaca, NY: Cornell University Press.

Hsu, G., & Hannan, M.T. (2005). Identities, genres, and organizational forms. *Organization Science*, 16, 474-490.

Hogan, R. (2007). *Personality and the fate of organisations*. Mahwah, NJ: Erlbaum.

Holland, J.H. (1998). *Hidden order*. Reading. MA: Addison-Wesley.

Huy, Q.N. (1999). Emotional capability, emotional intelligence, and radical change. *Academy of Management Review*, 24, 325-345.

Huy, Q.N. (2001). Time, temporal capability, and planned change. *Academy of Management Review*, 26, 601-623.

Jimmieson, N.L., Terry, D.J., & Callan, V.J. (2004). A longitudinal study of employee adaptation to organisational change: the role of change-related Information and change-related self-efficacy. *Journal of Occupational health Psychology, 9*(1), 11-27.

Jones, L., Watson, B., Hobman, E., Bordia, P., Gallois, C., & Callan, V.J. (2008). Employee perceptions of organizational change: impact of hierarchical level. *Leadership and Organisation Development Journal, 29*(4), 294-316.

Judge, T.A., Thoresen, C.J., Pucik, V., & Welbourne, T.M. (1999). Managerial coping with organisational change: a dispositional perspective. *Journal of Applied Psychology*, 84, 107-122.

Kauffman, S.A. (1998a). *At home in the universe*. New York: Oxford University Press.

Kauffman, S.A. (1998b). *The origins of order: self-organisation and selection in evolution*. New York: Oxford University Press.

Kets De Vries, M.F.R. (2001). *The leadership mystique*. London: Prentice Hall.

Kinnear, C., & Roodt, G. (1998). The development of an instrument for measuring organisational inertia. *Journal of Industrial Psychology, 24*(2), 44-54.

Landeweed, J.A., & Boumans, N.P.G. (1994). The effect of work dimensions and need for autonomy on nurses work satisfaction and health. *Journal of Occupational and Organizational Psychology*, 67, 207–217.

Laubscher, L. (2014). Human niche expert. Personal interview, Johannesburg, 16 July.

Lazarus, R.S. (1991). *Emotion and adaptation.* New York: Oxford University Press.

Lazarus, R.S., & Folkman, S. (1984). *Stress, appraisal, and coping.* New York, NY: Springer.

LeDoux, J. (1996). *The emotional brain: The mysterious underpinnings of emotional life.* New York: Simon & Schuster.

Le Fevre, M., Matheny, J., & Kolt, G.S. (2003). Eustress, distress and interpretation in occupational stress. *Journal of Managerial Psychology, 18*(7), 726-744.

Lewin, K. (1952). Frontiers in group dynamics. In D. Cartwright (ed.). *Field Theory in Social Science: Selected Theoretical Papers by Kurt Lewin.* London: Tavistock. pp 188-237.

Loh, S.Y., Than, W., & Quek, K.F. (2011). Occupational pressure: targeting organisational factors to ameliorate occupational dysfunction. *Journal of Occupational Rehabilitation,* 21, 493-500.

Lussier, R.N. (2002). *Human relations in organizations: applications and skill building* (5th ed.). New York: McGraw-Hill.

Marks, M.L. (2003). *Charging back up the hill: workplace recovery after mergers, acquisitions, and downsizings.* San Francisco, CA: Jossey-Bass.

Martin, A., Jones, E., & Callan, V. (2006). Status differences in employee adjustment during organisational change. *Journal of Managerial Psychology, 21*(2), 145–162.

Maslach, C.A., & Jackson, S.E. (1981). The measurement of experienced burnout. *Journal of Occupational Behavior,* 2, 99-113.

Maslach, C., Schaufeli, W.B., & Leiter, M.P. (2001). Job burnout. *Annual Review of Psychology,* 52, 397-422.

Mathers, C.D., Vos, E.T., Stevenson, C.E., & Begg, S.J. (2000). The Australian burden of disease study: measuring the loss of health from diseases, injuries and risk factors. *Medical Journal of Australia, 172*(12), 592-596.

Mayer, E.A. (2000). The neurobiology of stress and gastrointestinal disease. *Gut,* 47, 861.

Merriam-Webster Dictionary. (2013). [Online]. Retrieved from: <http://www.merriam-webster.com> [Accessed 22 October 2013].

Millar, C., Hind, P., & Magala, S. (2012). Sustainability and the need for change: organisational change and transformational vision. *Journal of Organisational Change Management, 25*(4), 489-500.

Mina, S. (2014). Managing the strategic decision in governmental organisation within chaos theory. *Managerial Challenges of the Contemporary Society,* 4.

Morris, W.N., Worchel, W., Bios, J.L., Pearson, J.A., Rountree, C.A., Samaha, G.M., Wachtler, J., & Wright, S.L. (1976). Collective coping with Stress. *Journal of Personality and Social Psychology, 33*(6), 674-679.

Noblet, A., Rodwell, J., & McWilliams, J. (2006). Organisational change in the public sector: augmenting the demand control model to predict employee outcomes under new public management. *Work and Stress,* 20, 335-352.

Ohman, A., & Mineka, S. (2001). Fears, phobias, and preparedness: toward an evolved module of fear and fear learning. *Psychological Review, 108*(3), 483-522.

Ormrod, J. (2014). *Human learning* (6th ed.). Harlow, Essex: Pearson.

Pearce, J.C. (2003). *Spiritual initiation and the breakthrough of consciousness: the bond of power.* Rochester, VT: Park Stress Press.

Péli, G.L., Pólós, L., & Hannan, M.T. (2000). Back to inertia: theoretical implications of alternative styles of logical formalization. *Sociological Theory,* 18, 195-215.

Penn, M.L. (1991). Memory, emotional processing, and anxiety: A critique. *Current Psychology: Research and Reviews, 10*(4), 253-262.

Pettigrew, A.M., Woodman, R.W., & Cameron, K.S. (2001). Studying organisational change and development. *Academy of Management Journal, 44*(4), 697-713.

Rafferty, A.E., & Griffin, M.A. (2006). Perceptions of organisational change: a stress and coping perspective. *Journal of Applied Psychology, 91*(5), 1154-1162.

Richmond, R.L., & Kehoe, L. (1999). Quantitative and qualitative evaluations of brief interventions to change excessive drinking, smoking, and stress in the police force. *Addiction*, 94, 1509.

Ringleb, A.H., Rock, D., & Ancona, C. (2013). Neuroleadership. In D. Rock & A.H. Ringleb (eds.). *Handbook of Neuroleadership.* London: NeuroLeadership Institute.

Rock, D. (2009). *Your brain at work: strategies for overcoming distraction, regaining focus, and working smarter all day long.* New York: Harper Business.

Rock, D., Siegel, D.J., Poelmans, S.A.Y., & Payne, J. (2013). The Healthy Mind Platter. In D. Rock & A.H. Ringleb (eds.). *Handbook of Neuroleadership.* London: Neuroleadership Institute. pp. 127–161.

Rosen, S., & Rosen, S. (2000). *The philosophers handbook: Essential readings from Plato to Kant.* New York: Random House, p. 536.

Rosenberg, S., & Mosca, J. (2011). Breaking down the barriers to organizational change. *International Journal of Management and Information Systems, 15*(3), 139-146.

Sapolsky, R.M. (2004). *Why Zebras don't get ulcers: an updated guide to stress, stress related diseases, and doping.* New York: Holt Paperbacks.

Schermerhorn, J.R. (2003). *Organizational Behavior* (8th ed.). New York: Wiley.

Selye, H. (1956). *The stress of life.* New York: McGraw-Hill.

Selye, H. (1964). *From dream to discovery.* New York: McGraw-Hill.

Selye, H. (1976). Forty years of stress research: principal remaining problems and misconceptions. *Canadian Medical Association Journal,* 115, 53-56.

Selye, H. (1983). The stress concept: past, present, and future. In C. L. Cooper (ed.). *Stress research.* New York: Wiley. pp. 1-20.

Selye, H. (1987). *Stress without distress.* London: Transworld.

Senior, B., & Swailes, S. (2010). *Organisational change.* Harlow, UK: Pearson Education.

Sirkin, H.L., Keenan, P., & Jackson, A. (2005). The hard side of change management. *Harvard Business Review, 83*(10), 108–118.

Speilberger, C.D. (1972). *Anxiety: current trends in theory and research.* New York: Academic Press.

Statistics SA. (2014). *Consumer price index March 2014.* [Online]. Retrieved from <http://www.statssa.gov.za>.

Strümpfer, D.J.W. (2006). The strengths perspective: Fortigenesis in adult life. *Social Indicators Research,* 77, 11-36.

Squire, L. (1987). *Memory and the brain.* New York: Oxford University Press.

Taleb, N.N. (2010). *The black swan: the impact of the highly improbable* (2nd ed.). London: Penguin.

Taleb, N.N. (2012). *Antifragile: how to live in a world we don't understand.* London: Penguin.

Tiong, T.N. (2005). Maximising human resource potential in the midst of organisational change. *Singapore Management Review, 27*(2), 25-35.

Tucker, P., Pfefferbaum, B., Nixon, S., & Dickson, W. (2000). Predictors of post-traumatic stress symptoms in Oklahoma City: exposure, social support, peri-traumatic responses', *The Journal of Behavioral Health Services and Research,* 27:406–416.

Ursano, R.J., Fullerton, C.S. & Norwood, A.E. (2002). *Psychiatric dimensions of disaster: patient care, community consultation, and preventive medicine.* Retrieved from: <http://www:psych:org/pract-of-psych/disaster:cfm>.

Van Knippenberg, B., Martin, L. & Tyler, T. (2006). 'Process-orientation versus outcome-orientation during organisational change: the role of organizational identification', *Journal of Organisational Behavior,* 27:685-704.

Vasse, R.M., Nijhuis, F.J. & Kok, G. (1998). Associations between work stress alcohol consumption and sickness absence. *Addiction,* 93, 231.

Viljoen-Terblanche, R.C. (2008). *Sustainable organisational transformation through inclusivity.* Master's Thesis. Pretoria: University of South Africa.

Weiner, B.J. (2009). A theory of organisational readiness for change. *Implementation Science,* 4, 1-9.

Werkman, R.A. (2009). Understanding failure to change: a pluralistic approach and five patterns. *Leadership and Organisational Development Journal, 30*(7), 664-684.

Yerkes, R.M., & Dodson, J.D. (1908). The relation of strength of stimulus to rapidity of habit-formation. *Journal of Comparative Neurology and Psychology*, 18, 459.

ENDNOTES

1   Rosen & Rosen, 2000, p. 536.
2   Bateh, Castaneda & Farah, 2013; Eisenbach, Watson & Pillai, 1999.
3   Taleb, 2012, p. 13.
4   Dahl, 2009.
5   Blom & Viljoen, 2015.
6   Terblanche, 2008.
7   Millar, Hind & Magala, 2012.
8   Sirkin, Keenan & Jackson, 2005.
9   Viljoen-Terblanche, 2008.
10   Di Virgilio & Ludema, 2009; Ford, Ford & D'Amelio, 2008; Martin, Jones & Callan, 2006.
11   Rosenberg & Mosca, 2011.
12   Werkman, 2009.
13   Lewin, 1952.
14   Kinnear & Roodt, 1998.
15   Cummings & Worley, 2005; Senior & Swailes, 2010.
16   Armenakis & Bedeian, 1999; Beer & Nohria, 2000; Pettigrew, Woodman & Cameron, 2001.
17   Carr & Brower, 2000.
18   Fleming & Spicer, 2003.
19   Atkinson, 2005.
20   Weiner, 2009.
21   Strümpfer, 2006.
22   Avey, Wernsing & Luthans, 2008; Bercovitz & Feldman, 2008.
23   Bateh et al., 2013.
24   Dahl, 2009, p. 4.
25   Tiong, 2005.
26   Jimmieson, Terry & Callan, 2004.
27   Tiong, 2005.
28   Huy, 1999.
29   Hogan, 2007.
30   Bernerth, Walker & Harris, 2011.
31   Rafferty & Griffin, 2006.
32   Huy, 2001.
33   Rafferty & Griffin, 2006.
34   Marks, 2003.
35   Bernerth et al., 2011.
36   Maslach & Jackson, 1981.
37   Cropanzano, Rupp & Byrne, 2003; Maslach, Schaufeli & Leiter, 2001.

38   Halbesleben & Buckley, 2004.
39   Loh, Than & Quek, 2011.
40   Dahl, 2009.
41   Loh et al., 2011.
42   Chen, 2011.
43   Corbitt, 2005.
44   Judge, Thoresen, Pucik & Welbourne, 1999..
45   Darling & Heller, 2011.
46   Coy, 2008.
47   Bloom, 2010.
48   Blom & Viljoen, 2015.
49   Blom & Viljoen, 2015.
50   Viljoen-Terblanche, 2008.
51   Viljoen-Terblanche, 2008.
52   Blom & Viljoen, 2015.
53   Fram, 1992.
54   Dahl, 2009.
55   Jones, Watson, Hobman, Bordia, Gallois & Callan, 2008.
56   Blom & Viljoen, 2015.
57   Statistics SA, 2014.
58   Hogan, 2007; Rock, 2009.
59   Hansson, Vingard, Arnetz & &erzen, 2008; Noblet, Rodwell & McWilliams, 2006; van Knippenberg, Martin & Tyler, 2006.
60   Bernerth et al., 2011.
61   Blom, 2015.
62   Ringleb, Rock & Ancona, 2013.
63   Jimmieson et al., 2004.
64   Bloom, 2010.
65   Rock, 2009.
66   Taleb, 2010.
67   Rock, Siegel, Poelmans & Payne, 2013.
68   Blom & Viljoen, 1015.
69   Certo, 2003.
70   Certo, 2003.
71   Certo, 2003
72   Certo, 2003.
73   Yerkes & Dodson, 1908.
74   Selye, 1987.
75   Le Fevre, Matheny & Kolt, 2003.
76   Yerkes & Dodson, 1908.
77   Le Fevre et al., 2003.
78   Certo, 2003; Lussier, 2002; Schermerhorn, 2003.
79   Huy, 2001.
80   Berceli, 2012.
81   Selye, 1956.
82   Mayer, 2000; Selye, 1956.
83   Selye, 1976; 1983; Code & Langan-Fox, 2001.
84   Richmond & Kehoe, 1999; Vasse, Nijhuis & Kok, 1998.

85   Selye, 1956.
86   Selye, 1956; 1964.
87   Selye, 1987, p. 17.
88   Pearce, 2003, p. 52.
89   Pearce, 2003.
90   Lazarus, 1991.
91   Lazarus, 1991.
92   Cohen, 2004; Squire, 1987; LeDoux, 1996.
93   Morris et al., 1976.
94   Merriam-Webster Dictionary, 2013, np.
95   Speilberger, 1972, p. 482.
96   Penn, 1991, p. 254.
97   LeDoux, 1996.
98   Sapolsky, 2004.
99   Ohman & Mineka, 2001.
100   Berceli, 2012, p. 35.
101   Mathers, Vos, Stevenson & Begg, 2000.
102   Carter, Williams & Silverman, 2008.
103   Ormrod, 2014.
104   Berceli, 2012.
105   Selye, 1956.
106   Penn, 1991.
107   Blom, 2015.
108   Grady & Grady, 2011.
109   Hannan & Freeman, 1989.
110   Dahl, 2009.
111   Hsu & Hannan, 2005; Hannan, Baron, Hsu & Koğcak, 2006.
112   Péli, Pólós & Hannan, 2000.
113   Corbitt, 2005.
114   Baumeister, Twenge & Nuss, 2002.
115   Beehr, Jex, Stacy & Murray, 2000.
116   L&eweed & Boumans, 1994.
117   Ursano, Fullerton & Norwood, 2002.
118   Tucker, Pfefferbaum, Nixon & Dickson, 2000.
119   Kets De Vries, 2001.
120   Le Fevre et al., 2003.
121   Lazarus & Folkman, 1984.
122   Blom, 2015.
123   Laubscher, 2014.
124   Blom, 2015.
125   Bar-Yam, 2002.
126   Hayles, 1991.
127   Mina, 2014.
128   Grant, 2008.
129   Kauffman, 1998a; 1998b.
130   Holl, 1998.
131   Kauffman, 1998a; 1998b.
132   Holl, 1998.

133   Einstein in Klein, 1967.
134   Ackoff, 2010.
135   Viljoen, 2015.
136   Beck, Larsen, Solonin, Viljoen & Johns, 2018.

Chapter

7

THE IMPORTANCE OF LEADERSHIP IN RADICAL CHANGE EFFORTS

Joyce Toendepi and Rica Viljoen

INTRODUCTION

Leadership in the 21st century needs a perspective with sufficient depth and breadth to allow a broader view of the complexities in which people live.[1] It is on the leadership agenda to consciously influence societal transformation to achieve consensus on the distribution of wealth and social norms. Societal transformation may indeed stimulate geo-political cohesion, which in turn influences global cooperation, hence the world would be a better place to live in. On the other hand, diversity of thought, thinking systems and differing agendas may present a challenging puzzle for leadership to construct. Likewise, leadership in South Africa needs to devise a concrete communicative process that will allow stakeholders to freely participate in the change process – both within organisations and in society at large.

The African continent is increasingly experiencing complex social problems at the societal, organisational and individual levels, which now demand complex solutions to adapt. New leadership efforts need to be crafted to deal with the increasing systemic dynamics to rewire systems in a more virtuous, sustainable manner. The aim of this chapter is to describe the dynamics that challenge leaders in the South African context from a social systems point of view. Further, the dynamics of complex adaptive systems are introduced, and those of societal transformation and social consciousness are explained. The importance of the role of leadership in this ever-changing social system is also underlined. The chapter concludes with a claim on leadership to step up and take authority for adopting new ways of doing business in South Africa, and the importance of finding alternative ways of dealing with internal and external stakeholders.

THE SOUTH AFRICAN CONTEXT AS BACKDROP

Since South Africa became a democracy in 1994, five presidents have served the country, yet social conditions on the ground have not changed significantly. In a recent study by Statistics South Africa (2016), several socio-economic challenges were recorded, including unemployment being measured at 24.5% in the first quarter of 2016. Ordinary citizens face inequality, poverty and poor education daily. The Gini coefficient has remained at 0.63[2] and the poverty indicators show that 45.5% of the population still live below the poverty datum line.[3]

The Global Competitive Index[4] ranked South Africa as one of the most developed African countries, however a World Economic Forum Report[5] stated that issues like labour unrest, labour lay-offs, service provision protests, xenophobia, corruption, personal security and poor education remain problematic for public and private sector leaders in South Africa. In a study on how transformational leadership can act as a catalyst to higher levels of consciousness in social systems, Toendepi[6] stated that the major threats to the South African democratic society include a lack of unity of purpose, insufficient social cohesion, and socio-economic exclusion. The social system does not seem to be focused on the issues mentioned above as the institutional capacity seems less developed. Muthein[7] explained that South Africa lacks a coherent model of public sector reform.

South Africa has committed to the eight Millennium Development Goals (MDG) targets, i.e. the eradication of extreme poverty and hunger; the achievement of universal primary education; the promotion of gender equality and empowerment of women; the reduction of child mortality; an improvement in maternal health; combating HIV/Aids, malaria and other diseases; ensuring environmental sustainability; and the development of global partnerships for development, all of which can be classified as socio-economic challenges (Millennium Development Goals Report, 2015). Private sector leaders should be actively involved in assisting the public sector to achieve these goals.

Not only is leadership in South Africa faced with socio-economic issues, but it is also challenged by the dynamics caused by the previous apartheid regime. There is a necessity to optimise cultural diversity, thus leaders require distinct leadership competencies and capabilities to be able to integrate the nation, organisations and communities into functional social systems. Toendepi[8] explained that higher levels of leadership consciousness are needed to achieve unity of purpose, which is the responsibility of the social system's leadership. She also passionately argued that leadership decisions need the support of those affected by such decisions, hence new ways of doing business and dealing with relations in and outside the boundary of organisations become important.[9]

Social transformation is happening at a slow pace in South Africa, due to the leadership quality of both the private and public sector. The World Economic Forum[10] stated that the retarded rate of social transformation in any society creates conditions that stimulate social tensions that can ignite global consequences. This is happening increasingly in South Africa, as demonstrations and marches about societal challenges take place regularly. Various international measurements and assessment indices report on the gradual deterioration of the democratic performance of South Africa. The GCI measure and assessment indicates similar trends for South Africa as described by the Ibrahim Index of African Governance (IIAG), the United Nations Development Plan (UNDP), the Human Development Index (HDI) and the Transparency International Index (TII), all of which identify trends of gradual worsening of performance from an average basis. Toendepi[11] highlighted the importance of social system understanding and the degree of complexity that the micro and macro factors introduce in making distinctions to guide decision-making.

As stated by Nkuna and Sebola[12], the task at hand for leadership in South Africa is to interact with the public through the application of different schemas and display different competencies. Kellis and Ran[13] reiterated that the new era requires leadership to effectively identify and support the public interests. Schwella, Botha, Brand, Engelbrecht and van Eijbergen[14] "described democratic and effective leadership as a transparent action involving the leader and followers in an inclusive setting to effectively realise legitimate, legal and socially valuable goals and objectives".

SOCIAL SYSTEMS AND THEIR DYNAMICS

The essence of complex adaptive systems

Merriam-Webster[15] defined a social system "as patterned series of interrelationships that result in a coherent whole", while Metcalf[16] referred to systems as having a lot to do with collective parts in some spatial relation to each other. The utility of systems thinking is in visualising and gaining insight into dynamic wholes; organisations are steeped in increasing complexity because of disruptors which are game changers such as big data. Leaders need to understand the levels and causes of complexity in their social systems and the wider environment.[17]

Whole societies and organisations are social systems consisting of individuals, teams, leaders and dominant coalitions. In complex adaptive systems like the South African social system, solutions do not reside with the executive but in the collective intelligence of people at all levels.

Cilliers[18] described the characteristics of complex systems thinking as:
- elements of the system interact dynamically with each other;
- elements in the system are not always aware of the behaviour of the whole;
- the interaction can be physical or it can be the exchange of information;
- the interactions are rich and impact other parts of the system;
- the interactions are non-linear and complexity theory principles apply;

- the principle of recurrency occurs – there are feedback loops in the system;
- the behaviour of individual elements does not impact the overall behaviour of a system;
- the boundaries of systems are open;
- these systems may operate in conditions that are far from equilibrium;
- a constant flow of energy is critical to ensure the organisation of the system; and
- systems like this emerge from history; they evolve and the past impacts current behaviour.

Metcalf[19] noted that what distinguishes these elements of a system is not their physical or spatial proximity, but rather the fact that the systemic elements are interdependent and behave as part of a system. Leadership is essential in catalysing consciousness so that participation becomes meaningful, Toendepi[20] explained, while Ungerer, Pretorius and Herholdt[21] stated that a shared meaning is a result of intense dialogue. Rica Viljoen[22] highlighted the importance for leaders to be self-aware, as well as able to dialogue and deal with difficult conversations.

In *Inclusive Organisational Transformation*, Viljoen[23] integrated the underlying theories that impact on social systems. First, paradox theory is at play in systems like this. This means that opposites are often contained somewhere in the system. Second, complexity theory explains that for every action there are a multitude of unintended implications and that nothing will be simplistic again. Third, social systems self-organise and the formal organogram of an organisation is often not aligned to what is really happening. Last, chaos theory explains that while you are in a system the chaos may be overwhelming, but by looking from a different stance about what created the dynamics in the first place, one can create new insights about systemic patterns and leverage points to intervene at.

Snowden and Boon[24] explained that social complexities morph into complex adaptive challenges, while Jordan (2011) described some properties of complex challenges as having complex causality and many stakeholders, to the extent that the issue cannot be delegated to one actor. Complex adaptive challenges are also chronic and require systemic adaptation, because quick fixes will not be effective.[25]

Social systems can self-organise when collective intelligence is utilised to foster commitment and willingness to change, explained Senge.[26] A social system involves interactions and interdependencies among its parts that have different functions and characteristics. Leaders must be aware of systemic dynamics, and their understanding of how complex social systems function is becoming crucial. The best leader may be the one that listens best to the whole organisation, as many organisations are over-managed and under-led. Traditional organisations create autocratic and rules-driven environments that stifle innovation, creativity, spontaneity, flexibility and responsiveness, and are based on the control and command of employees who are deemed untrustworthy. One of the most important lessons for leaders is to trust their people to do their work, i.e. trust is a pre-requisite in order to achieve an inclusive culture, which in turn is conducive for trust.

Concelman and Phelps[27] warned that leading is becoming increasingly difficult given the growing complexity, the need to do more with less, and the uncertainty that defines leadership roles and the state of the economy, while Musgrave[28] expressed the desperate need for women and men who can take charge and tackle socio-economic challenges effectively through identifying and supporting public interests. Beck[29], who was instrumental in the transformation of South Africa from 1989 to 1994 through his work with the political and business leaders of the time, still believes that South Africa, as one of the most diverse countries on the globe, will see new solutions emerge to solve the ongoing societal and systemic problems. The role of leadership in changing systemic dynamics in complex adaptive systems cannot be underestimated and will be discussed later in the chapter.

Societal transformation and social consciousness

For Kaufman[30], social transformation refers to a collective shift in the levels of consciousness of a whole society. The University of Johannesburg's Professor Alex Broadbent[31] described transformation in the South African context as a process of unlocking latent talent in the population, not as a fairness or redress for those who were previously disadvantaged. Castels[32] added that social transformation is a fundamental shift in the way society is organised that goes beyond the continual processes of incremental social change that are always at work. New models and ways of organising are needed to deal with these societal changes.

Dibrell, Craig, Kim and Johnson[33] explained that social consciousness is an indication of how the organisation is aware of its place and relevance, with Pavlidis[34] adding that social consciousness is the level of knowledge and objectivity that the collective has about reality. Furthermore, Viljoen[35] postulated that consciousness is the lens through which people view reality, saying that the object being viewed remains constant, yet different consciousness levels result in different informed interpretations. Kaufman[36] used the term 'collective consciousness' to describe a set of shared beliefs, ideas and norms that bind society. Raised levels of consciousness may be achieved through the unleashing of individual and collective voices to create a shared understanding.[37] It is thus clear that there is a direct relationship between the level of consciousness and the transformational process in social systems, whether it is at an individual or collective perspective.

In the inclusivity model discussed in Chapter 3, changes in the new world of work, the implications of systems thinking and rising levels of consciousness in society are positioned as drivers of change in the external environment, which leaders and the social systems that they represent should adapt to, to stay relevant and be sustainable. The bottom part of the model is incorporated below in Figure 7.1 for easy reference.

The way: How we adapt					
DYNAMICS OF CHANGE	Why we adapt		Essence of change		Awareness of adaption
DRIVERS OF CHANGE	New world of work		New sciences		Rising levels of consciousness
	Nature of the world				

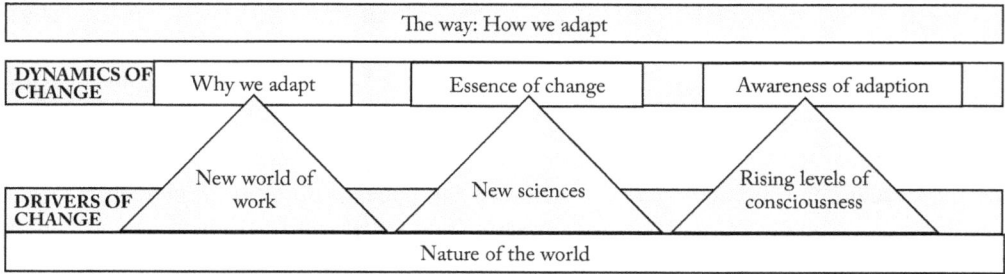

Figure 7.1: Inclusivity Model[38]

For Viljoen[39], consciousness is a lens through which reality is viewed. As people are now more aware than ever before, there has been a rising level of consciousness, thus it is the duty of leaders to adapt to the varying changes and diverse ways of dealing with such dynamics. Prinsloo (2012) noted that consciousness reflects the level of awareness or inclusiveness and extensiveness of uptaking of new information. Dibrell[40] viewed organisational social consciousness as the organisation's awareness of its place, social responsibility, ethics, culture, corporate values and stakeholders' interests, however Vilakati[41] argued that social consciousness refers to positionality and identity, i.e. we find ourselves at the southern part of Africa, impacted by our stance towards the history and the future of this space in time. Leaders should be acutely aware of how different layers of consciousness impact the sense making of individuals and the social systems in which they operate.

Internationally, current structures are challenged. The election of Donald Trump, the exit of the United Kingdom from the European Union, and South African cries that "Zuma must fall" and "Fees must fall", all highlight the rising level of consciousness in society. Organisations in South Africa are cut from the same social cloth, and the same dynamics inside organisations also impact on leaders in organisations. The old ways of leading are not congruent with current business problems, therefore new ways of doing business and interacting with different role players are required.

According to Achua and Lussier[42], for a transformational process to be a success it has to involve broader stakeholder participation, with the ultimate goal of establishing a shared purpose which is created through involvement and a process of inclusivity. A transformational process is the result of a congruent alignment of belief systems and values with a common goal. Beck[43] called this a "superordinate goal", drawing on the original definition by Muzafer Sherif[44] that common goals refer to goals which are compelling and highly appealing to members of two or more groups in conflict, but which cannot be attained by the resources and energies of the groups separately. In effect, it is a goal that is attained only when groups pull together. Co-determination and the corresponding slogan 'Ya Rona' (Ours/Belong to us)[i], as implemented by

---

i   Ya Rona is a concept in Sotho, which is one of the official languages in South Africa.

Interstate Bus Lines (IBL), can be described as a superordinate goal. The case study of IBL is shared in Chapter 9.

Kaufman[45] referred to social transformation as including the collective consciousness of a society to a level where reality can be defined by consensus. Pavlidis[46] explained that social consciousness and social action are inherently linked to education; as a result, the role that educators play in stimulating and moulding people's ability to transform social reality must be acknowledged. The next step is that the development of consciousness to such levels where it enables collective transformation and collective shaping of reality is an act associated with the acquisition of knowledge. Later in this chapter, the importance of leadership education and development is discussed.

Manley, O'Keefe, Jackson, Pearce and Smith[47] agreed that common purpose taps into people's needs and creates something bigger than our individual needs; it rallies peoples' emotional, cognitive and spiritual commitment around a cause. Something magical happens when people are consulted, involved and co-create in a process that can be described as inclusive. Diverse stakeholder groups are unified through shared purpose, enabling everybody to work creatively, embrace agreed values and foster shared decision-making. Collective intelligence is also achieved when all involved at any level in an organisation/society are consulted and involved in decision-making processes.[48] Senge et al.[49] added the dimension of collective wisdom, which results when a systems leader creates an enabling environment where the affected people come together to share their concerns, think more deeply about what is happening, and explore options beyond popular thinking.

Trends and impacts of external factors such as the fourth technological revolution and globalisation exponentially increase societal complexity, thus leaders need to engage people in matters that concern them and adapt consistently to changes in the external environment in order to survive in business. Laubscher[50] explained how changing life conditions require new thinking systems to evolve over time. Leaders are role models of the new value system and must encourage followers to approach the challenges in new and collective ways. In that process, trust is a critical element and the transformational leaders need to build support by being honest with their followers. Adaptive transformation becomes critical when our deeply held beliefs are challenged and our earlier versions of success factors are made obsolete by emerging dynamics.

THE DYNAMIC ROLE OF LEADERSHIP IN COMPLEX ADAPTIVE SYSTEMS

The purpose of leadership is to create a better future for all; leaders who truly care for their followers expose them to the painful reality of their condition and demand that they fashion a collective response. Based on the observations by Heifetz and Laurie[51], followers in general desire comfort, stability and solutions from their leaders, but unfortunately, that is "spoon-feeding". Veldsman[52] defined 'leadership' as a process where groups of people jointly create a shared desirable future within a specific context, while Liddle[53] described leadership as a complex social phenomenon that lacks clear definition. She added that leadership is central to good governance, and pointed out that there is confusion about what exactly leadership is or how leaders instigate transformation. At the same time, Laubscher[54] expressed the important role of a leader as a catalyst, defining their role as entering a system to effect change, only to move out later, unchanged him/herself. Without leadership, systems often attempt to create equilibrium but move back to the way of least resistance, i.e. the way things were.

Wilson[55] described how leaders needing to balance competing pressures for transformational change is at odds with the existing processes, with Hamel[56] adding that the notion that a leader is a heroic decision maker is untenable due to complexities. He proposes that leaders be recast as social systems architects who catalyse innovation and collaboration.

Viljoen-Terblanche[57] viewed leadership as a critical prerequisite to organisational and systemic change, and identified leadership doing and being as two symbiotic forces that can rewire dynamics in a virtuous manner through inclusivity. The voices of the individual, the group and the organisation can be woven around organisational strategy and values, yet industry and societal dynamics should also be considered in this integral tapestry that leadership is weaving.

Clawson[58] expressed the view that change and its related concepts and principles are intertwined with leadership. Toendepi[59] continued by saying that leadership in a social system means nothing if it does not attempt to facilitate change or lead to sustainable social transformation. Rising levels of consciousness in leadership can enable such a change. If there is no significant renewal within the social system, one could argue that there is no quality leadership, Toendepi[60] explained. Similarly, Ackoff[61] (cited in Metcalf[62]) noted that without purposefully designing human social systems, no change will happen. Senge[63] explained that in systems, the natural trend would be to return to equilibrium. New levels of consciousness can help leaders to identify and implement new solutions, as current solutions to systemic problems only maintain the current reality.

To be able to think systemically and holistically about the total transformation of a society and the companies in them, leaders need to first understand the properties of their social systems and lead from within the system. Social systems function on interrelations and feedback; different parts of a system rely on other parts for information, action and support. Inclusivity enables organisations to tap into the gifts and contributions from a diverse workforce. Participation in organisational decision-making creates not only shared vision, but also significance and buy-in into organisational strategies and plans.

It appears that the current organisational employee relationship paradigm is not able to resolve the modern socio-economic challenges of employees and societies, perhaps because of the current situation that Einstein originally explained. For this reason, Toendepi[64] argued that leadership in the South African context needs to encourage continuous learning through broader stakeholder engagement. During that process, leaders must ensure an inclusive co-creation culture, which is sensitive to individual differences such as personality, value systems, gender and thought processes.

Achua and Lussier[65] commented that a transformational leader seeks trust, commitment, and the respect of followers to transform a weak or declining organisation into a new social system. Good governance is also a critical element in social system transformation. Ali[66] highlighted that good governance is a process of competently managing a social system's resources and affairs in a manner that is transparent, equitable and responsive to the needs of the people, while Toendepi[67] stressed the importance of leaders being catalysts of creating inclusivity and listening to the voices of participants in the system. The fact that this catalysing process is not always happening stems not only from a lack of leadership capacity, but also from a deficiency of coherence in galvanising the consciousness necessary for the achievement of consensus for the development of a social system. According to van Wart[68], a leader needs to involve followers as much as possible and still retain the ability to use power for their benefit.

Integral leadership, as described by Kupers and Volckmann[69], is a leadership style that attempts to integrate other major styles of leadership, which involves understanding people's mind-sets, values, capabilities and situational dynamics. An integrated understanding of how individual thinking systems can be woven into a collective form the basis of leading from this stance. Beck[70] called this way of leading through the optimisation of the dynamics of various role players, meshwork. Without functional leadership, organisational goals are not meaningful and followers are not inspired to participate in the effort. Effective and congruent leadership is thus a critical pre-requisite for the sustainable transformation of social systems.

Crystallising leadership voice through development

From the previous discussion, diversity factors such as diversity of thought can be seen as forming an integral part of the unique quality of an individual, therefore it makes business sense to create opportunities for individuals to explore who they are, what their unique contributions are, and ways in which to optimise these unique contributions, while simultaneously minimising the impact of their individual growth areas.

Although everyone perceives and makes decisions based on diverse factors such as personality, this process is uniquely different for everyone. An awareness of an individual's unique style, preferences and skills is thus key for growth (Bar-On, 2003). Awareness of the self is situated within the boundaries drawn by culture, worldview and the individual habits of attention that contribute to cultural fluency. This awareness is an essential complement to the understanding of cultural dynamics.[71] As awareness filters through the understanding, which, in turn, passes, increases and informs, individuals can apply themselves with increasing fluency. A leader must crystallise his or her own leadership voice and gain the confidence to speak up - even in difficult times and conditions.

The late President Nelson Mandela was described by Senge et al.[72] as a known systems leader who managed to unite a nation once divided. A systems leader, according to the authors, has the ability to see reality through the eyes of people; build relationships based on deep listening; and create networks of trust and collaboration. A systems leader's core capabilities include the ability to see a holistic picture together with the people, which is essential for a collective shift of focus from problem orientation to participatory solution finding. A systems leader also helps people move beyond just reacting to these challenges to developing innovative solutions for the future. This shift involves confronting difficult truths about the current reality and fostering social learning that builds consensus about problems and innovative solutions.[73] Beck[74] described Madiba as a systemic, functional leader who spent most of his time designing, developing and transforming the social system that he led to be in tune with the current living conditions, as well as the conditions that were appearing on the horizon. Systems leader capacities, like those Madiba displayed, should be developed through formal, organisational and informal leadership development initiatives.

Unless leaders develop an awareness of divergent cultural starting points and insight into own dynamics, miscommunication and frustration may negatively influence interpersonal relationships. Organisational development interventions may enable leaders, firstly, to optimise individual strengths; secondly, to manage the unintended implications thereof; and lastly, to understand and optimise the strengths and development areas of others.

New ways of organising relationships, in and outside organisations, ask of leadership to be courageous and steadfast, disregarding distractions. Van Wart[75] described the dimensions of integrity in leaders as including honesty/truth telling, trustworthiness, fairness and conscientiousness. However, integrity also encapsulates ethical conduct to maintain a safe environment, which allows the disclosure of wrong doings. Effective leaders in the new world of work ensure the execution of strategy and plans through empowered employees. Significant mind shifts are needed for leadership to be able to transform social systems that were perceived to function well before.

In Table 7.1 below, some mind shift changes that are critical to survive in the new world of work are discussed.

Table 7.1: Mind shift changes critical to survival in a new world of work

Old leadership stance	New adapted leadership stance
Salaries are confidential	Radical openness towards remuneration
Strategy is confidential	Co-creation of strategy
Managers tell the rest what to do	All participate in how to achieve organisational outcomes
Profit benefits the shareholders	Profit benefits the stakeholders
Stakeholders are viewed as external forces with opposing agendas	Stakeholders are viewed as partners
Unions are viewed as disruptive	Unions are viewed as strategic partners
The human resources function is viewed as a cost	The human resource function is viewed as a strategic part of business
Culture is an unintended implication of leadership style	Culture is constructed in the strategic architecture of the strategy process
Management is responsible for discipline in a system	Social systems (management, workers and the unions) share in the governance of a system
Shares are sold to make money	Ownership of business is shared to ensure sustainability
Leaders ask "I-questions" or "WE-questions"[ii]	Leaders ask questions about both the "I" and the "WE"

In Table 7.1 above, the adaptive leadership stance that is a pre-requisite for the implementation of alternative engagement models with social systems is described. A radical, courageous thinking system is required in both leadership and in supporting functions to management to do things in a new way - a way that maintains the strengths of the old organisational systems yet transcends the unintended implications of the organising system. In Chapter 3, the differences between "I" questions and "WE" questions are explained, i.e. "I" questions are characteristic of leaders who want to gain power, succeed in business, or to achieve materialistically, while "WE" questions are asked by people who sacrifice to serve the tribe, to save now to gain later, or to follow rules to benefit all later. Beck et al.[76] referred to questions of existence that are based on both individual and collective questions as second tier leadership.

These thinking systems often occur in social systems. In the new world of work leaders need a systemic functional understanding that both "I" and "WE" questions must be asked in an inclusive space. The emphasis shifts from being egocentric or

---

ii   This question refers to spiral dynamics theory, as described in Chapter 3.

collectivistic to a position where both these thinking systems can co-exist in individual and collective leadership. A "both and" position is held, rather than an "either/or" position, and integral perspective is adopted rather than "my way is the only way". This transcendence to a more inclusive stance begs of courageous leaders to do alternative things to create new approaches in social systems, as doing what we have always done will perpetuate the current socio-economic dynamics that are obviously not achieving sustainability goals. Courageous leadership is needed to adopt the new leadership stance. The question to be asked is what will be the consequences if leadership do not adapt their thinking to a more inclusive way?

Universities and business schools have to study their curriculum for leadership development to ensure that the capabilities that leaders need in dealing with complex adaptive systems are developed. The same applies to Learning and Development departments in organisations. Keevy[77] advocated for an integrated approach to leadership development encompassing executive sponsorship and presence, experiential formal learning, coaching, and reflective processes both inside and outside the classroom to facilitate sustainable leadership practices.

In Table 7.2 below, the development of leadership theory is summarised for easy comparison with current learning outcomes. If companies and universities still train to develop leadership competencies based on theories of the 1980s, we may just be turning out leadership that is not prepared for the complex, systemic realities of the new world of work.

Table 7.2: Contributors to leadership development

Contribution	Who	When
Action-centred leadership	Adair	1973
Servant leadership	Greenleaf Trevor	1977 2007
Transforming leadership	Burns	1978
Transformational leadership	Tichy & Devanna Weathersby Engelbrecht & Chamberlain Yulk	1984 1998 2005 2006
Feminine leadership	Loden	1985
Charismatic leadership	House Musser Kets de Vries Maxwell	1977 1987 1991 1999
Situational leadership	Hersey & Blanchard	1982

Contribution	Who	When
Super leadership	Sims & Manz	1989
Visionary leadership	Nanus	1992
Spiritual leadership	Fairholm Vaill	1996 1998
Authentic leadership	Terry	1993
Ubuntu	Mbigi & Maree Van Niekerk Mbigi Ramose Van der Coloff	1994 1994 1995, 1997 1999 2004
Cognitive leadership	Gardner Collins	1996 2001
Result-based leadership	Ulrich, Zenger, Smallwood	1999
Strategic leadership	Drucker Kotter Buckingham & Clifton	1999 1999 2001
Systemic leadership	Allen & Cherry	2000
Conscious leadership	Renesh	2001
Complex leadership	Marion & Uhl-Bien	2001
Global leadership	Kets de Vries	2001
Janusian leadership	Parapone & Crupi	2002
Resonant leadership	Boyatzis & McKee	2005
African leadership	Banhegyi & Banhegyi	2006
Relational leadership	Uhl-Bien	2006
Ideal leadership	Stout	2006
Congruent leadership	Stanley	2008
Integral leadership	McGregor	2010
Shared leadership	Kellis & Ran	2013
Systems leadership Systematic leadership	Senge et al.	2015
Second tier leadership	Beck et al.	2018

It is important to enable leaders through development initiatives in the following areas:

- Emotional intelligence to deal with environmental demands.
- Adaptive intelligence to be able to adapt to changes in the external environment.
- Systemic intelligence to be able to understand systemic dynamics.
- Contextual intelligence to be able to understand the dynamics of the contextual variables in an event.
- Complexity intelligence to be able to see things for what they are.

Further, leaders should be assisted in the development of:

- meaning making – how they reach conclusions;
- patterning – how to read individual and social systems archetypes/organising patterns;
- understanding their own leadership philosophy and the unconscious assumptions they derive and base assumptions on;
- leading complex, adaptive social systems; and
- how to create inclusivity in their originations.

Organisations as social system structures morph as required in reaction to external conditions, thus leaders must constantly scan both the internal and the external environment to detect subtle changes and hear messages from the future. Leadership education and development is critical for ensuring rising levels of consciousness in social systems.

Governance in a new world of work

The new world of work demands that leaders be experts in contextual engagement; they are expected to attain contextual fit and harmony within their organisations. However, for one to be able to understand and manage contextual demands, certain leadership orientations are demanded in order to achieve a fit for purpose.[78] Organisations and societies are interactive social systems whose sub-systems have to be mutually supportive and reinforcing. Veldsman stressed the importance of competencies that enhance positive identification of the type of misfits present in the system and the suitable fit enhancing approach to be applied. With this ability to achieve contextual fit with their environments and situations, leaders are able to govern in a better way.

There is need to re-think the inclusive growth approaches and to prepare leaders in organisations as systems leaders for them to be able to anticipate systemic impact on the value creation within the system. One of the issues that keeps rearing its head in most social systems is the ability to govern well in view of the interconnectedness of economies. In that regard, adaptation for fit is increasingly being demanded because economies are not at the same developmental stages. As a result, leaders in social systems are expected to keep the common good both internally and externally to their sphere of influence and to devise innovative solutions with the people.

A practice of systemic good governance

Metcalf[79] referred to governance as a systemic practice that regulates decision-making in all spheres. The term 'governance' itself refers to the various ways through which social life is coordinated.[80] This presents governance as a multi-faceted concept, with the World Bank[81] referring to governance as the use of power, either politically exercised to manage the nation's affairs or in the management of a country's economic and social resources for development. Generally, the concept of governance defined above is concerned with the management of societal issues through interaction to achieve mutuality at any level of organisation[82], yet governance can be referred to as good when it serves the interests of the public or bad when it is to the contrary. For this reason, leadership is central to good governance and it is leadership's role to facilitate good governance in social systems.

Good governance attributes include legitimacy, accountability, transparency, corruption free, participation, consensus-oriented and all effective ways of using public power and resources for the benefit of society.[83] In most of the good governance definitions, serving the interests of the public features prominently.

Figure 7.2 below shows some of the important principles of good governance.

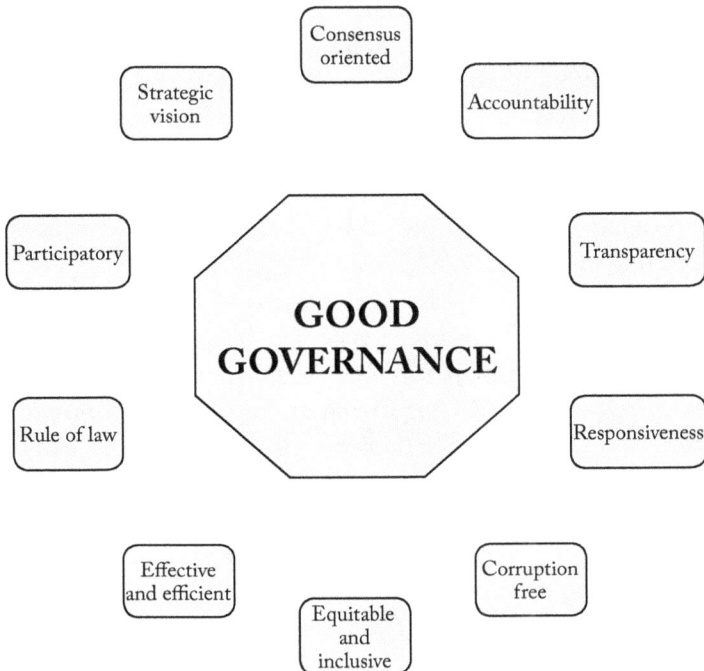

Figure 7.2: Good Governance Principles (Adapted from Ali[84])

These core good governance principles are interrelated and mutually reinforcing, to the effect that broader participation will eventually enhance the good information exchange needed for effective and inclusive decision-making processes.[85] The system requires mutual trust, reliability, openness and citizen empowerment to be central to good governance. On the other hand, bad governance is seen as the main cause of present day societal challenges. Bad governance has been seen to cause societal ills such as corruption, elevated unemployment and rising inflation rates, factors which can, in turn, cause civil unrest. In totality, good governance is participatory and responsive to both the current and future needs of social systems, i.e. it is a positive factor in developmental issues.

Accountability and corruption

Accountability within a good governance framework refers to holding individuals responsible for their actions and is exercised by those to whom one is accountable through participation in the regulation and implementation of policies.[86] Accountability presents itself as a measure of good governance that is available to triangulate and align the interests of stakeholders, corporations and society. Closely related to the issue of accountability is the concept of transparency, which is instrumental in the development of mutually agreed high principles that can drive good codes of conduct based on the ethical and equitable values set for the organisation. As a result, the accountability principle requires high levels of transparency and the recognition of laws that govern the land. Meritocracy goes hand-in-hand with accountability. According to Muthein[87], the new public management bureaucracies rely highly on skilled and deeply experienced professional administrators with the necessary competencies to successfully do the work. Sirisetti[88] explained that competencies are a set of behaviour patterns that an incumbent brings to a position to perform its task and functions competently. The incumbent has to have moral values in order to be able to distinguish what is right from wrong all the time.

However meritocracy is severely compromised by corruption, which is referred to as the misuse of an official position for personal gain and is a hindrance to good governance.[89] In 2013, the *Diagnostic Report* ranked South Africa 72 out of 178 countries, a drop from 54 in 2011, signifying an increased level of corruption in the country. Strict accountability and transparency were also found to be lacking. The recent event where South Africa was downgraded to junk status by the Standard and Poor's Global Rating (S & P), thereby lowering South Africa's creditworthiness to a sub-investment grade, was the result of a perceived lack of transparency, an alleged lack of meritocracy in the appointment of cabinet posts, and the presence of corruption in the system. The consequences of no investor confidence and capital flight to more investment grade economies has dire implications for the optimal functioning of local organisations, hence leadership in this environment need to be prepared for fundamental changes that may derail the development of positive economic growth pathways. However, it has to be acknowledged that the position of leadership in organisations in this situation becomes challenging when considering the interests of all stakeholders.

Weeding out corruption is not an easy task; it requires the whole society to be aware and report corruption to a level where everyone holds everyone accountable. According to Ossai-Ugbah[90] it is every citizen's duty to remove corruption from society, but this can only be achieved if the fight begins from each individual's inward self and is facilitated by political will. As a solution to issues that affect good governance in the new world of work, inclusive participation in the decision-making processes and a wider stakeholder involvement can mitigate the impact. Therefore, what is required are leaders who are willing and capable of making the necessary changes through pushing for the right policy regulation and reform.

INCLUSIVE PARTICIPATION

Schwella et al.[91] and Ali[92] agreed that participation by citizens either directly or through intermediate institutions is vital for good progress in the development process, emphasising that the voices of all people should be heard in decision-making. Ali added that mass participation fosters democracy, which in turn is a prerequisite for good governance. For Sayeed and Pillay[93], participation must be active, free and meaningful in order to be useful to the development process. The argument around citizen participation centres on the fact that active and realistic participation, which is inclusive, results in shared consciousness and improved decision-making that benefits the rest of the society (Mwanza et al.[94]). The thrust of good governance is geared towards the optimal functioning of societies where the quality of life for all citizens is guaranteed through the effective and efficient processes of decision-making.

The new world of work requires that the leader adopts bold steps to improve workforce conditions, promote diversity and promote multi-stakeholder dialogues. More fearless approaches are being demanded in order to achieve social changes through collaboration for the best future. Today, the processes of consensus orientation, progressive participation and inclusivity foster in organisations a situation where the collective agrees on their best interests. Employees have a major stake in the success of the enterprise, as their job security depends on its survival; they can gain from increased productivity and lose from high labour costs, as these affect the firm's ability to compete.[95] The emphasis on participation is that at most the voices of all people are heard in decision-making, thus fostering a democratic process, which in turn is a prerequisite for good governance.

The South African unitary corporate governance system has a shareholder orientation that limits the other key stakeholders from engaging in decision-making in the company. Key stakeholders contribute to the success of the company, and a socially responsible business attends to the legitimate interests of all its key stakeholders.[96] In a comparison between the South African corporate governance system and the German two-tier board system and its co-determination provision, the latter emerges as most effective in ensuring the perpetuation of stakeholder interests. However, the German system is silent on stakeholders (for example communities) other than shareholders and employees.

Some reformers argue that workers are not merely factory parts, they are citizens, hence there is an underlying ideology that employee participation in decision-making will promote trust, co-operation and harmony. Other internal issues that engage co-determination are changes in the organisation of work, the introduction of new work methods, mergers, and cut backs to the establishment. The main benefit of inclusive participation (co-determination) is mutuality, as it takes into account the interests of multiple stakeholders with the aim of creating sustainable value and long-term benefits within the organisation.[97] Employee representatives monitor the day-to-day business operations and influence the strategic significance of a company. Here leadership must paradoxically give power away to get power – the power of inclusivity and trust. All of these issues require courageous leadership.

In South Africa, leadership from all the stakeholders - including unions, shop stewards and employees - is required. This book focuses on what co-determination is and how it can successfully help South African organisations enhance labour relations and come up with unique African ways to co-create sustainable outcomes.

INTEGRATION AND CONCLUSION

People may display the technical expertise required to perform their functions, but rarely do they have the opportunity to understand the impact of the full potential of their experience, a previous study by Viljoen-Terblanche[98] found. Tacit knowledge may be replicated and recreated by placing greater emphasis on those learning opportunities that promote the acquisition of diverse viewpoints. In the new world of work, organisations that are successful in optimising the collective thinking processes of the people in their organisations will ensure the shared vision of all, create significance to transform and unleash human capacity to perform, ensuring sustainability in turbulent times.

Organisations need to create a space in which employees' wisdom, insights and gifts – the skills for which they were employed in the first place – are brought to the organisational table in order to create an environment in which diverse views, paradigms and perspectives can create a synergistic, sustainable outcome. Leadership should create an atmosphere that is conducive to inclusivity; only then can the benefits of diversity of thought be unleashed. Any leader within any organisation is confronted by different combinations of diversity factors, *inter alia*, diversity of thought, worldview, race, gender and generation.

In this chapter, an emphasis was placed on how leadership in South African businesses can catalyse social consciousness to higher levels to transform the societies in which they function, by devising innovative solutions together with the people. The same principles derived here can be transferred to other emerging economies. The task of leadership is to make sense of the nonsense; to attempt to leverage complex social systems to achieve sustainable performance; to make music out of the noise; and to facilitate growth in individuals, in groups, and ultimately in organisations, by enhancing the wisdom and unleashing the potential contained in the workforce.

REFERENCES

Achua, C.F., & Lussier, R.N. (2013). *Effective Leadership* (5th ed.). Nashville, TN: Southern Western.

Ali, M. (2015). Governance and Good Governance: A Conceptual Perspective. *Dialogue (Pakistan), 10*(1), 65-77.

Beck, D. (2013). *The Master Code. Spiral Dynamics Integral Accreditation*: Course Notes. Santa Barbara: Adizes Business School.

Beck, D., Larsson, T., Solomin, S., Viljoen, R.C., & Johns, T. (2018). *Spiral Dynamics In Action. Humanities Master Code*. London: Wiley.

Broadbent, A. (2015). *Transformation (UJ's Humanities Dean Prof Alex Broadbent speaks on transformation)*. [Online]. Retrieved from: https://www.youtube.com/watch?v=u0S6_lJPAmY.

Castels, S. (2010). Understanding Global Migration: A Social Transformation Perspective. *Journal of Ethnic and Migration Studies, 36*(10), 1565-1586.

Cilliers, P. (1998). *Complexity and Postmodernism: Understanding Complex Systems*. London: Routledge.

Clawson, J.G. (2003). Level Three Leadership: Getting Below the Surface. Upper Saddle River, NJ: Prentice Hall.

Concelman, J., & Phelps, M. (2014). *Lost in Translation*. Birmingham, Alabama: ASTD Enterprise.

Dibrell, C., Craig, J.B., Kim, J., & Johnson, A, J. (2015). Establishing How Natural Environment Competency, Organisational Social Consciousness and Innovativeness Related. *Journal of Business Ethics, 127*(3), 159-605.

Forman, J.P., & Ross, L.A. (2013). *Integral Leadership: The Next Half-Step*. New York: State University Press.

Hamel, G. (2009). *Moon Shots for Management*. Retrieved from: https://ai.wu.ac.at/~kaiser/literatur/moonshots-gary-hamel.pdf

Heifetz, R.A., & Laurie, D.L. (2001). The Work of leadership: Breakthrough Leadership. *Harvard Business Review, 79*(11), 131-141.

Howe, B.M., & Kamaruddin, N. (2016). Good Governance and Human Security in Malaysia: Sarawak's Hydro-electrical Conundrum. *Contemporary South-East Asia, 38*(1), 81-105.

Jordan, T. (2011). Skilful engagement with wicked Issues: A Framework for analysing the meaning making structures societal change agents. *Integral Review, 7*(20), 47-91.

Kaufman, P. (2005). Learning to not Labour: How working-class individuals construct middle-class identities. *Sociology Quarterly, 44*(3), 481-504.

Kellis, D.A., & Ran, B. (2013). Modern Leadership principles for public administration: Time to move forward. *Journal of Public Affairs, 13*(1), 130-141.

Keevy, Z. (2018). *Leadership architecture for Stratified Systems Theory for retail.* (Unpublished PhD thesis.) Johannesburg: University of Johannesburg.

Kupers, W., & Volckmann, R. (2009). A dialogue on Integral Leadership. *Integral Leadership Review, IX*(4), 1-11

Laubscher, L. (2013). *Human Niches: Spiral Dynamics for Africa.* (PhD dissertation.) Modderfontein: Da Vinci Institute.

Liddle, J. (2010). Twenty-first century public leadership with complex governance systems: some reflections. *Journal of Policy and Politics, 38*(4), 657-663.

Manley, K., O'Keeffe, H., Jackson, C., Pearce, J., & Smith, S. (2014). A shared purpose framework to deliver person-centred, safe and effective care: organisational transformation using practice development methodology. *International Practice Development Journal, 4*(1), 1-32.

Metcalf, G.S. (2014). *Social Systems and Design* (Vol 1). Tokyo and NY: Springer.

Musgrave Jr, A.W. (2014). Management vs. leadership in the Public sector. *The Public Manager,* 56-59.

Muswaka, L. (2014). The Two-Tier Structure and Co-determination: Should South Africa follow the German Example? *Mediterranean Journal of Social Science, 5*(9), 142-147.

Muthein, Y. (2013). Public Service Reform: Key Challenges of Execution. *Strategic Review for Southern Africa, 36*(2), 126-142.

Mwanza, L., Mwitwa, J., & Mukunto, K. (2014). Good Governance and the Media in Zambia between the Years 2008 and 2013. *Africa Insights, 44*(30), 82-96.

Nkuna, N., & Sebola, M. (2015). Coping with Leadership Persona in South Africa: Public Administration Practice: Implications on Macro-Policy Initiatives and Implementations. *Bangladesh e-Journal of Sociology, 12*(1), 6-19.

Ossai-Ugbah, C. (2011). Corruption and Societal Transformation: Exegesis. *Ogbomoso Journal of Theology, 16*(3), 137-158.

Pavlidis, P. (2015). Social Consciousness, Education and Transformative Activity. *Journal For Critical Education Policy Studies, 13*(2), 1-37.

Prenting, T. (1992). Co-determination: its practice and applicability to the United States of America. *S.A.M. Advanced Management Journal,* Corpus Christi Journal, 57(2).

Prinsloo, M. (2012). Consciousness Models in Action: Comparison. *Integral Leadership Review, 8*(1) 1-24.

Saydee, C.M., & Pillay, P. (2013). Assessing South Africa's Food Security Strategy through a good governance lens. *Politeia, 32*(2), 84-104.

Schwella, E., Botha, C., Brand, D., Engelbrecht, M., & van Eijbergen, R. (2015). *South African Governance.* Cape Town: Oxford University Press Southern Africa.

Senge, P.M., Hamilton, H., & Kania, K. (2015). The Dawn of Systems Leadership. *Sanford Social Innovation Review, 13*(1), 27-33.

Senge, P.M. (1996). *Leading Learning Organisations: The Bold, the Powerful and the Invisible.* Palo Alto, CA: Davies-Black Publishing.

Sirisetti, S. (2006). Quality Leadership in the Public sector: Strategies and Challenges. *Journal of Commerce, 3*(4), 45-48.

Snowden, D., & Boone, M.E. (2007). A Leader's Framework for Decision Making. *Harvard Business Review,* (November), 69-76.

Merriam-Webster.com. (2015). *Social system* [Online]. Retrieved from http://www.merriam-webster.com/dictionary/socialsystem.

Statistics South Africa. (2014). *Poverty Trends in South Africa. An examination of absolute poverty between 2006 and 2011.* Retrieved from: http://www.statssa.govt.za/.

Statistics South Africa. (2016). *Population Statistics Census.* Retrieved from: www.statssa.gov.za/publications/pop.

Summers, C. (1982). Co-determination in the United States of America: A projection of problems and potentials. *Journal of Comparative Corporate Law and Securities Regulation*, 4, 155-191.

Toendepi, J. (2017). *Transformational Leadership as a Catalyst to Higher Levels of Consciousness in Social Systems*. (Unpublished Masters' Thesis.) Johannesburg: University of Johannesburg.

Toendepi, J. (2013). *A Systemic Perspective to Wealth Creation in South Africa through Learning and Adaptation*. (Doctoral Thesis.) Saarbrücken, Germany: Lambert Publishing.

Ungerer, M., Pretorius, M., & Herholdt, J. (2011). *Viable Business Strategies: A Field book for Leaders*. Randburg: Knowres Publishing.

Van Wart, M. (2013). Lessons from Leadership Theory and Contemporary Challenges of Leaders. *Public Administrative Review*, 73(4), 553-565.

Veldsman, T. H. (2015). MPhil in Management: Lecture Notes Leadership Challenges in Emerging Countries.

Vilakati, V. M. (2013). *African Spirituality Consciousness within the Personal Interpersonal Professional leadership*. (Unpublished Master's Thesis.) Johannesburg: University of Johannesburg.

Viljoen, R. C. (2015). *Organisational Change & Development: An African Perspective*. Randburg: Knowres Publishing.

Viljoen, R. C. (2008). *Sustainable Organisational Transformation Through Inclusivity*. (Thesis Research Paper.) Retrieved from: http://uir.unisa.ac.za/bitstream/handle/10500/726/00thesis.pdf;jsessionid=7E4388C7BA63B3239F19DA46D876C751?sequence=2

World Economic Forum. (2015). Retrieved from: www.3weforum.org/doc/WEF-GlobalCom.

ENDNOTES

1 Forman & Ross, 2013.
2 Statistics South Africa, 2016.
3 Statistics South Africa, 2014.
4 The Global Competitive Index, 2015.
5 World Economic Forum Report, 2015.
6 Toendepi, 2017.
7 Muthein, 2013, p. 127.
8 Toendepi, 2017.
9 Toendepi, 2013.
10 The World Economic Forum, 2015.
11 Toendepi, 2013.
12 Nkuna & Sebola, 2015.
13 Kellis & Ran, 2014.
14 Schwella, Botha, Brand, Engelbrecht & van Eijbergen, 2015, p. 2.
15 Merriam-Webster, 2015.
16 Metcalf, 2014.
17 Keevy, 2018.
18 Cilliers, 1998.
19 Metcalf, 2015.
20 Toendepi, 2017.
21 Ungerer, Pretorius & Herholdt, 2011.
22 Viljoen, 2014.
23 Ibid.
24 Snowden & Boon, 2007.

25   Jordan, 2011, p. 48.
26   Senge, 1996.
27   Concelman and Phelps, 2014.
28   Musgrave, 2014.
29   Beck, 2013.
30   Kaufman, 2005, p. 481.
31   Broadbent, 2015.
32   Castels, 2010, p. 1576.
33   Dibrell, Craig, Kim & Johnson, 2012, p. 591.
34   Pavlidis, 2015.
35   Viljoen, 2015, p. 113.
36   Kaufman, 2003.
37   Viljoen, 2015.
38   Ibid
39   Ibid.
40   Dibrell, 2015, p. 591.
41   Vilakati, 2013.
42   Achua & Lussier, 2013.
43   Beck, 2013.
44   Muzafer Sherif, 1953.
45   Kaufman, 2005.
46   Pavlidis, 2015.
47   Manley, O'Keefe, Jackson, Pearce & Smith, 2014.
48   Toendepi, 2017.
49   Senge et al., 2015.
50   Laubscher, 2013.
51   Heifetz & Laurie, 2001, p. 131.
52   Veldsman, 2015, p. 90.
53   Liddle, 2015.
54   Laubscher, 2013, p. 242.
55   Wilson2000.
56   Hamel, 2009, p. 5.
57   Viljoen-Terblanche, 2008.
58   Clawson, 2003.
59   Toendepi, 2017.
60   Ibid.
61   Ackoff, 2004, cited in Metcalf, 2014.
62   Metcalf, 2014.
63   Senge, 2003.
64   Toendepi, 2017.
65   Achua & Lussier, 2013.
66   Ali, 2015, p. 67.
67   Toendepi, 2017.
68   van Wart, 2013.
69   Kupers & Volckmann, 2008.
70   Beck et al., 2018.
71   LeBaron, 2005.
72   Senge et al., 2015.

73   Senge et al., 2015.

74   Beck, 2013.

75   Van Wart, 2013, p. 560.

76   Beck et al., 2018.

77   Keevy, 2018.

78   Veldsman, 2016.

79   Metcalf, 2014.

80   Schwella et al., 2015.

81   World Bank, 2014.

82   Schwella et al., 2015.

83   Ali, 2015; Mwanza, Mwitwa & Mukunto, 2014.

84   Ali, 2015.

85   Schwella et al., 2015.

86   Sayeed & Pillay, 2013.

87   Muthein, 2013.

88   Sirisetti, 2006, p. 46.

89   Schwella, et al., 2015; Ali, 2015.

90   Ossai-Ugbah, 2011.

91   Schwella et al., 2015.

92   Ali, 2015.

93   Sayeed & Pillay, 2013.

94   Mwanza et al., 2014.

95   Summers, 1982.

96   Muswaka, 2014.

97   Ibid.

98   Viljoen-Terblanche, 2008.

8

CREATING SHARED VALUE THROUGH CO-DETERMINATION – SOUTH AFRICAN CASES

Rica Viljoen and Tonja Blom

INTRODUCTION

Most organisational development experts and strategies hold the view that if an organisation discards its traditional structures, titles, rules and controls, the chances of success and sustainability deteriorate significantly; it could even be reckless to trade in such a way. However, the cases below paradoxically ask for exactly this shift in thinking. An inclusive, shared and co-determined approach to organisational dynamics is proposed, which is described theoretically as an extreme stage of participative management.

In this chapter, a few attempts to implement co-determination in South Africa are shared. Although successful cases with proven success or sustainability are few and far between, evidence is presented of an alternative stance towards employee relations in companies. In cases where this strategy has been formalised and implemented, it seems as if the effects of the attempt result in an exponential growth in business indicators such as presentism, engagement, productivity and customer centricity. In cases where workers take authority of managing self and others in the organisation, a corresponding decline in indicators such as employee turnover, incidents, accidents and strikes are also indicated.

The cases discussed here, e.g. Eskom and Cashbuild, remind one of the sentiments of Steiner[1], who said passionately that:

> *Our highest endeavor must be to develop free human beings who are able to impart purpose and direction to their lives. The need for imagination, a sense of truth and a feeling of responsibility – these three forces are the very nerve of education.*

The case of Interstate Bus Lines is also briefly introduced; this case forms the foundation of this book and is presented in more depth in Chapter 9. Further, the story of Solms Delta is shared courtesy of its owners. In contrast, a story is shared of a farm where attempts towards empowerment failed, while Mangwanani Spa is used as an example where workers share in ownership. Lastly, themes that emerge through the various cases are analysed and meta-insights about co-determination are derived. The reader is invited to suspend their current thinking about ownership, profit share, power dynamics and employee relations and explore whether these cases could provide a new narrative – one that might re-write the way in which we can connect sustainably by creating shared values over boundaries of social systems.

ESKOM – THE UNFOLDING VISION INITIATIVE[i]

Background

Mid 1985, Eskom was "hit" by a revolution, which turned it inside out to become one of the top electricity utilities in the world.

This revolution came about as a result of the findings of the De Villiers Commission, which had been appointed by the PW Botha government two years prior as a result of the government's displeasure with Eskom's general performance. Eskom was then known as the Electricity Supply Commission, the ESC or ESCOM. In the media, ESC was said to mean *"easy, slow and comfortable"*.

This revolution was preceded by the appointment of Dr. Ian McRae as Chief Executive Officer and Dr. John Maree as Chairman. The previous six Commissioners were relieved of their duties and replaced by an Electricity Council as an oversight body of 14 representing various stakeholders. The day-to-day management vested in a Management Board consisting of Executive Directors managing different portfolios, which was chaired by Ian McRae.

In 1991, Eskom embarked on an internal review of its performance since 1985, which was facilitated by Deloitte Pim Goldby of London. The Eskom team was led by Jac Messerschmidt, Executive Director in the Chief Executive's Office, who was supported by three other Executive Directors. This team euphemistically became known in the organisation as *"The three blind mice plus one"* or the *"goofers"*. The outcome of this intervention was entitled *"Eskom's STRATEGIC REPOSITIONING"*, which focused on further cost reductions and restructuring post 1985.

This ignited a second revolution, led by Gwede Mantashe (then General Secretary of the National Union of Mineworkers) and other Eskom trade unions. They styled their resistance *"Save the Eskom Campaign"* and petitioned McRae that Eskom's Management Board and Electricity Council should abandon this new *"Eskom STRATEGIC REPOSITIONING"*, as the cost reductions and restructuring entailed further retrenchment of Eskom staff.

---

i Interview with Dr GF Lindeque, previously Executive Director (Human Resources) AT Eskom, by Dr Rica Viljoen of Mandala Consulting and the Henley School of Business

Ian McRae charged George Lindeque (Executive Director, Human Resources) to develop an implementable sustainable solution and to get Eskom out of this quagmire. *"George, fix it", Ian said firmly. "I do not want this to happen again!"* This was the birth of Eskom's Unfolding Vision (EUV) initiative. The Deloitte Pim Goldby intervention was a very expensive lesson for Eskom, i.e. that Eskom's Board of Management and the Electricity Council could not just do as they pleased.

Establishing the EUV process and what it entailed

After many hours and days of deliberations and consultations between Lindeque and Paul Semark (Executive Director - Generation) with corporates, consultants (particularly Christo Nel who provided valuable and insightful guidance), academics, politicians, and local and other experts from abroad, as well as lobbying Eskom's executive directors, John Maree, other management levels and the trade unions, it was agreed that the focus of the EUV would be to establish a process whereby trade unions could meaningfully influence decision-making in Eskom. In other words, it was the establishment of a process of co-determination between management and the trade unions. An implementation team, superbly led by Riaan Neethling (General Manager - Human Resources) and consisting of Eskom management and trade union representatives, developed the implementation and communication processes.

For a variety of reasons, this implementation process and the communication thereof was difficult and tiresome, and it had its fair share of diversions, bumps, potholes, boycotts and walkouts. It was also extremely complicated to establish buy-in and acceptance on both sides of the table, and it was very necessary to unlock many unexpected conundrums to progress. The philosophical bases were experienced as very foreign, after all, why would you trust your archrivals at the workplace to co-determine your work future? Despite this, the Eskom and trade union teams did a magnificent job maintaining the momentum.

The process started with a plenary consisting of more than 300 managers, trade union leaders and shop stewards. Facilitated mixed (Eskom management and trade union representatives) small groups initially had to indicate what activities and matters in Eskom should be stopped, what activities should be maintained, and what new activities should be initiated. After moderating all the outputs, these small groups generated 150 different matters to be further debated and considered.

Subsequently these 150 matters were packed into six "baskets", namely governance, equal opportunities, training and development, housing, information sharing, and process and structural matters. Six joint task groups produced action plans and monitoring mechanisms. The end result of these deliberations was that comprehensive structures and supporting processes and procedures were jointly designed and established concerning the following matters:

- Three trade union representatives would be appointed to the Electricity Council, Eskom's governing body.
- The establishment of a forum to deliberate on future strategic matters and direction.
- The establishment of a national negotiating forum to deal with major national matters like wages, salaries and conditions of service.
- The establishment of fora at different sites to deal with the day-to-day on-site matters.
- The establishment of ad hoc fora when required, for instance the appointment of Ian McRae's successor was intensely discussed before the appointment was announced.

The main impact of the unfolding vision process on Eskom

In reviewing the EUV initiative, the following matters needed to be considered:

- **Some general thoughts**
  This was not a "rational", quick fix process. It took a long time, was difficult and required extensive information sharing and consultation. It required maximum consensus seeking and constrained management prerogative and led to protracted decision-making. It required a fundamental shift in management thinking. It did not mean an end to disagreements and disputes.

- **Relationship matters**
  A foundation was laid for new partnership relationships with a greater tolerance and pragmatism. It also developed a greater capacity to address differences and conflict and significantly reduced adversity and rhetoric. Trade unions also developed a greater Eskom business understanding.

- **Substantive matters**
  Many restructuring agreements were concluded and a greater understanding of the management of surplus staff resulted. Participative structures, processes and procedures were developed and implemented and local dispute settling was accepted. Eskom and its unions moved out of the political spotlight.

- **Some concerns**
  Communicating the EUV initiative was difficult because it was seen as Eskom 'giving away the family silver'. It would also appear as if the importance of balancing "rights and responsibilities" was not fully resolved.

What made this work?

The seven main critical success factors were:
- Bold and disciplined insightful leadership from management and trade unions.
- Continued and extensive administrative support.
- Develop the common ground and unfold a shared vision with open minds.
- Consult before taking action and keep to the agreements.
- The process has to be continuously managed at all levels.
- Energy and the will to do it but with patience.
- Rights have responsibilities and obligations.

Close

Through the EUV, it was Eskom's intent to establish a mutually beneficial relationship between Eskom and the trade unions that would contribute to Eskom becoming a top performing viable electricity utility internationally. This was achieved in early 2000 and maintained for some years thereafter.

Today the notion of the EUV is probably not known at all in Eskom. This could mean that the EUV was embedded, that the imperative of sound trade union relations has become less important, or that the HR game in South Africa has completely changed.

CASHBUILD

Albert Koopman was appointed Managing Director of Cashbuild in 1982. Early in his career he attended one of Don Beck's workshops in Johannesburg and also interacted with Loraine Laubscher on understanding thinking systems of South African people with a PURPLE centre of gravity. He truly understood PURPLE[ii] thinking systems and implemented a tribal system in Cashbuild where everybody was viewed as part of a collective. A real South African version of participative management was implemented by Cashbuild, and the company experienced great success.

Koopman believed in visibly-felt leadership, and spent a lot of time interacting with the workforce. He was known as a leader who really listened, and became aware of the lack of business understanding of workers, the perceived arrogance of leadership, and distrust in the system. In interacting with the system, Koopman became aware that workers really wanted to be involved in running the organisation. The need for participation could not be denied. Workers were committed to skills development and the creation of a culture that was conducive to diversity, and also wanted equality ownership. Ultimately, Koopman found that workers did not feel that they were treated with dignity and respect.

---

ii   Thinking systems are explained in Chapter 2.

Koopman acted on what he had heard. He reduced status symbols in the organisation and management started to assist workers with difficult tasks. He also implemented a profit-share scheme, and through involvement in decisions, ultimately increased the productivity and commitment of his workforce. Workers were even given the power to contribute to the dismissal of management members who did not deliver. Management information was widely shared, and a work committee had the authority to run the business, make appointments and conduct dismissals. He adopted the philosophy that nobody would steal anything that they already owned, and staff members were trusted with keys to the stores that contained significant levels of stock.

When Koopman left Cashbuild, more than a third of the staff owned shares in the business, and trust and openness had taken the place of control and secrecy. Koopman combined innovation and risk in an inclusive approach of co-creation, participation and commitment, with the business results including a decline in staff turnover from 126% to 9%.[2] Later, Koopman sold all his interests in Cashbuild and emigrated.

Laubscher explained that for years the assumption was that engineers or business strategists built the best companies, which was wrong. Tjaart van Staden attempted to continue with the model, but according to Laubscher, he was too impatient. An in-depth understanding of PURPLE especially, but also of other thinking systems as described by spiral dynamics, is required to ensure that organisational solutions are deep and accurate.

Almost four decades ago, after initial attempts to find new ways of doing business, Laubscher[3] says:

> *"Your country has great resources, much envied by others, in industrial metals, precious metals, chemicals, diamonds and some fuels. Now that I can observe that you are planning a course, which will also put you among the world leaders in productivity of management, I will prepare to salute you people among the top winners."*

Even though a new political model, namely democracy, was formed in South Africa, it seems as though initial attempts to implement co-determination in the 1980s were forgotten.

INTERSTATE BUS LINES

Interstate Bus Lines is a private bus company that is based in Bloemfontein. Over the last 25 years, the organisation has invested annually in individual, group and organisational development. Although the company faced difficult times over the years, it managed to construct a culture of inclusivity and trust; everyone in the organisation was exposed to interventions that assisted them to understand their own personality type. They engaged in emotional intelligence development work and teams now regularly do team-building sessions. Organisational culture studies are completed at regular intervals, and the results of these studies are integrated into strategies, business plans and ultimately performance management. The Benchmark of Engagement (BeQ) is used in the diagnostic phase of these studies as it consists of multi-cultural and diagnostic organisational development properties that describe the human energy to perform in the system. The BeQ further has the philosophy of consciously listening to different voices in the system – both qualitatively and quantitatively.

Twice, during national strikes of COSATU, the workers at Interstate did not strike. This resulted in organisational benefits that largely outweighed the anticipated loss of one day's participation in a strike. Further, relationships with key stakeholders are engaging and positive, which ensures a license to operate in an industry that is reliant on the awarding of tenders.

Every three to five years a full strategic process is facilitated. Scenario planning is done, business architecture is constructed and a strategy map is co-created. This map is used to indicate strategic goals that are translated into operational goals, operational initiatives, and ultimately, performance indicators. Over the years, the number of people who were involved in these strategic sessions increased. The boundaries of these strategic sessions are permutable and union shop stewards, board members and different levels of management are invited and welcomed to co-create.

Spiral dynamics principles were introduced in the organisation, and for the last eight years, different thinking structures have been considered in the translation of strategy. Loraine Laubscher facilitated spiral dynamics sessions with management, workers and union members, and Viljoen's philosophy of Inclusivity has been followed. Diversity of thought is not only respected, but also stimulated and promoted.

Four years ago, the Human Resources manager, Henk van Zyl, managed to implement the concept of co-determination, which was an idea that had occupied his thinking for an extended period. Since then he has been actively involved with various unions, wage negotiations and bargaining councils. During his career, Henk became sure that alternative options of managing employee relationships existed. For him, the principles of inclusivity and spiral dynamics made intuitive sense. Later, when conducting a Psychological Map, it became clear that Henk was YELLOW. A YELLOW leader is considered to be an integral, functional leader who is not scared to speak the truth in a system, and has the capability of weaving together different thinking systems into an integral tapestry of being. This complex thinking system allowed him to consider alternative options of organising, overcoming the risk of not having enough, understanding the paradox that to receive one must give, and having the ability to identify the potential gifts of all the different people with different thinking in the Interstate system. He became aware that more than 90 per cent of the workers of Interstate were PURPLE, i.e. they were tribal, collective and very concerned about family and traditions; it was important to them to be respected and treated with dignity. He also realised that the management team was largely BLUE and ORANGE. This is a blend between people who are risk adverse, rule-following, risk-taking and enterprising. Henk knew that the time was right to propose co-determination; the levels of trust in the organisation were high, the internal capacity had been built due to the various developmental initiatives, and the management and other stakeholders were accustomed to participating in the strategic planning process.

The process of co-determination was constructed during a strategic session with three members of national unions, the management team and shop stewards. Members of the taxi industry were also incorporated. Through a facilitative process of appreciation, Inclusivity and spiral dynamics, a joint strategy was co-created and agreed upon. Union members thoroughly enjoyed the process, yet voiced a concern that workers would think that they joined management. Management, meanwhile, was concerned that they had to share responsibility in terms of planning, discipline and reward, and that they might lose control. The workers, on the other hand, felt that although they trusted management, they might lose representation if the union joined management. Finally, the national representation felt that it was progressive, but idealistic. Little did the participants of this process know that history was set in motion that day, and that the co-created strategy that emerged had such a powerful integrative power, that it could only be described as magical and transformational.

The successful implementation of co-determination forms the crux of the rest of this book. Henk van Zyl not only shared the strategy of Interstate as a case study, but he also made all the relative supporting documents and templates available to other practitioners to follow. In 2016, Henk was awarded the SABPP's HR practitioner of the year award for his contribution to the profession. He also acted as ambassador for the SABPP and actively continues to share his insights, memories and practices. The case of IBL is shared in more detail in Chapter 9, while further practical advice for practitioners is given in Chapter 10.

SOLMS-DELTA: A CASE OF CO-DETERMINATION IN SOUTH AFRICA

Solms-Delta is more than just a wine estate. In many ways it is a pioneering farm, but most importantly, it is the first 50/50 co-ownership farm in South Africa. This farm involves much, much more than mere winemaking. Solms-Delta embraced diversity splits to emerge with a unique package of wines, music, cuisine, environment, museums, and most importantly, shared ownership.

Professor Mark Solms spent many years abroad and is best known for his landmark discovery of the brain mechanisms of dreaming, as well as the integration of modern neuroscience with psychoanalytic theories and methods, however the South African roots of this world-renowned neuroscientist brought him back home. In 2001, Solms purchased the historic Delta wine estate with a mission to revitalise it, but also to fundamentally rethink Cape winemaking traditions in the process. After assuming custodianship of the 320-year old estate, Solms started to re-establish the vineyards and cellars. However, very soon, Solms realised that he was partaking in division, us-

and-them and oppression. To keep the dream alive, current thinking had to change radically.

With his rich knowledge of neuroscience and psychology, Solms looked at this dilemma as he would look at a sick patient. He realised the importance of doing something actively about the legacy of his European forebears (who had settled in the Cape six generations before) and thereby addressing the pressing social and economic problems facing South Africa today.

Solms really wanted to make a difference at the grass-roots level. He sponsored better education, medical care, social work and a crèche even before the business was profitable. The inevitable by-product of this was that in conjunction with all the other physical building activities on the farm, trust was slowly being rebuilt, and workers are still supported in this regard today.

The Delta farm was originally a wine farm, but at the time Solms bought it, it was producing fruit. Solms-Delta started operations in 2002, and a major operational overhaul commenced to convert the fruit farm back into a wine farm. From the onset, working conditions, living conditions and communication posed tremendous challenges. Solms tried to convince the farm's virtually indentured tenants that his intentions to institute land reform were genuine. However, realisation hit hard as Solms admitted to himself that he was becoming the "white boss", resulting in poor work ethics, poor communication, theft and unmotivated staff. This broken social dynamic confounded Solms, and he attempted to explore ways for dealing with this dynamic in a different way. That meant seeing the project as a patient, and not a wine farm.

He embarked upon a medical strategy as he decided to diagnose problems with his newly-purchased wine farm. That meant he had to start with the patient's history, then current symptoms, and finally a diagnosis. Of course that meant taking a look at what was happening on this piece of land, and the result was an archaeological dig.

Solms[iii] persuaded his long-time friend, British philanthropist Richard Astor, scion of a celebrated Anglo-American family, to buy the neighbouring farm in order to increase the estate's development capital. Solms and Astor partnered, resulting in each controlling one third of the modern-day Delta estate. Solms and Astor, in an unprecedented move, then both put their farms up as collateral so that a third adjoining farm could be purchased for the workers. Together they tackled the social realities of South African agriculture.

In South Africa's rural agricultural areas, the children of farm workers have been obliged to become farm workers themselves. The logical choice of vehicle to enable shared ownership was through the establishment of a Trust. Established in 2005, the mission of the Wijn de Caap Trust was to break the cycle of poverty and dependency among historically disadvantaged tenants and employees on the Solms-Delta estate. The Trust aimed at broadening its horizons by creating educational opportunities and

---

iii Interview conducted by Dr Tonja Blom

minimising the burdens on the parents, while simultaneously improving the quality of life on the farm. The Wijn de Caab Trust now had a 33% equity stake in Solms-Delta, and the profit from wine sales has been used to build attractive houses for workers and their families, as well as refurbishing and upgrading existing houses. All houses are fitted with satellite televisions, and social programmes have greatly improved the workers' health, education and general quality of life. To make this three-way partnership work, Solms and Astor put their own assets on the line, reasoning that without a realistic wealth-sharing model their own privileges were both indefensible and unsustainable.

As the shared ownership structure came into existence, the Trust identified the primary goals of shared ownership such as land tenure, housing, education and skillfully equipping the next generation. Placing the business into a Trust was both difficult and important, as nobody gained direct financial remuneration from it. Farm workers are represented on the Board of the Trust, however, thus they share in the decision-making and the Trust is safeguarded against misuse and abuse.

With the Wijn de Caab Trust solely benefiting their employees and farm residents, Solms and Astor then turned to the Franschhoek Valley and broader Cape Winelands district. In 2007, the two families established the privately funded Delta Trust, which seeks to facilitate an inclusive sense of community through educational, cultural, sporting and social programmes. The Trust founders believed that what happened on local Franschhoek farms could have a ripple effect throughout the valley, the winelands, the country and beyond.

As mentioned previously, archival diggings started in 2005. Everybody on the farm assisted with the dig as archaeologists uncovered the ruins of what was believed to be the original farm dwelling from 1690. As the diggings progressed, a deep realisation hit home.

"We have to tell the story first", Solms explained. He refers here to the life stories of all the workers and of the farm. Production and operations have to take a back seat, as the story must become the first priority. From a business perspective, this can be interpreted as poor business sense, organisational suicide or even insanity. It meant that a historian had to be appointed to research the factual information of the past, and this information was added to the archeological findings to create a picture of what really happened in this area. One day, a farm worker who took part in the dig and who saw himself as a part of the patient that was being examined, found an artefact and said to Solms: "Sien jy meneer, ons mense was voor joune hierso".[iv] This was the first verbal contact between the farm worker and Solms; the conversation was the trigger point that drove Solms to ensure that the farm had to stand for everything that was authentic and traditionally South African. From here on, the farm would enable the stories and histories of all the inhabitants to be heard and honoured.

---

iv An Afrikaans comment meaning: "Do you see Sir? Our people were here before yours".

Right from the onset everybody on the farm was consulted. As workers saw tangibly what was happening around them – archaeological digs, a museum and the building of houses – trust slowly grew and increased. Although hesitant at first, active dialogue grew with trust. Everybody's voice and story had to be heard. This was no small undertaking, however Solms was committed to the goal. Every employee now had an interest in making Solms-Delta a success and all experienced high levels of trust. The purpose of creating trust was to contribute to greater social cohesion and inclusiveness in South African communities through careful, patient and creative local cultural work. Because of this purpose, the Trust currently supports a broad range of projects, including education, heritage, social upliftment, sports and recreation.

In those early days, a musician and good friend of Solms often visited the farm and played his guitar for the farm workers. The music and culture, as a vehicle for transformation on the farm, emerged. A music museum, The Music Van de Caab Centre, was even erected on the farm. Why? "Because music, which is one of humanity's most primal means of communication, crosses boundaries and has the power to heal and unite; a power which is terribly necessary in post-apartheid South Africa", explained Solms. "Exploring the musical aspect of our heritage also celebrates the many influences and peoples who put their own stamp on what we now call South African music. No single part is more important than the whole, and that's what we hope we've put into a lively, fun and educational package." Music is continually used as a manner of social therapy. A woman's choir and brass band play at local events, provide activities and allow for the expression of feelings and emotions. All guides of the music centre are Solms-Delta farm residents or from the local communities, and are involved in some musical ensembles on the estate. They have all been involved in the making of replica instruments, which they demonstrate and answer questions about, or just chat about the meaning of music in their own lives. They all bring their authentic views and personal involvement to this musical experience.

Shared ownership is an expensive strategy. Benefits, in particular, are expensive. The scope of this almost overwhelmed Solms, as everything that happened on the farm was funded privately. Education, the crèche, housing, social enterprises and all other benefits were privately sponsored. These included four teachers, a full-time social worker, a full-time health-care practitioner, salaries and education, to name but a few. Needless to say, this resulted in enormous pressure on the business.

Ultimately, the estate raised huge expectations in the industry in terms of their progressive activities, however they never really had outside or government support. A pressing question to this day is how to communicate the story of Solms-Delta to the end consumer, given the large number of wines available in the retail space. Things like rack space for "ethical wine production" is one idea, yet retailers are slow to buy into this as South African consumers are not really concerned about ethics.

In 2012 a radical shift happened in terms of what was viable for the business, where costs could be cut, and how this model could urgently become sustainable.

In a radical effort to upscale the business, operations were restructured and controls were tightened. The estate's commercial footprint had to be enlarged and wine production had to increase. Discussions with the government took place from 2012 to 2014, and the then Minister of Agriculture (who made statements about 50/50 land ownership) acknowledged the huge contribution made by Solms-Delta. This led to an acknowledgement by the government in July 2015 that Solms-Delta was the first 50/50 land ownership business in the wine industry. On 10 December 2016, an official launch ceremony took place on the estate with the Minister of Agriculture in attendance.

As affairs took a turn for the worst, a meeting was called with everybody in typical Solms-Delta fashion to discuss cash flow and the possible cutting of benefits. Immediately, everybody agreed to cut satellite television – they all wanted to work to get the farm and the business on track and make the business successful. Workers were even prepared to use the local clinic again instead of the private clinic on site.

The support that the workers showed in this crisis spoke of the level of responsibility they felt to make this business a success for the betterment of all.

This model is a showcase that shared ownership in the farming industry is possible. Hard work is being done to ensure the viability and sustainability of this model. In total there are 98 people on the farm, and roughly 250 beneficiaries further benefit from this model. Retrospectively, the Solms venture indicates that this model is extremely expensive, and it would perhaps have been easier to establish the business first, become profitable and then create shared ownership and all the related benefits. In such a case, the pressing question would be how trust could be earned. Starting up a new business by using the Solms-Delta model will no doubt be extremely difficult (if at all possible), however the estate bears testament to an idealistic, entrepreneurial venture that is starting to come into its own, 15 years after commencement. The business hopes to break even in 2018. As do all new businesses, they struggle with difficulties related to incremental benefits versus growth. Production doubles every two years, but coupled with a 30% profit margin this creates cash flow difficulties. According to Solms, growth is needed to cover overheads and to ensure a sustainable company structure. Being able to balance growth and cash flow will thus be instrumental to ensuring a sustainable future.

There are projects in the pipeline to ensure future sustainability, all of which are aimed at positive transformation. One of these is a large cellar incubator, focused on the facilitation of black-owned brands. Generally, the large outlay of buying a farm is a huge hindrance given the prohibitive cost for new brands to enter the market; it would have been easier to window-dress wholesale purchase and rebranding under a black brand or just by using a different label. The idea for this facility is to cater for and subsidise production costs for these brands, with key underpinning tenants that can carry most of the operational costs, ensuring shared knowledge, a grape source and key suppliers to create an effective production leg. A second leg will involve business and marketing, as well as sales support in order to build the brand. Once the brand has established momentum, a third leg will constitute will entail partnership with large banks and funding to secure land ownership for black brands.

Solms believes that the only real way to transform the industry is to ensure that brand owners and decision makers who are not white, enter into the industry. Solms-Delta will be an underpinning tenant, again subsidising that which is required to transform the wider industry. Further future plans include a packing shed, which will not only result in instant job creation, but also in home ownership and shared ownership in the longer term.

THE DEVASTATING CONTRAST: THE STORY OF A CHICKEN FARM

On 11 December 2016, Nel[4] wrote about yet another productive farm outside Brakpan that had been destroyed by mismanagement. The Department of Rural Development and Land Reform had purchased the land, assets, chickens and all vehicles from the previous owner when he retired, and various previously disadvantaged and aspiring farmers could apply for this land. The Department selected six applicants and on 27 November 2015, handed the farm over to them at absolutely no cost - they received the farm and 34,000 chickens. Within a few months, they had sold all the chickens and wasted the money on pleasure and holidays.

The state supplied them with a further 30,000 chickens in the hope that the farmers would use this second incentive to buy chicken feed. The six farm recipients sold most of these chickens as well, whilst they allowed the remaining chickens to die of hunger. In less than a year, on 15 November 2016, the SPCA (Society for the Prevention of Cruelty to Animals) came upon a gruesome sight where hundreds of dead chickens were lying in cages, and the rest of the birds had no feathers left and hardly any flesh on their bodies. Live chickens sat on chicken carcasses. The SPCA had to kill the remaining 3,000 chickens.

The 23 workers (some of whom had been on the farm for more than 12 years) were complaining bitterly. They had not received wages in five months, and were unable to feed their families.

The six land beneficiaries were unable to uphold contracts with Checkers and Spar (which generated a monthly income of between R800,000 and R900,000), and insisted on working only with cash and writing invoices by hand, even though a worker knew how to capture everything on a computer. The result of this empowerment effort was that 23 workers and their families were without work and income, and thousands of chickens died.

The above story clearly indicates the dark, damaging side of empowerment. In these situations, it is clearly not a good idea to give ownership away for free. The importance of heritage and culture can also not be underplayed. If shared owners are proud of their culture and heritage (as opposed to having received a handout), they will take better care of ensuring sustainability. Receiving land without any attached heritage will be doomed from the start, however given the financial burden of purchasing a farm, equipment and other assets, a Trust seems to be the obvious answer. As in the case of Solms-Delta, the land deed is kept in the Trust, and is only handed over once the farm is profitable.

Communication, consultation and shared decision-making have to form part of daily operations, as this implies some form of shared responsibility and/or accountability when things start to go wrong. This will also ensure accountability and action, and that the strategy is adjusted in time.

THE STORY OF MANGWANANI, THE AFRICAN SPA

Erin Limbert met Virginia in 1998, who expressed her desire to work part time to earn an extra income. Limbert assisted her in studying massage and physiology, borrowing books from the library and making her family, friends and relatives available for Virginia to practice on. Virginia went on to study head and body massage.

Mangwanani – the African Spa – came into existence in 2002 when Limbert (the CEO) set the wheels in motion to give birth to her dream. The dream was to create a retreat which embraced the ethos of revitalisation with an African flavour that was specifically directed at uplifting rural women.

As this was a unique concept, it presented quite a challenge. At the time, Virginia was well on her way to becoming one of Mangwanani's first therapists. The spa opened and catered for six guests a day, however with dedication and the hard work of Virginia and other staff members, this soon grew to nine guests a day. Virginia's story became a model for success as Mangwanani continued to invest in people and their education. Simultaneously, the business slowly grew; today they cater for 84 guests every day.

It has never been the intention of Mangwanani to hold back its employees. Virginia received R50,000 to join her husband's take-away business, however she returned to Mangwanani, and thanks to the financial and practical help she received, she is now the manager of the Palazzo Boutique Spa at Mangwanani.

Nelson was employed as a bus driver who requested funding to start his own glass-glazing company. He received R108,000 from Mangwanani to start up his new venture, and his business is doing well with three employees. Nelson is a successful entrepreneur thanks to his Mangwanani start. Not surprisingly, Nelson's wife Sarina still works for Mangwanani.

Mangwanani African Spa has an average of 120,000 visitors annually and employs over 1,000 people, 95% of which are previously disadvantaged individuals.

The following dominates the Mangwanani story:

- Further education and innovative ideas are always encouraged (even if it could mean resignation).

- Employees are encouraged to accept authority and to do their jobs with full commitment and responsibility.
- The larger environment benefits from their model.
- Mutual trust and respect.

By investing in education, involving workers in their own business realities, and creating an environment of trust and respect, human energy blossoms in the Mangwanani system.

EMERGING INSIGHTS

The stories of Cashbuild, Solms-Delta, Interstate and Mangwanani are steeped in idealism, yet this necessarily begs some questions:
- Is an approach of shared ownership truly transferable?
- Is this strategy realistic without extensive monetary availability (private or public)?
- Is this long journey worth the effort?
- What are the prerequisites for the successful implementation of such a process?

In all the cases shared in this chapter the following themes are presented:
- The intent of leadership to do things differently is evident.
- An understanding of the social-economic conditions of the containing environment or overculture is clear.
- A real and almost tangible desire is felt to involve and include employees not only in decision-making, but also in discipline and ownership.
- Trust is a critical prerequisite for the success of such a strategy.
- It is not a quick- fix, but rather focuses on social innovation.[v]
- Leadership cannot be scared, but must walk the talk.
- An understanding of letting go in order to get, as well as insights into the dynamics of other paradoxes, should be present.
- The approach is based on hope and not on fear – second tier leadership (YELLOW) is a requirement as a catalyst for transformation.
- If one looks carefully, one may be surprised by the goodwill and willingness in the system to co-create.
- Education, training and development are critical prerequisites for building capacity in a system to transform.
- The human energy in the system can be unleashed through inclusivity.
- Empowerment cannot be free – people feel respected and entrusted when they are deserving and legitimate owners of a business.

---

v   In all the cases the process of building trust emerged over 15 years or more.

IN SUMMARY

In the preface to his book, *Holism and Evolution*, General Jan Smuts (1925) said:

> *"The old concepts and formulas are no longer adequate to express our modern outlook. The old bottles of wine will no longer hold the new wine. Management*[vi] *of the future, while it will be built largely of the well-proved materials, will require new and ampler foundations in the light of the immense extension of our intellectual horizons."*

This chapter illustrates that different options are indeed possible. It is critical that leaders develop new understandings and perspectives of their ecologies, and gain an integral insight into the manner in which different people think, and think differently. Massive changes are occurring on the socio-economic level in emerging economies, thus it is crucial for the survival of organisations as ever-changing complex systems for leadership to adjust at every level of a business. Problems need to be addressed fully and on a mutual basis, and leadership should accept and recognise that every individual in the organisation is capable of making a positive contribution, and wants to do so. This, in turn, unleashes meaning in people's lives, individually and collectively, and makes the previous dysfunctional items in systems constructive. Strong leadership is required to create a meaningful future not only for their organisations, but also for humanity at large. This statement is made in the light of international competition and strife for limited resources and conflicting agendas worldwide.

Plato said that those who are able to see beyond the shadows and lies of their culture will never be understood, let alone be believed by the masses. Leadership like this is required to make bold decisions as they hold the key to the salvation of the globe.

In the next chapter, the story of Interstate Bus Lines is presented in more depth. Insights gained through implementing co-determination are presented, and practical advice for implementation follows.

REFERENCES

Beck, D.E., & Van Heerden, H.K. (1987). *The cutting edge of tomorrow*. Pretoria: Jet Set.

Koopman, A. (1991). *Transcultural Management*. Blackwell: Oxford.

Mangwanani. (2018). *Mangwanani*. Retrieved from: http://www.Mangwanani.co.za.

Laubscher, L.I. (2013). *Human Niches: Spiral Dynamics for Africa*. Ph.D dissertation. Modderfontein: Da Vinci Institute. Retrived from: https://www.mandalaconsulting.co.za/Documents/Thesis%20-%20 Loraine%20Laubscher.pdf.

Nel, J. (2016). *So sink jy 'n plaas*. Retrieved from http://www.netwerk24.com/Nuus/Algemeen/so-sink-jy-n-plaas-20161210.

Viljoen, H. (November 2016). *Personal Interview*.

---

vi Don Beck and Keith van Heerden replaced the world 'spiritual temple' with 'management' in the quote above.

ENDNOTES

1   Steiner, (n.d.)
2   Koopman, 1991.
3   Laubscher, 2013.
4   Nel, 2016.

9

PREPARING INTERSTATE BUS LINES FOR THE RADICAL, INCLUSIVE STRATEGY OF CO-DETERMINATION

Rica Viljoen and Henk van Zyl

INTRODUCTION

PART 1: BACKGROUND OF INTERSTATE BUS LINES

The concept of co-determination and the complex social systems within organisations have been discussed in previous chapters. In this chapter, the authors attempt to describe the reason why Interstate Bus Lines (IBL) explored a different Employee Relations (ER) model, and how the principles of the German Co-determination Model were adapted to comply with the company's objectives. An attempt at balancing the thinking patterns between PURPLE and BLUE human niches in such a model is also presented. The IBL case was originally published in *Organisational Change and Development*.[1]

This chapter consists of three sections. The first part deals with the background of Interstate Bus Lines, the second describes the cornerstones and building blocks of the IBL Co-determination Model , and the third part examines IBL's approach and mechanisms to co-determination. The purpose of this chapter is to discuss the broad underlying approach and principles of agreement. Details contained as examples of agreements are attached as Appendices.

BACKGROUND OF IBL

In the book, *Employee Engagement in a South African Context*, Viljoen[2] devoted an entire chapter to the concept of co-determination. She also presented a comprehensive case study on Interstate Bus Lines. Based on that case study, the authors will refer to extracts of relevant issues for the purposes of the topic under discussion.

HISTORY OF EMPLOYEE RELATIONS AT IBL

IBL is a private commuter passenger transport company operating from Bloemfontein and covering Botshabelo, Thaba Nchu and the surrounding areas. The company was established in 1975 with four buses, and has grown to 243 buses and 730 employees. The bus industry plays a vital role in transporting workers, yet over the years this mode of transport has been targeted by militants who have voiced their demands by stoning or burning buses in an attempt to force the industry governing bodies to accede to their demands. The period from 1980 to 1990 witnessed unrest in the labour and trade union movements in South Africa. Workers formed themselves into various unions and during the early part of the decade, numerous strikes broke out across a number of industries. Over that time the labour movement consolidated itself into the Congress of South African Trade Unions (COSATU)[i], however the vibrancy of trade unionism in the 1980s was accompanied by increased strikes and policy brutality.[3]

During 1986, members of COSATU embarked on a series of strikes. In January alone, 185,000 members went on strike. Many Mondays were lost to industrial action and by the end of March 1986, the number of COSATU members on strike had risen to 550,000 - significantly higher than the total of the 450,000 who went on strike in 1984.[4]

Conflict between the Government and labour movements increased to such an extent that the Government raided COSATU House on 29 April 1986 and detained 2,700 unionists throughout the country. On 12 June 1986, COSATU House was barricaded by the South African Defence Force (SADF). From then on, the trade unions carried on with strike action across all industries, and in November 1987, the Union of South African Railways and Harbours (SARHWU) embarked on a six-week strike. During 1988 the Government banned 17 labour organisations; although COSATU was spared, it was prohibited from engaging in political activities. During the same year, the Labour Relations Amended Bill was passed and COSATU embarked on a three-day national strike from 6 to 8 June 1988, which was labelled as a National Peaceful Protest. Between 2.5 and 3 million people observed the stay-away call.[5]

During those turbulent times, IBL was also affected by work stoppages, strikes and the burning of buses. In 1989, the Mass Democratic Movement and other parliamentary groups took action against the government in which IBL did not participate, hence it was seen as an instrument of the state. Disrupting the bus service then would have negatively impacted on the economy of Bloemfontein and IBL decided to continue with operations, disregarding the protests. Unfortunately, during the same year, IBL workers embarked on a strike that lasted for five months. Boycotts and strikes were the order of the day, buses were burned, and roads were blocked and destroyed. Management dismissed all workers and employed casual labour to keep the buses running. The dismissed workers intimidated and even killed some of the casual workers, burned buses and the premises, and threatened management.

---

i   COSATU has since disintegrated.

The turning point in the history of IBL was the re-employment of the dismissed workers after extensive consultation and negotiations with the community, unions and political leaders' structures. Reflecting on this period, Abel Erasmus, the then MD and owner of IBL said during an interview:

> *"Employees were emotional and political and the Union influence was significant. I had to look at productivity in the systems. It was then when I realised that we, as Management, were not aligned with the rest of the organisation. I had a meeting with my team and I realised that there was a 50% compliance with procedures. We were not doing everything right."*

It was evident that trust within IBL had to be ensured and inclusive management strategies and internal HR initiatives had to be put in place. The relationship between management and shop stewards was still based on formal traditional recognition agreements, and periodic work stoppages and strikes took place as a result of the way collective grievances, disciplinary action, and the dismissal of employees were handled. Erasmus sold his shares in the organisation and a 63% Black Broad Based Shareholding was introduced, where employees were granted the opportunity to buy shares in an employee Share Trust. The Company further empowered employees by allocating five sub-contractor buses to an employee ownership Trust scheme.

Inclusive engagement strategies and internal HR initiatives

Abel Erasmus felt very serious about investing in the employees of Interstate Bus Lines. Further, he wanted the full organisation to be part of the transformational process and not only a select few. From 1994, for more than a decade all the workers participated in various organisational development processes. Leon Lategan of Tsumkwe Consulting and Rica Viljoen of Mandala Consulting facilitated strategic sessions, team-building and leadership development initiatives, and a range of interventions were implemented over the years. Lategan and Viljoen facilitated most of the interventions, with every bus driver and various other employees in IBL participating in high rope interventions at Wintershoek Wild. A wide range of experiential training sessions were facilitated, such as a team-building session in the Namib desert with the management team. As a result, management noticed a change in the attitudes and behaviours of both shop stewards and management, and realised that an investment in human resources could make a significant contribution to the success of the organisation.

Inclusive engagement interventions at IBL

As documented by Viljoen[6], in 1998, management decided to conduct an engagement study to describe the organisation and to determine areas in the system where intervention was required to enhance individual, group and organisational dynamics.

The findings of the initial study were as follows:
- Energy in the system was indicated as disillusioned, tired, overstretched and disengaged.
- Trust levels were depleted.
- Top management and middle management were divided.
- Younger supervisors struggled to take the lead over older workers.
- Bus drivers were not treated with dignity.
- Departments blamed each other for breakdowns, the late arrival of buses and poor service delivery.
- Enforcing discipline resulted in mistrust.
- There was a division between the bus drivers and the mechanics.
- High levels of suspicion were experienced at different levels in the organisation.
- Top management were afraid to have a different opinion from that of the CEO.

The BeQ theory indicated that there was not enough energy in the system to deal with the tasks at hand, and without intervention the situation would deteriorate to negatively impact performance indicators such as productivity, turnover and a lack of absenteeism. The Company contracted Viljoen to develop an inclusive turn-around engagement strategy together with the HR Department. The following interventions were carried out:

- **A psycho-analytical team-building session**
  It was important to begin with the alignment of top management, thus a psycho-dynamic Tavistock team-building session was facilitated at Mount Everest outside Harrismith in the Orange Free State in 1998. The team engaged in high-rope facilities with the intention of enhancing levels of trust in the system.

- **Strategic planning session**
  A strategy was co-created after a strategic map was designed by the top 24 people. This strategic map was rolled down the organisation and translated into business plans. Together with the results of the engagement study, the strategic map was implemented throughout the organisation. After the successful finalisation of the strategic plan in 1999, management reviewed the initiatives and embarked on strategic planning for the next five years. The strategic plan was then translated throughout the organisation.

- **Middle management team-building**
  Middle management teams from each department were engaged in team-building activities, with personality types being used to describe diversity of thought initiatives. Bar-On emotional intelligence (EQi) assessments were also conducted as a pre-measure and diagnostic tool for identifying individual development plans, upon which the intervention focused. At this time middle

management indicated that they did not believe that top management was serious about fixing the relationships and reported that they did not feel supported. In this way it became clear that it was necessary to restore trust between the middle management and top management teams.

- **Systems thinking joint session**

  Russell Ackoff's systems thinking process was used to integrate the thinking of the top and middle management, with 78 people participating in the process at Wintershoek Wild for two and a half days. Both top and middle management co-created visuals on the current reality, and realised that without trust among different levels and departments, the vision of IBL would never be achieved. This intervention restored the trust issues between top and middle management in the organisation, and today the organisation does not speak about levels of management in an effort to steer away from a hierarchical structure.

- **Emotional intelligence development**

  Over a period of four years, an intensive emotional intelligence development plan was executed, with every driver being exposed to a journey of soft skills development. This included communication skills, stress management, presentation skills, personality-type analysis and conflict management. Later Oubaas Jooste, a consultant to IBL, continued with this journey and each bus driver and their immediate family were exposed to the process of self-development.

- **Team development**

  Team development processes followed, with natural teams participating in a three-day workshop. To the lowest level in the organisation, everyone worked with personality type analysis. Further experiential learning sessions assisted natural group dynamics to surface and assisted the facilitators to address and consult to the manifested dynamic. Action plans on ways of enhancing engagement at each level in the organisation were drawn up, and roles and responsibilities were contracted. Each team used clay to portray their unique contribution to the larger organisation, before the plans were linked to strategy which then was linked to performance management.

The Bar-On EQi describes the way in which an individual copes with environmental demands; a mean of 100 shows that an individual is coping as expected at his or her age. Four years following the intervention, the Bar-On EQi was used as a re-measure and the average increase in emotional leadership of top and middle management was 12 and 14 points to 114 and 108 points respectively.[ii]

---

ii   According to Multi Health Systems (MHS), the consulting psychologists that distribute the EQi internationally, a five point increase is seen as significant.

Summary of interventions

Table 9.1 shows an overview of all the OCD and engagement initiatives utilised.

Benchmark of engagement (1998) Joint action planning throughout organisations	
Psychometrics of top management team and middle management	
Inclusive engagement strategy	Psycho-analytical team-building with EXCO
	Strategic planning session (early 1999)
	Middle management teaming session
	Systems thinking process with EXCO and middle management
	Intensive soft skills development – all employees (2000 – 2004)
	Teaming and joint action planning – all natural teams (2002 – 2006)
	Emotional intelligence re-measure
	Human resources strategies and aligned practices
Strategic planning sessions (every four years)	
Translation of strategy to everyone in the organisation	
Benchmark of engagement (2009) Joint action planning throughout organisation	
Spiral dynamics session with management, supervisors and unions (2012)	
Sessions with the unions and management every four years	
Team-building and strategy translation – all natural teams (2014)	
Emotional intelligence development – all employees (2015)	
Co-determination strategy with management, unions, national leaders (2015)	

Source: Viljoen, 2016[7]

THE EMPLOYEE RELATIONS MODEL AT IBL: WHERE IBL IS TODAY

In 2010, Clive Thompson, professor at the Faculty of Law of the University of Cape Town (UCT), delivered a working paper on *Dispute Prevention and Resolution in Public Services and Labour Relations* at the International Labour Office in Geneva, as well as at a CCMA Indaba in 2011.[8] In advising on good policy and practice when dealing with dispute prevention and resolution, as well as collective bargaining, he outlined the following guiding propositions for the institutional framework and its supporting processes:

- Bargaining and consultation should promote best-practice features.
- Ethos is more important than machinery. The cultivation over time of an ethos of cooperative workplace relations geared towards productive outcomes on employee equity is key.
- Great workplace: those that are productive and rewarding have great working relationships founded on trust and respect, which are geared towards sustainable business success.
- Good workplace relations need to be pressed into the service of organisational performance.
- Collective bargaining is not the main game and should not feature as the primary channel of labour management engagement.
- Value creation (better goods, services or service delivery) through continuous interaction (intensive consultation) should be the main game.

For the significant, sustainable successes that followed this approach in IBL, please refer to the original case study in *Employee Engagement in a South African Context*, by Nienaber and Martins.[9]

CONCLUSION

Over many years, Interstate invested in creating a culture of inclusivity. Everyone in the organisation was regularly exposed to soft skill interventions, and the Benchmark of Engagement was regularly used as the basis to diagnose additional areas of development and to quantify the return on investment (ROI). These areas were immediately addressed, laying the groundwork for the successful implementation of a radical, inclusive strategy - co-determination.

Based on the above, IBL has developed its own institutional framework and supporting processes that have contributed to the success of the company and formed the basis of its ER Model. These processes are discussed in the next chapter.

REFERENCES

Koopman, A.D., Nassar, M.E., & Nel, J. (1987). *The Corporate crusaders.* Isando: Lexicon Publishers.

SA Government. (1995). *Labour Relations Act No. 66 of 1995 with amendments.* Pretoria: Government Printers.

SA History Online. 2013. *History of Labour Movements in South Africa – Timeline of the Labour and Trade Union Movement in South Africa.* [Online]. Retrieved from: www.Sahistory.org.za.

SA History Online. 2016. *History of Labour Movements in South Africa – Timeline of the Labour and Trade Union Movement in South Africa.* [Online]. Retrieved from: www.Sahistory.org.za.

South African Board of People Practices. (2013). *HR Management Standards for South Africa.* [Online]. Retrieved from: http://www.sabpp.co.za/wp-content/uploads/2017/05/HR-Standards-Schools-10-May-2017.pdf

Viljoen, R. (2016). Engagement – The critical pre-requisite for co-determination, p148. In H. Nienaber, & N. Martins. *Employee Engagement in a South African Context.* Bryanston: KR Publishing.

ENDNOTES

1   Nienaber & Martins, 2016.
2   Ibid.
3   SA History Online, 2013.
4   Ibid.
5   Ibid.
6   Viljoen, 2016.
7   Viljoen, 2016.
8   Ibid.
9   Ibid.

10

CO-DETERMINATION MADE PRACTICAL AT INTERSTATE

Henk van Zyl

INTRODUCTION

This chapter is a summary of how Interstate Bus Lines put the concept of co-determination into practice. Co-determination operates on the basis that employee participation in the decision-making process of the organisation positions them as owners, which positively influences the effectiveness and efficiency of operations. At IBL, owning shares and having the opportunity to co-decide enhanced trust and created a sense of collectiveness in the system, i.e. the Co-determination Model at IBL is a success because it is built on inclusive engagement processes that foster trust and harmony in the social system. Today, IBL has a high-performance culture because co-determination assisted them to tap into their diversity and take advantage of the gifts that individuals and teams brought into the system. The following is a collection of the approaches and experiences of IBL in the successful implementation of co-determination.

HIGH STANDARD OF HR PRACTICES

The company established an HR Department to comply with all HR functions and appointed professional human resources personnel to implement and maintain the required policies, procedures and processes. IBL also implemented initiatives to ensure employee engagement in the company processes. The SABPP developed a national HR Standards Model through an inclusive and transparent process that was supported by national and international HR professionals. The IBL HR Department participated in this development process of HR Standards to ensure that the Company benchmarked, implemented and complied with the SABPP's HRM standards. The model was presented for inputs to the HR community in 2013, and was rolled out in Interstate Bus Lines in 2014 and 2015.

The HR Manager also submitted a motivation to convince the executive to embark on a process of adapting all HR practices, policies and procedures in order to comply with the national HR standards. All members of the HR team were involved and due process was followed to align all HR practices to comply with national standards.

Compliance with the HR standard forms the basis of all HR initiatives, programmes and practices to ensure that the HR department plays a vital role in the business strategy and success of the company. The HR department was audited in 2016 by the SABPP and received a favourable audit report in all 13 standards. IBL received the following awards:

- Best achiever in HR standards exemplary practice.
- Best practice award exceeding 65% overall.
- Finalist in Workforce Planning.
- Finalist in Service Delivery.
- Finalist in Organisational Development.
- Employee Relations.

The awards motivated IBL to continue the journey of complying with the HR standards, as maintenance of and compliance with these standards are life-long journeys. After receiving the awards, the CEO, George Mokgothu, commented:

> "The extensive audit, a first not only for the Transport Industry but also for a Free State based company, undertaken by the reputable SABPP, allows me to say with absolute confidence that receiving this quality assurance certificate confirms the high quality of our HR systems, processes and practices.
>
> I can now with absolute confidence say that our HR practices are of such a high standard, the department is professionally and ethically managed and surely adds positive value to our bottom line. The SABPP HR standard audit certification is a stamp of approval on our people, our pride."

UNDERSTANDING PEOPLE AND MANAGING DIVERSITY

Managing diversity has been defined by Ting-Toorney and Chung[1] as acquiring the necessary knowledge and dynamic skills to manage such differences appropriately and effectively. It is also about developing a creative mindset to see things from different angles without pre-judgement.

The basis of managing diversity at IBL is based on the Spiral Dynamics or Human Niche theory, which was introduced to the company by Viljoen and Laubscher in 2013. This theory refers to different thinking systems that inform diversity of thought in systems. Viljoen[2] stated that "at IBL, the BeQ indicated that 89% of the people in the organisation had a Purple thinking system, 3% Red, 5% Blue, 2% Orange and 1% Green and Yellow combined. For the organisation to be successful and to execute Blue strategies such as following standard operating procedures, safety first and being on time without breakdowns, the hearts and the minds of Purple people had to be convinced to do Blue".

In Chapter 3, the human niches and their manifestations and importance in organisations were described. According to Viljoen, different thinking systems ask different questions and therefore behave differently, judge differently and differ in meaning-making. In particular, the archetypal thinking systems/human niches should be considered when engaging with them. This aspect is so critical to leadership that it cannot be ignored. If leaders can understand the thinking structures of people in their systems, then they can adapt the communication strategy, reward, recognition, discipline and cultural issues accordingly. This understanding is extremely important for creating the conditions in which employees in multi-cultural settings can engage.

LEADING IN THE RAINBOW NATION SETTING

In the previous section, inclusive engagement initiatives that aligned the top management team, restored trust between top and middle management, and assisted in implementing personal and leadership development programmes at IBL were discussed. It has been observed that the same leadership crisis that affected IBL management is currently affecting the labour unions in South Africa; leadership mistrust is prevalent among union leaders in the same unions, amongst different unions, and between leaders and their constituencies.

In the Co-determination Model where union leaders are treated as equal partners in business, their development will be the focal point for the success of engagement initiatives; the future of companies and the achievement of their goals and objectives depend on the quality of their leadership practices. The companies will have to invest in, and assist unions with, team-building and leadership development on an ongoing basis to sustain sound relationships for the future.

CREATE OWNERSHIP AND A SENSE OF BELONGING

The concept of share ownership in companies in South Africa dates back to 1983, when Koopman turned Cashbuild around and profitability rose from R700,000 in 1982 to R1.6m in 1984, and nearly R4m in 1986. As part of the turnaround strategy, Koopman introduced drastic changes to the organisational culture and management styles, and encouraged full worker participation. Along with his new perception grew a strong sense of urgency on the part of top management for EEO (Every Employee and Owner). This philosophy of EEO derived from his discovery that every employee has a desire to contribute meaningfully in the workplace and longs for a sense of belonging in the business.

According to Pierce[3], the roots of psychological ownership can be found in the following three main motives of efficiency and effectiveness, self-identity, and having a place.

Efficiency and effectiveness

To a large extent the motive underlying possession is to be in control. Ownership and the rights that come with it allow individuals to explore and alter their environment, thereby satisfying their innate need to be efficacious. The desire to experience causal efficiency in altering the environment leads to attempts to take possession and the emergence of ownership feelings.

Self-identity

Possessions also serve as symbolic expressions of the self since they are closely connected with self-identity and individuality. It is through our interactions with our possessions, coupled with a reflection upon their meaning, that our sense of identity, and our self-identifications are established, maintained, reproduced and transformed.[4] Thus, we suggest that people use ownership for the purpose of defining themselves, expressing their self-identity to others, and ensuring the continuity of the self across time.

Having a place

Ownership and the associated psychological state can also be explained in part by the individual's motive to possess a certain territory of space; to have a home in which to dwell. To have a place is important - it is a need of the human soul. When we inhabit something, it is no longer an object for us but becomes part of us. It is because of this motive and the possibility to satisfy it through ownership that people devote significant energy and resources to targets that can potentially become their homes. In summary, feelings of ownership allow individuals to fulfill these three basic human motives, which are the reasons for psychological ownership.

According to Olckers[5], psychological ownership has been associated with the following:
- Greater commitment to the organisation.
- Greater accountability.
- Greater job satisfaction.
- Better organisational behaviour.
- Better organisation – based on self-esteem.
- More effort on the part of the individual to engage in organisational citizenship behaviours.
- Increase in extra-role behaviours, meaning that individuals with higher levels of psychological ownership are more likely to engage in extra-role behaviour.
- Intention to stay in organisations.

It is most likely that employee ownership will encourage employees to think and act like owners, which can enhance organisational performance and effectiveness. As an attempt to promote ownership and a sense of belonging, IBL introduced a Bus Ownership Scheme and a Share Trust Scheme. In 2009 the company also empowered its employees by allocating them four sub-contractor buses to manage through an Employee Trust Scheme. The Trust and the buses are known as 'Basebetsi Transport', which means 'Workers Transport'. It is owned by the workers and they provide services on behalf of IBL in line with the tender specifications that the company has with Government.

From a PURPLE niche perspective, the concept of owning shares in a company may raise suspicion as the concept of share principles and the dynamics thereof belong to a BLUE thinking system. In a PURPLE niche, ownership of tangible assets that are managed by the owners themselves enhances a sense of collectiveness and trust in the system. The Share Trust Scheme was therefore introduced for employees in the higher positions in the organisation who were predominantly from the BLUE niche. In 2011 after strategic sessions that were translated throughout the company, the words 'Ya Rona' were added to the Company's logo, which means 'Ours'. The success of the Company is thus a result of the combined efforts of all the employees and loyal passengers for the benefit of the community. This was done with the support of the Department of Transport, which is viewed as the overall employer.

ENERGISE AND INVEST IN EMPLOYEES

IBL uses the BeQ Model as an organisational enquiry that describes organisational culture levels of engagement in the social system. It is an attempt at understanding not only what the need for an individual to bring his or her voice to the organisation table is, but it is also of paramount importance to the understanding of the contextual lens through which perceptions of respect, trust, support and other engagement factors are typically measured. Without understanding the thinking structures that create the perceptions in the first place, and ultimately causally determining the behaviour of a workplace, interventions will be designed and implemented based on symptoms and not primary causes.

In 2009, IBL embarked on a BeQ study to determine the levels of human energy in the system to perform. The BeQ indicated a workforce that was ENGAGED, i.e. there was enough positive human energy in the system to implement the organisational strategy. There were still areas that could be improved, but the management team immediately took action to enhance those areas. It should, however, be noted that the levels of engagement that were measured in IBL were seldom detected. It became evident that the employees trusted management now that they were included in decision-making, took personal responsibility, and acted as owners of IBL.

As a result of the BeQ study, supervisory skills, diversity, emotional intelligence and wellness initiatives were identified as development areas that should be addressed. In 2014, Loraine Laubscher facilitated Spiral Dynamic sessions called human niche interventions with various IBL groups. The work continued under Dr Oubaas Jooste, with emotional intelligence work being conducted with all employees.

The health condition of employees, especially those of bus drivers, was identified as a risk area for the safe and reliable transportation of commuters. The Company therefore employed the services of Life Hospital to provide a daily occupational health clinic on the premises. IBL conducted a Benchmark of Engagement (BeQ) study through Mandala Consulting in 2016 to identify development areas and initiatives as part of the Company's strategic plan for the next five years. The BeQ is an instrument that measures the interplay between assumptions and perceptions in organisations around constructs that contribute to the unleashing of individual voices, contributions and gifts.

PERFORMANCE AND CULTURE

Company culture is at the heart of competitive advantage because it determines the way in which things are done and how people behave[6]; it is the hardest item for competitors to copy or imitate. High performers create an environment with a unique personality, soul and passion for performance, so that people can make the right decisions and do the right things no matter what positions they hold in the business. This culture inspires people to go the extra mile – to make and execute good decisions without supervision.[7]

At IBL, the performance culture is driven by an incentive scheme that has been developed over the years with group as well as individual targets that are reviewed on an annual basis. The targets are linked to the key performance areas in job profiles as well as with objectives and targets that are linked to the overall success of each department and have an impact on the bottom line. The Company values the impact of the incentive scheme to its overall success, to such an extent that it spends 13% of the payroll on monthly incentive payments on an individual and group basis. The principle of incentive payments is based on cost savings and income generated as a result of meeting targets.

The bus drivers are the first contact with IBL customers, thus their driving habits and conduct have a direct impact on reputation, accidents, fuel savings, tyre usage, safety, ticket theft and the whole process of service delivery. For this reason, the criteria selected and targets set are directly linked to the above. Drivers are divided into teams and a concept of self-regulating teams has been established, where they select a team leader who manages the achievements of the teams.

In the book *Organisation Culture, Organisational Performance*, Rick describes the following 10 key elements for creating a high-performance culture, which were incorporated at IBL:

- Clearly define what winning looks like.
- Spell out your "preferred culture" – establish preferred behaviours that support your values.
- Set stretch targets – the more you expect, the more they will achieve.
- Connect to the big picture – how individual efforts fit into the broader company strategy.
- Develop an ownership mentality – think and act like an owner.
- Improve performance through transparency – increase a sense of ownership.
- Increase performance through employee engagement.
- Storytelling – use stories to motivate employees to achieve more than they thought possible.
- Internal communication – need to be on top of the agenda
- Take time to celebrate – celebrate milestones, acknowledge hard work, boost morale and keep up the momentum.

High-performing organisations do not take culture for granted; they plan it, monitor it and manage it so that it remains aligned with what they want to achieve. As per the famous words of Peter Drucker: "Culture eats strategy for breakfast."

PART 2: CORNERSTONES AND BUILDING BLOCKS OF IBL CO-DETERMINATION

CO-DETERMINATION

The cornerstones and building blocks of the IBL Co-determination Model , as well as the approach and mechanisms thereof, are discussed in the following sections. The institutional framework of the ER Model (see Figure 5.6), as well as the supporting processes that enabled IBL to consider the implementation of the Co-determination Model, are examined in this section of the chapter. The model is based on inclusive engagement processes that not only contribute to the success of a company, but also promote and sustain peace and harmony.

Through the Co-determination Model, the parties are committed to engage each other on the following:
- Co-creating the future.
- A high level of engagement.
- Sharing power and responsibilities.
- Joint strategy formulation.
- Growth and expanding.
- Joint problem solving.
- Having a voice.
- Pro-active dispute prevention and resolution.
- Managing disputes.

CORNERSTONES OF THE IBL CO-DETERMINATION MODEL

Through the interactions between the trade unions and management at IBL over the years, key issues were identified that urged management to explore alternative ways of engaging with the unions. The design of the Co-determination Model for Interstate Bus Lines emanated from an in-depth study of the principles and objectives of the German Co-determination Model, as well as from lessons learned from case studies published in South Africa where companies implemented some form of union participation in joint committees.

CASE STUDIES – A TREND TOWARDS CO-DETERMINATION

Professor Eddie Webster of the University of the Witwatersrand[7] selected companies on which the Sociology of Work Unit (SWOP) had conducted research, and where the existence of institutions for worker participation were known, in order to study workplace representation. The findings from these case studies can be divided into the following four themes:
- What powers forums have.
- How forums deal with conflict.
- Why forums were introduced.
- What form they take.

Based on the findings of these surveys, a number of general issues were identified concerning the functioning of the forums. These were taken into consideration during the development of Interstate Bus Lines' Co-determination Model, namely:
- Companies, especially large companies, are spending considerable amounts of time and resources in running and servicing forums.
- In some cases there is a dependence on individuals, like the charismatic individual manager who initiates a forum and later leaves the company.
- Forums arise from their close links with union structures, and owing to these links, white-collar workers and middle managers are excluded from the forums.
- A dual structure of collective bargaining emerges: wage bargaining took a sectoral approach and bargaining over production at the plant level became a separate issue. This dual structure made it easier to separate wage bargaining from negotiating over issues related to production and productivity. This dual structure of bargaining offers the real prospect of articulation, namely increased labour–management interaction at several levels.
- Forum members have limited capacity to engage in joint problem solving.

- Union representatives complained that decisions made at the forum are never implemented. They argued that the forum have no teeth, that management controls the agenda and uses the forums to lecture forum members, that meetings are not held regularly, and that management only calls the unions when they need them and uses them as rubber stamps.
- Management draw up the agenda when they call a meeting and unions do not have the opportunity to meet as a group. Most union officials come from political backgrounds with limited understanding of business principles and processes of production. The high turnover of union officials and inadequate training of workplace representatives exacerbates this. A second and related limitation concerns the reluctance of employees and their representatives to identify with the goals of the enterprise. This is deeply rooted in the low trust dynamic that arises from the apartheid workplace regime, and has resulted in suspicion of any involvement in decision-making.
- The shop stewards saw the role that works councillors play in the German system as being in conflict with their role as worker representatives. The act of joint decision-making for the shop stewards meant that the works councils had been co-opted into management and not that workers are being involved in decision-making. As a result of this suspicion, worker representatives find themselves in difficult positions when companies engage in cost-cutting exercises.
- Both management and shop stewards are well versed in adversarial bargaining and find it difficult to adjust to co-determination.
- Forums are not based on legal rights but on the sheer power (or lack thereof) of union representatives in the workplace.
- At the core of the unions' caution lies the concern that new forms of workplace representation will undermine established union structures.
- Management's uncertainty, especially in terms of the statutory forums, arises from their fear that the proposed forums will substantially curtail their prerogative to make unilateral decisions by giving workers statutory rights to consultation and co-decision-making.

Comparative research has, however, concluded that institutions such as workplace forums offer a secure basis on which to construct an effective partnership with employees at the plant level. Moreover, such institutions hold out the prospect for enhancing efficiency by improving the operations of firms. The research also suggests that workplace forums could strengthen unions, firstly by exercising their rights in unitary bodies on behalf of the workplace as a whole, and secondly, unions can strengthen themselves by gaining access to information from their members on the forum. The forums also offer unions the opportunity to increase their capacity through training, paid time off, full-time representatives and administration facilities.

OBSERVATIONS AND LESSONS LEARNT BY IBL MANAGEMENT THROUGH UNION RELATIONSHIPS

Prior to the implementation of the Co-determination agreement, the Company had all the relevant ER-related policies and procedures in place. It was obvious that this ER model was outdated and did not serve the purpose of engaging organised labour in a pro-active manner. Conflict and mistrust still prevailed, irrespective of attempts by management to build relationships between themselves and union leaders. The format in which the recognition agreements, the structure of meetings and the interactions with unions and shop stewards was structured proved to be counterproductive in resolving issues and engaging employees in the joint decision-making processes. Over the years, IBL understood the following tendencies and behaviour of organised labour.

Union leadership and the role of shop stewards

The struggle mentality of unions is common; they often regard employers as oppressors, which has historically resulted in electing militant and arrogant shop stewards to fight for employee rights and benefits. In many instances, the election of competent leaders who can make positive contributions to the well-being of their members are overseen.

Due to the South African Road Passenger Bargaining Council's central bargaining model, the shop stewards' ability to improve their members' conditions of employment and benefits are restricted at the company level. The shop stewards were therefore frustrated, owing to their inability to participate meaningfully at company level negotiations. The only real contribution at company level was their presence in disciplinary hearings and grievance resolution meetings. It was obvious to IBL's management that new ways had to be explored to engage shop stewards meaningfully in joint decision-making forums.

The level of supervision, management and leadership capacity in unions is of great concern. If union leaders and shop stewards participate in the decision-making process in companies, they need to understand business principles, industry dynamics, company values, strategic initiatives and company policies. The traditional role of shop stewards thus needs to be re-defined and shop stewards, like managers, should be elected based on scientific job requirement selection criteria.

Strikes and labour unrest

In many of the cases where employees embarked on strike action, it was observed that a large proportion of employees did not want to participate, but due to their collective thinking pattern, as well as intimidation, they were forced to take part. There is no democratic process that allows employees to vote on strike action and collectively decide whether to strike or not; in many instances, strike action is dictated by union officials without considering the wishes of employees. The controlling authorities of labour must be prepared to take into consideration the wishes of the majority of their members when organising strikes or sanctioning any other industrial action, for example they could use the strike ballot system.

Who has the power?

The Company has the right and authority to determine profit margins and manage the Company accordingly; to develop and implement strategy to reach stakeholders' expectations; to set rules and standards to obtain productivity targets; and to continuously assess company effectiveness and market relatedness and impose corrective measures.

MOBILISING THE WORKFORCE

Management can only achieve the above by mobilising and aligning the workforce to execute what has been planned. If workers are not engaged and do not buy into management's objectives, there are few options that management can use to force labour to do what they want. In the case of IBL, labour is aware that strike action is detrimental to the operations of the company, as it is difficult to replace 300 bus drivers during or even after a strike. In contrast with other industries, IBL cannot recoup any losses after a strike as customers may permanently make use of other transport modes and Government may terminate the Company's contract. Due to this, employees know that they can dictate to and manipulate management by embarking on illegal and unprotected strike action to achieve what they demand, irrespective of complying with legal obligations. The Company therefore had to reconsider the traditional perception of labour as a liability and find alternative ways to engage labour in improving work standards, productivity, work ethics and company effectiveness.

Management's commitment to change

Management perceived trade unions as being destructive and unrealistic in their demands, with the aim of opposing the company in its endeavour to run the business[i]. The view of "them" and "us" existed in the minds of both management and labour.

Executive management had to change their perceptions of unions and their leadership and accept that they are an essential partner and key stakeholders in the business, while management had to be prepared to engage labour on strategic as well as company level issues and accept that their contributions are vital for company performance. Management had to know the extent to which they can engage labour in the decision-making processes without losing control over the management of the Company.

i   This was the case before co-determination was implemented.

Communication with labour

Over the years, management abdicated their responsibility to communicate directly with their labour force and used the unions to carry messages to their constituents. Management thus had no control over what message was communicated and the different unions used this opportunity to manipulate the messages to their advantage. This resulted in even greater divisions between management and employees, therefore new communication strategies had to be explored to keep employees informed on company matters and the decisions that were taken.

Disciplinary matters

Disciplinary matters were the most common reasons behind the dissatisfaction that resulted in unprotected strikes and work stoppages. Labour believed that disciplinary chairpersons were dictated to by management in their findings, and that management used this forum to dismiss their members. It was obvious that a different approach was required to instill trust and consistency in the system; the use of external independent chairpersons was one of the options that had to be considered.

Grievances and disputes

Labour was of the opinion that management protected certain managers against whom grievances were lodged, and that there was no fair arbitration as the chairpersons who handled grievances were being manipulated by management. Management must thus be prepared to revise dispute procedures and develop a transparent and accommodative process that will prevent favouritism and build trust when dealing with grievances and disputes.

Relationships between unions

At IBL there are three recognised trade unions with competition for membership. Management's relationship with each union, as well as the relationships among the unions, are extremely difficult to manage and make it challenging to ensure that management remains unbiased and fair according to the perceptions of the employees. Although a recognition agreement with each union exists, a collective approach to this situation needs to be developed. The rivalry of outside unions always seems possible, which endangers the stability of union leadership as well as the relationships between unions and the company.

Disclosing of information

Management have to consider to what extent they are prepared to disclose relevant information that will allow labour to engage effectively in consultation and joint decision-making, without running the risk that privileged information will be misused.

Philosophy of trade unions and their members

Trade unions need to reconsider their freedom ideology urgently and stop regarding companies as oppressors or enemies; they need to change their philosophy and commit themselves as business partners that can make meaningful contributions to the success of the company. If labour wants to share in the prospects and profits of a company, they must co-create and participate meaningfully in that company's decision-making processes.

Union members must understand the new role of their shop steward representatives. When shop stewards participate in management structures, they are often regarded as "sell outs" or managements puppets. Shop stewards thus find themselves in difficult situations when they are engaged in contributing to controversial decisions. Union members must understand that if they enjoy representation on management structures, their leaders will act in their best interests, while employees need to understand that their ultimate existence and prosperity lies with the company and not with the unions.

Understanding business principles

Shop stewards, managers, supervisors and employees must understand the business models of their companies as well as their industries. They must further understand how income is generated by their companies, and their expenses and obligations.

Ownership

The historic owner/worker mentality prevailed in labour's perception of work, and they never regarded themselves as part of the business. To create a sense of ownership and belonging, management had to explore the extent to which they were prepared to introduce initiatives to share profits with employees through incentive schemes, profit sharing, shares or ownership.

Restructuring the relationship

In observing the lessons learnt by IBL above, as well as the company's attempt to find a different approach to sustainable employee relations, it is clear that management and labour had to be introspective about what needed to be considered to restructure the relationship.

PART 3: IBL APPROACH AND MECHANISMS TO CO-DETERMINATION

In an attempt to change a current practice and introduce alternative models, one must distinguish between designing a model and the process of negotiating for such a model. One can design a "state-of-the-art" model, but if an inclusive engagement process is not followed correctly, the chances of implementing such a model become very remote.

When working with people who are predominantly from the PURPLE human niche, great caution and patience should be practiced, and time and financial constraints should not be of significance; it is most unlikely that negotiations will reach a fruitful conclusion in one session. In the case of IBL, three unions were involved and a reputable and knowledgeable facilitator who was trusted by both management and labour facilitated the engagement sessions. It is also important to engage union leaders at both the national and provincial levels, as well as all shop stewards. Management should also be represented at the executive level, not only by the ER or HR executives.

The discussions in the section *Cornerstones of the IBL Co-determination Model* above formed the basis for designing the Co-determination Model at IBL. In the IBL case where multiple unions were involved, it was necessary to compile other relevant agreements in support of the co-determination agreement, namely the Collective Recognition Agreement, Closed Shop Agreement and Dispute Prevention and Resolution Agreement.

CO-DETERMINATION AGREEMENT

Two-tier structure

As in the case of the German Co-determination Model, this principle of a two-tier meeting structure is followed at IBL. Employee representation and participation take place at two levels, i.e. at the workplace level, which is a workers' representative council (WRC) where operational issues are pursued, and at the executive level, which is a joint forum (JF) with legal capacity pursuing economic, strategic and substantive issues. The two levels of co-determination complement each other and the JF oversees the functioning of the WRC.

Objectives of the Co-determination Agreement and commitment of the parties

The objectives of a Co-determination Agreement are of vital importance as they form the basis for the conduct and commitment of the parties. As will be discussed in detail later, any party that does not subscribe to or endeavour to comply with the objectives, terms and conditions of the Co-determination Agreement are denied involvement.

The following are some of the objectives of the Co-Determination Agreement:

- Creating a climate in which disagreements are settled through dialogue and co-decision and not by force or conflict.
- Pro-actively engaging as parties in decision-making processes.
- Developing and training leaders and representatives to make meaningful contributions to the process and take responsibility for decisions taken.
- Creating communication structures to ensure that decisions taken are communicated to all employees.
- Increasing productivity and company effectiveness, and in return the working conditions, benefits and living standards of employees.
- Creating a spirit of mutual trust by discussing matters with an earnest desire to reach an agreement.

The parties acknowledge and are committed to the following:

- The effective running of the company is fundamental to reaching every party's objectives.
- Honouring agreements.
- Maintaining sound relationships based on trust and respect.
- Considering the values and objectives of the Co-determination Agreement in all the parties' dealings and deliberations with each other.
- Recognising and adhering to the contractual obligations that the company has entered into with the Government of South Africa.

Meeting structure

The meeting structure as summarised in Table 10.1 below gives an overview of the functioning of the different forums.

Table 10.1: Co-determination meeting structure

FORUMS	LEVEL	COMPOSITION	MEETINGS
JOINT MANAGEMENT/UNION FORUM (JF) ← WORKPLACE REPRESENTATIVE COUNCIL (WRC) ← Dispute Resolution Committee (DRC); ← Discipline Committee (DC)	**EXECUTIVE** — Economic planning, Strategic focus, Collective agreements, Non-substantive issues, Dispute resolution, Financial and operational performance, Empowerment schemes **MANAGEMENT** — Productivity and efficiency, Structural changes, Shop floor issues, Restructuring, Company policies, Welfare issues, Communication **CONSULTATION** — Resolve disputes, Resolve conflicts, Monitor risks, Monitor compliance, Arbitration panelists, Discipline chairpersons	CEO/COO and Executives, Provincial Union Officials, Leadership of Shop Stewards Council Departmental Heads, Managers, Supervisors, Shop stewards, Non-Union members Company and Union Representatives	Objectives and duties, Disclosure of information, Confidentiality, Chair and Secretarial functions, Meeting intervals, Agenda and meeting arrangements, Preparations and mandate for meetings, Removal and replacement of members, Voting procedures, Communication of decisions, Levels of bargaining, Dispute procedures, Strike ballot procedures

Joint Management/Union Forum (JF)

The JF operates at an executive level; its primary focus is economic planning, strategic issues, collective agreements and non-substantive matters. It is also the highest authority that interacts with unions.

Workplace Representative Council (WRC)

The WRC operates at the managerial level, with a primary focus on discussing and resolving all operational matters that affect both the company and employees. It seeks to promote the interests of all the employees in the workplace, whether they are union members or not.

Disciplinary Committee (DC)

The primary focus of the DC is to assist and encourage compliance with disciplinary procedures and to code and attempt to resolve matters of a disciplinary nature. It also contributes to matters regarding the appointment and training of disciplinary chairpersons, and monitors compliance with company policies, disciplinary codes and procedures by chairpersons, company representatives and union representatives. The DC does not have the authority to discuss merits of cases, overturn rulings, or act as an appeal committee.

Dispute Resolution Committee (DRC)

The primary focus of the DRC is to assist and encourage compliance with the dispute resolution policies and procedures pro-actively in order to resolve conflicts through non-adversarial means, as well as to assist in managing the process of resolving formal and informal disputes. The DRC does not have the authority to discuss the merits of individual disputes, overturn outcomes, or act as an appeal committee, but can advise individuals or parties on issues of procedure.

Confidentiality and disclosure of information

The company has an obligation to disclose relevant information that will allow the parties to engage effectively in consultation and joint decision-making with certain provisos. Every member of the JF who has access to the information shall sign a confidentiality agreement, and any breach of the confidentiality shall be dealt with in terms of the dispute or disciplinary procedure.

Members attending meetings

Members appointed to meetings shall serve for a period of not less than two years, and may not be represented by a proxy if they cannot attend a meeting. The continuity and consistency of discussions and decisions taken at meetings are key, and it is important to maintain a high level of professional conduct. It is also important in the case of a board of directors meeting that the same members attend all meetings.

Communication of decisions

Prior to the close of every meeting, the group shall formulate a communiqué or briefing letter that will serve the purpose of a standardised message that will be communicated to all employees, posted on all notice boards, and e-mailed to all members who access emails. The importance of this clause is that a standardised brief is received by all unions and that the same message is communicated throughout the company.

Strikes and lock-outs

The parties acknowledge that strikes and lock-outs have a detrimental effect on the company, and agree that the employees and the parties will not organise or embark on such action without first discussing the intended action in the JF meeting. The controlling authority of a trade union shall take the wishes of the majority of its members into consideration when organising or participating in sanctioning or supporting a strike or any other industrial action. The unions shall obtain a mandate for strike action from all eligible employees in the company of at least 60% in favour of a strike by conducting a strike ballot in accordance with procedures agreed in the JF.

Development of shop stewards

It is agreed and recorded in the Co-determination Agreement that the JF shall identify the training needs of members and request management to arrange training as identified. All members will attend training sessions as identified. Since the inception of the Co-determination Agreement, a comprehensive training and development programme for shop stewards was compiled and they were put through training sessions, which included the following:
- LRA;
- discipline;
- business principles;
- company policies;
- computer literacy;
- supervisory training;
- emotional intelligence; and
- co-determination, collective recognition, closed shop and dispute prevention and resolution agreements.

A full-time shop steward attended a CCMA Commissioners course and after certification, the IBL awarded him time off to act as a commissioner on behalf of the CCMA on various bargaining councils. He would then plough back the knowledge and experience he gained in advising the employees at IBL.

Dispute procedures

A comprehensive Dispute Prevention and Resolution Agreement supplements the Co-determination Agreement, and parties agree not to declare a dispute or embark on a strike or lock-out unless the internal dispute procedures have been exhausted. One of the objectives of the Co-determination Agreement is to create an atmosphere in which disagreements and disputes are settled through dialogue and co-decision, and not by force and/or conflict.

Discontinuation of a party to this agreement

The successful implementation and maintenance of agreements depend on the manner in which parties adhere to and honour the collective agreements. A union shall therefore be discontinued as a member if its recognition is cancelled in terms of the Recognition Agreement, if it has been deregistered as a union in terms of the LRA, and/or if it does not subscribe or endeavour to comply with the terms and conditions of the Recognition Agreement.

Collective Recognition and Procedural Agreement

To maintain sound and fair employee relations with all three unions, it was to the mutual benefit of the parties to formulise and regulate their relationship with clearly stated rules and procedures, in order to reduce the possibility of conflict between management and employees. It was therefore necessary to agree on a collective procedural agreement that would apply to all unions. The advantage of having such a collective agreement is that all parties are subjected to the same rules, benefits and procedures, which minimises conflict between parties and builds trust in the system.

Closed Shop Agreement

The Company and unions have entered into collective Recognition and Co-determination Agreements that regulate the relationship between the parties through engaging unions and worker representatives in joint decision processes. The successful implementation and maintenance of the agreements depend on the stability of union participation; the Closed Shop Agreement will assist in achieving these objectives. This agreement is subject to Section 26 and all other relevant provisions of the LRA, as well as the collective Recognition and Co-determination Agreements.

The most controversial part of the agreement is that if a union ceases to be a party to this agreement, members of that union shall have 30 days to join one of the remaining unions; failure to do so results in the employees facing dismissal from the company. The advantage of having a Closed Shop Agreement is that it forces a union to remain party to the agreements, which brings stability to the ER processes in the company.

DISPUTE PREVENTION AND RESOLUTION AGREEMENT

Objective

The objective of this agreement is to supplement the Co-determination Agreement with procedures to prevent and resolve grievances and disputes, as well as to complement other relevant company policies in preventing and resolving disputes. It also assists the company, unions and employees to speed up the resolution of disputes by being transparent, without the interference of any party that may have an adverse interest in the dispute. The agreement addresses areas relating to grievances, disputes and discipline, and applies procedures that prevent and resolve disputes pro-actively by engaging all parties in a transparent process.

Tribunal

To bring transparency to the dispute resolution and grievance procedure, a Tribunal Committee was introduced. This committee consists of a chairperson, an independent professional with relevant experience and legal expertise, as well as a union official and management representative with relevant knowledge and expertise as recommended by the Dispute Resolution Committee. The tribunal procedures and conduct are in accordance with the arbitration and conciliation proceedings and principles of the Bargaining Council dispute procedures.

THE ROLE OF THE WORKPLACE REPRESENTATIVE COUNCIL (WRC)

The WRC is the first filter of dispute prevention or resolution, and deals with issues referred to them by the various departments and/or unions. Issues such as employment practices, racism, training, unfair treatment, discrimination of a group, structural changes, disciplinary matters and company policies and procedures are referred to the WRC. The WRC may decide to refer matters for further investigation to other forums, and if still unresolved, shall refer the matters to the JF.

THE ROLE OF THE JOINT FORUM (JF)

The JF is the highest authority in the prevention and resolution of disputes, and will discuss and consult on unresolved issues referred to them. The JF may also decide to refer issues that require further investigation to appropriate forums such as the WRC, DC, DRC, union parties, management parties or ad hoc committees. Unresolved issues and/or disputes relating to non-substantive conditions of employment shall be referred to the tribunal for conciliation/arbitration, and the outcome shall be binding to all parties (see Figure 10.1 below). All unresolved disputes that may lead to a strike or lock-out shall be discussed in the JF. In the event of a strike, the JF shall appoint an election officer and a committee to prepare and conduct a strike ballot.

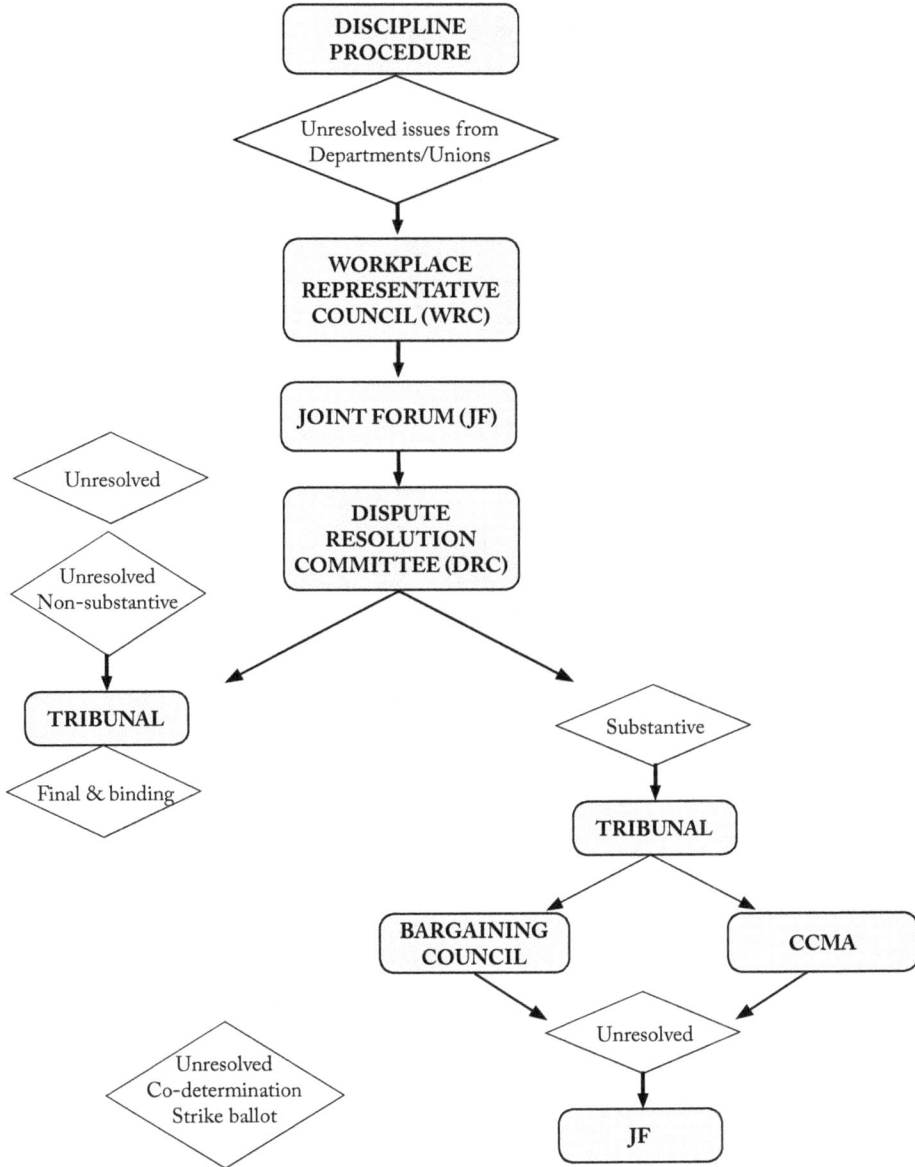

```
                        ┌─────────────────┐
                        │   DISCIPLINE    │
                        │   PROCEDURE     │
                        └─────────────────┘
                              ◇ Unresolved issues from
                                Departments/Unions
                        ┌─────────────────┐
                        │   WORKPLACE     │
                        │ REPRESENTATIVE  │
                        │  COUNCIL (WRC)  │
                        └─────────────────┘
                        ┌─────────────────┐
                        │ JOINT FORUM (JF)│
                        └─────────────────┘
     ◇ Unresolved       ┌─────────────────┐
                         │    DISPUTE      │
     ◇ Unresolved        │  RESOLUTION     │
       Non-substantive   │COMMITTEE (DRC)  │
                         └─────────────────┘
    ┌──────────┐
    │ TRIBUNAL │                    ◇ Substantive
    └──────────┘
     ◇ Final & binding
                                    ┌──────────┐
                                    │ TRIBUNAL │
                                    └──────────┘
                         ┌──────────────┐        ┌──────┐
                         │  BARGAINING  │        │ CCMA │
                         │   COUNCIL    │        └──────┘
                         └──────────────┘
     ◇ Unresolved                    ◇ Unresolved
       Co-determination
       Strike ballot                 ┌──────┐
                                     │  JF  │
                                     └──────┘
```

Figure 10.1: Dispute procedures

GRIEVANCES

The Company's grievance procedures or relevant company policies and procedures shall be applied to resolve grievances. Unresolved grievances shall be referred to a tribunal/grievance committee, as described above. Should the aggrieved employee not be satisfied with the decisions of the tribunal, he or she may refer the matter to the Bargaining Council's dispute resolution mechanisms or those of the CCMA. Figure 10.2 below is flow diagram of the grievance procedures.

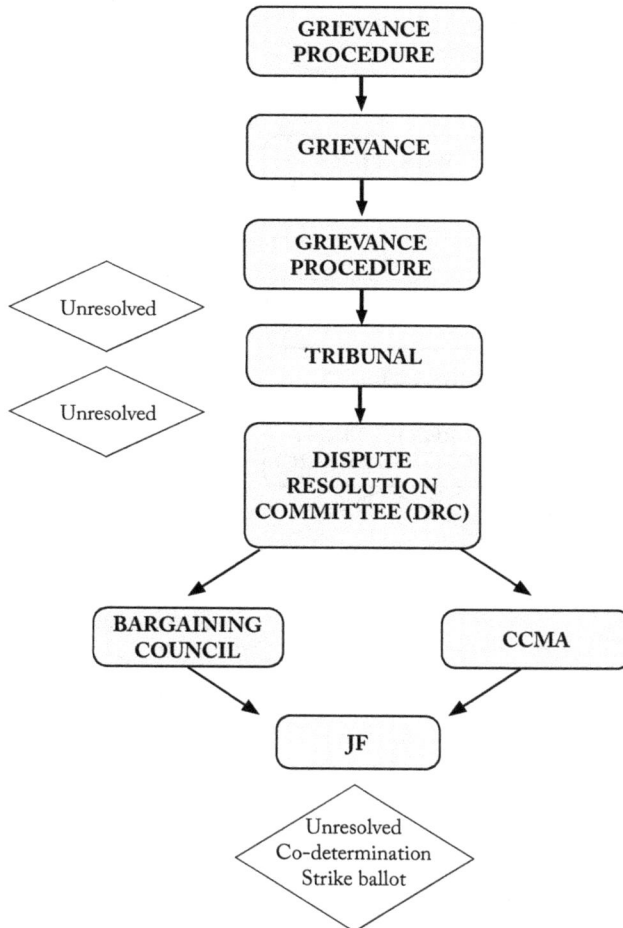

Figure 10.2: Grievance procedures

DISCIPLINE

Due to the historic disputes, dissatisfaction, unprotected strikes and work stoppages that resulted from disciplinary matters, the company had to find a different approach for dealing with these matters in order to instil trust and consistency in the system. The Company negotiated a disciplinary procedure and code with the unions, which is viewed as a collective agreement. All parties accepted ownership and all proceedings and dissatisfaction were dealt with in terms of the agreement.

The introduction of the Disciplinary Committee further assisted in building trust in the system, whereby members of the DC could make presentations for the appointment of chairpersons, monitor the conduct of chairpersons and representatives, and recommend corrective actions. The DC could also make recommendations to the WRC on the appointment and removal of arbitrators on the panel.

In the past disciplinary hearings were disrupted and postponed due to delaying tactics on procedural issues that frustrated the process. It was therefore agreed that the company's representative, a shop steward and the accused have a pre-disciplinary consultation meeting to clarify procedural requirements, exchange and acknowledge the bundle of documents, gather additional information required, and clarify any disputes regarding the charges. Any party that fails to attend the meeting as arranged waives the opportunity for the chairperson to consider requests that are addressed in the meeting. However, this arrangement can only be agreed on when there is enough trust in the system.

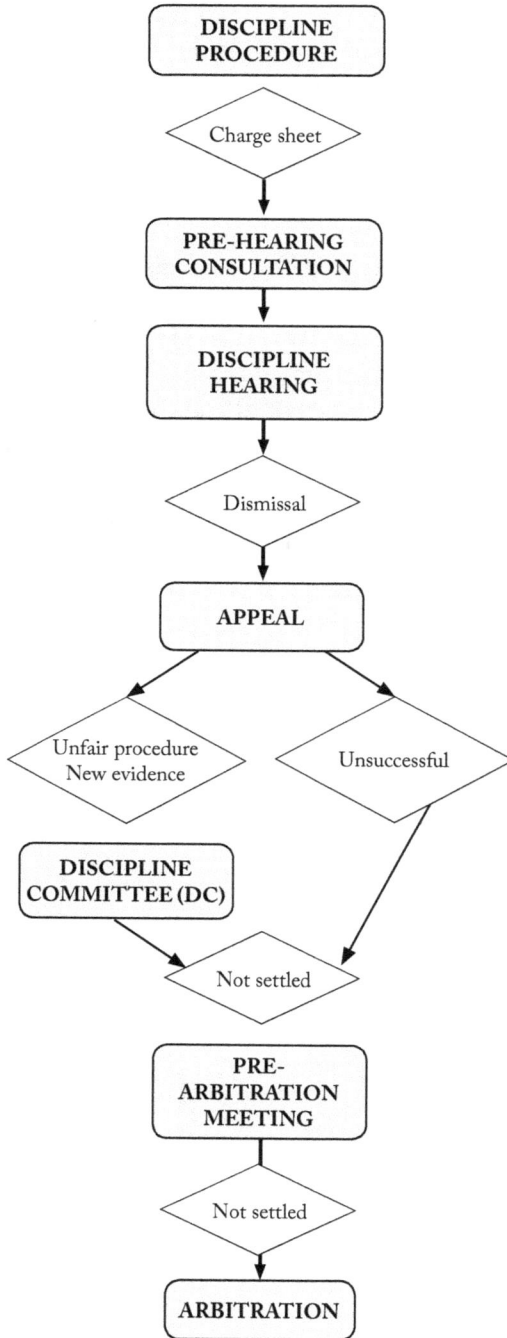

Figure 10.3: Disciplinary procedures

CONCLUSION

In this chapter, the author described the ways in which the principles of co-determination were adapted to a South African context, and how the mechanics and approach manifested into the agreements. The high levels of trust and respect in the system that resulted from engagement initiatives and strategies helped to build an institutional framework in an ER model. Other South African organisations can gain valuable insights from the manner in which IBL managed the different human niches in high-level engagement strategies to build a prosperous enterprise.

REFERENCES

Olkers, C. (2011). *A Multi-Dimensional Measure of Psychological ownership for South African Organisations.* PhD Faculty of Economic and Management Sciences at the University of Pretoria. [Online]. Retrieved from: https://repository.up.ac.za/bitstream/handle/2263/28730/Complete. pdf?sequence=8.

Pierce, J.L, Kostova, T., & Dirks, K.T, (2001) Towards a theory of Psychological Ownership in Organizations. *The Academy of Management Review* Vol. 26, No. 2 (Apr.), pp. 298-310

Ting-Toorney and Chung (2005). Understanding Intercultural Communication. Los Angeles: Roxbury Publishing Company.

Viljoen, R.C. (2017). *Multicultural Research. In H. Nienaber and N. Martins: Employee Engagement in a South African Context.* Bryanston: KR Publishers.

Viljoen-Terblanche, R.C. (2009). *Sustainable organisational transformation through inclusivity.* Master's Thesis. Pretoria: University of South Africa.

Webster, E., & Macun, I. (1998). A trend towards co-determinati0n? Case studies of South African Enterprises. *Law, Democracy & Development*, 2(1), 63 - 84.

ENDNOTES

1   Ting-Toorney & Chung, 2005.
2   Viljoen, 2017, p. 29.
3   Pierce, 2001, p. 298-310
4   Pierce, 2001.
5   Olckers, 2011.
6   Viljoen-Terblanche, 2009.
7   Webster & Macun, 1989.

Chapter

11

CO-DETERMINATION – A PRACTICAL APPROACH

Henk van Zyl

INTRODUCTION

In this chapter, a practical approach towards the implementation of a Co-determination Model for an organisation will be discussed.

"The gurus of the management world agree, and readers who are acquainted with outstanding organisation noted for their cohesion and team spirit will know from their own experience, that there is no standard package that can be had straight off the shelf. Participated management can be adopted by any organisation which acknowledges the need to change. Its implementation does not depend on specific circumstances, nor does it depend on the personality of one individual."[1]

The purpose of this chapter is to assist Human Resources practitioners with practical guidelines to design and implement a management/employee engagement model based on the principles of co-determination.

This chapter will not address the implementation of HR practices, interventions and/or measurements of engagement to build trust, develop leadership, create a sense of ownership and manage diversity; it is assumed that the HR practitioner will apply these to transform the corporate environment to set the scene for implementing a co-determination approach to ER, as discussed in Chapter 5. The case study of IBL's successful implementation of co-determination was discussed in Chapter 10. In this chapter, the practical process to implement co-determination is shared.

Supporting documents for the implementation of co-determination are attached below, including a Gantt Activity Schedule used by Interstate Bus Lines as an example of the overall implementation process.

STEP BY STEP EXPLANATION OF HOW TO IMPLEMENT CO-DETERMINATION IN YOUR ORGANISATION

Table 11.1: Gantt chart/activity schedule used by Interstate Bus lines (IBL) to implement the Co-determination Model

PROJECT: CO-DETERMINATION MODEL — ACTIVITY SCHEDULE / GANTT CHART — HUMAN RESOURCES – INDUSTRIAL RELATIONS

Milestone Leg: — Compiled by: H.A. VAN ZYL — Page: 1 of 2

Date Initiated: JUNE 2014 — Approved by: — Chart date/Rev. No:

ActId.	Activity Description	Responsible person
1.	Conduct research and compile proposal	HvZ
2.	Present proposal to Executive Management/buy-in of management	HvZ
3.	Consult with shop stewards/unions and proposal/buy-in of shop stewards/unions	HvZ
4.	Arrange workshop with stakeholders	HvZ/Mandala
5.	Feedback session with shop stewards	HvZ
6.	Feedback session with middle management	HvZ
7.	Roadshow to all employees	GN
8.	Develop/Amend Co-determination Model	HvZ

Milestone Leg: — Compiled by: H.A. VAN ZYL — Page: 2 of 2

ActId.	Activity Description	Responsible person
9.	Compile Recognition/Closed Shop Agreement/ Dispute Procedure	HvZ/Marie Bloem
10.	Facilitate signing of agreements	HvZ/Roy Els
11.	Attend Spiral Dynamic/value engineering course	HvZ/Mandala
12.	Secure Union office facilities	HvZ
13.	Design business simulation training model	B Gie
14.	Elect shop stewards	GN
15.	Feedback to steering committee	HvZ
16.	Communicate progress to delegates	HvZ
17.	Implement new model	HvZ
18.	Design supervisory course for committee members	HvZ/Learn Corp
19.	Train all employees in business simulation model	Training
20.	Unions elect committee members	GN
21.	Train committee members	GN
22.	Install committees	HvZ

STUDY THE PRINCIPLES OF CO-DETERMINATION

The HR practitioner must have a thorough knowledge and understanding of formal employee engagement models, with special reference to the concepts and principles of co-determination. The insights in this book can form the basis of the knowledge and understanding of the advantages and mechanisms that are required to implement such a model.

He/she must believe that the new approach will not only result in enabling management/employee engagement, joint decision-making and information sharing, but will form the basis of an agreed scope to achieve organisational growth and sustainability. This belief will form the basis of their promotion of the advantages of such an approach, as well as help them to convince management and labour constituencies about those advantages.

Management buy-in

Fundamental to the success of a new approach is the acknowledgement of management that the current ER systems and practices are outdated and do not make any meaningful contribution to engaging employee representative structures in joint decision-making processes. Management need to recognise the importance of viewing labour as a business partner by involving them at the core of business decision-making, sharing power where it effects the well-being of workers, creating a sense of ownership, and improving the standard of living of employees. As Koopman[2] put it, "Management and labour need to have a common focus, so that the purpose become not separable. The structures that emerge should be between the organisation and individual and not between management and labour. Surely the usefulness of work, dignity and self-respect can only be achieved through a true democratic right to have a say in one's destiny".

Management's greatest concern when it comes to the concept of sharing of power is that it will violate their rights of authority in such a manner that it will infringe their prerogatives to manage the company.

Management need to be assured, therefore, that whatever worker participation model they implement, their rights authority and prerogatives are protected and that the model will ultimately lead to an increase in productivity, company effectiveness and profit margins, with a decrease in work stoppages, strikes and labour unrest. Management should also be assured that the model will comply with the South African Board for People Practices' professional practice standards for co-determination, which are described in Chapter 8.

Labour buy-in

The level of trust that exists in the organisation will determine the manner and effort that will be applied to introduce the new way of involving labour in participating in decision-making structures. As discussed in Chapter 3, it is critically important to measure levels of trust with a statistically valid, culturally sensitive instrument like the one IBL has adopted, namely the Benchmark of Engagement (BeQ).

The most difficult part is to change the mind set and thinking patterns of union representatives to put on a "management cap" and accept the idea of making unpopular management decisions that might not always find favour with all the employees they represent. Union representatives might see their new role as being in conflict with their traditional role as worker representatives, and be concerned that they will be viewed with suspicion by their constituencies.

The unions may also be concerned that their legal rights to act as independent entities according to the union's constitution will be infringed, as well as their rights to participate collectively as organised labour at the Bargaining Council level.

The relationship and trust levels between union representatives and their constituencies must be managed in such a way that trust levels are not depleted and that representatives are not regarded as "sell outs", but will always act in their best interests.

The most common questions asked by unions are why the need for participative decision-making and what's in it for us? As in the case of management, labour needs to be assured that their rights will be protected and that the model will ultimately lead to an increase in productivity and company effectiveness, which will in turn improve their working conditions, benefits and standards of living.

Workshop/Developing the Co-determination Model

When arranging for representatives from all the parties to attend the workshop, the protocol of inviting the respective representatives from all levels should be observed. The importance of the exercise warrants union representatives from the national, provincial and company levels, from all the unions, to be involved. Management must also be represented by all levels in the organisation, from executive to supervisory level, as must people in the organisation who can give meaningful input to the process. Further, it is important that an independent, reputable and knowledgeable facilitator be appointed by agreement between labour and management to facilitate the process. In the case of IBL, representatives from the Bargaining Council, independent academics and a representative from the CCMA were also invited by agreement to give input into the process of designing a Co-determination Model.

In the case of IBL, Dr. Rica Viljoen from Mandala Consulting, who is a specialist in organisational change and development from an African perspective, as well as employee engagement in diverse workplaces, facilitated the process over a period of three days. The details of the actual session are discussed below.

Prior to the session, Dr. Viljoen was briefed on the objectives as well as the guidelines with regard to the required outcomes.

During the workshop different scenarios were discussed and it was obvious that all the parties recognised the need for a different approach to deal with employee relations in future. The parties were also asked to sketch the scenario for 2020 if they were to carry on in the same manner without any interventions. The following insights transpired during the process.

Management response
- Mistrust between management and employees.
- More illegal strikes/disputes.
- Company sustainability at risk.
- Circle of us and them becomes bigger.
- Less productivity.
- Employees not engaged in decision-making.
- More money spend on IR/dispute resolution.
- Lack of ownership mind set.
- More absurd demands from unions.
- No common goal/focus.
- Unreliable service delivery due to labour unrest.
- Blame shifting/blaming will continue.

Labour response
- Lack of capacity of shop stewards.
- Employees will lose confidence in the dispute resolution process.
- Biased chairpersons of disciplinary hearings.
- Conflict between unions.
- Disputes not effectively dealt with.
- Lack of leadership skills, both management and unions.
- Lack of vision for the industry at large.
- Huge disparity in wealth creation between management and employees.
- Increase in disputes.
- Mistrust between labour and management.
- Rivalry between unions.
- Poor service delivery.

During the session, the fear of both parties that their rights would be violated had to be addressed and the following was agreed:

Rights/prerogatives of unions
- Constitutional and legal rights and duties to act as independent entities in accordance with the unions' constitutions.
- Agreements shall be within the scope of all relevant legislation.
- Operate within the scope of the collective agreements that regulate the relationship between the parties.

Rights/prerogatives of management
- Determine profit margins and manage the company accordingly.
- Develop and implement a strategy to meet shareholders' expectations.
- Determine minimum working conditions and salary scales.
- Set rules and standards to obtain productivity targets.
- Continuously assures company effectiveness and to impose corrective measures.
- Set minimum employment requirements and appoint employees accordingly.
- Determine business processes.

The World Café technique, as originally described by Brown and Cooperrider[3] and adapted by Viljoen[4], was used to create the Co-determination Model. The advantage of this technique is that it ensures that the outcome is co-created. Co-creation and a shared understanding lead to significance, which, in turn, manifests in commitment. The outcome of the exercise resulted in having an in-principle understanding and broad guidelines for the following attached agreements:
- Co-determination – Appendix A
- Closed Shop – Appendix B
- Collective Recognition – Appendix C
- Dispute Prevention and Recognition – Appendix D
- Qualitative Research Report – Appendix E

Towards the end of the process, the parties were requested to discuss what they should start doing, continue doing and stop doing. The response from the parties, especially union leaders, demonstrated their maturity, willingness and enthusiasm to commit themselves to a process of venturing into a new era of co-determining the future of the company.

Start doing:
- We must work together in order to achieve what we have decided.
- Honest communication to build trust.
- Finalise agreements and start communication process.
- Set up proper communication structures.
- Sell the idea as a collective.
- Start building trust.
- Engage employees about what was agreed upon for the future of the company and employees.

Continue doing:

- Keep on working as a team.
- Improve communication with shop stewards and officials.
- Empower employees.
- Engage shop stewards and maintain good relationships.
- Treat all people with respect to build trust.
- Continue to build good relationships amongst ourselves for the good of our business and shareholders.
- Continue with the trust that was established at the workshop.

Stop doing:

- Blaming others.
- Conflict.
- Thinking 'us' and 'them'.
- Mistrusting.
- Stop fear and believe we can do it.
- Stop mistrust and doubts about the process.
- Stop conflict, allegations and fighting each other.

GET EVERYBODY ON BOARD

No philosophy, strategy, action or decision, however good and well-meant, can survive or prosper if all the relevant stakeholders are not well-informed and given the chance to buy into it. The entire workforce needs to believe that the new system is intended to pro-actively engage parties in a decision-making process that will affect their well-being, and that it will provide a better and more meaningful quality of work life for everyone.

During the workshop, it was decided that representatives from labour and management should collectively embark on a roadshow throughout the company and collectively give feedback on the decisions taken. This action demonstrated to all employees the commitment from both management and organised labour. Feedback sessions were held with shop stewards, middle management, management and all employees.

DESIGNING OF AGREEMENTS

Every organisation has a unique history of how the relationship between organised labour and management manifested over the years, and depending on circumstances and needs, specific issues can be captured in the agreements to regulate behaviour between the parties.

In the case of IBL, the following had to be taken into consideration:
- Unions are party to a Bargaining Council.
- The company is a member of an employer's association and Bargaining Council.
- Protect the rights of parties.
- Each union must comply with its own constitution.
- Involvement of provincial/national union leadership.
- What information to be disclosed?
- How will information be kept confidential?
- How will unions be represented as forums?
- Voting procedures if no consensus exists.
- How will decisions taken be communicated?
- What can be negotiated on the company level versus the council level?
- How will disputes be handled in the various forums?
- How to deal with strikes – secret ballot.
- What formal structures exist and what are their powers, objectives, duties and representation?
- What will happen if a party does not comply with an agreement?

The existence of three unions in the company, as well as the danger of additional rival unions, threatened the implementation and maintenance of a Co-determination Model. This prompted the company to convince the parties to enter into a Closed Shop Agreement to limit and ring-fence parties to the agreement, as displayed in Appendix B. The purpose was to ensure stability in the joint decision-making process.

The prevailing Recognition Agreements with the unions were cancelled and one Collective Recognition Agreement was drafted (see Appendix C) which regulates the relationship between the company and the union. Depending on the membership figures, a union enjoys certain privileges, for example the majority union is entitled to a full time shop steward. The collective nature of this agreement has resulted in a fair and transparent relationship between the parties. If, in the future, any union applies for recognition at IBL, the same agreement will apply.

Due to the historic disputes, dissatisfaction, unprotected strikes and work stoppages that resulted from unresolved grievances and disciplinary matters, a Dispute Prevention and Resolution Agreement, as per Appendix D, was drafted. This assists the aggrieved parties to speedily resolve disputes by being transparent, and to proceed without the interference of any party that might have an adverse interest to the dispute. As part of the process of resolving disputes, the parties agreed to establish a tribunal that consists of a chairperson, an independent professional with relevant experience and legal expertise, as well as a union and management representative with relevant knowledge and experience. The details of the functioning of the tribunal is contained in the Dispute Prevention and Resolution Agreement.

IMPLEMENTING THE PROCESS

The fundamental principle of the new system was that management's exclusive right to control and their autocratic management style, through which they reserved the right over power, decision-making, authority, accountability, innovation and the dissemination of information, was replaced with organisational processes and philosophies that nurture interdependent rather than independent or confrontational relationships with organised labour. Organised labour, by agreement, is involved in all decisions that may affect their work and well-being.

Organised labour, which was used to criticising management for decisions made, and had demonstrated militant and destructive behaviour in their fight for certain rights and benefits, now had to play a different role and act as co-responsible leaders in the decision-making process. They needed to understand business principles, industry dynamics, company values, strategic initiatives and company policies.

"The successful implementation of participative systems will depend on the extent to which management and workers understand each other's perceptions of life, both within and outside the organisation. Managers who respect the dignity of the people and perceive them to be making a valuable contribution towards the business must demonstrate this overtly. In other words, managers will have to actively involve workers in decisions, allow them to experiment and innovate, allow errors in decisions as part of the growth process, and show interest in workers' needs and ideas by walking around and maintaining meaningful contact. Common perceptions regarding the importance of self-worth and respect for the other's human dignity now become a common purpose, which channels the energy of both parties towards mutual growth and success."[5]

LEADERSHIP DEVELOPMENT

In designing a supervisory/leadership course for committee members, the HR practitioner must not only ensure that the members have a thorough knowledge and understanding of the contents of all the agreements, but also that the principles of participative management, human dignity, respect, values and creating a common purpose based on common perceptions are present, which will drive parties to a common objective. All managers and union representatives who serve on the various forums must be subjected to a comprehensive training and development programme.

In the case of IBL, the training programme for shop stewards was designed and the parties agreed on the following contents of the programme.

- Union-related:
  o Constitution of unions.
  o How to represent a member in a disciplinary hearing.

- Management/leadership:
  o Management and supervision.
  o Emotional intelligence.
  o Business principles.
  o Computer literacy.

- Bargaining Council collective agreements:
  o South African Road Passenger Bargaining Council (SARPAC)
  o SARPAC Constitution
  o SARPAC Dispute Procedure
  o SARPAC Main Agreement

- Company's collective agreements:
  o Co-determination.
  o Closed Shop.
  o Recognition.
  o Dispute Prevention and Resolution.

- Legislation:
  o Labour Relations Act.
  o Employment Equity Act.
  o Skills Development Act.
  o Empowerment Schemes.
  o Basebetsi Trust (employees' ownership scheme).
  o Initiative Scheme.

- IR policies and procedures.

- Training and development policies and procedures.

- HR policies and procedures.

- Departmental policies and procedures.

UNDERSTANDING BUSINESS PRINCIPLES

The implementation of a Co-determination Model is doomed if employees, especially union representatives, do not understand how the business functions. They must understand how income is derived, what expenses and financial obligations the company has, what the company's business model looks like, as well as details of the industry the company operates in.

If all employees and leaders are subjected to lectures and training sessions on why profits are made and how business functions, over time they will have more and more reason to trust the company and will become part of it.

SELECTION CRITERIA FOR SHOP STEWARDS/COMMITTEE MEMBERS

Union members must elect shop stewards who will be able to make meaningful contributions in the various forums.

As per the Co-determination Agreement, members of the various forums/committees must maintain a high level of professional conduct and subscribe to the spirit of the agreements. Members may not infringe any of the terms of these agreements or act in a manner that is detrimental to the parties. If a member is guilty of misconduct during a meeting, he/she will be removed and the relevant constituency will be asked to deal with the matter in terms of their constitution of good practice. If a member is unable to correct his/her misbehaviour, the relevant constituency will be required to remove and replace the member. Members are privileged to certain relevant confidential information that will allow them to engage effectively in consultation and joint decision-making, thus they need to sign a Confidentiality Agreement and any dispute regarding a breach will be referred in terms of the disciplinary procedure.

In terms of the Collective Recognition Agreement, the union shall endeavour to elect trade union representatives that have the ability to actively participate, make meaningful contributions, and subscribe to the objectives and commitments of the Co-determination Agreement. The criteria for the election of shop stewards are discussed and agreed upon by the JF prior to the election of shop stewards. The recognition of a shop steward may be revoked by the company if a representative fails to comply with certain provisions of the agreement or displays bad conduct.

At IBL, the traditional role of shop stewards has changed; they now carry out their responsibilities by always acting in the best interests of the company and their members.

EMPLOYEE ENGAGEMENT AND TRUST IN PRACTICE

Employee engagement, from a theoretical and academic point of view, is described in *Employee Engagement in a South African context*.[6] The BeQ methodology applied in IBL by Rica Viljoen is also described here (see Appendix E). What makes the BeQ approach unique is that it is a diagnostic, integrated, multi-culturally sensitive tool that also describes spiral dynamics as per Chapter 3 of this book. In comparison to other approaches, it describes engagement from not only the individual and the organisational domains, but also from the team and the contextual domains.

In Chapter 9 of the above-mentioned book, the case study of IBL is described. Viljoen noted that "not only did leadership in this organisation over the years invest in engagement studies and OCD initiatives such as strategy translation and team-building; they also allowed leadership to give away decision-making powers to worker representatives. This courage was repaid with employees that trusted leadership even more".[7]

For the purpose of this discussion, a practical approach to engaging employees and union representatives from shop floor to board level, with reference to Interstate Bus Lines, will be described.

Executive level

The ultimate demonstration of trust in union leadership that goes beyond participative management and joint decision-making is to trust the union representatives as business partners in sharing and co-creating the future of the company. The company executives embark on a strategic formulation exercise every five years, and during the session in 2015, invited the union representatives and officials that serve on the Joint Forum to participate. This act by the executive team acknowledged the contribution of the labour representatives and recognised their value as stakeholders, while living up to the true meaning of co-determination. This also placed a responsibility on the shoulders of the union representatives to actively participate in the translation and cascading of the business strategy to their constituencies at large, and to demonstrate responsibility.

The Joint Forum (JF) is the highest authority of the Executive, and has a primary focus on economic planning, strategic issues, collective agreements and non-substantive issues. This forum meets quarterly and is entitled to consult on any matter related to the above.

Management level

An IBL Workplace Representative Council provides management and shop stewards with an opportunity to meet monthly to discuss and resolve all operational matters that affect both the company and its employees. It seeks to promote the interests of all employees in the workplace, whether or not they are trade union members.

The Dispute Resolution and Discipline Committees are a forum where management and union representatives meet to proactively assist and encourage compliance with agreements and procedures, and attempt to speedily resolve matters and disputes.

Each functional department meets monthly with their respective union representatives to discuss problem areas and issues of activities and production.

As per legal requirements, union representatives participate in and contribute to the Skills Development and Employment Equity meetings.

Functional level

Union representatives participate as members on a selection panel to interview candidates for positions in the bargaining unit.

The company's incentive scheme is target based and inputs from employees/team members in setting and reviewing targets demonstrates management's level of trust in the system. Each employee receives his/her results and is rewarded monthly, and can monitor his/her progress accordingly.

Prior to every day's shift in the technical department, each functional unit starts with a "green area meeting" to plan and review the daily schedule. Employees are engaged on productivity issues and the joys and sorrows of team members are addressed. The same meeting is held in other departments on a weekly or monthly basis.

In terms of the company's bus ownership scheme, employees are elected as trustees in terms of the rules of the Trust. The trustees exercise their rights and duties and engage the workplace to obtain feedback regarding the financial performance of the trust.

Social level

The stakeholder relations function in the company arranges a host of social activities on a monthly basis, and depending on the event, engages employees from all levels of the organisation. Events such as sports days, thanksgiving, prayer days, donations to child care homes, school and old age home visits, pensioner days, etc. give true meaning to the company's slogan, "Ya Rona", which mean "our company".

THE COW PHILOSOPHY

According to spiral dynamics (see Chapter 3) and the Motivational Theory of Clare Graves and Don Beck, people in the PURPLE human niche have a copying analogue thinking system, which means that in order to enable PURPLE to be productive, examples must be given repetitively in the form of stories or metaphors.[8] PURPLE was conceptualised by Laubscher and Viljoen in the book *Indigenous Spiritual Consciousness*[9], which describes indigenous wisdom from all around the world.

In IBL, the metaphor of the cow (Table 11.2) is used to describe the company. The slogan, "Don't kill the cow", is often used in cases where actions can have a negative impact on the company, such as work stoppages, poor service delivery, strikes etc. The slogan "Feed the cow" is used when initiatives are implemented that result in growth. When a cow produces milk, it is a result of the quality of food that it was fed, e.g. an increase in production. When incentive bonuses are paid out, it is a result of the amount of milk that the cow produced. The demand for more benefits depends on the amount of milk produced, thus management need to invest the milk in purchasing more cows or maintaining the cow. IBL therefore doesn't "kill the cow", but rather fights for milk. This metaphor is accepted and understood by both union representatives and employees; everybody understands that their livelihood depends on the condition of the cow.

Traditional engagement

The metaphor can also be used to describe traditional engagement models in relation to co-determination. In traditional engagement, initiatives for enhancing teamwork and efforts to work more effectively and increase productivity result in the cow producing more milk. The result of these engagement initiatives are obtained through a process of consultation and contributions made by employees. This results in having ownership of your jobs and your team. These engagement initiatives are short-term, however, and are therefore not sustainable because of the lack of co-creating and ownership in the company. When engaging employees or shop stewards in the resolution of disputes, it is reactive and parties seeking alternatives to resolve existing disputes.

Co-determination engagement

In co-determination, the emphasis is on high level engagement and holds both parties, management and labour, responsible for committing themselves to the growth and sustainability of the cow - and even to put the company in a position to purchase more cows.

   These high level engagement initiatives take place at the executive level and make both parties responsible for joint strategic formulation. This emphasises the long-term nature of the relationship and results in employees having a sense of psychological ownership in the company. The parties pro-actively manage disputes and grievances by identifying risk areas and jointly seeking alternatives to prevent and resolve disputes.

   Ultimately, the parties jointly own the cow, feed the cow and monitor the amount of milk that it produces (see Tables 11.2 and 11.3 below).

Table 11.2: The metaphor of the cow

FEED THE COW	MILK THE COW
Executive level	Team/job level
Ownership in company	Ownership team/job
Sharing responsibility	Making a contribution
Strategic formulation	Strategic translation
Expansion/growth	Increase productivity
Long-term	Short-term
Co-determine	Consult
Proactive management of disputes	Reactive resolving of disputes
Sustainable	Non-sustainable

Table 11.3: Co-determination figuratively described as a cow

Co-Determination	Engagement
Sustainable	Non-sustainable
Feed the cow	Milk the cow
Executive management level	Team/Job level
Ownership in company	Ownership team / job
Sharing responsibility	Making a contribution
Strategic formulation	Strategic translation
Expansion/growth	Increase productivity
Long-term	Short-term
Co-determine	Consult
Proactive management of dispute prevention and resolution	Reactive resolving of disputes

In Table 11.2 above, two archetypes can be seen. The benefits of co-determination and engagement are made real through the use of commonly understood metaphors. In the Sotho culture, a man must have a few cows from a cultural perspective, i.e. some people relate spontaneously to the metaphor.

REFERENCES

Koopman, A.D., Nassar, M.E., & Nel, J. (1987). *The Corporate crusaders*. Isando: Lexicon Publishers.

Brown J., & Isaacs D. (2005). *The world cafe: shaping our futures through conversations that matter*. San Francisco: Berret-Koehler.

Viljoen, R. (2015). *Organisational Change & Development: an African Perspective*. Bryanston: KR Publishing.

Nienaber, H., & Martins, N. (eds.). (2016). *Employee Engagement in a South African context*. Bryanston: KR Publishing.

Laubscher, L.I., & Viljoen, R.C, (2014). African Spirituality, Insights from the Cradle of Mankind. In C. Spiller & R. Wolfgramm (eds.). *Indigenous spiritualties at work: Transforming the spirit of business enterprise*. Information Age Publishing. Charlotte, NC.

ENDNOTES

1   Koopman, 1987, p. 94.
2   Koopman, 1987, p. 171.
3   Brown & Isaacs, 2005.
4   Viljoen, 2015.
5   Koopman, 1987, p. 136.
6   Nienaber & Martins, 2016.
7   Nienaber & Martens, 2016, p. 150.
8   Viljoen, 2015, p. 66.
9   Laubscher & Viljoen, 2014.

Chapter

12

A DIFFERENT KIND OF HUMAN:
Essentials for the Success of Co-determination in South Africa

Nceba Ndzwayiba

INTRODUCTION

This chapter adopts a transdisciplinary approach and draws from decolonial and post-colonial critical theories to call for a re-conceptualisation of co-determination in ways that respond effectively to the local contextual imperative of reimagining what it means to be human together. I call this a "different kind of human". This call emanates from a painful history that continues to shape the present, in which humanity has been dissected into hierarchies to secure positionalities of superiority, power and privilege for some, and to relegate others to a sub-human status.

The chapter is located within the post-modernist, post-structuralist critical philosophical school of thought. It thus transcends the prevailing ahistorical and apolitical theories and models of diversity, inclusion and multi-culturalism that abound in management sciences. Rather, it draws from a variety of critical transformative theories to illuminate the persistent oppression and inequality that implicates social identities. The intent is to raise consciousness and mobilise the collective to change these norms so as to advance social justice and equality for all. This approach is congruent with the rising student voice in institutions of higher learning, and most recently in critical management studies that draw from decolonial philosophy to compete with what Davies[1] called the "unfinished activisms".

The author identifies as a black, able-bodied, pro-queer, un-practising Christian middle class male. He is a social justice scholar and activist and a head of transformation in a corporation. The views expressed in this chapter mainly draw from an extensive literature review conducted for the findings of his doctoral thesis entitled, *Doing Human Differently*.

SOUTH AFRICA IN CONTEXT

South Africa is a fascinating place and space of transitions, with a myriad of successes, failures, challenges, activisms, contradictions, contestations, opportunities and possibilities. Samantha Vice[2] aptly described this emerging democracy as a "strange place". Vice advanced that despite the efforts by politicians and public relations officials to persuade its citizens otherwise, the country remains a visibly divided, suspicious and morally tangled land to live in. Indeed, complexity and constant sense making have become the new norm. This goes along with a great sense of delusion described by Sizwe Mpofu-Walsh[3] as the state in which the self-evident is not necessarily the case.

This new democracy is contending with external factors that it needs to respond to swiftly, including globalisation, the shifting geopolitical power dynamics, the unwavering hegemony of neo-liberal economics juxtaposed with an unexplained shift away from the communist bloc by the ruling African National Congress following the collapse of the communist Soviet Union at the end of the Cold War, and the fourth industrial revolution technological advancements. Internally, the new democracy is under fire from the younger generation of so called "born frees" who are critical of the CODESA settlement and the so-called Rainbow Nation of former President Nelson Mandela and Archbishop Bishop Desmond Tutu. Issues of land reforms, widening inequality, high levels of unemployment and poverty are precipitating the social implosion and labour unrest that former President Thabo Mbeki foretold in his "dream deferred" speech.[4] Mistrust and impatience are setting in[5], contrasted with the meagre gains of broad-based black economic empowerment and affirmative action, amongst other transformative laws, that are opening up economic participation opportunities for a handful of previously marginalised groups.

Existing and being impactful in this complex space demands the transcending of the parochial singular paradigm thinking that draws artificial distinctions between business, society and humans (or biography). This needs to be exchanged for transdisciplinary and undisciplinary ways of thinking and doing. Such a move has huge potential for opening space for what Viljoen[6] called diversity of thought and Grosfoguel[7] called pluriversality of thought, so as to respond effectively to the real societal problems rather than being preoccupied with singular disciplinary mastery.

Diversity of thought[8] and pluriversalism[9], in turn, demand the reconnecting of history, business, society, biography and power.[10] Thus, stakeholders (rather than shareholders) need to transcend ideological essentialism. They also need to, as Steyn[11] argued, surpass a simplistic singular view of history in order to appreciate human and social reality as multi-layered and multi-dimensional, fluctuating, ambivalent, and open to new possibilities. Co-determination is, therefore, a solution that is presented in this book which fits perfectly into this new social imaginary.[i]

---

i   Steyn uses the word "social imaginary" to denote the envisioning of a possible "new" future that is characterised by the antithesis of everything wrong about the present.

The efficacy and credibility of co-determination, however, in the context of inequalities that intersect with social identities, rest heavily on the extent to which co-determination can facilitate the altering of the well-established unequal power relations that produce, reproduce and embed hierarchies of human superiority and inferiority. Simply put, co-determination has to enable stakeholders to work tirelessly towards rooting out structurally and psychologically embedded racism, sexism, homophobia, ableism, patriarchy, xenophobia and Christionormativity, amongst other "-isms", so as to produce a "different but equal" humankind.

THE SOCIAL CONSTRUCTION OF SUPERIOR AND INFERIOR HUMANS

Re-imagining a "different yet equal" humankind requires what Ndlovu-Gatsheni[12] described as the revisiting of the ugly past, in order to make sense of the murky present, so as to design a better future for all. This begs the question why some human bodies and subjectivities are accepted as the ideal form of being human, while others are looked down upon (dehumanised) as not "normal" or "fully" human – not only historically but in the present day epoch of democracy and universal human rights. Relatedly, why do organisational processes (though often denied) sustain these superior – inferior binary positionalities?

In *Pedagogy of the Oppressed*, the Brazilian Marxist critical theorist and educational scholar, Paulo Freire[13], posited that although the challenge of humanisation has always been, from an axiological perspective, a central problem to humankind, it has recently taken an inescapable concern as it leads to the recognition of dehumanisation, not only as an ontological possibility but as a historical reality.

Freire's[14] views align with Fanon's[15] sociogenesishypothesis. Fanon declared that besides the ontogeny and the phylogeny of being human stands sociogeny. The sociogenesis hypothesis questions ontogenesis and phylogenesis models for being preoccupied with biological – evolutionary contestations of human origins and ignoring the socio-historical-economic and political contexts that shaped the development of societies. This offers a revolutionary mode of rethinking the human category. Fanon, together with his fellow anti-colonial Francophone and Guinea Bissauan colleagues, Césaire and Cabral, presented the human as a mode of being and becoming that is shaped within a precise yet timeless history of coloniality of power and being.[16]

Steyn[17], a South African thinker who combined France Winddance Twine's concept of racial literacy and Freire's[18] notion of "conscientizacao" to develop critical diversity literacy, added that the human is indeed not a self-evident category, but has always been a site of contestation and shaped within the context of unequal power relations. Steyn[19], Fanon[20], Freire[21] and others point to the importance of locating the question of "Where did it all go wrong?" to the hypothesis of the European philosopher, Rene Descartes' (1596 - 1650) "Cogito Ergo Sum", the Cartesian Dualism hypothesis, and the related scientific racism epoch (1650s – 1780s).

In this epoch, European enlightenment scholars produced pseudo-scientific epistemologies that overly glorified white European abled-bodied Christian heteropatriachal masculine bodies (thus themselves) as the epitome of being human.[22] These scholars ordained themselves and those who looked like them as the pure gene (eugenics), and therefore the natural embodiment of intelligence, authority and godliness.

In this production of what Hegel (1808 - 1811) called the "Other", the enlightenment clique associated the thinking "mind" with "man", thereby ordaining themselves as superior beings who could be in the public space; and associated woman with inferiority, powerlessness, and as emotional beings who should belong to the domestic sphere.[23] In fact they undermined their own wives, mothers, sisters and fellow family members, who could have been bi-racial, had a disability and/or been non-gender binary identifying. The dark or brown skinned people of the global South were not only excluded in this world-changing decision-making process, but they were actually constructed as the naturally inferior, primeval, barbaric and savage "Others". The "others" were thus relegated into a sub-human category that Fanon[24] called the "zone of non-being". This production of centres of "normal" humans and margins of "different" sub-humans were epistemologically systematised in the 19th century through claimed "neutral", "objective", "universal" scientific truths that informed the construction of the modern world order as we know it today, including its systems and institutions such as democracy, industrialisation, urbanisation, division of labour and pedagogy. Hence feminists, critical race scholars, critical management scholars, critical disability theorists, post-colonial scholars[25], decolonial thinkers and subaltern studies[26] relentlessly call out the modernity project as having been an inherently racist, Eurocentric, ableist, sexist, heterosexist and androcentric project.

This appropriated right to be exclusively human informed the logic of Western modernity and its discourses such as colonialism, imperialism, capitalism, division of labour, urbanisation, individualism, rationality and scientific knowledge, amongst many.[27] The outcomes of this logic have been evident in multifarious dehumanising discourses, including the conquests of the Americas and the Restern[ii] periphery[28], the trans-Atlantic slave trade, the holocaust, apartheid, and in the contemporary global structure of coloniality of power and being. Steyn[29] reminds us that as far back as 1441, ten Africans from the northern Guinea coast were shipped to Portugal as a gift to Prince Henry. Likewise, after colonising the Americas and renaming the Tahinos humans of the Americas "Red Indians", Christopher Columbus brought spices, gold and some "Red Indians" as a gift to the Spanish monarchy as evidence of his discovery of the new world.

---

ii   Professor Sampie Terblanche refers to the rest of the non-western world as the "Restern periphery"

THE HUMAN IN SOUTH AFRICAN ORGANISATIONS

Acker[30] thoughtfully postulated that inequality regimes are produced and entrenched in a reciprocal relationship between society and the labour market. The labour market, as the microcosm of society, is thus an ideal space for observing and confronting, with the intent of ridding organisations of what Ramphele[31] referred to as the ghosts of racism, sexism and patriarchy.

In the organisational context, the division of labour mirrors the Cartesian ideologies of humanism. Even in the United Nations member countries that ratified affirmative action, employment opportunities for marginalised groups are created at lower levels of occupations than in the upper echelons.[32] Blacks, women, lesbians, gays, transgender people and disabled people, amongst other marginalised groups, constantly contend with micro-aggressions, marginalisation, and forms of indignities and inequalities. On the contrary, whiteness, particularly white masculinity, is beheld as the unquestionable attribute of being a business leader. Thus, this identity is evaluated as having more inherent leadership potential than "other" racial groups.[33] Professor Liz Booysen[34] summed this up well when she said "White is Right", "West is Best", "Think Manager, Think Male".

Indeed, South Africa's Commission on Employment Equity's[35] successive annual reports have affirmed the fact that the division of labour is racialised, gendered and able-bodied. The following graphs summarise the recent statistics reported by the Commission in its latest report:

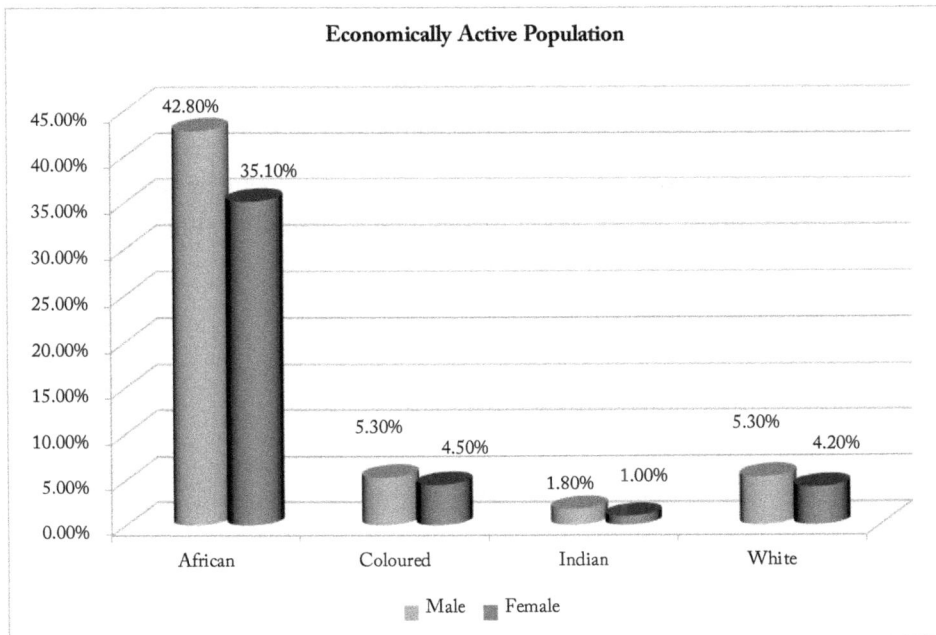

Figure 12.1: Economically Active Population per race and gender

Top management 2017

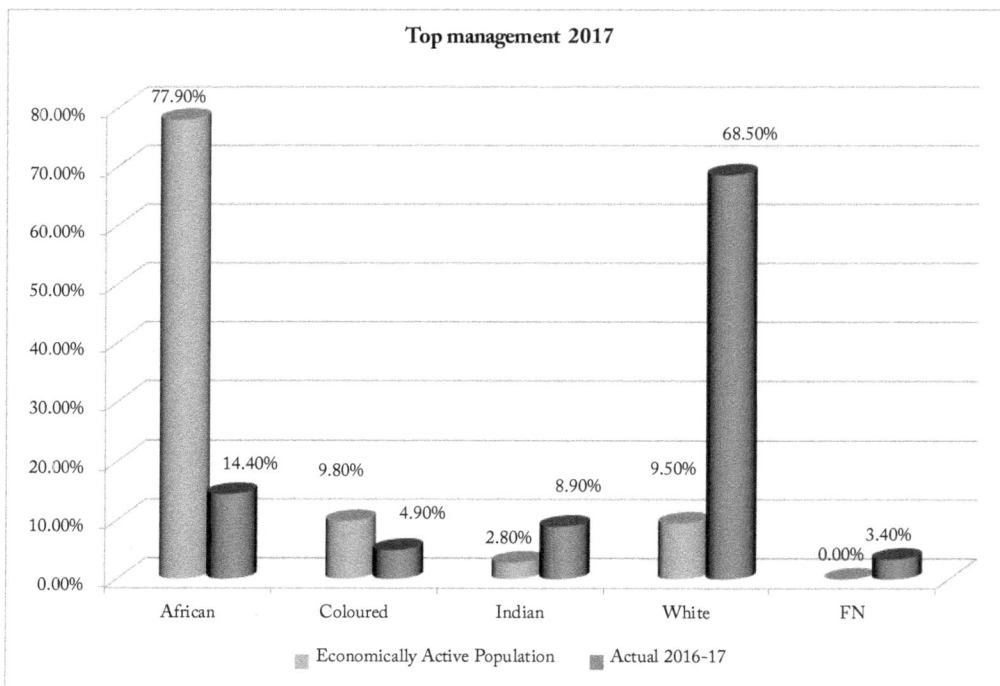

Figure 12.2: Top management 2017 per race

The graphs show that white people make up nearly 10% of South Africa's economically active population, yet they occupy nearly 70% of the decision-making positions, and the majority of these are white males. White females, as Booysen[36] argued, gain access to these protected white masculinity enclaves by virtue of their proximity to whiteness. Blacks, who constitute nearly 90% of the economically active population, are subservient to white masculinity, which continues to preside over them as prescribed in the enlightenment hierarchy of being. Regrettably, the replacement trends shown in the figure below demonstrate the intention to maintain this order of things:

Workforce Movement: Top Leadership

	Terminations	Recruitment	Promotions	Development
African	21.70%	29.00%	20.80%	69.40%
Coloured	5.30%	5.20%	8.40%	3.00%
Indian	6.70%	9.10%	12.50%	4.50%
White	60.70%	50.70%	55.10%	23.10%

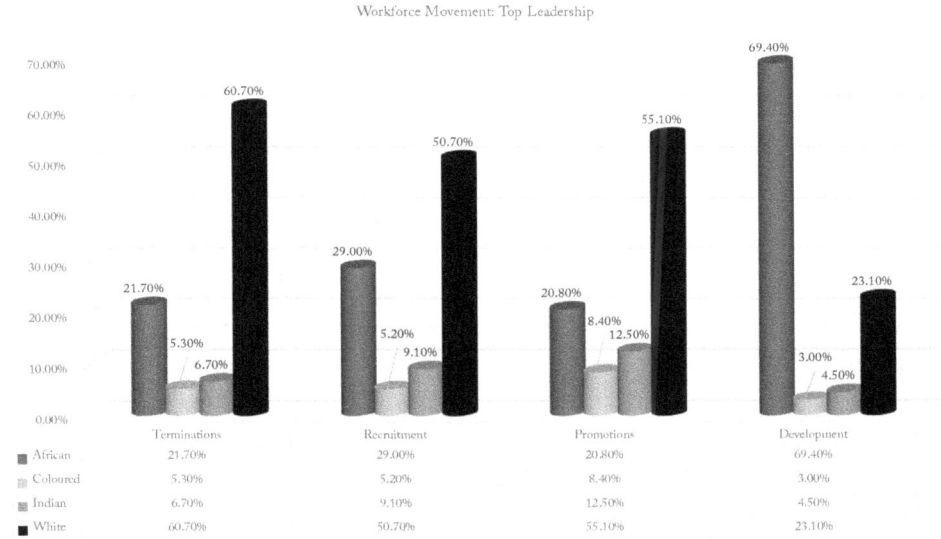

Figure 12.3: Workforce movement: Top leadership

Interestingly, the enlightenment ideas of who is fully human and who is not are also visible in the representation of women and persons with disabilities, as illustrated in the graphs below:

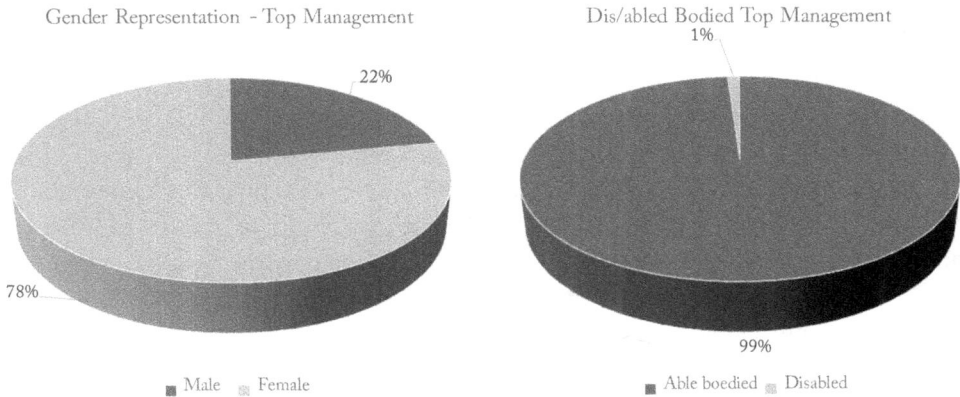

Gender Representation - Top Management

Dis/abled Bodied Top Management

- Male
- Female

- Able boedied
- Disabled

Figure 12.4: Top management: Gender representation

This is the case for masculinity/femininity and able-bodiness and disabledness, with women making up only 22% of positions of authority while disabled persons make up a mere 1%.

Beyond the representational dominance, when the positively appraised dominant groups assume these leadership roles, they also take up responsibility and authority for influencing and shaping organisational culture and norms. Often, this leadership prototype does not critically think about these historically embedded oppressive systems. This is mainly due to the fact that they are not so self-evident, therefore they are assumed to be non-existent. Further, if this leadership prototype does not critically confront its own unconscious bias, it is more than likely to preside over workplaces that "intentionally or unintentionally" propagate marginalisation, inferiorisation and silencing of the subordinated groups. Madi[37] explained the effects of such environments for bodies that are different to the dominant norm when he likened it to "surviving in the jungle". In conceptualising co-determination, it is crucial that we do not "consciously or unconsciously" reproduce these problematic discourses.

In a study that critically examined appraised diversity discourses amongst Johannesburg Stock Exchange-listed corporations, Ndzwayiba[38] found that most organisations pay lip service to transformation and equality. The diversity initiatives in the studied organisations regarded inequality, oppression and dominance as historical legacies rather than present day phenomena that are tied to coloniality of power and being and reproduced through neoliberalism. Consequently, the diversity initiatives were mostly minimalistic and impelled identity siloism, race and gender blindness, medicalisation and hyper-individualisation of disability, nurturing of white fragility, and reproduction of gender binaries. Relatedly, blacks, women, queer persons and persons with disabilities were barely visible in positions of power, strategic influence and high income. These subjugated groups had to constantly perform whiteness, normative masculinity, able-bodiedness and heteronormativity in order to fit in. This performance is systematised under the guise of merit without recognising its dehumanising effects.

MAPPING THE WAY FORWARD

The inequalities outlined in the preceding section persist in the era of legislation. This is evidence of the fact that legislation alone is never enough to transform hearts and minds, or to transform ideological processes that have become deeply systematised. This is the reason why it is often difficult to prescribe a set of bullet proof answers.

The ensuing suggestions form part of incomplete work that I am still busy with, which intends to provide a framework that can guide the analysis and exploration of possible solutions. These include transcending singular paradigm thinking; critical reflexivity; being true and sensitive to the voice of lived human experiences; adopting transversal politics; being an activist and/or aligning to movements that illuminate the marginalised voices, which include but are not limited to feminism, critical race, critical disability, gender and queer movements; and most importantly, understanding ways in which the matrix of domination is upheld so that individuals and collectives can exercise agency to disrupt these patterns wherever they emerge. In concluding this chapter, I will focus on understanding business complicity in oppression, critical diversity literacy, intersectionality and the matrix of domination.

BUSINESS COMPLICITY IN OPPRESSION

Perhaps one of the fundamental reasons for business complicity in the status quo is the belief in classical economics theories which position businesses as merely the phenomenon of the markets and therefore untouched by socio-political realities in the very environment from which they derive profits.

Beder[39] explained that the classical economics view, fuelled by the increased prominence accorded to markets, has led to a situation in which (transnational) corporations eclispse the nation state as the driving force behind policy making. She added that these corporations gain political power through resources and influence, market ideology, public relations and political mobilisation, leading to the distortion of the idea that governments need to protect citizens against exploitation and the excesses of free enterprise, and replacing it with the idea that government should protect business activity against the excesses of democratic regulation.

Debunking this classical idea of a socially free floating business, Lazarus[40] argued that corporations serve as mechanisms by which different social, cultural, political and economic systems confront each other. Thus, corporations import and impose knowledge systems, cultural values and practices that routinely conflict with existing ones in the social environments in which they operate.[41] These imported and imposed knowledge and cultural systems, as argued above, often draw from oppressive normalised ideas of what it means to be human. By so doing, they produce, reproduce and embed forms of oppressive "-isms" that do not only become deeply interwoven into organisational systems and culture, but flow through to the society. This is particularly true in the South African context, where Ubuntu forms an integral of the social fibre. Contrarily, classical economics theory is based on individualistic Darwinist "survival of the fittest" ideas.

CRITICAL DIVERSITY LITERACY

Critical diversity literacy is useful for reading, analysing and responding to these deeply internalised oppressive systems. Professor Melissa Steyn[42] has been developing this framework over the last two decades. She defined critical diversity literacy (CDL) as "an enabled mode of existence" that is consistent with the requirements of the 21st century".

In developing the CDL framework, Steyn[43] borrowed from Winddance Twine's concept of racial literacy and Freire's[44] notion of "conscientizacao". Steyn thus saw CDL as the process of conscientisation. CDL can be understood as a reading practice that recognises and reacts to multi-faceted social, political and economic climates and prevalent structures of oppression that implicate social identities. The intention is to take a firm stand against such practices wherever and however they manifest. As a reading practice, CDL offers an angle for reading the patterns of power and oppression, the analytical tools to read the intricacies of such patterns, the vocabulary to name the ideological systems and hegemonic discourses that produce such patterns, and the competence to challenge these in the interest of deepening democracy for all.

Steyn[45] provided ten criteria that can be applied in evaluating the presence of CDL in any social context, which included:

- an understanding of the role of power in constructing differences that make a difference;
- a recognition of the unequal symbolic value and material value of different social locations, including acknowledging hegemonic positionalities and concomitant identities such as whiteness, heterosexuality, masculinity, cisgender, ablebodiness, middleclassness etc., and how these dominant orders position those in non-hegemonic spaces;
- an analytical skill at unpacking how these systems of oppression intersect, interlock, co-construct, and constitute each other, and how they are reproduced, resisted and reframed;
- a definition of oppressive systems such as racism as current social problems and not only historical legacy;
- an understanding that social identities are learned and an outcome of social practice;
- the possession of a diversity grammar and vocabulary that facilitate a discussion of race privilege and oppression;
- the ability to translate (see through) coded hegemonic practices;
- an analysis of the ways that diversity hierarchies and institutionalised oppressions are inflected in specific social contexts and material arrangements;
- an understanding of the role of emotions, including our own emotional investment, in all of the above; and
- an engagement with issues of the transformation of these oppressive systems towards deepening social justice in all levels of social organisation.

INTERSECTIONALITY

Crenshaw's[46] idea of intersectionality is to social justice what Marxism is to labour theory. This black feminist from a legal background explored the experiences of black migrant workers in the United States of America, leading to the production of an analytical theory that brings together critical race theory, gender politics and sociological political theory. Intersectionality clarifies that individuals embody multiple identities, and that one can simultaneously be privileged and oppressed on the basis of these multiple intersecting identities. In so doing, Crenshaw[47] assisted us to analyse, study and make sense of ways of understanding oppression beyond singular identities.

Crenshaw[48] also postulated that these silo approaches are incapable of adequately addressing the nuances involved in the subordination of black women. Hill-Collins[49] and Crenshaw[50] stated that cultural patterns of oppression are not only interrelated, but are bound together and influenced by intersectional social systems, such as race, gender, social class, citizenship status, sexuality, ability and other identity categories. Lanehart[51] demonstrated the complex and intertwined identity categories that make up an individual's identity.

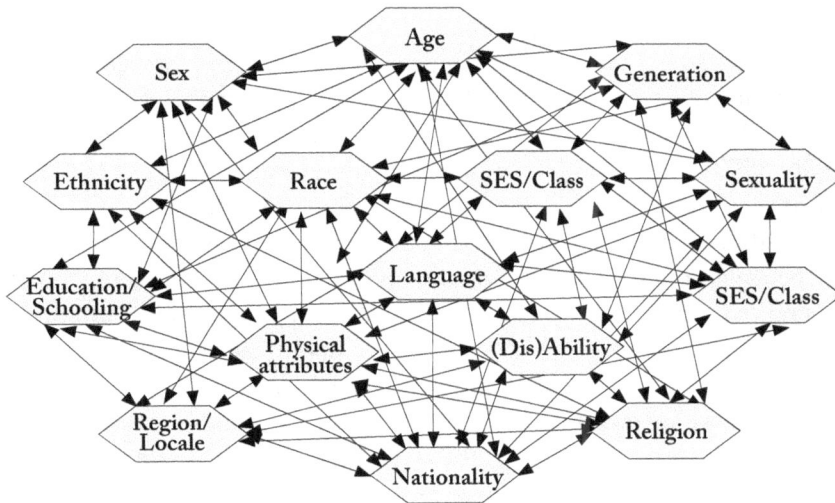

Figure 12.5: Depiction of intersectionality
Source: Adopted from Lanehart[52]

McCall[53] clarified that intersectionality is a technique or method of studying complex relationships between multiple dimensions and modalities of social relationships and subject formations. Thus, intersectionality permits the examination of how ways in which social and cultural categories interlock. It also makes it possible to study and challenge oppressive systems within a group that shares similarities and differences.[54]

This implies that gender, race, ethnicity, disability, sexuality, class and nationality are not essentially autonomous of one another; rather, they are interrelated. Therefore, a person may experience various forms of oppression on multiple levels, depending on their positionality in the hierarchy of being.[55] Knudsen[56] explained that intersectionality is instrumental in analysing the production of power and oppressive processes between and within social identity categories.

MATRIX OF DOMINATION

Hill-Collins[57] specifically explained that these oppressive systems are organised and sustained through four interrelated domains of power:

- Structural domain.
- Disciplinary domain.
- Hegemonic domain.
- Interpersonal domain.

Hill-Collins[58] went on to explain the structural domain as comprising social structures such as policies, culture, the economy, law, and religion; the disciplinary domain as the mechanism of managing oppression through the institutional regulation of human behaviour, routinisation, rationalisation and surveillance; the hegemonic domain as legitimising oppression, which may include symbols, images, language, values, media images, curricula and textbooks; and the interpersonal domain, which is made up of the personal relationships we maintain as well as the different interactions that make up our daily life. This includes how an individual understands the self and others, and how they in turn oppress or uphold the oppression of the others.

Once routinised, these systematised oppressive ideas of who is more human than the other become normalised and virtually invisible, such that they form part of the taken for granted order of things and daily routine. When questioned or unroutinised, they are always justified through ahistorical and apolitical responses that blame the victim and accuse them of being delusional and possessing an inherent inadequacy by positioning these inequalities and injustices as the inevitable outcome of just and fair meritocratic systems. In so doing, the responder fails to account for the structural barriers put in place to deny the different others access to resources that would enable them to acquire merit.

CONCLUSION

This chapter demonstrates the centrality of disrupting normalised ideas about human differences. Drawing on critical philosophical thought, the chapter elucidated the history and ideological systems that created, reproduced and entrenched these ideas, and the invisible ways in which they operate nowadays to create situations of unequal power, privilege and domination. The chapter further illustrates that if these remain unchanged, co-determination will simply create another platform of engagement of unequal human subjects, thereby opening itself up to being ineffective and to the arising revolt by the decolonial activists. The main contribution of the chapter is to show that the idea of a non-racial and non-sexist democracy rests on ongoing efforts that will challenge the status quo in the interest of reinstating a different humankind that is characterised by empowering differences.

REFERENCES

Acker, J. (2006). Inequality Regimes: Gender, Class, and Race in Organizations. *Gender & Society, 20*(4), 441-464.

Atkins, R. (1993). *Art Spoke. A guide to contemporary ideas, and buzzwords, 1848 - 1944.* New York: Abbevile Press.

Barrett, T. (1997). Modernism and Postmodernism: An Overview with Art Examples. In J. Hutchens & M. Suggs. *Art Education: Content and Practice in a Postmodern Era* (pp. 17-30). Washington DC: NAEA.

Beder, S. (2009). Neoliberalism and the Global Financial Crisis. *Social Alternatives, 8*(1), 17-21.

Booysen, L. (2007). Societal power shifts and changing identities in South Africa: Workplace implications. *South African Journal of Economic and Management Sciences, 10*(1), 1– 20.

Booysen, L. (2007). Societal Power Shifts and Changing Identities in South Africa: Workplace Implications. *South African Journal of Economic Sciences*, 1-20.

Commission on Employment Equity. (2015). *Employment Equity Report.* Pretoria: Department of Labour.

Crenshaw, K. (1989). Demarginalizing the Intersection of Race and Sex: A Black Feminist Critique of Antidiscrimination Doctrine, Feminist Theory and Antiracist Politics. *The University of Chicago Legal Forum, 140*, 139-167.

Crenshaw, K. (1991). Mapping the Margins: Intersectionality, Identity Politics, and Violence against Women of Color. *Stanford Law Review, 43*(6), 1241-1299.

Davies, A.Y. (2016). *Unfinished Activisms and Contemporary Struggles for Justice.* 17th Steve Biko Memorial Lecture, University of South Africa, Pretoria.

Fanon, F. (1967). *Black Skin White Masks: Get Political.* New York: Grove Press.

Freire, P. (1978). *Pedagogy of the Oppressed.* New York: Penguin Random House.

Gevisser, M. (2007). *The Dream Deferred: Thabo Mbeki.* Johannesburg: Jonathan Ball.

Grosfoguel, R. (2009). A Decolonial Approach to Political Economy: Transmodernity, Border Thinking and Global Coloniality. *Epistemologies of Transformation, The Latin American Decolonial Option and its Ramifications,* (Fall), 10-38.

Grosfoguel, R. (2009). A Decolonial Approach to Political Economy: Transmodernity, Border Thinking and Global Coloniality. *Epistemologies of Transformation,* 10-38.

Habib, A. (2014, April 23). *Inequality is South Africa's Greatest Challenge.* Retrieved from: http://www.ngopulse.org/blogs/adam-habib-inequality-south-africa-s-greatest-challenge.

Healy, G. (2016). The Politics of Equality and Diversity: History, Society, and Biography. In R. Bendel, I. Bleijenbergh, & A. Mills. *The Oxford Handbook of Diversity in Organisations* (p. 15). Oxford, UK: Oxford University Press.

Herbut, J. (2013, March 17). *Reasons for Spanish Exploration: God, Gold or Glory?* Retrieved from: https://prezi.com/cvegrahy_37m/reasons-for-spanish-exploration-god-gold-or-glory/.

Hill-Collins, P. (2000). *Black Feminist Thought: Knowledge, Consciousness, and the Politics of Empowerment.* New York: Routledge.

Hymer, S. (1976). *The International Operations of Nation Firms: A Study of Foreign Direct Investment.* Cambridge: MLT Press.

Knudsen, S.V. (2006). Intersectionality - A Theoretical Inspiration in the Analysis of Minority Cultures and Identities in Textbooks. In B. B. Aamotsbakken, S. V. Knudsen, & M. Horsely. *Caught in the Web or Lost in the Textbook?* (pp. 61-67). Caen: IARTEM.

Lanehart, S.L. (2009). *Diversity and Intersectionality.* The Seventeenth Annual Symposium About Language and Society (pp. 1-8). Austin: Texas Linguistics Forum.

Lazarus, A.A. (2001). *Multinational Corporations.* New York: Elsevier Science.

Leornadelli, G.J., Rosette, A., & Phillips, K.W. (2008). The White Standard: Racial bias in leadership categorization. *Journal of Applied Psychology, 93*(4), 758-777.

Lyon, D. (1999). *Postmodernity*. Buckingham: Open University Press.

Madi, P.M. (1993). *Affirmative Action in Corporate South Africa: Surviving in the Jungle*. Kenwyn: Juta.

Malala, J. (2012, August 17). The Marikana Action is a strike by the poor against the state and the haves. *The Guardian*. Retrieved from: https://www.theguardian.com/commentisfree/2012/aug/17/marikana-action-strike-poor-state-haves.

McCall, L. (2005). The Complexity of Intersectionality. *The University of Chicago Press Journals, 3*(3), 1771-1800.

Mignolo, W., & Escobar, A. (2013). *Globalisation and the Decolonial Option*. New York: Taylor & Francis.

Mpofu-Welsch, S. (2017). *Democracy and Delusion*. Tafelberg, Cape Town.

Ndlovu-Gatsheni, S. (2013). *Coloniality of Power in Postcolonial Africa: Myths of Decolonisation*. Senegal: CODESRIA.

Ndlovu-Gatsheni, S. (2015). Decoloniality as the Future of Africa. *Africa Development, 40*(3), 13-40.

Ndzwayiba, N. (2017). *Doing Human Differently: A Critical Analysis of Appraised Diversity Discourses in Corporate South Africa*. PhD Thesis, University of the Witwatersrand, Johannesburg.

Ndzwayiba, N.A. (2012). *Challenges of Transformation Managers in Corporate South Africa*. Johannesburg: University of Johannesburg.

Ndzwayiba, N., Ukpere, W., & Steyn, M. (2016). *Debunking The Fable of Job Hopping Amongst Black Professionals in Corporate South Africa*. (Unpublished article.) Johannesburg.

Netshitenzhe, J. (2013). *Why Inequality Matters: South African Trends and Interventions*. Johannesburg: Mapungubwe Institute for Strategic Reflection.

Prasad, P. (2003). The Return of the Native: Organizational Discourses and the Legacy of the Ethnographic Imagination. In A. Prasad (ed.). *Postcolonial Theory and Organizational Analysis: A Critical Engagement*. New York: Palgrave, pp. 149–170.

Quijano, A. (2000). Coloniality of Power, Eurocentrism, and Latin America. *Nepantla: Views from South: Duke University Press*, 533-580.

Ramphele, M. (2009). *Laying Ghosts to Rest: Dilemmas of the transformation in South Africa*. Cape Town: Tafelberg.

Roach, S. (2010). *The Next Asia: Opportunities and Challenges for A New Globalization*. New Jersey: Wiley.

Said, E. (1978). *Orientalism: Western Conceptions of the Orient*. London: Penguin.

Samantha, V. (2010). How Do I Live in this Strange Place? *Journal of Social Philosophy, 41*(3), 323-342.

South Africa's Commission on Employment Equity. (2017). *Department of Labour*. Pretoria: Government Printers.

Spivak, G. C. (1988). Can the Subaltern Speak? In C. Nelson & L. Grossberg (eds.). *Marxism and the Interpretation of Culture*. London: Macmillan.

Steyn, M. (2001). *Whiteness Just Isn't What It Used To Be: White Identity in a Changing South Africa*. New York: State University of New York.

Steyn, M. (2007). As the Postcolonial Moment Deepens: A response to Green, Sonn and Matsebula. *South African Journal of Psychology, 37*(3), 420-424.

Steyn, M. (2015). Critical diversity literacy: Essentials for the twenty-first century. In S. Vertovec. *Routledge Handbook of Diversity Studies* (p. 379). New York: Routledge.

Supski, S. (2007). *It Was Another Skin: The Kitchen in 1950's Australia*. Bern: Peter Lang.

Vice, V. (2010). How Do I Live In This Strange Place? *Journal of Social Philosophy, 41*(3), 323-342.

Viljoen, R. (2014). *Inclusive Organisational Transformation: An African Perspective to Human Niches*. Farnham: Gower Publishing.

Wits Centre for Diversity Studies. (2015, April 11). *Doing Human Conference*. Retrieved from: https://www.wits.ac.za/news/latest-news/general-news/2015/2015-04/wicds-hosts-doing-human-conference.html

ENDNOTES

1   Davies, 2016.
2   Vice, 2010.
3   Mpofu-Walsh, 2017.
4   Gevisser, 2007.
5   Malala, 2012; Netshitenzhe, 2013; Habib, 2014.
6   Viljoen, 2014.
7   Grosfoguel, 2009.
8   Viljoen, 2014.
9   Grosfoguel, 2009.
10 Healy, 2016.
11 Steyn, 2015.
12 Ndlovu-Gatsheni, 2015.
13 Freire, 1978.
14 Freire, 1978.
15 Fanon's, 1967.
16 Quijano, 2000.
17 Steyn, 2015.
18 Freire, 1978.
19 Steyn, 2015.
20 Fanon, 1967.
21 Freire, 1978.
22 Mignolo & Escobar, 2013; Wits Centre for Diversity Studies, 2015.
23 Supski, 2007.
24 Fanon, 1967.
25 Said, 1978; Prasad, 2003.
26 Spivak, 1988.
27 Barrett, 1977; Atkins, 1993; Lyon, 1999.
28 Herbut, 2013; Grosfoguel, 2009; Ndlovu-Gatsheni, 2013; 2015.
29 Steyn, 2001.
30 Acker, 2006.
31 Ramphele, 2009.
32 Leonardelli, Phillip & Rosette, 2008.
33 Leonardelli, Phillip & Rosette, 2008.
34 Booysen, 2007.
35 South Africa's Commission on Employment Equity, 2017.
36 Booysen, 2007.
37 Madi, 1993.
38 Ndzwayiba, 2017.
39 Beder, 2009.
40 Lazarus, 2001.
41 Lazarus, 2001.
42 Steyn, 2015.
43 Steyn, 2007; 2015.
44 Freire, 1978.
45 Steyn, 2015.
46 Crenshaw, 1989; 1991.

47   Crenshaw, 1989.
48   Crenshaw, 1991.
49   Hill-Collins, 2000, p. 42.
50   Crenshaw, 1989; 1991.
51   Lanehart, 2009.
52   Lanehart, 2009.
53   McCall, 2005.
54   Knudsen, 2006.
55   Lanehart, 2009.
56   Knudsen, 2006, p. 62–63.
57   Hill-Collins, 2000.
58   Hill-Collins, 2000.

Appendix A

CO-DETERMINATION AGREEMENT

Entered Into Between

ITUMELE BUS LINES (PTY) LTD T/A INTERSTATE BUS LINES
(Hereiafter referred to as "the Company")

And

TIRISANO TRANSPORT AND SERVICES WORKERS UNION
(Hereinafter referred to as TASWU)

And

SOUTH AFRICAN TRANSPORT AND ALLIED WORKERS UNION
(Hereinafter referred to as SATAWU)

- The Company, TASWU And SATAWU are collectively referred to as "the Parties".
- TASWU And SATAWU are collectively referred to as "the Unions".

The Parties hereby agree as follows:

1. **Preamble**:

The parties to this Agreement acknowledge and recognise that:

1.1 This Agreement is subject to the relevant provisions of the Labour Relations Act, Provisions of the Constitution and Agreements of the South African Road Passenger Bargaining Council (SARPBAC) as well as the Closed Shop and Recognition Agreement that regulates the relationships between the parties.

1.2 The Unions exercise their constitutional and legal rights and duties to act as individual independent entities in accordance with the Union's respective Constitutions as well as collectively as organized Labour in terms of the Bargaining Council Constitution and according to the Collective Agreements that regulates the relationship between the parties to this Agreement.

1.3 The Company exercises its authority and duty to:
- Determine profit margins and manage the Company accordingly;
- Develop and implement strategy to reach shareholders' expectations;
- Determine minimum working conditions and salary scales;
- Set rules and standards to obtain productivity targets;
- Continuously assess company effectiveness and market relatedness and impose corrective measures;
- Set minimum employment requirements and appoint employees accordingly;
- Determine business processes.

2. **Objectives of the Co-determination Agreement**:

The objectives of the Agreement is to:

2.1 Create a climate in which disagreements and disputes are settled through dialogue and co-decision and not by force.

2.2 Pro-actively engage as parties in the decision making processes which affect their well-being, instead of wasting energy and resources on re-active problem solving.

2.3 Empower individual employees to engage them in business processes in their sphere of operations so that they are enabled to become innovative problem solvers and pro-actively and positively influenced by giving them correct information to make decisions.

2.4 Manage the conflict of interests and consciously addressing and resolving disputes between the Company and the Unions/Employees.

2.5 Create a spirit of mutual trust discussing matters with an earnest desire to reach an agreement.

2.6 Develop and train parties (leaders and representatives) to take responsibility for decisions taken and make meaningful contributions to processes.

2.7 Create communication structures to ensure that decisions taken are communicated to all employees.

2.8 Increase productivity, company effectiveness and in return working conditions, benefits and living standards of employees.

3. Commitments of parties to the agreement:

The parties to this Agreement acknowledge that the successful implementation and maintenance of this Agreement depend on the following:

3.1 Notwithstanding the inherited ideologies and differences between the Unions and the Company, the parties acknowledge that the effective functioning of the Company is fundamental to reach each party's objectives.

3.2 Parties shall recognise and honour the rights of other parties.

3.3 Parties shall honour agreements.

3.4 Parties shall value and maintain sound relationships built on trust and respect.

3.5 The parties shall consider the values and objectives of the Co-determination Agreement in all their dealings and deliberations with each other.

3.6 The Parties shall familiarize themselves with, recognize and ensure adherence to the contractual obligations that the Company has entered into with the Government of South Africa.

4. Employee participation in management structures:

4.1 Employee participation in terms of this Agreement takes place at two levels; on the workplace level where operational purposes are pursued (operational performance, public relations, administration, services) as described in paragraph 6; and at Executive level with legal capacity pursuing economic or substantive issues as described in paragraph 5. The two levels of Co-determination complement each other.

5. Joint Management / Union Forum (JF):

5.1 Objective and Duties:

5.1.1 The primary focus of the JF is on economic planning, strategic issues, collective agreements and non-substantive matters.

5.1.2 The JF is entitled to be consulted by the employer about proposals relating to any of the following matters, but not limited to:

- New ventures;
- Dismissal of employees based on operational requirements;
- Exemptions from any collective agreements or any law;
- Employee empowerment trusts and incentive schemes;
- Strike, lockout and picketing procedures;
- Disciplinary procedures;
- Financial and operational performance of the company;
- Administration of agency fee funds;
- Disciplinary rules and codes of conduct;
- Non-substantive conditions of employment (not covered by the Bargaining Council);
- Collective Agreements;
- Co-determination Agreement;
- Unresolved issues deriving from the Workers Representative Council (WRC);
- Relationship between parties; and
- Criteria for merit increases and discretionary bonuses

5.1.3 Management representatives in the JF will consult and endeavour to reach consensus with the representatives of other stakeholders in the JF before implementing any proposal concerning but not limited to:
- Disciplinary procedures;
- Dismissal of employees for reasons based on operational requirements;
- Exemptions from any Collective Agreement or any law;
- Non-substantive conditions of employment; and
- Co-determination and Collective Agreements.

5.1.4 Disputes deriving from the above, will be dealt with in terms of paragraph 5.10.

5.2 Disclosure of information:

5.2.1 The Company will disclose to the JF upon request all relevant information that will allow the JF to engage effectively in consultation and joint decision making.

5.2.2 The Company shall not disclose information:
- That is legally privileged;
- That the company cannot disclose without contravening a prohibition imposed on the employer by any law or order of any court;
- That is confidential and, if disclosed, may cause substantial harm to an employee or the employer; or
- That is private personal information relating to an employee, unless that employee consents to the disclosure of that information.

5.2.3　The Company shall notify the JF in writing if of the view that any information disclosed as above is confidential.

5.2.4　If there is a dispute about the disclosure of information, any party to the dispute may refer the dispute in terms of the dispute procedure as per paragraph 5.10.

5.2.5　Any documented information that is required to be disclosed by the company shall be made available on request to the members of the JF.

5.3　Confidentiality:

5.3.1　Each member of the JF shall sign a confidentiality agreement. In any dispute about an alleged breach of confidentiality, the dispute will be referred in terms of the dispute or disciplinary procedure as per the confidentiality agreement.

5.4　Reporting structure:

5.4.1　The Company Executives shall, within their mandate from the Board of Directors, strategic objectives and business commitments endeavour to engage the Unions through dialogue to explore alternatives with an earnest desire to reach agreements.

5.4.2　The Unions shall, within the aims and objectives of each of their respective constitutions as well as the mandate from their constituencies participate in the JF's by making meaningful contributions to improve the company's effectiveness.

5.5　Meetings:

5.5.1　Composition of the JF meeting:

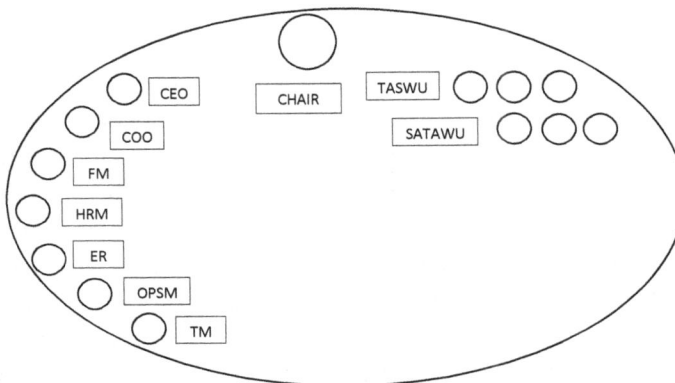

The members of the meeting shall be constituted as follows:

5.5.1.1 **Company Members**:
- Chief Executive Officer (CEO);
- Chief Operating Officer (COO);
- Financial Manager (FM);
- Human Resource Manager (HRM);
- Employee Relations Maanager (ERM);
- Operations Manager (OPSM); and
- Technical Manager (TM).

5.5.1.2 **Union Members**:
- A Union Official from each of the respective Unions (SATAWU, TASWU);
- Chairperson of Shop Steward Council or a Shop Steward appointed by the Union (SATAWU, TASWU);
- Secretary of Shop Steward Council or a Shop Steward appointed by the Union (SATAWU, TASWU);
- Each Union may appoint one (1) Shop Steward as an alternate who may attend a meeting in the event of a main member not being available.

5.5.2 **Chairperson and Secretary**:
- The Company shall provide Secretarial functions.
- The Chairperson will be appointed by the JF from time to time.

5.5.3 **Meeting intervals**:

5.5.3.1 Meetings shall be arranged on a quarterly basis and four (4) meetings shall be held per year. In extraordinary circumstances, any party may request a special meeting should the urgent matter at hand may warrant it.

5.5.3.2 In the event that a matter needs further investigation, the JF may form an ad hoc small committee to investigate and make a recommendation to the JF.

5.5.4 **Agenda and meeting arrangements**:

5.5.4.1 During the first meeting of the year, members shall determine the dates for the rest of the year. The Secretary shall notify members two (2) weeks, under normal circumstances, prior to the meeting to forward items for discussion. The Secretary shall finalize the agenda and distribute the same to the members not less than seven (7) days prior to the meeting. No items other than items on the agenda will be discussed unless the opposing party gives consent to discuss the extraordinary issues requested or a party is able to motivate that the extraordinary developments dictate that the issue should be discussed.

5.5.4.2 The Secretary shall compile and distribute minutes at least seven (7) working days after the meeting unless otherwise agreed in the meeting.

5.5.4.3 The Secretary shall keep and ensure availability of minutes of the meeting and all resolutions adopted at the meeting

5.5.4.4 At every meeting, the minutes of the previous meeting shall be read, corrected if necessary and signed by the Chairperson as well as a representative from each of the parties.

5.5.4.5 The proceedings of any meeting shall not be invalidated by reason of non-attendance of any of the representatives providing that the quorum is reached.

A quorum constitutes the Company and two of the Unions, regardless the number of representatives from any of the parties.

5.5.5 Preparations and mandates for meetings:

5.5.5.1 Members shall ensure that timeous mandates are obtained prior to the JF meetings from constituencies and where required, consolidated mandates are obtained to promote constructive consultations and speedily finalizations of matters at hand.

5.6 Membership:

5.6.1 The Company shall appoint the members of the JF as per paragraph 5.5.1.1 or as otherwise decided to have representatives from each functional department within the organization at the meeting. It is however compulsory that the CEO and COO shall not be substituted as members.

5.6.2 The Unions shall appoint members as per paragraph 5.5.1.2 as well as according to the union's constitution regarding the appointment of union officials and the election of office bearers from time to time.

5.6.3 The Company and the Union shall submit the names of their members at the first meeting of each year and members shall hold office for a period of not less than two years unless removed by their respective constituencies in terms of their constitutions or as per paragraph 5.6.6.

5.6.4 The members of the meeting shall be standing members and may only be alternated in terms of paragraph 5.5.1.2 or unless he/she is permanently removed and replaced. If any person, for whatever reason, fails to attend a meeting, he/she may be alternated only in terms of paragraph 5.5.1.2 and will otherwise be noted as absent with or without reasons whatever the case may be.

5.6.5 The JF may, from time to time, identify training needs of JF members and shall request Management to arrange training as identified. JF members shall avail themselves for training as identified.

5.6.6 Members of the JF shall maintain a high level of professional conduct and subscribe to the spirit of the Co-determination Agreement. Members shall not infringes any of the terms of this Agreement or acts in a manner which is detrimental to the interests of the Parties. If a member is guilty of misconduct during a meeting, he/she will be removed or requested to excuse him/herself from the meeting and the relevant constituency will be requested to deal with the matter in terms of their constitution or good practice. If a member is unable to correct his/her behaviour, the relevant constituency will be requested to remove and replace the member.

5.7 Voting procedures:

5.7.1 It may be required from time to time to establish whether sufficient consensus exist between the Union regarding items as per point 5.1.3 or any other item that may constitute a dispute between the Company and Unions.

5.7.2 If sufficient consensus in terms of 5.1.3 exist between Unions, a dispute may not be declared by one Union and dispute procedures will not be instituted as per paragraph 5.10. All Unions (and their respective representatives and officials) will accept the resolution by the majority decision of the Unions.

5.7.3 Sufficient consensus will be regarded as the support of not less than (60%), sixty percent of the eligible votes cast.

5.7.4 In determining the number of eligible votes to which a Union is entitled at any point in time, there shall be taken into account the number of employees that subscribe to the union membership as reflected on the most recent monthly union membership list provided by company's payroll.

5.7.5 The number of eligible votes to which Unions are entitled shall be based on one (1) vote per each employee as per paragraph 5.7.4.

5.8 Communication of decisions:

5.8.1 Prior to closure of the meeting, the meeting shall formulate a communique/ briefing letter that will serve the purpose of a standardized message that will be communicated to all employees, posted on all notice boards and e-mailed to all computer recipients.

No member of the JF shall communicate with the media or any matter discussed in the JF except the spokesperson who shall be authorized with the approval of the CEO or his delegate and as approved by the JF.

5.9 Levels of bargaining:

5.9.1 The South African Road Passenger Council is the exclusive forum for the negotiation and conclusion of agreements on substantive issues between employers and employers' organisations, on the one hand, and the trade unions on the other hand.

5.9.2   Despite clause 5.9.1, trade unions may consult with the employer at JF level on non-substantive conditions of employment, operational procedures, bonuses or incentive schemes that are directly related to profit or productivity, or both. A matter contemplated in this sub-clause is not intended to be negotiated in the Bargaining Council.

5.9.3   In the event of a deadlock in negotiations on an issue contemplated by clause 5.9.2, the dispute will be dealt with in terms of clause 8 of this Agreement as well as Appendix D no. 4 of the Dispute Prevention and Resolution Procedure.

5.9.4   The Parties to this Agreement specifically undertake not to call a strike or lock-out or in any other way seek to induce or compel negotiations on the issues referred to in clause 5.9.2.

5.10   Dispute procedures:

5.10.1 Unless a Collective Bargaining Council Agreement or LRA provides otherwise, any party to this Agreement may refer the dispute to the Bargaining Council/ CCMA in writing after the internal dispute procedures as per paragraph 8 has been exhausted.

5.10.2 The Bargaining Council must attempt to resolve the dispute through conciliation.

5.10.3 If the dispute remains unresolved, the dispute shall be referred to the Dispute Prevention and Resolution Procedure.

5.10.4 The Parties to this Agreement specifically agree not to call out a strike or a lock-out on issues that are tabled at the JF unless the internal dispute procedure as per paragraph 5.11 and 8 have been followed.

5.11   Strikes and Lock-outs:

5.11.1 The parties acknowledge that strikes and lock-outs are a basic right in terms of the provisions of the LRA.

5.11.2 Notwithstanding the above, the parties acknowledge that strikes and lock-outs always have or has the potential to have a detrimental effect on the company and the employees. The Parties will not organize or embark upon such action without first discussing the intended action in the JF meeting.

5.11.3 The controlling authority of a trade union shall take the wishes of the majority of its members in consideration when organizing, participating in, sanctioning or supporting a strike or other industrial action.

The unions shall obtain a mandate for strike action from all eligible employees in the Company of at least 60% in favour of a strike.

5.11.4 The JF shall appoint an Election Officer and a committee to prepare and conduct the ballot. The ballot shall be done according to procedures agreed to by the JF.

5.11.5 If sufficient consensus does not exist between the Unions, a dispute may not be declared by one Union and dispute procedures will not be instituted as per paragraph 5.10. All Union Parties will accept the resolution of the majority decision of the Unions.

5.11.6 All unresolved disputes that may lead to a strike or a lock-out shall be dealt with in terms of paragraph 5.11.

6. Workplace Representative Council (WRC):

6.1 Objectives and duties:

6.1.1 The primary focus of the WRC is to discuss and resolve all operational matters which affect both the Company and employees and seek to promote the interest of all employees in the workplace, whether or not they are trade union members.

6.1.2 The WRC is entitled to make recommendations and proposals relating to any of the following matters:
- Enhancement of efficiency and productivity in the workplace;
- Any work and structural changes in the organisation;
- Job grading;
- Social / medical / welfare issues;
- Implementation of new products/plans;
- Subject to the applicable legislation and company policies:
  - Education and training
  - Employment equity
  - Health and safety
- Deviations from disciplinary procedures;
- Company policies;
- Appointments and staff movements;
- Collective grievances;
- Shop floor issues;
- Communication;
- Relationship between parties; and
- Restructuring the workplace, including the introduction of new technology and new work methods.

6.1.3   The Company representatives must allow the WRC an opportunity to make representations and to advance recommendations and proposals and must consider and respond to the proposals.

6.1.4   Any party may refer an issue to the JF that is deemed to be discussed or warrant deliberations on a high level. This will however not prevent the Company to implement issues after discussions are concluded as per paragraph 6.1.5.

6.1.5   The Company may implement proposals concerning the following without being obliged to reach an agreement after discussions:
- Enhancement of efficiency and productivity in the workplace;
- Changes in the organisation of work;
- Structural changes;
- Job grading;
- Product development and plans;
- Criteria for merit increases or payment of discretional bonuses;
- Company policies;
- Appointments and staff movements; and
- Restructuring the workplace, including the introduction of new technology and or work methods.

6.1.6   The WRC shall refer all disciplinary matters to the Disciplinary Committee as per paragraph 7 that fall within the scope and terms of reference of the Disciplinary Committee.

6.1.7   The WRC shall refer all matters to the Dispute Resolution Committee as per paragraph 8 that have a potential risk in damaging the relationship between the parties on matters that may result in a formal dispute such as:
- Collective grievances;
- Relationship between parties; and
- Matters that fall within the scope of the DRC.

6.1.8   No Party to this Agreement may call a strike or lock-out on issues that derived from the WRC unless covered in paragraph 5.10.1.

6.2   Meetings:

6.2.1   Composition of the WRC:

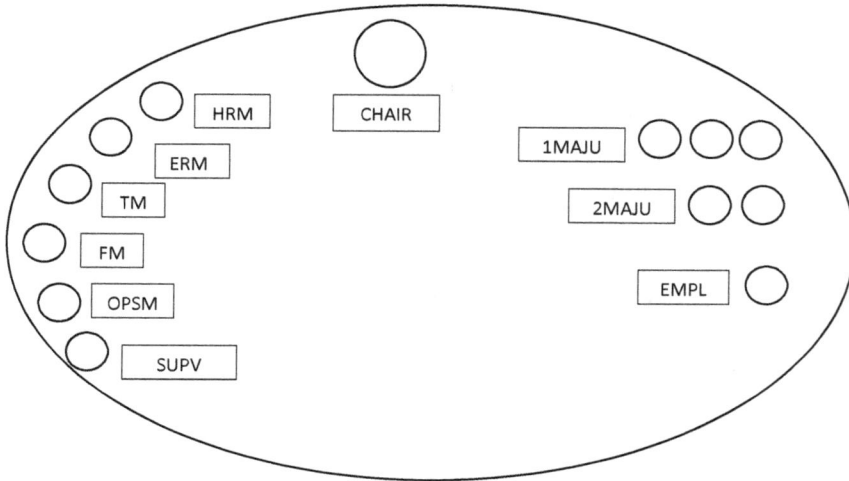

The members of the meeting shall be constituted as follow:

6.2.1.1 Company members / representatives:
- Human Resource Manager (HRM);
- Employee Relations Manager (ERM);
- Technical Management (TM);
- Financial Management (FM);
- Operations Manager (OPSM); and
- Supervisor (SUPV).

6.2.1.2 Union / Worker members:
- 3 Union representatives of the 1st majority union:
  - 1 Full time shop steward;
  - 2 Union representatives;
- 2 Union representatives of the 2nd majority union;
- 1 Employee representative.

6.2.2   Chairperson and Secretary:
- The Chairperson position shall rotate between the Parties; and
- The Company shall provide secretarial functions.

6.2.3 Meeting intervals:

6.2.3.1 Meetings shall be held on a monthly basis. In the event that a matter needs further investigation, the WRC may form an ad hoc small committee to investigate and make recommendations to the WRC.

6.2.4 Agenda and meeting arrangements:

6.2.4.1 The date and time of the next meetings will be decided upon in each meeting.

6.2.4.2 The secretary shall notify members at least two (2) weeks prior to the meeting. The secretary shall finalize the agenda and distribute same to members one (1) week prior to the meeting. No items other than items on the agenda will be discussed unless the opposing party gives consent to discuss the extraordinary issue/s requested.

6.2.4.3 The secretary shall keep and ensure availability of minutes of the meeting and all resolutions adopted at the meeting.

6.2.4.4 At every meeting, the minutes of the previous meeting shall be read, corrected if necessary and signed by the chairperson and a representative of each union confirmation.

6.2.4.5 The proceedings of any meeting shall not be invalidated by reason of the non-attendance of any of the representatives providing that the quorum is reached.

A quorum constitutes the Company and two of the Unions, regardless the number of representatives from any of the parties.

6.2.4.6 The secretary shall compile and distribute minutes at least (1) one week after the meeting unless otherwise agreed in the meeting.

6.2.5 Preparations and mandates for meetings:

6.2.5.1 Members shall ensure that timeous mandates are obtained prior to the WRC meeting from constituencies and where required, consolidated mandates are obtained to promote constructive discussions and speedily finalization of matters at hand.

6.3 Membership:

6.3.1 The Company shall appoint the members of the WRC as per paragraph 6.2.1.1.

6.3.2 The Unions and workers shall elect the required number of representatives as per paragraph 6.2.1.2 from amongst their various constituencies.

6.3.3 The election of union representatives shall be in accordance with each of their respective unions' election procedures as contained in their constitution.

6.3.4   The process of election of non-unionised worker representatives shall be arranged and supervised by the Industrial Relations Manager.

6.3.5   The Company and the Unions shall submit the names of their members at the first meeting of the year and members shall hold office for a minimum of (2) two years unless removed by their respective constituencies in terms of their constitutions or as per paragraph 6.3.8.

6.3.6   The members of the WRC shall be standing members and shall only be substituted or alternate by a specific nominated person unless he/she is permanently removed and replaced. If any person, for whatever reason, not attend a meeting, he/she will not be substituted and will be noted as absent with or without reasons whatever the case may be.

6.3.7   The WRC may, from time to time, identify training needs of WRC members and shall request Management to arrange training as identified. WRC members shall avail themselves for training as identified.

6.3.8   Members of the WRC shall maintain a high level of professional conduct and subscribe to the spirit of the Co-determination Agreement. Members shall not infringe any of the terms of the Agreement or act in any manner which is detrimental to the interests of the parties. If a member is guilty of misconduct during a meeting, he/she will be removed or requested to excuse him/herself from the meeting and the relevant constituency will be requested to deal with the matter in terms of their constitution or good practice. If a member is unable to correct his/her behaviour, the relevant constituency will be requested to remove and replace the member.

6.4   Communication of decisions:

6.4.1   Prior to closure of the meeting, the meeting shall formulate a communique/ briefing letter that will serve the purpose of a standardized message that will be communicated to all employees, posted on all notice boards and e-mailed to all computer recipients. No member of the WRC is allowed to engage outside parties on internal discussions of the WRC as per company policies.

7.   Discipline Committee (DC):

7.1   Objectives and duties:

7.1.1   The primary focus of the DC is to productively assist and encourage compliance with the disciplinary procedures and code of the company and to attempt to resolve matters of a disciplinary nature.

7.1.2   The DC shall keep abreast of changes in Labour Law, Legislation, Case Law and organisational requirements that necessitate amendments to Disciplinary Procedure and Codes and make recommendations to the JF in this regard.

7.1.3   The company shall appoint suitable qualified chairpersons as per the Disciplinary Procedures and will disclose the proposed names of the panel of chairpersons to the DC. The DC shall be allowed to make presentations in terms of candidates and selection criteria but will not prevent the company to appoint chairpersons after deliberations are concluded.

7.1.4   The DC shall make recommendations on the minimum training requirements for chairpersons, company and union representatives, monitor training and observe compliance.

7.1.5   All complaints, alleged deviations from the Disciplinary Procedure and Code or any matter or conduct that have a negative effect on the smooth running of disciplinary matters caused by a chairperson, shop steward, company representative, employee representative or employee shall be referred to the DC for investigation. The DC shall forward recommendations to the WRC.

7.1.6   The DC shall make recommendations to the WRC regarding the appointment and removal of arbitrators for the panel of arbitrators in terms of the Bargaining Council's constitution.

7.1.7   The DC shall pursue all weekly disciplinary reports and assist in rectifying deviations that cause unnecessary delays, postponements and dismissal of cases.

7.1.8   The DC shall not have authority to discuss the merits of individual disciplinary cases, overturn chairpersons' rulings or act as appeal committee but can recommend to the appeal chairperson on issues of procedure.

7.2   Disclosure of information:

7.2.1   The company will disclose to the DC upon request all relevant information that will allow the DC to engage effectively as per paragraph 5.2 of this Agreement.

7.3   **Meetings**:

7.3.1   **Composition of the DC meeting**:

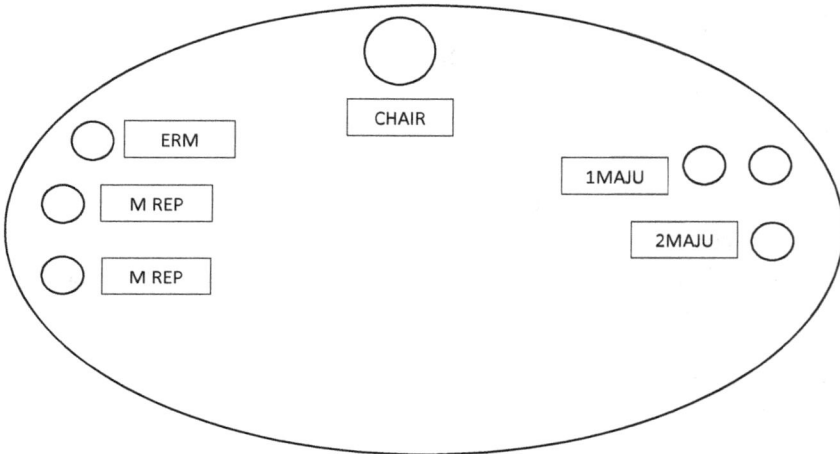

The members of the meeting shall be constituted as follow:

7.3.1.1 **Company members / representatives**:

- 1 Employee Relations Manager; and
- 2 Management Representatives.

7.3.1.2 **Union members**:

- 2 Union representatives of the 1st majority union
  - 1 Full time shop steward; and
  - 1 Union representative.

- 2 Union representatives of the 2nd majority union
  - 1 Technical representative
  - 1 Operations representative

7.3.2   **Chairman and Secretary**:

7.3.2.1 The Company shall provide the chair and secretarial functions.

7.3.3 Meeting intervals:

7.3.3.1 Meetings shall be held as per matters referred from the JF, WRC or upon request from the Unions or the Company.

7.3.4 Agenda and meeting arrangements:

7.3.4.1 A party that wishes to convene a meeting shall notify the secretary in writing, indicating the urgency and time frame required as well as details of issues to be discussed.

7.3.4.2 The secretary shall finalize the agenda and distribute to all relevant parties and finalize arrangements.

7.3.4.3 No items other than items in the agenda will be discussed unless the opposing party gives consent to discuss the extraordinary issues requested.

7.3.4.4 The secretary shall keep and ensure availability of the minutes of the meeting and all resolutions adopted at the meeting.

7.3.4.5 At every meeting, the minutes of the last meeting shall be read, corrected if necessary and signed by the chairperson as well as representatives of each union confirmation.

7.3.4.6 The proceedings of any meeting shall not be invalidated by reason of non-attendance of any of the representatives providing that the quorum is reached.

A quorum constitutes the Company and two of the Unions, regardless the number of representatives from any of the parties.

7.3.4.7 The secretary shall compile and distribute minutes at least (1) one week after the meeting unless otherwise agreed in the meeting.

7.4 Preparations and mandates for meetings:

7.4.1 Members shall ensure that timeous mandates are obtained prior to the DC meeting from constituencies and where required, consolidated mandates are obtained to promote consecutive discussions and speedily finalization of matters at hand.

7.5 Membership:

7.5.1 The Company shall appoint the members of the DC as per paragraph 7.3.1.1.

7.5.2 The Unions and workers shall elect the required number of representatives as per paragraph 7.3.1.2 from amongst their various constituencies.

7.5.3 The election of union representatives shall be in accordance with the respective union's election procedures as contained in their constitution.

7.5.4 The Company and the unions shall submit the names of their members at the first meeting of the year and members shall hold office for a minimum period of (2) two years unless removed by their respective constituencies in terms of their constitutions or as per paragraph 7.5.7.

7.5.5 The members of the DC shall be standing members and shall only be substituted or alternated by a specific nominated person unless he/she is permanently removed or replaced. If any person, for whatever reason, fails to attend a meeting, he/she will not be substituted and will be noted as absent with or without reasons whatever the case may be.

7.5.6 The DC may, from time to time, identify training needs of DC members and shall request Management to arrange training as identified. DC members shall avail themselves for training as identified.

7.5.7 Members of the DC shall maintain a high level of professional conduct and subscribe to the spirit of the Co-determination Agreement. Members shall not infringe any of the terms of this Agreement or act in a manner which is detrimental to the interests of the parties. If a member is guilty of misconduct during a meeting, he/she will be removed or requested to excuse him/herself from the meeting and the relevant constituency will be requested to deal with the matter in terms of their constitution or good practice. If a member is unable to correct his/her behaviour, the relevant constituency will be requested to remove and replace the member.

7.6   Confidentiality

7.6.1 Each member of the DC shall sign a confidentiality agreement. In any dispute about an alleged breach of confidentiality, the dispute will be referred in terms of the dispute or disciplinary procedure as per the confidentiality agreement.

7.7   Communications of decisions

7.7.1 Prior to closure of the meeting, the meeting shall formulate a communique/ briefing letter that will serve the purpose of a standardized message that will be communicated to all employees, posted on all notice boards and e-mailed to all computer recipients.

8. **Dispute Resolution Committee (DRC):**

8.1 **Objectives and duties:**

8.1.1 The primary focus of the DRC is to proactively assist and encourage compliance with the Dispute Prevention and Resolution procedures to resolve conflicts through non-adversarial means and also to assist in managing the speedily resolving of formal and informal disputes.

8.1.2 The DRC shall monitor the number and nature of disputes recorded and advise the company of the risks and consequences of unresolved disputes. The DRC shall make recommendations regarding amendments of the Dispute Resolution Policy to the JF.

8.1.3 The DRC shall assist in clarifying disputes and make recommendations to employees and parties on the method to resolve the dispute as contained in the Dispute Resolution Policy.

8.1.4 The company shall appoint a panel of internal and external facilitators, conciliators and mediators in terms of the Dispute Prevention and Resolution procedure and disclose the proposed names and credentials to the DRC. The DRC shall be allowed to make presentations in terms of candidates and selection criteria and members of the DRC shall endeavour to reach consensus on the appointment of facilitators and mediators. The Company shall have the right to appoint the panel members after deliberations are concluded.

8.1.5 All complaints, alleged deviations from the Dispute Prevention and Resolution procedures and or any matter or conduct that have a negative effect on the timeous and effective resolving of disputes, shall be referred to the DRC for investigation. The DRC shall forward their recommendations to the WRC.

8.1.6 The DRC shall pursue dispute resolution reports and assist in rectifying deviations that cause unnecessary delays and postponements of disputes.

8.1.7 The DRC shall not have authority to discuss the merits of individual disputes, overturn outcomes or act as appeal committee but can recommend to the individual or parties on issues of procedure.

8.2 **Disclosure of information:**

8.2.1 The company will disclose to the DRC upon request all relevant information that will allows the DRC to engage effectively as per paragraph 5.2 of this Agreement.

8.3   Meetings:

8.3.1   Composition of the DRC meeting:

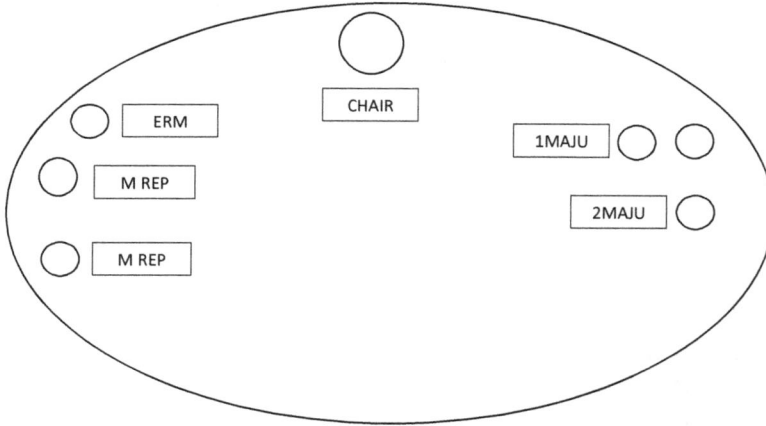

The members of the meeting shall be constituted as follow:

8.3.1.1 Company members / representatives:

- 1 Employee Relations Manager; and
- 2 Management Representatives.

8.3.1.2 Union members:

- 2 Union representatives of the 1st majority union
  - Full time shop steward
- 1 Union representative
- 1 Union representatives of the 2nd majority union

8.3.2   Chairman and Secretary:

8.3.2.1 The Company shall provide the chair and secretarial functions.

8.3.3   Meeting intervals:

8.3.3.1 Meetings shall be held as per matters referred from the JF, WRC, DC or upon request from the Unions or the Company.

8.3.4   Agenda and meeting arrangements:

8.3.4.1 A party that wishes to convene a meeting shall notify the secretary in writing, indicating the urgency and time frame required as well as details of issues to be discussed.

8.3.4.2 The secretary shall finalize the agenda and distribute to all relevant parties and finalize arrangements within the directed time frame.

8.3.4.3 No items other than items in the agenda will be discussed unless the opposing party gives consent to discuss the extraordinary issues requested.

8.3.4.4 The secretary shall keep minutes and ensure availability of the meeting and all resolutions adopted at the meeting.

8.3.4.5 At every meeting, the minutes of the last meeting shall be read and signed, corrected if necessary by the chairperson as well as representatives of each union confirmation.

8.3.4.6 The proceedings of any meeting shall not be invalidated by reason of non-receipt by any member of the notice of the meeting or of non-attending meetings as notified.

8.3.4.7 The secretary shall compile and distribute minutes at least (1) one week after the meeting unless otherwise agreed in the meeting.

8.4   Preparations and mandates for meetings:

8.4.1   Members shall ensure that timeous mandates are obtained prior to the DRC meeting from constituencies and where required, consolidated mandates are obtained to promote consecutive discussions and speedily finalization of matters at hand.

8.5   Membership:

8.5.1   The Company shall appoint the members of the DRC as per paragraph 8.3.1.1.

8.5.2   The Unions and workers shall elect the required number of representatives as per paragraph 8.3.1.2 from amongst their various constituencies.

8.5.3   The election of union representatives shall be in accordance of the union's election procedures as contained in their constitution.

8.5.4   The Company and unions shall submit the names of their members at the first meeting of the year and members shall hold office for a minimum period of (2) two years unless removed by their respective constituencies in terms of their constitutions or as per paragraph 8.5.8.

8.5.5   The members of the DRC shall be standing members and shall only be substituted or alternate by a specific nominated person unless he/she is permanently removed and replaced. If any person, for whatever reason, fails to attend a meeting, he/she will not be substituted and will be noted as absent with or without reasons whatever the case may be.

8.5.6　The DRC may, from time to time, identify training needs of DRC members and shall request Management to arrange training as identified. DRC members shall avail themselves for training as identified.

8.5.7　Members of the DRC shall maintain a high level of professional conduct and subscribe to the spirit of the Co-determination Agreement.

8.5.8　Members not infringe any of the terms of this Agreement or acts in a manner which is detrimental to the interests of the parties. If a member is guilty of misconduct during a meeting, he/she will be removed or requested to excuse him/herself from the meeting and the relevant constituency will be requested to deal with the matter in terms of their constitution or good practice. If a member is unable to correct his/her behaviour, the relevant constituency will be requested to remove and replace the member.

8.6　Confidentiality

8.6.1　Each member of the JF shall sign a confidentiality agreement. In any dispute about an alleged breach of confidentiality, the dispute will be referred in terms of the dispute or disciplinary procedure as per the confidentiality agreement.

8.7　Communication of decisions

8.7.1　Prior to closure of the meeting, the meeting shall formulate a communique/ briefing letter that will serve the purpose of a standardized message that will be communicated to all employees, posted on all notice boards and e-mailed to all computer recipients.

9.　Discontinuation of a Union Party to the Agreement

A Union shall be discontinued as a party to this Agreement under the following circumstances:-

9.1　The recognition of a Union is cancelled in terms of the Recognition Agreement.

9.2　The Unions registration is cancelled by the registrar from the appropriate register in terms of Section 106 of the Labour Relations Act and or other relevant Sections of the Act.

9.3　A union does not subscribe or endeavour to comply with the objectives, terms and conditions of the Co-determination Agreement or is in material breach of the Agreement. A dispute with regards to this paragraph will be referred to an internal tribunal to be determined by the JF.

10.   Dissolution of the Co-determination Agreement

The Co-determination Agreement will be dissolved under the following circumstances:-

10.1   The Unions may request a ballot to dissolve the Co-determination Agreement.

10.2   If sixty (60) percent of the total eligible votes of members, who are entitled to vote as per paragraph 5.7, are cast in favour of a resolution to dissolve the Co-determination Agreement.

10.3   The JF shall appoint an Election Officer and a committee to prepare and conduct the ballot as per paragraph 5.11.4.

10.4   By the Company if the relationship between the parties to this Agreement is detrimental to the sound relationship between employees and the company.

10.5   In the event of the dissolution of the Co-determination Agreement, the Company and Unions will negotiate new Agreements governing the relationship between the parties. The new Agreements which will be effective upon the effective date of the dissolution of the Co-determination Agreement.

The dissolution resolution will be effective sixty (60) days after the decision has been taken to allow the parties to negotiate new Agreements.

Thus signed and dated at Bloemfontein on this _____ day of _____ 2017.

THE PARTIES: **WITNESSES:**

_____   1. _____
THE COMPANY   WITNESS

_____   2. _____
TASWU   WITNESS

_____   3._____
SATAWU   WITNESS

Appendix B

CLOSED SHOP AGREEMENT

Entered Into Between

ITUMELE BUS LINES (PTY) LTD T/A INTERSTATE BUS LINES
(Hereiafter referred to as "the Company")

And

TIRISANO TRANSPORT AND SERVICES WORKERS UNION
(Hereinafter referred to as TASWU)

And

SOUTH AFRICAN TRANSPORT AND ALLIED WORKERS UNION
(Hereinafter referred to as SATAWU)

* The Company, TASWU And SATAWU are collectively referred to as "the Parties".

* TASWU And SATAWU are collectively referred to as "the Unions".

1. PREAMBLE

The parties to this Agreement recognise that:

1.1 This Agreement is subject to Section 26 and all other relevant provisions of the Labour Relations Act, provisions of the South African Road Passenger Bargaining Council as well as the Collective Recognition and Procedural and Co-determination Agreements that regulates the relatonship between the parties.

1.2 The Unions exercise their constitutional and legal rights and duties to act as individual independent entities as per the respective union's constitutions as well as collectively as organized Labour in terms of the Bargaining Councils Constitution.

2. OBJECTIVE AND SCOPE

2.1 The Company and Unions have entered into a Collective Recognition and a Co-determination Agreement that regulates the relationship between the parties through engaging Unions and worker representatives in joint decision processes.

2.2 The successful implementation and maintaining of the Co-determination and joint decision making processes depends on stability in Union participation and the Closed Shop Agreement will assist in achieving these objectives.

2.3 The terms of this Agreement shall apply to all eligible employees that are employed by the Company that fall within the bargaining unit as defined in the Main Collective Agreement of the South African Road Passenger Bargaining Council. This Agreement shall therefore not apply to union members that fall outside the Bargaining Unit.

3. COMMENCEMENT OF THE AGREEMENT

3.1 This Agreement shall come into operation on the date of signature and shall be subject to a ballot held by eligible employees covered by this Agreement of which two thirds (66%) must vote in favour of the Agreement.

3.2 The Company and Unions shall appoint an Election Officer and Committee to prepare and conduct the ballot.

4. MEMBERSHIP OF UNIONS

4.1 Eligible employees who are employed by the Company prior to the date of signature of this Agreement who are not Union members shall not be required to be members of a Union.

4.2 Eligible employees who are employed by the Company after the date of signature of this Agreement shall be obliged to apply for membership to one of the Unions that is party to this Agreement and shall within thirty (30) days from the date of appointment submit proof of Union membership to the Company. An employee shall only be allowed to join one of the Unions as per the Recognition Ageement.

4.3 No Union may refuse an employee membership or expel an employee from the Union unless:-

4.3.1 refusal or expulsion is in accordance with the Union's constitution; and

4.3.2 the reason for the refusal or expulsion is fair, including but not limited to, conduct that undermines the Union's collective exercise of its rights.

4.4 The Company shall include the provisions of paragraph 4.2 in the job offer and Contract of Employment prior to employment and disclose the provisions of the Closed Shop Agreement during induction training to all newly appointed employees.

5. DISMISSAL OF EMPLOYEES IN TERMS OF THIS AGREEMENT

5.1 An employee may be dismissed if the employee: -

5.1.1 was informed of the provisions of this Agreement in terms of paragraph 4.4 and;

5.1.2 refuse to join a Union as per paragraph 4.2; and

5.1.3 was refused membership or expelled as a member of all two (2) Unions in terms of paragraph 4.3.

5.2 An employee may not be dismissed for not joining a union: -

5.2.1 In terms of paragraph 4.1 and

5.2.2 on grounds of conscientious objection provided that a motivation for such objection has to be put in writing and submitted to the Company within thirty (30) days of appointment.

The Company will consider and respond to the objection, and if rejected, the employee may refer the matter in terms of the internal dispute resolution procedures.

6. UNION SUBSCRIPTION FEES OR LEVY PAYMENTS

6.1 The Unions agree that no membership subscription or levy deducted may be: -

6.1.1 Paid to a political party as an affiliation fee;

6.1.2 Contributed in cash or kind to a political party or a person standing for election to any political office; or

6.1.3 Used for any expenditure that does not advance or protect the socio-economic interests of employees.

6.2 Employees who are not Union members as per paragraph 4.1 and 5.2.2 shall pay an agency fee equvalent to the average amount of the two (2) union's subscription that would apply to an employee.

Such agency fee may be deducted from the wages of an employee without the employee's authorisation.

6.3 The amount deducted as per paragraph 6.2 will be paid into a separate account for the purpose of protecting socio-economic interests of employees and the fund shall be administered by the Joint Forum Committee as contemplated by the Co-determination Agreement.

7. DISCONTINUATION OF A PARTY TO THIS AGREEMENT

7.1 A Union shall cease to be a party to this Agreement under the following circumstances:

7.1.1 The Recognition of a union is cancelled in terms of the Recognition Agreement.

7.1.2 The union registration is cancelled by the registrar from the appropriate register in terms of Section 106 and or other relevant Sections of the LRA.

7.1.3 The union does not subscribe or fails to comply with the objectives, terms and conditions of the Co-determination Agreement or is in material breach of the Agreement.

7.2 In the event of a Union Recognition with the Company being cancelled as per paragraph 7, the Union shall automatically be expelled from the Closed Shop, and Co-determination Agreements.

7.3 The Closed Shop Agreement shall then apply to the remaining parties in good standing and the employees of the expelled union shall be granted thirty (30) days to join one of the remaining unions, failing to which employees may face dismissal as per paragraph 5.

8. TERMINATION OF THE CLOSED SHOP AGREEMENT

8.1 The Closed Shop Agreement may be terminated under the following conditions: -

8.1.1   By agreement between the parties.

8.1.2   If one third of the employees covered by this Agreement sign a petition calling for the termination of the agreement and three (3) years have lapsed since the date on which the Agreement commenced or the last ballot was conducted.

The Company and the Unions shall then appoint an Election Officer and Committee to prepare and conduct a ballot of the employees covered by the Closed Shop Agreement. If the majority of the eligible employees who voted, have voted to terminate the closed shop agreement, the agreement will be terminated.

8.1.3   By the Company if the relationship between the parties to this agreement is detremental to the sound relationship between employees and the Company.

Signed at Bloemfontein on this _____ day of _____ 2017 in the presence of the undersigned Witnesses.

WITNESSES:

_____   1. _____
For and on behalf of the Company
being duly authorised

_____   2. _____
For and on behalf of TASWU
being duly authorised

_____   3._____
For and on behalf of SATAWU
being duly authorised

Appendix C

COLLECTIVE RECOGNITION AND PROCEDURAL AGREEMENT

Entered Into Between

ITUMELE BUS LINES (PTY) LTD T/A INTERSTATE BUS LINES
(Hereiafter referred to as "the Company")

And

TIRISANO TRANSPORT AND SERVICES WORKERS UNION
(Hereinafter referred to as TASWU)

And

SOUTH AFRICAN TRANSPORT AND ALLIED WORKERS UNION
(Hereinafter referred to as SATAWU)

* The Company, TASWU And SATAWU are collectively referred to as "the Parties".

* TASWU And SATAWU are collectively referred to as "the Unions".

1.   PREAMBLE

The Company and the Unions that are parties to this Agreement acknowledge and recognise:

1.1   the importance of sound and fair employee management, industrial and/or labour relations and enter into this Agreement with the declared intent of continuing to promote and ensure such a relationship;

1.2   that it is to the parties' mutual benefit to formalise and regulate their relationship and to have clearly stated rules and procedures which will reduce the possibility of conflict between Management and Labour (workers);

1.3   the right of the Unions to represent the interests of their members in accordance with their respective constitutions;

1.4   the authority of Management to direct and manage the Company.

2.   OBJECTIVE AND SCOPE

The objective of this Agreement is to regulate the relationship between the Company and the Union to ensure a healthy and productive working environment free of labour unrest.

This Agreement is subject to the relevant provisions of the Constitution of the Republic of South Africa, Labour Relations Act, Act 66 of 1995, as amended from time to time, the provisions of the Constitution and Agreements of the South African Road Passengers Bargaining Council (SARPBAC) as well as the Closed Shop and Co-determination Agreements signed by the parties.

3.   RECOGNITION

3.1   The Company shall grant each of the Unions recognition on the following basis:-

3.1.1   Where the Union is a signatory to the Collective Recognition and Procedural Agreement, the Closed Shop Agreement and the Co-determination Agreement.

3.1.2   Where the Union's recognition has not been terminated due to non-compliance with the terms of this Agreement or the Closed Shop Agreement or the Co-determination Agreement.

3.2   The Union's position in terms of majority shall be determined by the number of employees that subscribe to the Union membership as reflected in the most recent monthly Union membership list provided by the Company's payroll.

3.3 Recognition of a Union is always subject to due registration of the Trade Union withteh Registrar of Labour Relations in terns of the Labour Relations Act.

3.4 Recognition of a Union will be subject to membership threshold of 30% with cognisance of the stipulations of the Labour Relations act.

3.5 A Union is admitted by adjudication by the Labour Court or by agreement by the Joint Forum as contemplated by the Co-determination Agreement

4. PEACE OBLIGATION

The parties shall endeavour to ensure that no victimisation by the Company, the Union, Union members and non-members take place or are allowed.

The parties undertake not to propagate, intice or embark on any industrial action without compliance with the provisions of the Labour Relations Act, Co-determinations, Closed Shop and the Collective Recognition Agreement.

The parties further undertake to subscribe, actively participate and comply with the provisions of the Co-determination, Closed Shop and Collective Recognition Agreement.

The parties agree that the above mentioned is a material term of this Agreement and that breach thereof can result in termination of this Agreement.

5. ACCESS

5.1 Union Officials and Office Bearers as defined in the Act shall have reasonable access to the workplace to meet with members during members' own time or to conduct Union business. Prior arrangements must be made with the Human Resources Department on each occasion before the right of access may be exercised.

5.2 General meetings during working hours may only be held under special circumstances and with the prior consent of the Human Resources Department. Such request should be made at least 24 hours before any proposed meeting, unless otherwise agreed to.

5.3 Reasonable access by Union Officials to meet Union Representatives elected in terms of this Agreement shall be afforded upon prior arrangement with the Human Resources Department.

5.4 Access in terms of sub-clauses 5.1 to 5.3 above shall not interrupt normal operations of the business. The Company is entitled to set any reasonable conditions as to time and place of access so as to safeguard life and property and to prevent the undue disruption of work.

6.   NOTICE BOARDS

6.1   The Union may display appropiate Union communications and notices save for political party's notices, on official Company notice boards provided such notices have been co-signed by a nominated Company Official. 6.2 Trade Union Representatives may place official union notices and announcements concerning union activities on the Company's notice boards provided that such notice or announcement shall first be cleared with the Company's Employee Relations Manager.

6.1   Whilst Management shall maintain normal custody of official notice boards, nothing contained in this clause should be construed so as to make the Company responsible for the contents of any notice displayed, its unauthorised removal and/or liable for its replacement.

7.   UNION SUBSCRIPTIONS

7.1   The Company agrees to deduct Union subscriptions from the wages and salaries of workers who are Union Members provided it receives a signed authority from individual employees to do so. An Employee shall only be allowed to be a member of one of the recognized Unions as per the provisions of the Closed Shop Agreement.

7.2   Subscriptions thus deducted shall be remitted to the Union on or before the 7th working day of the month following the month in which deductions were made with a list of employees whose subscriptions have been deducted.

7.3   The Union shall give the Company one calendar month's written notice of any change in its membership fees and levies in accordance with the its constitution. The Company shall deduct the new amount in the first week following the expiration of the notice period .

7.4   Members who have signed a written authority to deduct Union fees and who resign from the union, have the right to cancel such authorisation upon one (1) calender month written notice. Cancellation shall be in writing and a copy of the cancellation letter of an employee shall be sent to the Union with the remittance of trade union subscription fees deducted for the month in which the notice was received.

7.5   Upon receipt of a notice of resignation from the Union, the Union may be afforded the opportunity, with the consent of a withdrawing employee, to interview such an employee. All arrangements with regard to such exit interview shall be made by the union with the employee and such interview shall take place in the employee's own time.

7.6   The Company shall not be responsible for collecting subscriptions that are in arrears save where such arrears arise through the failure or refusal of the

Company to deduct the subscriptions. Subscriptions will only be deducted at the end of the month in which notice was received, if it was submitted to the Company before the last weekday of the first week of that month.

7.7 Union membership fees that are in arrears may, on receipt of a written request by the employee, be deducted from the salary/wage of the employee over a period not exceeding three (3) months and remitted to the union in the same payments.

8. TRADE UNION REPRESENTATIVES

8.1 RECOGNITION OF UNION REPRESENTATIVES

8.1.1 The company agrees to recognize the number of trade union representatives according to the formula provided for in section 14 of the LRA only.

8.1.2 The parties furthermore agree that in the event of the number of employees increasing or decreasing with more than 50 employees, the number of trade union representatives will be adjusted accordingly in terms of the formula as provided for in section 14 of the Labour Relations Act, Act 66 of 1995.

8.1.3 To ensure equal spread of representation, the parties agree that more than one representative shall not be elected from a section/team within a Department other than Bus Drivers unless otherwise agreed upon by the JF. The number of representatives per Department/Depot elcted shall be in proportion to the number of members in a Department/Depot unless otherwise agreed upon by the JF.

8.1.4 The election and terms of office of trade union representatives shall be regulated by the Union's constitution and the provisions of this Agreement.

8.1.5 Election of trade union representatives shall take place on the Company's premises in normal working hours during the employees' lunch time or off period and provided that the normal functioning of the Company shall not be effected or disrupted. Management will be allowed to have a Management representative present during these elections.

8.1.6 The Union shall inform the Company of the results of the elections in writing within seven (7) days of such elections.

8.1.7 The Unions should endeavor to elect trade union representatives that have the ability to actively participate, make meaningful contributions and subscribe to the objectives and commitments of the Co-determination Agreement.

8.1.8 The criteria for the election of Shop Stewards shall be discussed and agreed upon (in line with the respective constitutions of the Unions) upon by the Joint Forum prior to the election of Shop Stewards.

8.2 TERMINATION OF OFFICE OF TRADE UNION REPRESENTATIVES

A trade union representative shall cease to hold office in the following circumstances:

8.2.1 Upon termination of such office as provided for in the Union's constitution;
8.2.2 Upon resignation from the Company;
8.2.3 Upon termination of the Contract of Employment by the Company;
8.2.4 Upon termination of trade union membership;
8.2.5 Upon termination of this Agreement;
8.2.6 Upon withdrawal of recognition by the Company as provided for in clause 8.4.

8.3 MEETINGS

8.3.1 UNION REPRESENTATIVES COUNCIL MEETING

8.3.1.1 Union representatvies shall be entitled to hold a meeting amongst themselves for one hour to coincide with their lunch break once a month without loss of remuneration, for the purpose of preparing agendas for monthly council meetings with Management, considering unresolved complaints and other Union business. Prior arrangements must be made with Human Resources and the Departmental Head concerned.

8.3.2 JOINT TRADE UNIONS/DEPARTMENTAL MANAGEMENT MONTHLY MEETINGS

8.3.2.1 The joint Trade Unions/Departmental Management monthly meetings will be attended by Union Representatives who have members in that department. If Unions have members in that department, Unions are entitled to attend, and shall be proportianately represented with not more than five (5) shop stewards in total.
8.3.2.2 These meetings will be held on a monthly basis and departmental matters of mutual interest will be discussed as well as addressing problem areas and to give feedback on activities and production.
8.3.2.3 Secretarial services will be provided by Management.

8.3.3 INTERSTATE BUS LINES/UNION MEETINGS

The purpose of this meeting is to discuss issues of concern that relates to a specific Union. Any of the parties may request a meeting at this level. The party requesting such meeting will provide the other party with a notice and agenda for such a meeting at least one week prior to the date of the proposed meeting, unless otherwise agreed to.

8.3.4 MASS MEETINGS

The Unions shall be entitled to hold Mass Meetings as per paragraph 9.5.

8.3.5 CO-DETERMINATION MEETINGS

Union representatives shall attend meetings as per the Co-determination Agreement.

8.4 REVOCATION OF RECOGNITION OF A TRADE UNION REPRESENTATIVE

The recognition of a trade union representative may be revoked by the Company if, a representative fails to comply with the provisions of clause 4, 8.1.7 and clause 9 of this Agreement and only after the employee and union has been given written notice to this effect and failed to remedy the breach within two weeks after receipt of such notice.

9. RIGHTS AND DUTIES OF UNION REPRESENTATIVES

9.1   Union representatives are employees of the Company and thus remain subject to the Company's rules and regulations.

9.2   Union representatives shall perform their duties in terms of section 14(4) of the Labour Relations Act, Act 66 of 1995, the Union Constitution, procedures and provisions of this Agreement and shall make every effort to ensure that the Union's obligations in terms of this Agreement are honoured.

9.3   Union representatives shall be entitled to represent their members in cases of discipline and grievances as per the weekly roster of cases scheduled.

9.4   Union representatives shall not leave their places of work without prior permission of their Supervisors as per the following procedure:-

9.4.1 The Shop Steward shall notify the Supervisor two (2) days in advance of the arrangements with regards to his/her absence under the following circumstances:-

- Represent members in cases of discipline and grievances as per paragraph 9.3.
- Hold meetings in terms of paragraph 9.5.
- Attend meetings as per prior approval in terms of paragraph 9.6, 9.7 and 9.8.
- Attend meetings as per paragraph 8.3.
- Election of union representatives in terms of paragraph 8.1.5.
- As well as any other reason not covered above.

If a union representative fails to make prior arrangements as per this paragraph or fails to provide evidence of approval of meetings the Supervisor may not unreasonably withhold permission. In the event of extraordinary circumstances where a Shop Steward cannot be released from his duties, the Supervisor and the Shop Steward shall notify the IR Manager who will consult with the union official and make alternative arrangements.

9.5   Union representatives shall be entitled to hold a meeting with their members for one (1) hour to coincide with their lunch break once a month without loss of remuneration, for the purpose of preparing agendas for monthly meetings with Management, considering unresolved complaints and other Union business as per paragraph 8.3.4. Prior arrangements must be made with Human Resources and the Departmental Head concerned. This paragraph shall not apply to operational personnel.

9.6   The Trade Union Representatives as a group shall be entitled to a five (5) workdays special leave with full pay per annum per union representative to be used for any of the purposes as set out in section 14 (5) of the Labour Relations Act, 1995; Provided that no one trade union representative shall be allowed to take more than ten (10) days special leave per annum; Provided further that such special leave shall expire at the end of the calender year.

9.7   Each Union official or office bearer as defined in the Act, shall be entitled to a maximum of five (5) working days special leave per calender year to fulfil the functions of that office as set out in Section 15 of the LRA. Such leave shall not be transferred to another official or office bearer and leave not granted during the year shall expire at the end of that year.

For purposes of this clause official or office bearer refers to such office in the regional or national structures of the Union. The number of days that Union Officials or Office Bearers participate in Bargaining Council matters shall not be deducted from the number of special leave days.

9.8   In the event that more than the maximum amount of special leave days are required by one/more unions, the matter will be referred to the JF for consideration which may not be unreasonably withheld.

9.9   The recording of special leave refered to in 9.6 and 9.7 above shall be kept by the Industrial Relations Manager.

9.10   Depending on the requirements of the operation schedule, the duties of a bus driver trade union representative, duly elected in terms of the Agreement may be reduced to shorter morning an dafternoon duties/shifts, to afford him/her time for representation purposes and/or other union business.

9.11 Where the operational requirements of a depot cannot accommodate the arrangements referred in 9.9 suitable arrangements will be made between the depot Management and the trade union representatives in the depot.

9.12 All duly elected trade union representatives of eth Union, will be afforded tim eoff with pay at normal rate during working hours to perform the functions of the trade union representative in accordance with this Agreement. Any form of time off for such trade union representative shall be by mutual consent and prior approval by Management as per prescribed procedure, between Management and the affected trade union representative as per paragraph 9.4. granted.

9.13 To avoid a possible conflict of interest the following persons, including but not limited to an Inspector, Traffic Superintendent, Management, Supervisor, Management Support Staff (as per definitions contained in the constitution of the South African Road Passenger Bargaining Council) and/or any person who may perform an inspection function and/or any person who may inspect a bus and/or the above mentioned persons being a union representative will not represent a bus driver in a disciplinary hearing, appeal or arbitration case under the following circumstances:

- if the misconduct relates to dishonesty of ticket related offences as contained in **rule 10** in the disciplinary code; and
- if the above mentioned persons are the complainant or a witness or being appointed as a complainant and to be used as a witness in instituting disciplinary action against an employee.

10. APPOINTMENT OF A FULL-TIME UNION REPRESENTATIVE

10.1 Subject to the Union representing the majority of employees and at least fourty (40) percent of all the employees employed within the Bargaining Unit, and in addition to the trade union representatives referred to in clause 8.1.1, the parties may agree on the election of one (1) full time trade union representative.

10.2 The election, terms of office and all relevent matters pertaining to such full time representative shall be regulated in a separate agreement to be entered into between the parties if and when the required level of representation is obtained. Such agreement shall be entered into within six (6) months of signature of this Agreement.

10.3 In the event of the two majority unions having equal membership, the full time union representative position will be abolished.

11. DURATION AND TERMINATION OF THE AGREEMENT

11.1 This Agreement shall come into effect on the date of its signing by the parties and shall be binding on parties until terminated.

11.2 The Agreement may be terminated by either party if the other party is in material breach of the terms of this Agreement. The aggrieved party must give the offending party written notice of the intention to terminate the Agreement and also indicate what corrective action the offending party must undertake to avoid this termination. Failure by the offending party to remedy the breach within thirty (30) days of receipt of such notice will result in the termination of this Agreement.

11.3 This Agreement shall also be terminated under the following circumstances: -

11.3.1 The unions registration is cancelled by the registrar from the appropriate register in terms of Section 106 or other relevant sections of the LRA.

11.3.2 A union does not subscribe or fails to comply or is in material breach with the objectives, terms and conditions of the Co-determination Agreement.

11.3.3 A union ceized to be a party to the Closed Shop Agreement.

11.4 The Unions recognition will be terminated with immediate effect in terms of paragraph 11.3.1 and 11.3.3.

11.5 The non-compliance of paragraph 11.3.2 is regarded as a material term of this Agreement and that a breach thereof may result in the termination of this Agreement as per paragraph 11.2.

12. AMENDMENTS TO THE AGREEMENT

Any proposed amendments may be forwarded in writing to the other party and will be discussed in a Joint Forum Committee meeting as per the Co-determination Agreement.

13. DEFINITIONS

Any expression used in this Agreement which is defined in the Labour Relations Act, 66 of 1995, shall have the same meaning as in the Act. Any reference in this Agreement to the male gender shall include the female gender and vice versa. Furthermore, unless inconsistent with the context:

13.1 **ACCESS**

means the right of an accredited union officials or office bearers to enter the business premises, provided that such access shall not disrupt the normal operations of the Company and shall always be subject to the provisions of this Agreement.

13.2 **REGISTERED AND ACCREDITED UNION OFFICE BEARER**

means a person who is an office bearer on the National Executive Committee or Regional Executive Committee or any such structures as the Union may have and who is not an official and whose name will be submitted to the Company in writing.

13.3 **REGISTERED AND ACCREDITED UNION OFFICIAL**

means a person employed in the National or Regional structure of the Union as the secretary, assistant secretary or organiser of the Union, whether or not that person is employed in a full time capacity, and whose name was submitted to the Company in writing and added to a list of Accredited Union Officials.

13.4 **ACT**

means the Labour Relations Act (No. 66 of 1995), as amended from time to time and includes regulations made thereunder.

13.5 **COMPANY**

means Interstate Bus Lines (Pty) Ltd.

13.6 **DISPUTE**

means any matter which is declared a dispute by written notice from one party to the other in terms of of this Agreement.

13.7 **GRIEVANCE**

means a dissatisfaction or feeling of injustice affecting an employee and/or union which arises out of his particular conditions of work or employment, or the employment relationship and dealt with in terms of the Grievance Procedure.

13.8 MANAGEMENT REPRESENTATIVE

means any person nominated by the Company to represent it in its dealings with the Union internally.

13.9 MEMBER

means any employee who is a member in good standing of the Union in terms of its constitution.

13.10 TRADE UNION REPRESENTATIVE

means an employee of the Company that was elected from amongst the employees in the workplace in terms of this Agreement, to represent the Union and its members that are employed by the Company in dealings with the Company.

13.11 UNION

means the SA Transport and Allied Workers Union, Tirisano Transport and Services Workers Union as constituted according to its constitution, lodged with the Registrar and registered in terms of the Act.

13.12 WORKPLACE

means all premises of Interstate Bus Lines (Pty) Ltd, namely Head Office and Workshop, Botshabelo Depot, Fairways Terminus, Thaba'Nchu Depot, Zone 1 Depot, Phomolong Depot and Central Park or any other premises that the Company may acquire to conduct their business in future.

13.13 EMPLOYEES

for the purpose of this Agreement when referring to determining the representivity of the union refers to all employees as defined in the Labour Relations Act, Act 66 of 1995, whether inside or outside the bargaining unit.

Signed at Bloemfontein on this _____ day of _____ 2017 in the presence of the undersigned Witnesses.

WITNESSES:

_____   1. _____

For and on behalf of the Company
being duly authorised

_____   2. _____

For and on behalf of TASWU
being duly authorised

_____   3._____

For and on behalf of SATAWU
being duly authorised

Appendix D

DISPUTE PREVENTION AND RESOLUTION AGREEMENT

Entered Into Between

ITUMELE BUS LINES (PTY) LTD T/A INTERSTATE BUS LINES
(Hereiafter referred to as "the Company")

And

TIRISANO TRANSPORT AND SERVICES WORKERS UNION
(Hereinafter referred to as TASWU)

And

SOUTH AFRICAN TRANSPORT AND ALLIED WORKERS UNION
(Hereinafter referred to as SATAWU)

* The Company, TASWU And SATAWU are collectively referred to as "the Parties".

* TASWU And SATAWU are collectively referred to as "the Unions".

The Parties hereby agree as follows:

1. PREAMBLE

The parties to this Agreement acknowledge and recognise that:

1.1   This Agreement is subject to the relevant provisions of the Labour Relations Act, Provisions of the Constitution ang Agreement of the South African Road Passenger Bargaining Council (SARBPAC) as well as the Closed Shop, Recognition and Co-determination Agreements that regulates the relatonship between the parties.

1.2   The objective of this Agreement is to: -
- Supplement the Co-determination Agreement with procedures to prevent and resolve grievances and disputes.
- Complement other relevant Company policies in preventing and resolving disputes.
- Assist the Company, the Unions and employees with the speedily resolving of disputes by being transparent without the inteference of any party that might have an adverse interest to the dispute.

1.3   All Employees, Management Employees and the Unions shall comply with the provisions as contained in this and other relevant policies and procedures and shall by no other means resolve disputes.

1.4   Where the current available policies, agreements and procedures have shotcomings in dealing with disputes, the specific case shall be referred to the Workplace Representative Council (WRC) for amending current policies and procedures or drafting new policies and procedures.

1.5   This Agreement contains the following Annexures relating to dispute prevention and resolution procedures: -

- Annxeure 1   -   Grievances
- Annexure 2   -   Workplace Representative Council
- Annexure 3   -   Joint Forum
- Annexure 4   -   Discipline
- Annexure 5   -   Pre-Hearing Minutes
- Annexure 6   -   Pre-Arbitration Minutes

Annexure 1

GRIEVANCE
DISPUTE PREVENTION AND RESOLUTION PROCEDURE

NO	PERSON/ FORUM	ACTIVITY	DOCUMENT
1.		The Company's Grievance Procedure, LRA'S relevant codes of good practice and dispute resolution mechanisms and company policies serves as guideline for dealing with the resolving of grievance i.e: - Individual grievances regarding: • Sexual harassment • Personal grievances • Discrimination • Unfair treatment • Salary disparity	Policies LRA
2.		The Company's grievance procedure or relevant company policies and procedures shall be applied to resolve the grievance.	
3.	Grievance Committe	Unresolved grievances shall be referred to a Grievance Committee which is an advisory body to the CEO. The Committee serves as a neutral three-person panel including a chairperson, a union organizer and management representative. The Committee Chair, an independent professional with relevant experience and legal expertise as well as the union official and management representative with relevant knowledge and expertise is recommended by the Dispute Resolution Committee and appointed by the CEO. The Committee's proceedings and recommendations to management are strictly confidential. The Grievance Committee normally holds oral hearings but with the parties consent, may consider a grievance on written record alone. At a hearing on merits, both parties may present evidence, and examine and cross examine witnesses. Following the hearing, the parties generally submit written briefs. After consideration and consultation with panel members, the Chairperson issues his/her report and recommendations to the CEO who issues a decision.	Chairpersons report
4.	Aggrieved Employee	Should the aggrieved employee not be satisfied with the decision of the CEO, the employee may refer the grievance as per the South African Road Passenger Bargaining Council or the LRA dispute resolution mechanisms.	Dispute referral document

Annexure 2

WORKPLACE REPRESENTATIVE COUNCIL (WRC) DISPUTE PREVENTION AND RESOLUTION PROCEDURE

NO	PERSON/ FORUM	ACTIVITY	DOCUMENT

1.	Union Rep. Company Rep. Employee Rep.	Parties shall refer the following issues, but not limited to, to the WRC for discussion and consultation.
		➤ Unresolved issues from Departmental, Management and Shop Stewards Meetings:
		  • Shop floor issues
		
		➤ Unresolved issues from Employment Equity Meeting:
		  • Racism
		  • Employment practices
		  • Promotions and staff transfers
		
		➤ Unresolved issues from Training Meeting:
		  • Training needs
		
		➤ Unresolved collective grievances:
		  • Grievance against Supervisor/Manager
		  • Unfair treatment of a group
		  • Salary disparities of a group
		  • Discrimination of a group
		
		➤ Deviation from policies and procedures
		➤ Workplace restructuring
		➤ Changes in organization of work
		➤ Structural changes
		➤ Relationship between parties
		➤ Communication
		➤ Appointment of Mediators/Arbitrators
		➤ Conduct of Chairpersons, representatives and accused employees
		➤ Company policies and procedures
		➤ Job grading
			Agenda
			
			Departmental minutes
			
			Employment Equity minutes
			
			Training minutes
			
			Grievance complaints
			
			Policy documents

2.	WRC, Secretary	The Workplace Representative Council (WRC) may decide to refer issues that requires further investigations to the appropriate forums such as but not limited to: - ➤ Departmental Management/Shop Stewards meeting ➤ Disciplinary Committee ➤ Ad-hoc committees ➤ Management ➤ Shop Stewards Councils	Minutes of WRC

NO	PERSON/ FORUM	ACTIVITY	DOCUMENT
3.	Unions, Management Committees	Report back findings and recommendations to the Workplace Representative Council (WRC)	Reports Minutes
4.	DRC	Discuss issues and if unresolved, refer to the Dispute Resolution Committee (DRC)	Minutes of WRC
5.	DRC	Report back findings and recommendations to the Workplace Representative Council (WRC)	Minutes of the DRC
6.	WRC	Discuss issues and if unresolved refer the issue to the Joint Forum (J.F)	Report

Annexure 3

JOINT FORUM (JF)
DISPUTE PREVENTION AND RESOLUTION PROCEDURE

NO	PERSON/ FORUM	ACTIVITY	DOCUMENT
1.	Company Officials Union Officials	Parties shall refer the following, but not limited to, to the Joint Forum (J.F) for discussion and consultation: ➢ Unresolved issues from the Workplace Representative Council (WRC) ➢ Recommendations from the Dispute Resolution Committee (DRC) ➢ Collective Agreements ➢ Relationship between the parties ➢ Non-substantive conditions of employment ➢ Employee Empowerment trusts and incentive schemes ➢ Dismissals on operational requirements ➢ Agency fee funds ➢ Disciplinary rules and code of conduct ➢ Strikes and lock-outs ➢ Deviation from collective agreements ➢ Implementation and exemption collective agreements	JF Minutes
2.	Joint Forum (J.F)	The Joint Forum (J.F) may decide to refer issues that require further investigation to appropriate forums such as but not limited to, to the: - ➢ Workplace Representative Council (WRC) ➢ Dispute Resolution Committee (DRC) ➢ Union/Union parties ➢ Company/Management ➢ Ad-hoc Committee	JF Minutes
3.	Company Officials Union Officials Committee	Report back findings and recommendations to the Joint Forum (J.F).	Report
4.	Joint Forum (J.F) Tribunal	Unresolved issues and or disputes relating to non-substantive conditions of employment, operational procedures, bonuses or incentive schemes that are directly related to profit or productivity, shall be referred for conciliation/ arbitration by a tribunal and the outcome shall be binding on the parties. Parties shall not call a strike or lock-out on issues referred above.	JF Minutes

NO	PERSON/ FORUM	ACTIVITY	DOCUMENT
4.	Joint Forum (J.F) Tribunal (Cont.)	The Tribunal normally serves as a three-person panel, including a chairperson, a union organizer and a management representative. The Tribunal consists of a chairman, an independent professional with relevant experience and legal expertise, as well as the union official and management representative with relevant knowledge and experience as recommended by the Dispute Resolution Committee (DRC) and appointed by the CEO. The Tribunal proceedings and conduct of panelists shall be in accordance with the arbitrations proceedings and principles as contained in the South African Road Passenger Bargaining Council dispute procedures. At the hearing on the merits, both parties may present evidence and examine and cross-examine witnesses. Following the hearing, the parties generally submit written briefs. After consideration, and consultation with panel members, the chairperson issues its report and recommendations to the company.	JF Minutes
5.	Parties Tribunal	Unresolved issues other than above, shall be referred to for conciliation/arbitration by a tribunal which findings shall serve as an advisory award.	
6.	Parties	In the event that a party not accepting the outcome of the award as in paragraph 5, may refer the matter as per the South African Road Passenger Bargaining Council or the LRA dispute resolution mechanism.	
7.	Parties	All unresolved disputes that may lead to a strike or lock-out shall be dealt with in terms of Clause 5.11 of the Co-determination procedure.	

Annexure 4

DISCIPLINE
DISPUTE PREVENTION AND RESOLUTION PROCEDURE

NO	PERSON/ FORUM	ACTIVITY	DOCUMENT
1.		The Company's collective disciplinary procedure agreement as well as the South African Road Passenger Bargaining Council dispute procedure serves as guideline for dealing with disciplinary matters.	Disciplinary Procedure and Code SARPBAC Constitution LRA
2.		Unfair dismissals regarding misconduct, incapacity, poor performance, and ill-health will be dealt with according to this procedure.	Disciplinary Procedure and Code
3.	Company Representatives Union Representatives Accused Representatives Accused	Prior to the date of the disciplinary hearing, the Company Representative and the Union/ Accused Representative shall meet and agree on the following:- 1. Securing the presence of any witness at the hearing. 2. Whether an interpreter is required and is arranged by the Union Representative. 3. The necessity for in loco inspection. 4. Expert evidence required to be arranged by the Company. 5. The exchange of witness statements. 6. The resolution of any preliminary points that are intended to be taken. 7. The availability of a Union/Accused Representative at the hearing. 8. The Union Representative had enough time to prepare for the hearing. 9. Any procedural matters that are in dispute. 10. Any disputes in lumine. 11. Exchange and acknowledgment of bundle of documents of both parties. 12. Any additional documents/photos or other information needed to conclude the hearing. 13. Objections to chairperson. 14. Any dispute regarding the charges formulated. The purpose of the above is to assist parties in preparing for the hearing to ensure the smooth and timeous conclusion of disciplinary hearings.	Pre-hearing consultation document

NO	PERSON/ FORUM	ACTIVITY	DOCUMENT
4.	Company Representatives Union Representatives Accused Representatives Accused	The document shall be used by any party and submitted to the Chairperson at the hearing as part as the bundle of documents.	Pre-hearing consultation document
5.	Company Representative Union/Accused Representative	A party that fails to attend a pre-hearing consultation session as arranged shall have waived the opportunity for the chairperson to consider requests that are addressed in the pre-hearing.	Pre-hearing consultation document
6.	Accused/ Union Representative Accused/ Accused Representative	After the hearing, the appellant shall complete and submit the appeal document as per the disciplinary procedure. In extraordinary circumstances, where the appellant is of the opinion that the hearing was procedurally unfair and or in the event of new evidence or evidence that was not considered during the hearing, that might warrant and independent opinion and or a new hearing, the appellant shall motivate their reasons and grounds for a re-hearing in writing and submit to the appeal Chairperson. The Chairperson shall consider the evidence before him and depending on the merits, refer the matter to the DC. The DC shall consider the recommendation and arrange for the tribunal to hear evidence, as per the tribunal proceedings described in paragraph 4 of the JF Dispute Prevention and Resolution Procedure. If the accused is still not satisfied, with the outcome of the tribunal, he/she may refer the matter for arbitration.	Request for appeal against a disciplinary hearing

NO	PERSON/ FORUM	ACTIVITY	DOCUMENT
7.	Company Representatives Union Representatives Accused Representatives	Prior to the date of the arbitration, te Disciplinary Coordinator shall arrange a date for the pre-arbitration meeting by e-mail and telephone confirming arrangements. The parties to arbitration must hold a pre-arbitration meeting dealing with the under mentioned matters. In a pre-arbitration meeting, the parties must attempt to reach consensus on the following: - 1. any means by which the dispute may be settled; 2. facts that are agreed between the parties; 3. facts that are in dispute; 4. the issues that the panelist is required to decide; 5. the precise relief claimed and if compensation is claimed, the amount of the compensation and how it is calculated; 6. the sharing and exchange of relevant documents, and the preparation of a bundle of documents in chronological order with each page numbered; 7. the manner in which documentary evidence is to be dealt with, including any agreement on the status of documents and whether documents, or parts of documents, will serve as evidence of what they appear to be; 8. whether evidence on affidavit will be admitted with or without the right of any party to cross examine the person who made the affidavit; 9. which party must begin; 10. the necessity for any *in loco* inspection; 11. securing the presence at the hearing of any witness; 12. the resolution of any preliminary points that are intended to be taken; 13. the exchange of witness statements; 14. expert evidence; 15. any other means by which the proceedings may be shortened; 16. an estimate of the time required for the hearing; 17. the right of representation; and 18. whether an interpreter is required and, if so, for how long and for which languages.	Pre-Arbitration minutes
8.	Company Representatives Union Representatives Accused Representatives	Unless a dispute is settled, the parties must draw up and sign a minute setting out the facts on which the parties agree or disagree and may also deal with any other matter listed in above. The parties must ensure that a copy of the pre-arbitration meeting minutes is submitted to the panelist at the conciliation/arbitration.	

NO	PERSON/ FORUM	ACTIVITY	DOCUMENT
9.	Arbitration Panelist	If any party to the dispute fails to attend a pre-arbitration meeting as arranged, the panelist may refer the matter back to the parties for a pre-arbitration meeting or make an order of cost against that party in terms of the SARBPAC Agreement. If the panelist decides to continue with the arbitration without the pre-arbitration minutes, the party tha fails to attend the consultation session as arranged shall have waived the opportunity for the Chairperson to consider requests that are to be addressed in the pre-arbitration meeting and concentrate on the merits of the case only.	

Annexure 5

INTERSTATE BUS LINES
PRE-HEARING MINUTES

IN THE HEARING BETWEEN

NAME: _____ (ACCUSED)

AND

NAME: _____ (COMPANY REPRESENTATIVE)

Alledged transgression _____

_____

_____

Minutes of the pre-hearing held on _____

1. Accused and Representative notified to attend a pre-hearing meeting on _____by _____by means of _____

2. Names of witnesses required at the hearing:

_____

_____

_____

3. Interpreter required and arranged by the Union: _____

_____

_____

_____

4. The necessity for in loco inspection: _____

_____

_____

_____

5. Expert evidence required to be arranged by the Company or the Union:

_____

_____

_____

6. Exchange of witness statements: _____

_____

_____

_____

7. Resolution of any preliminary points that are intended to be taken: _____

_____

_____

_____

8. The availability and name of a Union/Accused Representative at the hearing:

_____

_____

_____

9. Union/Company Representative notified in time to prepare for hearing: _____

_____

_____

_____

10. Any procedural matters that are in dispute: _____

_____

_____

_____

11. Any disputes in limine: _____

_____

_____

_____

12. Exchange and acknowledgement of bundle of documents of both parties:

_____
_____
_____

13. Any additional documents/photos or other information needed to conclude a hearing: _____

_____
_____
_____

14. Objection to a Chairperson: _____

_____
_____
_____

15. Any disputes regarding the charges formulated: _____

_____
_____
_____

REMARKS

_____
_____
_____
_____
_____
_____

COMPANY REPRESENTATIVE: _____ **DATE:** _____

ACCUSED REPRESENTATIVE: _____ **DATE:** _____

Annexure 6

INTERSTATE BUS LINES
PRE-ARBITRATION MINUTES

IN THE ARBITRATION BETWEEN

NAME: _____APPLICANT

AND

INTERSTATE BUS LINES   **RESPONDENT**

MINUTES OF PRE-ARBITRATION MEETING HELD ON:_____

Applicant and the Respondent notified to attend the Pre-Arbitration meeting on
_____ by _____ by means of _____

1. Any means by which the *dispute* may be settled:
    _____
    _____
    _____

2. Facts that are agreed between the parties:
    _____
    _____
    _____

3. Facts that are in dispute:
    _____
    _____
    _____

4. The nature of the dispute:

_____

_____

_____

5. The issue/s that the arbitrator is required to decide:

_____

_____

_____

6. The precise relief claimed and if compensation is claimed, the amount of the compensation and how it is calculated:

_____

_____

_____

7. The sharing and exchange of relevant documents, from both parties and the preparation of bundle of documents in chronological order with each page numbered:

_____

_____

_____

8. The manner in which documentary evidence is to be dealt with, including any agreement on the status of documents and whether documents, or part of documents, will *serve* as evidence of what they appear to be:

_____

_____

_____

9. Whether evidence on affidavit will be admitted with or without the rigt of *any party* to cross-examine the person who made the affidavit:

_____

_____

_____

10. Which party must begin:

_____

_____

_____

11. The necessity for any on-the-spot inspection:

_____
_____
_____

12. Securing the presence at the arbitration of any witness:

_____
_____
_____

13. The resolution of any preliminary points that are intended to be taken:

_____
_____
_____

14. The exchange of witness statements:

_____
_____
_____

15. Expert evidence required:

_____
_____
_____

16. Any other means by which the proceedings may be shortened:

_____
_____
_____

17. An estimate of the time required for the hearing:

_____
_____
_____

18. The right of representation:

_____
_____
_____

19. Whether an interpreter is required and, if so, for how long and for which languages:

_____

_____

_____

REMARKS

_____

_____

_____

_____

_____

_____

_____   _____

APPLICANT   **RESPONDENT**

DATE: _____**DATE:**_____

Signed at Bloemfontein on this _____ day of _____ 2017 in the presence of the undersigned Witnesses.

WITNESSES:

_____   1. _____
For and on behalf of the Company
being duly authorised

_____   2. _____
For and on behalf of TASWU
being duly authorised

_____   3. _____
For and on behalf of SATAWU
being duly authorised

Appendix E

QUALITATIVE
RESEARCH REPORT

IBL Combined 2017

BeQ™ Measurement, April 2017

- Introduction

Thank you for participating in the 2017 BeQ™ Benchmark measure.

The format of the 2017 report is in a PowerPoint format with additional report information that provides a more detailed explanation around a concept where required.

The report has been designed in this way to assist with specific business unit feedback and action plan sessions that you could set up so as to focus on specific developmental areas in lieu of any initiatives that you might need to implement. The action plans that you arrive at within your business unit could be translated into Performance Score Card actions so as to provide easy measurable outcomes to put into practice before embarking on a re-measure to monitor for progress and improvements.

If you have any difficulty in the application of the report, please feel free to contact us at any time.

- Our Contact Details

Report compiled by Dr Rica Viljoen and Mr Stefan Viljoen of Mandala Consulting.

Contact details:

Prof Rica Viljoen
+27 82 449 5846
rica@mandalaconsulting.co.za

Mr Stefan Viljoen
+27 76 907 3277
stefan@mandalaconsulting.co.za

| 1. | The philosophy of Engagement and the BeQ™ Model |

- The philosophy of Engagement

"Individual engagement to a group effort – that is what makes a team work, a company work, a society work, a civilization work"

Vince Lombardi

Benson (2006) described the true meaning of commitment as the ability to commit with passion to a noble pursuit. Engagement can be described as *"the act of committing, pledging or engaging oneself"* or *"the state of being bound emotionally or intellectually to a course of action or to another person or persons".*

Viljoen (2007) defined engaged commitment as "the trait of sincere and steadfast fixity of purpose, a person of energy and commitment" and "the act of binding oneself to a course of action". In the model that will be presented, the terms commitment and engagement will be used interchangeably. EMPLOYEE ENGAGEMENT, thus, is a concept that is generally viewed as managing discretionary effort, that is, when employees have choices, they will act in a way that furthers their organisation's interests. An engaged employee is a person who is fully involved in, and enthusiastic about, his or her work.

- The BeQ™ Model

The BeQ™-model measures the interplay between assumptions and perceptions alive and well in organisations around constructs that contribute to the unleashing of individual voices, contributions and gifts. Since the organisational and the country climate as well as the employees' worldview also influence these perceptions, they are also explored. The BeQ™ is a diagnostic method that identifies critical pre-requisites for organizational sustainability.

- The primary objective of the BeQ™ is to:

  - understand the underlying mental models of the employees;
  - explore the relations between perceptions that influence organisational commitment and the unleashing of individual voices and compare these to previous findings where appropriate;
  - understand the underlying assumptions as they pertain to the individual, the various teams, and the greater organisation; and to
  - determine the level of engagement within the organisation that will manifest in optimal productivity, business objectives and safe behaviour.

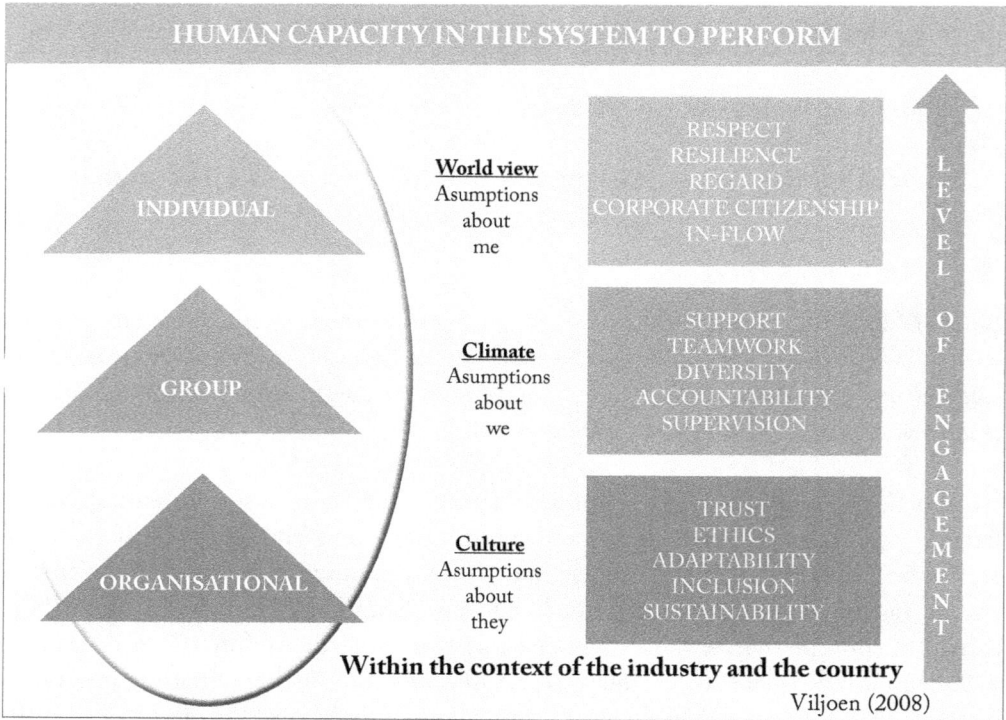

HUMAN CAPACITY IN THE SYSTEM TO PERFORM			
INDIVIDUAL	**World view** Asumptions about me	RESPECT RESILIENCE REGARD CORPORATE CITIZENSHIP IN-FLOW	
GROUP	**Climate** Asumptions about we	SUPPORT TEAMWORK DIVERSITY ACCOUNTABILITY SUPERVISION	L E V E L O F E N G A G E M E N T
ORGANISATIONAL	**Culture** Asumptions about they	TRUST ETHICS ADAPTABILITY INCLUSION SUSTAINABILITY	

Within the context of the industry and the country

Viljoen (2008)

Scientific correlations have been found between people having "voice" and levels of engagement. The benefits of engagement are:

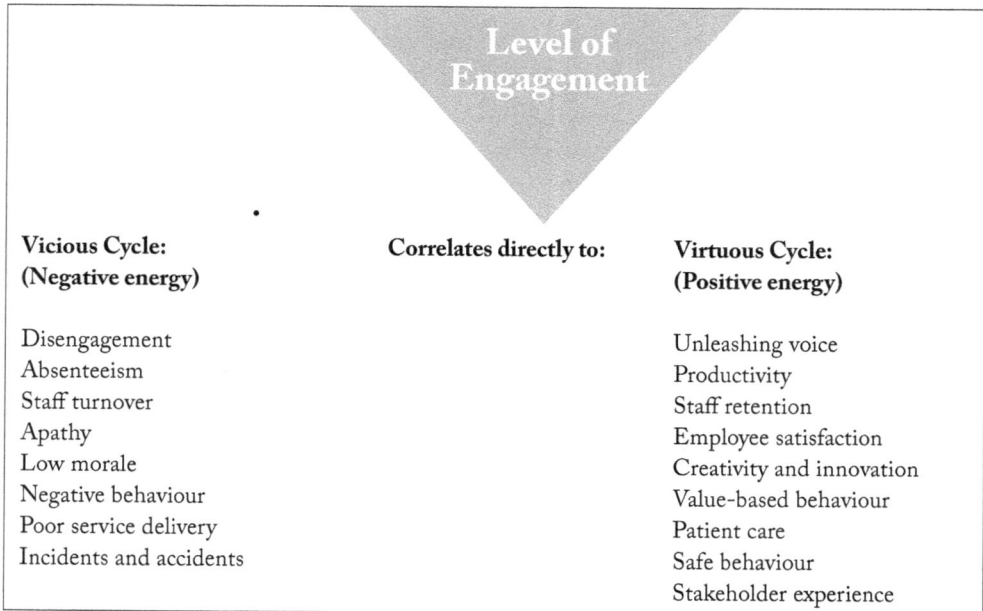

Level of Engagement

Vicious Cycle: (Negative energy)	**Correlates directly to:**	**Virtuous Cycle:** (Positive energy)
Disengagement		Unleashing voice
Absenteeism		Productivity
Staff turnover		Staff retention
Apathy		Employee satisfaction
Low morale		Creativity and innovation
Negative behaviour		Value-based behaviour
Poor service delivery		Patient care
Incidents and accidents		Safe behaviour
		Stakeholder experience

- The process of Inclusivity:

Inclusivity defined:

*"…a radical organisational transformational methodology which aligns **the doing** and **the being** side of the organisation around commonly defined principles and values, co-created by all.*

"It is a systemic approach that focuses on underlying beliefs and assumptions and challenges patterns in the individual, group and organisational psyche, to spend energy and engage in a sustainable, inclusive manner with the purpose to achieve shared consciousness."

Viljoen, 2007.

2.	Sample size and overall BeQ™ score	
Total size of population		
Number of questionnaires administered		359
Number of questionnaires captured		359
Percentage participation		100%

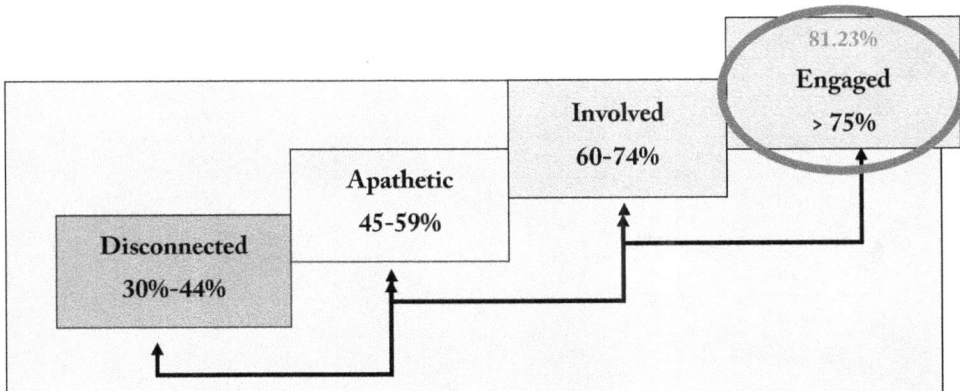

3. Staff Sample Breakdown

Department	No. of participants
Administration	41
Bus Drivers	94
HR	21
Management (P3-P8)	15
Operations staff (P11-P18)	65
Operations Seniors (P9-P10)	7
Technical staff (P11-P18)	88
Technical Seniors (P9-P10)	24
Good to Great Project	4
TOTAL	359

Gender	
Male	267
Female	87
Unspecified	5
Age group	
<25	17
25-32	58
33-40	82
41-50	108
>50	89
Unspecified	5
Time with organisation	
0 - 1 year	41
1 - 3 years	75
3 - 5 years	48
>5 years	187
Unspecified	8

4. BeQ Results

Respect		73.83
Resilience		88.07
Regard	**Emotional Presence 84.65%**	92.07
Corporate citizenship		85.98
In-flow		85.05
Support		80.88
Teamwork		85.22
Diversity	**Emotional Containment 79.90%**	83.08
Accountability		77.33
Supervision		75.56
Trust		71.00
Ethics		68.82
Alignment		84.24
Inclusion	**Organisational Gestalt 79.86%**	78.90
Production orientation		86.65
Adaptability		80.00
Wellbeing		83.41
Caring orientation		85.97
BeQ		**81.23**

When the results of the BeQ Survey are integrated a specific story for each Department unfolds. In the spirit of Appreciative Inquiry, a narrative is used to explain a dynamic, where the focus is not on good-bad, right-wrong, but more on what needs to be put in place to enable a system to unleash its energy so that it can function optimally. In this respect the story comprises three flows:

- It identifies the **Evident Enablers** already present in the team that will aid in unleashing the energy if allowed to continue to operate,
- It highlights the **Outcome Compromisers** that presently "block" or paralyse the system to function optimally, and
- It indicates what the **Manifested Dynamic** will be (as is already evident), if left alone or not addressed.

The story speaks about the "unsaid" things that play out in a variety of behaviours daily that add to the frustration of the task. These behaviours are "clustered" into a concept that simplifies something which often appears very complex.

The purpose of highlighting the manifested dynamic is to create awareness of the often unintended consequences that will play out if no intervention is entered into.

By managing the Outcome Compromisers and finding ways of overcoming the obstacles, and even more positive and truly committed energy will ensue – which in guaranteed to have a significant impact on teamwork, morale, accountability, ownership and fundamentally, operational excellence.

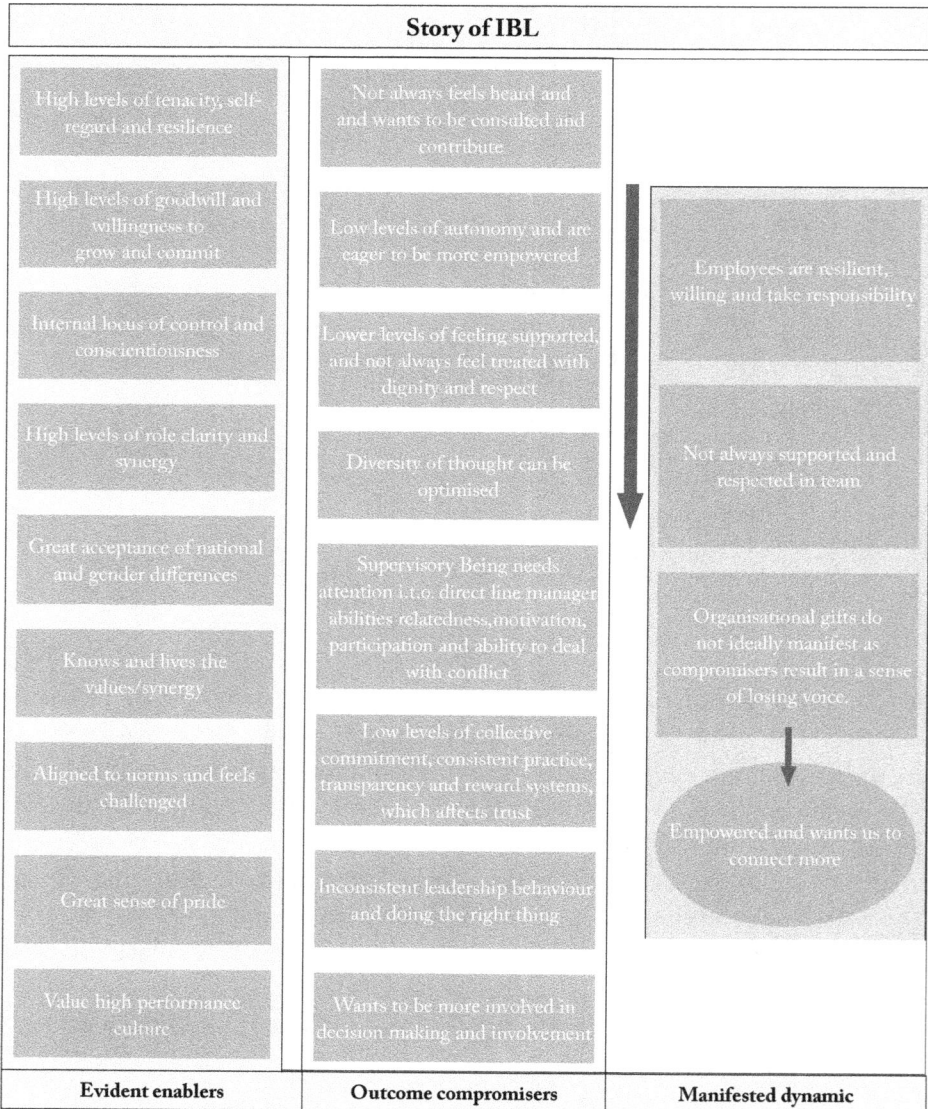

Story of IBL		
High levels of tenacity, self-regard and resilience	Not always feels heard and and wants to be consulted and contribute	
High levels of goodwill and willingness to grow and commit	Low levels of autonomy and are eager to be more empowered	Employees are resilient, willing and take responsibility
Internal locus of control and conscientiousness	Lower levels of feeling supported, and not always feel treated with dignity and respect	
High levels of role clarity and synergy	Diversity of thought can be optimised	Not always supported and respected in team
Great acceptance of national and gender differences	Supervisory Being needs attention i.t.o. direct line manager abilities relatedness, motivation, participation and ability to deal with conflict	Organisational gifts do not ideally manifest as compromisers result in a sense of losing voice.
Knows and lives the values/synergy	Low levels of collective commitment, consistent practice, transparency and reward systems, which affects trust	
Aligned to norms and feels challenged		Empowered and wants us to connect more
Great sense of pride	Inconsistent leadership behaviour and doing the right thing	
Value high performance culture	Wants to be more involved in decision making and involvement	
Evident enablers	**Outcome compromisers**	**Manifested dynamic**

IBL Combined: BeQ™ Emotional Presence analysis

AREAS OF STRENGTH
- Individuals have high levels of tenacity, self-regard and resillience.
- People show goodwill and are willing to grow and commit.
- Individuals at IBL have a high locus of control and a great sence of conscientiousness.

AREAS OF DEVELOPMENT
- Individuals here do not always feel heard and wants to contribute and be consulted.
- Individuals have lower levels of autonomy and are eager to be more empowered.
- Individuals do not always feel supported and individuals here do not always feel treated with dignity and respect.

IBL Combined: BeQ™ Emotional Containment Analysis

AREAS OF STRENGTH
- At IBL there are high levels of role clarity and synergy.
- People here have great acceptance for national and gender differences.

AREAS OF DEVELOPMENT
- People feel the supervisory being needs attention in terms of direct managers abilities, relatedness, motivation,participation and ability to deal with conflict.
- Diversity of thought can be optimised.

IBL Combined: BeQ™ Organisational Gestalt Analysis

AREAS OF STRENGTH
- People knows and lives the values of IBL.
- At IBL people are alligned to the norms and feels challenged.
- Individuals have great sence of pride.
- People here value the high performance culture at IBL.

AREAS OF DEVELOPMENT
- There are lower levels of collective comittment, consistent practice, transparency and reward systems wich affects trust.
- Individuals here feel that there is inconsistent leadership behaviour and lower levels of doing the right thing.
- People here wants to be more involved in decision making.

5.	BeQ™ 2017 Measure: Emotional Presence Data Sheet

•   Emotional Presence Data Sheet Constructs

Domain	Construct	Sub-Construct	BeQ
Emotional Presence	Respect	Dignity	74.07
Emotional Presence	Respect	Being heard	76.10
Emotional Presence	Respect	Consulted	70.17
Emotional Presence	Respect	Having voice	69.23
Emotional Presence	Respect	Feeling competent	79.54
Emotional Presence	Resilience	Adaptability	87.55
Emotional Presence	Resilience	Tenacity	89.03
Emotional Presence	Resilience	Resilience	88.07
Emotional Presence	Resilience	Self-regard	91.97
Emotional Presence	Resilience	Confidence	83.72
Emotional Presence	Regard	Awareness	89.83
Emotional Presence	Regard	Willingness to grow	90.14
Emotional Presence	Regard	Goodwill	94.06
Emotional Presence	Regard	Willingness to commit	94.24
Emotional Presence	Corporate Citizenship	Locus of control	93.20
Emotional Presence	Corporate Citizenship	Conscientiousness	95.22
Emotional Presence	Corporate Citizenship	Challenge	88.18
Emotional Presence	Corporate Citizenship	Empowered	78.44
Emotional Presence	Corporate Citizenship	Autonomy	74.87
Emotional Presence	In-flow	Opportunity to grow	82.31
Emotional Presence	In-flow	Belonging	87.78

•   Emotional Presence Constructs defined:

Individual domain:

Perceptions around the self are scored according to dynamics identified around respect, resilience, regard and the taking up of personal authority or responsibility. Each of these constructs are analysed and information with respect to the group being evaluated are found:

RESPECT

- Respect: This construct measures the degree to which employees report having a good sense of self awareness and feelings of being respected when they are allowed to air their views (have voice) and are heard or listened to. Perceptions around employees' sense of the organisation's efforts in demonstrating care for their well-being, is also measured here.

In sum: Respect refers to an assumption/showing of good faith and value towards another person

Experiences:

- I feel listened to
- I feel valued by others within my organisation
- I feel respected

Underlying Assumption:

Individuals within the organisation feel accepted, respected and valued.

RESILIENCE

- Resilience: This construct refers to the degree to which employees: report feeling competent and validated in the work they do, are given opportunities for growth and development and feel that they are able to perform a variety of tasks. Employees' levels of perseverance in terms of their ability to perform well under pressure, is also measured here.

In sum: Resilience refers to the ability of the organisation and individuals to deal with challenges effectively

Experiences:

- Changes are communicated effectively within the organisation
- Change is welcomed in the organisation
- The organisation is flexible to adapt to the challenges of the external environment

Underlying Assumption:

Change is managed effectively with-in the organisation and accepted by employees.

REGARD

- Regard: This construct pertains to the degree to which employees report on their sense of self regard, - to what extent do they feel that they can contribute and add value in their work and thereby build their sense of self-worth and ability to add value. The construct also notes whether employees value personal feedback and whether they see the need for personal growth and development. Employees' feelings of confidence are also evaluated here especially with regard to the way employees experience their level of confidence to act on their own (either where they might need to be empowered or guided, or to the extent to which they are comfortable to take their own initiative).

In sum: Regard refers to having a positive self-view and self-awareness. It further refers to both the perceived weak and strong points of an individual and how he or she deals with them.

Experiences:

- I have positive self regard
- I am aware of my capabilities
- I am confident about the value that I bring to the organisation

Underlying Assumption:

Employees that have a positive self regard will perform and contribute more optimally towards the goals of the organisation.

CORPORATE CITIZENSHIP

- Corporate Citizenship: The analysis of this construct relates to information shared with respect to employees' locus of control, sense of corporate citizenship and a willingness to want to contribute to the success of their organisation. It also refers to employees' level of willingness to engage and take responsibility for their role or employees' inclination to not do this and rather want to blame others if things go wrong, or if things are not done, rather than take up personal authority and initiative.

In sum: Corporate Citizenship refers to the degree to which an individual will take personal authority over a situation, act with goodwill and conscientiousness and behave like an owner towards his/her company.

Experiences:

- I am in control of my own environment
- I am responsible for my own outcomes
- I display organisational citizenship behaviour
- I do not feel powerless
- I am willing to go the extra mile in order to contribute
- I am committed to making my organisation a success.

Underlying Assumption:

Employees with a high level of personal responsibility and corporate citizenship have an internal locus of control and will take up space to sort out problems at hand. When corporate citizenship is high, the blaming culture will be low.

IN-FLOW

- In-flow: This construct measures the degree to which employees report being able to do their work in a synergized way so that work feels enabling and rewarding. People that feel challenged and stimulated by their work, have opportunities to grow and develop themselves, are able to do their work efficiently within reasonable time frames and that are mandated to make decisions within their sphere of influence, generally will report feeling "in-flow" with their work.

In sum: In-flow refers to one's ability to do one's work in a reasonably seamless, yet energizing/enabling way.

Experiences:

- I feel that I am empowered to make decisions within my sphere of influence.
- I feel that there are opportunities to grow and develop myself within my work.
- I feel challenged by my work and enabled to get through my work within reasonable time-frames allowed.
- I feel that I belong to my organisation – feel that I can add value and be valued for my contribution here.

Underlying Assumption:

Individuals with high levels of being "in-flow" will be efficient, effective and energized/motivated by their work.

6.	BeQ™ 2017 Measure: Emotional Containment Data Sheet

- Emotional Containment Data Sheet Constructs

Domain	Construct	Sub-Construct	BeQ
Emotional Containment	Support	Feeling supported	83.85
Emotional Containment	Support	Connected	79.25
Emotional Containment	Support	Informed	77.87
Emotional Containment	Support	Equipped	82.54
Emotional Containment	Teamwork	Role clarity	90.87
Emotional Containment	Teamwork	Synergy	87.47
Emotional Containment	Teamwork	Departmental Interdependence	83.00
Emotional Containment	Teamwork	Language differences	83.29
Emotional Containment	Teamwork	Teamwork	81.45
Emotional Containment	Diversity	Gender differences	86.71
Emotional Containment	Diversity	National differences	87.48
Emotional Containment	Diversity	Valuing age differences	82.68
Emotional Containment	Diversity	Diversity of thought	75.45
Emotional Containment	Accountability	Fair performance management	70.35
Emotional Containment	Accountability	Underperformance acceptance	71.33
Emotional Containment	Accountability	Reliability	76.23
Emotional Containment	Accountability	Translation of goals	78.09
Emotional Containment	Accountability	Performance Feedback	90.67
Emotional Containment	Supervision	Direct line-manager abilities	77.61
Emotional Containment	Supervision	On the job coaching	76.30
Emotional Containment	Supervision	Acknowledgement	78.02
Emotional Containment	Supervision	Motivation	77.17
Emotional Containment	Supervision	Participation	75.65
Emotional Containment	Supervision	Personalised Feedback	74.57
Emotional Containment	Supervision	Relatedness	69.62

•   Emotional Containment Constructs Explained:

Group domain:

The group-domain describes the climate in the organisation. Perceptions on this construct indicate how the group experience and perceive the feel (weather) of the organisation and reflect, to a large extent, the perceptions about the leadership of the organisation. Constructs that comprise the information gleaned about the group domain include Accountability, Diversity, Supervision and Support. The following can be learned after analysing the results:

SUPPORT

•   Support: This construct refers to the degree to which employees feel that teamwork, rather than working in a silo or isolation, in general is encouraged and the level to which they feel they have access to the equipment/training they need to perform their tasks.

In sum: Support refers to the extent that individuals feel encouraged, cared for and assisted by others

Experiences:

•   I feel supported by my team employees and managers
•   I feel acknowledged for my contribution
•   I feel listened to

Underlying Assumption:

High levels of support lead to a higher willingness to engage.

TEAMWORK

•   Teamwork: This construct refers to the degree to which employees feel that teamwork is encouraged and present in their team. Members that work together in a team rely and depend on one another, work together towards a common goal, feel accepted and supported by one another and have clearly defined roles and responsibilities both towards the team and themselves.

In sum: Teamwork refers to the degree to which team members work together and support one another as they work towards a common goal.

Experiences:

- I feel supported by my team members
- I feel accepted by my team members and know that they have my back.
- I feel we all know what is expected of us and that we work together to achieve the goals set for us.

Underlying Assumption:

High levels of teamwork lead to the effective and speedy attainment of set goals and enable team members to feel part of something meaningful, accepting and rewarding.

VALUING DIVERSITY

- Diversity: This construct evaluates the degree to which the group feels that diversity components such as gender, nationality, race, age, level of social standing, level of education etc. and the differences experienced around these are respected, or are sources of conflicts or divides amongst groups.

In sum: Valuing diversity refers to the degree to which differences due to language, race, gender and diversity of thought are valued and allowed in the workplace.

Experiences:

- Differences are seen as positive and enhancing to work relationships
- People are treated fairly and equally
- It is allowed to differ from others

Underlying Assumption:

Diversity is valued and accepted as good within the organisation. Valuing diversity leads to innovation, creativity and effective decision making.

ACCOUNTABILITY

- Accountability: This construct evaluates employees' view of leadership's level of reliability in terms of the consistency of their performance management practices in terms of contracting and delivering outcomes. In this regard, tolerance towards underperformance is seen as allowing employees not to be held accountable for mistakes or unproductive behaviour, whereas focus on a performance driven culture would breed a more accountable team.

In sum: Accountability refers to the degree to which we hold each other accountable for contracted outcomes and promises made.

Experiences:

- I am held responsible for my output
- I will want to contribute to the success of the organisation
- People that commit to something are held accountable to do it

Underlying Assumption:

This construct refers to whether individuals are being kept accountable for what was contracted with them. It refers to the degree of tolerance with non-performance that exists in organisations. A low level of accountability will result in a blaming culture.

SUPERVISORY LEADERSHIP

- Supervisory Leadership: Leadership in this context refers to the leadership capability that is needed by managers to effectively manage and lead employees. It also specifically applies to the depth of leadership on supervisory level since effectiveness on this level has a direct impact on the achieving of organisational goals.

Experiences:

- My manager is a good leader
- My manager has the necessary leadership skills
- My manager does a good job at leading the job at hand

Underlying Assumption:

Managers in this company are good leaders and have the necessary leadership skills to lead effectively.

- Supervision: is linked to support, but specifically focuses on the level of support experienced by staff with regard to their supervisory leadership. This construct evaluates the extent to which respondents feel that their supervisory leaders have good motivational ability, actively participate in tasks, and provide hands on coaching and performance feedback, encouragement and assistance to team employees and the degree to which they lead by example.

7.	BeQ™ 2017 Measure: Organisational Gestalt Data Sheet

• Organisational Gestalt Data Sheet Constructs

Domain	Construct	Sub-Construct	BeQ
Organisational Gestalt	Trust	Collective Commitment	74.41
Organisational Gestalt	Trust	Consistent Practices	72.01
Organisational Gestalt	Trust	Transparency	66.01
Organisational Gestalt	Trust	Reward system	63.92
Organisational Gestalt	Trust	Trustworthyness	78.67
Organisational Gestalt	Ethics	Doing the right thing	70.76
Organisational Gestalt	Ethics	Leadership behaviour	67.23
Organisational Gestalt	Ethics	Consistency	68.49
Organisational Gestalt	Alignment	Vision	78.56
Organisational Gestalt	Alignment	Strategy	79.94
Organisational Gestalt	Alignment	Business Plan	81.38
Organisational Gestalt	Alignment	Translation	80.93
Organisational Gestalt	Alignment	Know the values	89.94
Organisational Gestalt	Alignment	Role clarity	78.40
Organisational Gestalt	Alignment	Norms	92.82
Organisational Gestalt	Alignment	Challenged	91.93
Organisational Gestalt	Inclusion	Decision making	71.10
Organisational Gestalt	Inclusion	Involved	74.52
Organisational Gestalt	Inclusion	Pride	91.06
Organisational Gestalt	Production orientation	High Performance culture	88.69
Organisational Gestalt	Production orientation	Green	84.61
Organisational Gestalt	Adaptability	Supportive policies and procedures	80.00
Organisational Gestalt	Wellbeing	Health	80.12
Organisational Gestalt	Wellbeing	Employee of choice	86.71
Organisational Gestalt	Caring orientation	Drive to efficiency	84.43
Organisational Gestalt	Caring orientation	Patient care orientation	84.32
Organisational Gestalt	Caring orientation	Health and safety orientation	88.42
Organisational Gestalt	Caring orientation	Working Conditions	86.71

- Organisational Gestalt Constructs Defined:

Organisational domain:

The organisational domain is determined by the perceived levels of trust, inclusivity, ethics and alignment in the organisation, as well as the focus on production, safely and wellness. Collectively this contributes to the perceived sustainability and perceived culture of the organisation. Information on the individual constructs reveals the following:

TRUST

- Trust: This construct evaluates the degree to which information about the business is adequately and openly communicated to employees and whether efforts pertaining to performance are fairly and transparently rewarded. Management intent is also evaluated and employees' perceptions of how problems are dealt with and trust is instilled - especially in terms of fair performance management practices - are screened.

The degree to which people give others the benefit of the doubt and trust the intentions of others.

Experiences:

- This construct refers to the experience of the individual that he/she are trusted with the task that the organisation assigned to him/her. It further explores the sense that the organisation and management can be trusted.

Underlying Assumption:

Trust is the lens through which behaviours are interpreted. If trust is high, people are allowed to be themselves. If not, each action is hyper-analysed and interpreted by the untrusting party.

ETHICS

- Ethics: This construct measures the participants' perceptions around management ethics and consistency in decision-making, rewarding the right things, the degree to which important problems are addressed and managed and how the management of all these factors translates into tolerance/non-tolerance of underperformance. It alludes to the level of trust the leadership instils in its workforce through the level of fairness, transparency and consistency in which things are done.

This refers to the sense of the individual that the right things are done in the organisation

Experiences:

- We will do the right thing if nobody is watching
- Management will do the ethical thing
- We follow the moral high ground here

Underlying Assumption:

Ethical behaviour is part of the culture and is acknowledged and practiced by all within the organisation. An individual with similar ethical values to the organisation will experience a sense of belonging.

ALIGNMENT

- Alignment: This construct reports how employees see the organisation as being aligned in terms of the strategic intent, vision, significance and purpose thereof and the extent to which this strategy of intent is translated to all the various departments and reflected in the values and associated behaviours seen throughout the organisation.

Alignment refers to the degree to which people in the organisation are on the same page regarding the task and the way they engage with each other and the task at hand. It is measured on the extent to which the Being and the Doing side of the organisation is aligned.

Experiences:

- I understand the strategy of the organisation
- I know how my work links to the overall goals and strategy of the organisation
- My values are aligned with that of the organisation

Underlying Assumption:

The alignment of the doing (strategy) and value systems (the being) in the organisation contribute directly to productivity, and other economic factors.

INCLUSIVITY

- Inclusivity: This construct evaluates the degree to which participants feel that they are consulted about the things that directly affect them or are asked to give their opinion on important decisions, and whether differences of opinion are allowed and encouraged. The level of inclusion often translates into the level of belonging that team employees experience within their organisation. The more part of the organisation they feel, the more likely they would be to want to contribute and engage.

- Refers to the extent to which individuals are involved and consulted on issued that directly pertain to them.

Experiences:

- I am included in business discussions that are important to me
- I am consulted when something influences me directly
- I can influence decisions that are important

Underlying Assumption:

If employees of the organisation feel included, and a part of the organisation, they are more likely to engage and contribute. This construct shows the highest correlation with trust.

ADAPTABILITY

- Adaptability: This construct refers to the degree to which the organisation has grit, and can adapt to changes in the external environment. It is balanced by the human niche distribution in the system as employees with different world views/thinking systems have different perspectives of adaptability.

Experiences:

- The organisation easily adapts to change
- The transformation process that the organisation has embarked on is visionary
- Policies and procedures are supporting strategy

Underlying assumption:

The belief that an organisation can adapt to changes in the external environment, leads directly to an increase in a sense of safety and future job stability.

CARING ORIENTATION

- Caring Orientation: This construct refers to the degree to which the caring intent of top management translates into a sense that IBL is a caring organisation.

Caring refers to the degree to which attitudes and behaviours translate into a contextual framework that is characterised by supportive, responsive actions and reactions and a conceptual orientation that is focused on health and safety and care – both in the inner world and the external world (as patient care).

Experiences:

- IBL cares for my wellbeing
- People can work here for a long time

Underlying assumption:

As within so without. If we care inside our customers will mirror this sense.

8.	BeQ™ National Cultural Dynamic

- National Context

The worldview of the country in which an organisation operates can provide valuable context to the dynamics reported by the BeQ™-study. Hofstede advised management operating across country boundaries to have both knowledge and empathy with the local scene. National cultures differ on the following scales:

- Power distance (the degree to which people in a country view inequality among people of the country as normal),
- Individualism focuses on the degree the society reinforces individual or collective, achievement and interpersonal relationships.
- Masculine versus feminine (the extent to which a culture is conducive to dominance, assertiveness and acquisition of things versus a culture conducive to people, feeling and quality of life). Jung (1953) agreed with this view and he described Germany as the white "fatherland", and spoke of dark "Mother Africa",
- Uncertainty avoidance (the degree to which people in a country prefer structured over unstructured solutions), and

- Long-term versus short-term orientation (long-term implying a future orientation, like savings, versus short-term, implying a past and present perspective, like fulfilling social obligations and showing respect for tradition).

The following constructs are included aligned with Globe studies (2012):

- Performance Orientation the degree to which a society encourages high standards of performance, and rewards innovation and improvement.
- Assertiveness the degree to which individuals are assertive, tough, dominant and aggressive in social relationships.
- Future orientation the extent to which members of a society or an organisation believe that their actions will influence their own future.
- Humane Orientation the degree to which a collective encourages and rewards individuals for being fair, tolerant, altruistic, kind and caring to others.
- Institutional Collectivism the extent to which a society's organisational and institutional norms and practices encourage and reward collective action and collective distribution of resources.
- In-group/Individual Collectivism the degree to which individuals express pride, loyalty of cohesiveness in their organisations and families.
- Gender Egalitarianism the degree to which the collective minimises gender inequality.

The 2017 BeQ™-results obtained for "client" on Hofstede's national context indicates the following regarding the worldview of the respondents:

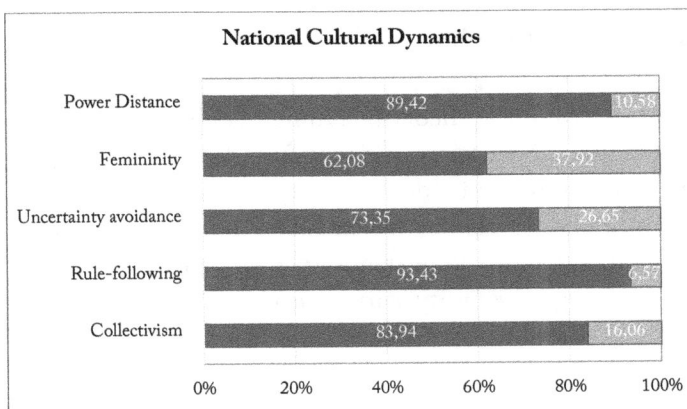

National Cultural Dynamics

Power Distance	89,42	10,58
Femininity	62,08	37,92
Uncertainty avoidance	73,35	26,65
Rule-following	93,43	6,57
Collectivism	83,94	16,06

0%   20%   40%   60%   80%   100%

- 89.42% of respondents believe that people in authority positions should be respected.
- 62.08% believe in more feminine values, which ascribe to harmonious relationships, nurture, creativity, caring and concern for the wellbeing of everyone which links to the humane orientation.

- 73.35% believe that taking risks should be avoided.
- 93.43% believe that it is important to follow rules.
- 83.94% believe that the community is more important than the individual.

A breakdown of the International ranking of South Africa in relation to other countries evaluated on the Hofstede constructs are represented in the table provided below for context.

South Africa 2014

International Rankings

Organization	Survey	Ranking
Heritage Foundation/The Wall Street Journal	Index of Economic Freedom	75 out of 178
Reporters Without Borders	Worldwide Press Freedom Index	42 out of 180
Transparency International	Corruption Perception Index	72 out of 175
United Nations Development Programme	Human Development Index	121 out of 207
Vision of Humanity	Global Peace Index	121 out of 162
World Economic Forum	Global Competitiveness Report	Not ranked

9. Human Niche Dynamics

Laubscher (2012) describes the theory of Human Niche development. She defines a human niche as a level of consciousness that an individual, a group, organisation or society starts to develop over time due to the questions of existence that the entity asks and the corresponding coping mechanisms in the brain, that moderate the innate quest. Due to authentic understanding of the dynamics that asking a specific existential question brings, the entity starts to excel at corresponding behaviours and attributes.

The theory of Human Niches draws heavily on the theory of spiral dynamics as described by Graves (1974), Cohan and Beck (1994) and Wilber (2004). Lessem (2012) described it as spiral dynamics for africa and a non-western description of spiral dynamics.

Human niches oscillate from an individualistic worldview to a collective worldview impacting significantly on the way in which a specific entity functions – either as an expressive individual or as a sacrificial group member. Each human niche can be categorised by a specific theme. These themes are listed below:

BEIGE:	How can I survive?
PURPLE:	How can we sacrifice for our community?
RED:	How can I get power?
BLUE:	How can we sacrifice for the future?
ORANGE:	How can I conquer the financial world?
GREEN:	How can we sacrifice to save the earth?

Although more categories are identified in theory, Laubscher (2012) argues that it is rarely, if ever, visible in a corporate setting.

The Transparent Human Niche describes the attitudinal dynamics of a work force in the here and now. The slide below is representative of the Transparent Human Niches that manifest presently. Business Unit/Department manifestations can be derived from what is described and then be compared to this overall dynamic.

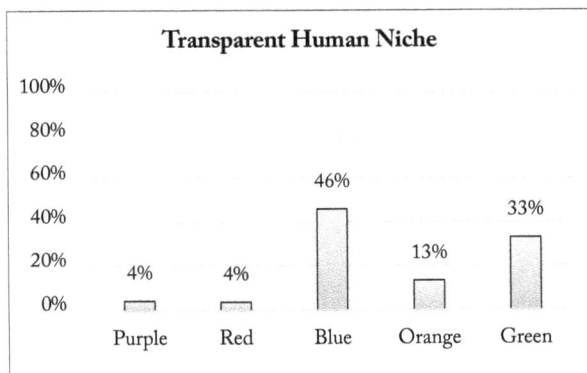

Transparent Human Niche

	Purple	Red	Blue	Orange	Green
	4%	4%	46%	13%	33%

4% do everything that they do for their community. This category is described by the colour Purple. Employees of this group enjoy speaking in parables and metaphors. The idioms of their speech are largely symbolic. Their worldview considers past trends and tendencies and lessons learned from their forefathers. People who excel at the human niche of purple are excellent in keeping the old ways, saving face and respecting elders and leaders.

4% of the sample group indicated a preference for Red – for getting personal power. In the case of IBL Combined, it appears that there will be judgement from the greater group on individuals that strive to get more power and that take visible risks. People engaging in this behaviour will be viewed as ego-centric and as going against the wishes of the greater community.

46% of the population of IBL Combined falls into the Blue category. People that have a Blue attitudinal value system sacrifice today so that they can receive later. They are rule following. Hierarchy is very important to them to sustain order and structure. In organisations, career paths become specifically important. They will try and do the right thing. Typically, people in the Blue niche are very religious. As Blue people strive to do the right thing, they follow strategies such as Behavioural Based Safety philosophies and other organized policies and practices.

13% of the population indicated a preference for an Orange human niche - individuals that take calculated risks, and want to make money. Being successful in their job and "making it" in the financial world is on top of mind. Typically, an Orange Niche is visible in individuals that follow the latest technological trends.

33% of the sample indicates a Green Human Niche preference. Green describes worldview where the emphasis is placed on the survival of the collective and the earth. In a Green environment, individuals have a humanistic ontology and truly visualize the growth potential of others.

Graves (1974) describes the phenomenon that individuals strive towards a future value system. It is not sure whether an individual will develop in this way – it depends on situational dynamics and on the specific crises that present themselves to the entity and then how the individual responds to it. Laubcher and Viljoen (2012) refer to this dynamic as emergent human niches.

The Emergent Human Niches for the IBL Combined group are visible in the graph below.

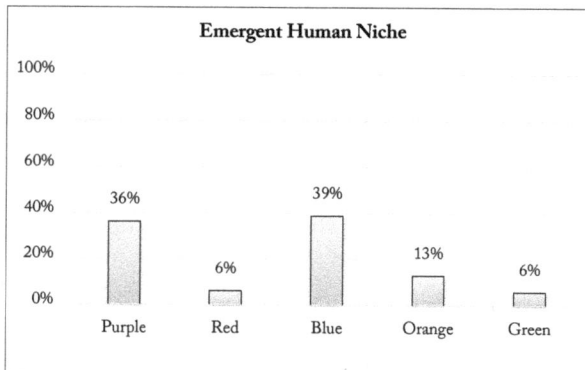

Emergent Human Niche

	Purple	Red	Blue	Orange	Green
	36%	6%	39%	13%	6%

It is clear that a Purple and Blue view will emerge under stress. Green will drain out and more people will ask "what is in it for themselves". Blue will become more detailed, strict and rigid. More Purple will emerge – more people will be concerned about their family and their security.

It is very significant to note that the emerging human niches are mainly focused toward a collective niche, in contrast to that of the transparent niches. Management should take this dynamic into account when translating strategy, when communicating with the organisation and when conducting training interventions. Reward structures and Human Resource strategies should also align to this dynamic.

10.	BeQTM Proposed Next Steps

- Provide feedback to participants so that people feel that their issues and contributions to the survey have been acknowledged.
- Joint action plans to build on any existing initiatives.
- Integration into business plans.
- Embark on interventions identified – greater team work. Encourage innovation and listen to inputs of employees on optimising delivery.
- Monitor monthly progress.
- Re-measure in 12 months.

Our Contact Details

Report compiled by Dr Rica Viljoen and Mr Stefan Viljoen of Mandala Consulting.

Contact details:

Prof Rica Viljoen
+27 82 449 5846
rica@mandalaconsulting.co.za

Mr Stefan Viljoen
+27 76 907 3277
stefan@mandalaconsulting.co.za

Mandala Consulting:
Postnet 24, Private Bag X10015, Randburg, 2125. 17 Friar Tuck Road, Robindale, Randburg, 2194.
Tel: +27 (0) 11 782 3651/754. Fax: +27 (0) 11 888 7657.
Website: www.mandalaconsulting.co.za.
Email: info@mandalaconsulting.co.za. Reg: 2006/029659/07.

The BeQ™ is the Intellectual capital and property of Prof Rica Viljoen.

No unauthorised copying of information may be used without acknowledgement or consultation with her.

Kindly ensure confidentiality of this report by observing adequate storage security, and request permission before publishing any results contained within prior to doing so. We also hereby request your consent to add you to our list of clients on our business website.

NATIONAL DYNAMICS

"It's not that we need to form new organisations. It's simply that we have to awaken to new ways of thinking. I believe it makes no sense to spend a lot of time attacking the current realities. It is time to create the new models that have in them the complexity that makes the older systems obsolete. And to the extent that we can do that, and do that quickly, I think we can provide what will be necessary for a major breakthrough for the future."

~Dr. Don Beck

Spiral dynamics is a way of thinking about the complexities of human existence and understanding the order and chaos in human affairs. It explains deep forces in human nature which shape our values, and lays out both a pattern and trajectory for change. It helps to enable greater understanding of how people, organisations and cultures function from the inside out, and will empower you to help them work, learn, and live better.

The term "spiral dynamics" refers to the cycling, expanding nature of this interactive emergent process, illustrated in many of Dr. Graves' diagrams, as well as the energetic forces which drive transformative change. There are two helixes. The first describes the questions of existence that an entity is struggling with. The second describes the coping mechanisms that the entity employs to cope with the challenge of existence.

It is an expansive sequence in some respect; this is not a hierarchy of wisdom or decency or even intelligences, much less happiness and worth. Instead, it delineates a series of different ways of prioritising and framing those things as solutions to one set of problems, creating new ones which require new thinking to resolve. First congruence then, if necessary or possible, growth. There is an increase in cognitive complexity as we move through the systems, but not in intelligence. Different intelligences are valued differently at different levels, just as different levels have their own sense of the spiritual, of the social, and of the essential.

The eight levels identified by Graves can be summarised as follows:

Level 1: Beige (Reactive/Survival Sense) • Sharpen instincts and innate senses

Level 2: Purple (Tribal/Kin Spirits) • Seek harmony and safety in a mysterious world

Level 3: Red (Egocentric/Power Gods) • Express impulsively, break free, be strong

Level 4: Blue(Absolutistic/Truth force) • Find purpose, bring order and ensure future

Level 5: Orange (Materialistic/Strive drive) • Analyse and strategise to prosper

Level 6: Green (Personalistic/Human kind) • Explore inner self, equalise others

Level 7: Yellow (Existential/Flex Flow) • Integrate and align systems

Level 8: Turquoise (Holistic Organism/Global/New) • Synergise and macro-manage

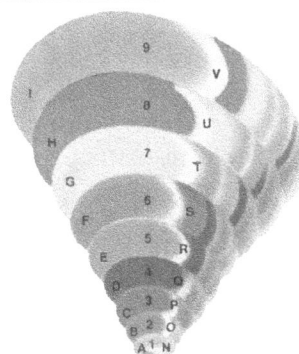

The worldviews oscillates from individual to collective views of the world. The colours used indicate this too – it oscillates from a cool to a warm colour. The warm group (beige, red, orange, and yellow) describes an internal "I-focused" locus of control and a way of living centered on self-expression and the ability to change and master the external world. These tend to be change-oriented.

The various levels are differentiated by how this expression of self takes place and the foundation of other systems on which it rests. The cool group (purple, blue, green, and turquoise) describes a "we-oriented" locus of control and a way of living centered on self-sacrifice and the ability to stabilise and come to peace with the inner world. These tend to be stabilisation-oriented and emphasise attention to external anchors and authorities. They, too, are differentiated in their forms of collectivism and the self-express systems subsumed within them.

	Question of Existence			Coping Mechanism
A	State of nature and biological urges and drives: physical senses dictate the state of being.	**BEIGE**	N	Instinctive: as natural instincts and reflexes direct; automatic existence.
B	Threatening and full of mysterious powers and spirit beings that must be placated and appeased.	**PURPLE**	O	Animistic: according to tradition and ritual ways of group: tribal; animistic.
C	Like a jungle where the tough and strong prevail, the weak serve; nature is an adversary to be conquered.	**RED**	P	Egocentric: asserting self for dominance, conquest and power. Exploitive; egocentric.
D	Controlled by a Higher Power that punishes evil and eventually rewards good works and righteous living.	**BLUE**	Q	Absolutistic: obediently as higher authority and rules direct; conforming; guilt.
E	Full of resources to develop and opportunities to make things better and bring prosperity.	**ORANGE**	R	Multiplistic: pragmatically to achieve results and get ahead; test options; maneuver.
F	The habitat wherein humanity can find love and purpose through affiliation and sharing.	**GREEN**	S	Relativistic; respond to human needs; affinitive; situational; consensual; fluid.

ACKNOWLEDGEMENTS

To: Henk van Zyl

What a joyful opportunity it is to write this dedication to Henk van Zyl, the *incidental writer*. Henk was the Senior Human Resources Manager in the first company I consulted at. I learned from him how to put the "human" back into human resources.

For as long as I have known him, he has claimed to be a practical man, not an academic. This facade was, however, deconstructed when Marius Meyer found Henk indeed to be deeply theoretically anchored, while he was doing a presentation as newly-appointed ambassador to the South African Board of People Practices.

Henk passionately insisted that he would NEVER write; that he would rather be as a doer, a fisherman or a retiree. However, to keep the appointment with his inner need to contribute, not to his company alone, but to the field of study and ultimately to South Africa and other emerging economies, he selflessly shared more in this book than could ever have been expected. A theoretical, academic and practical approach is interwoven with the purpose to share the actual functioning of the co-determination approach in a case organisation. Between these pages, the evidence of his corporate life work unfolds in a way that is humble, unassuming and real. It has proven that he has the potential to be catalytic, inclusive, integral and transformational.

Henk, you are an author after all, and this book cannot be dedicated to anyone but you.

Henk masterfully painted a new way of creating space where the dynamic interplay of different humans can be interwoven in the fabric of the social system at hand. His thinking pattern, his integration of organisational development and employee relations, and his deep, soulful insight, resulted in a conceptual framework that can give life to those involved in it. When people frowned at his initiatives and said that they did not make business sense or that the risk was too high, he was immovable in his intent and action. One wonders what they are saying now, when, owing to their involvement and because they trust management, his workers do not strike like those in the rest of the industry.

His actions left deep imprints in the hearts of many employees at Interstate, but also in the community in Bloemfontein. His authenticity, steadfastness and humane ability made him a respected senior manager, as well as an example of continuously encouraging healing and wholeness of not only his organisation, but also of society at large. Peter Salovay said: "In our complex and interconnected world, we need leaders of imagination, understanding and emotional intelligence – men and women who will move beyond polarizing debates and tackle the challenges we face. To cultivate such leaders, we must value and invest in humans."

Henk, you are such a leader, and to the beautiful people of Interstate you are an elder – a chieftain.

I asked Henk's daughter, Martie Bloem, a lecturer in private law at the University of the Free State, to write a few words about working with her dad. Here is her response:

About Henk van Zyl

I am fortunate to have known Henk my entire life, as his daughter and in a professional capacity.

Henk is a big fan of Winston Churchill's quotes, which is indicative of his sense of humour. A famous quote of Churchill which describes my father best is: "Courage is what it takes to stand up and speak; but courage is also what it takes to sit down and listen."

One of the first things I remember is that he taught me the difference between an autocratic and democratic style of management before I could ride a bicycle, and I grew up with this concept of participatory management.

According to Henk, almost everything is negotiable except one thing: respect. You can say what you want, to and about other people, but you have to do so with respect.

I have been part of his journey in discovering a solution for the labour challenges and ongoing strikes in South Africa, and to Henk it was simple: if everyone is included in decision-making, then disputes will automatically be limited and employees will be uplifted. His outlook on life in general and his extensive experience in labour relations were instrumental in this research. He knows and appreciates that co-determination is not an overnight solution, and that it is not achievable without a great deal of education and a fundamental change of mind-set.

Henk is without a doubt an expert in this field and his passion, insights and contribution to this work is invaluable.

Martie Bloem

Thank you for the honour of letting me journey with you through all these years. My respect for you has increased with time. Thank you that I could be a witness to the magic of co-determination. The impact that you and the people of Interstate had on my own thinking is profound and sacred.

I hope the writing bug has bitten you seriously enough to write another book!

Rica Viljoen

To Rica Viljoen

How better than in the words of Proverbs 31 can one dedicate a piece of work to a phenomenal woman?

"She is a hard worker, strong and industrious
She knows the value of everything she makes, and works late into the night
She is generous to the poor and needy
She doesn't worry when it snows, because her family has warm clothing
She is strong and respected and not afraid of the future
She speaks with gentle wisdom
Her children show their appreciation, and her husband praises her
Charm is deceptive and beauty disappears, but a women who honours the
Lord should be praised
Give her credit for all she does
She deserves the respect of everyone."

Thank you, Rica, for making sacrifices to enrich our lives with your knowledge and wisdom.

Henk van Zyl

To Jan Nel

"Sometimes," said Pooh, *"the smallest things take up the most room in your heart."*

South Africa has a Baasverteller[i] whose name is Jan Nel. Over the years, many stories, published in five books, on radio programmes, in a weekly newspaper column and in poems, came from his pen. Jan worked behind the scenes to remind South Africans about the power of storytelling by underlying its importance on culture, and illustrating the healing properties thereof. His stories triggered Ollie Viljoen to create the programme Spies and Plessis – a popular Afrikaans TV show that drew hundreds of viewers. To me he is OJ, a fond abbreviation for Oom Jan.

In time his storytelling capability transformed the writings of numerous ethnographic and auto-ethnographic masters and doctoral students into well-edited, richly presented and authentic documents. For books that were multi-cultural of nature, he did the same. Through his unique ability to work, not from within his own paradigm, sentence construction and specific understanding of the written text, but rather from within the writing style, ontology and epistemology of the author, meaningful pieces of work have been created. He practices his craft to deliver magical, descriptive narratives that impact all that read them.

OJ, you did this yet again with this book. What an honour to work with you. Your

---

i   An award-winning, renowned and expert storyteller

understanding of multi-culturalism not only stems from your own thesis for your Master's degree in ethnology, or your years of farming with diverse groups of people, but you also edited and co-authored all the work published in the last five years on spiral dynamics in Africa. This work includes the enrichment of the international understanding of PURPLE in spiral dynamics, and more recently your contribution to our inquiry into BEIGE can only be described as sacred and remarkable.

Jan Nel long ago transcended the role of editor, and in this book, illustrates his wisdom, insight of social phenomena, and his ability to manoeuvre written text into almost visible imagery.

OJ, without your assistance and the quiet support of your wife, Lynette, we will all be poorer.

I, particularly, would like to honour you; but also to everyone that you touch and have interacted with over the years. Thank you!

Rica Viljoen

INDEX

A

accountability and corruption, 136

adaptability, 87–88, 274, 277, 280, 288, 291

anxiety, 99–100, 102, 104–7, 111–12

approach and mechanisms to co-determination, 163, 184

archetypes of different thinking systems, 51–52

ASC and organisational development, 40

B

background of Interstate Bus Lines, 163

benchmark of engagement, 59, 87, 90, 92, 95, 151, 168–69, 176, 200

BeQTM Measurement, 272

BeQ™ Emotional Presence analysis, 279

build inclusivity, 87

business complicity in oppression, 220–21

C

caring orientation, 277, 288, 292

Cashbuild, 145, 149–50, 159, 173

changing world of work, 11, 109

characteristics and limitations, 74

closed shop agreement, 184, 189, 198, 204, 252–56, 258, 260, 266

co-determination, culture and structures, 76

co-determination agreement, 180, 184–85, 188–90, 207, 229–32, 235, 242, 246, 250–51, 253, 255, 258–59, 261, 263, 266

co-determination engagement, 83, 210–11

co-determination figuratively described as a cow, 211

co-determination framework, 95–96

co-determination in your organisation, 198

co-determination model, 23, 40, 42, 46, 163, 171, 173, 177–78, 184, 197–98, 200, 202, 204, 206

collaborative approach to labour market development, 20

collective recognition, 94, 184, 188–89, 202, 204, 207, 253, 257–59

commitment of the parties, 184

communication of decisions, 188, 236, 242, 250

communication with labour, 182

complex adaptive system, 109–10, 112

complex adaptive systems, 110–11, 121, 123, 125, 127, 132

concept of co-determination, 71, 151, 163, 171

confidentiality and disclosure of information, 187

contributors to leadership development, 132

cornerstones and building blocks, 163, 177

corporate citizenship, 28, 88, 274, 277, 280, 282–83

the cow philosophy, 209

create ownership and a sense of belonging, 173

critical diversity literacy, 215, 220–21, 226

critical to survival, 131

crystallising leadership, 129

D

depiction of intersectionality, 223

designing of agreements, 203

devastating contrast, 157

development of shop stewards, 188

Disciplinary Committee (DC), 187

disciplinary matters, 182, 190, 192, 204, 239, 243, 304

disciplinary procedures, 187, 194, 232, 238, 242–43

discipline, 58–59, 67, 83, 90, 94, 152, 159, 166, 173, 186, 188, 190–92, 194, 263, 271

dispute prevention, 94, 169, 177, 184, 188–90, 202, 204, 206, 211, 237, 247, 270–71, 299–300, 302, 304–5

dispute prevention and resolution, 94, 169, 177, 184, 188–90, 204, 206, 211, 237, 247, 270–71, 299–300, 302, 304–5